Gracious Goodness

... Charleston!

Bishop England High School
Endowment Fund
Charleston, South Carolina

The information contained in this book is true to the best of our knowledge. All recommendations are made without any guarantees on the part of the authors. The authors and publisher disclaim all liability in connection with the use of this information.

First Printing	7,000
Second Printing	10,000
Third Printing	15,000
Fourth Printing	15,000
Fifth Printing	10,000
Sixth Printing	8,000

ISBN 0-9629477-0-9
LCCN 91-065567

All proceeds from the sale of this book will go to the
Bishop England High School Endowment Fund.

Printed in the United States of America
TOOF COOKBOOK DIVISION

670 South Cooper Street
Memphis, TN 38104

Alma Mater

Inspired by your glorious name,
Ennobled by your love
Our yet unchallenged joyous hearts
Raise your banner high on high
And rally to your faintest call
For we know your worth,
O Alma Mater, strong and true,
We pledge our love to you.

Through youth's fair spring,
Unclouded skies,
Made brilliant by your light,
Have sheltered well your boys and girls,
Thus to send us bravely on,
Reflecting ever by our lives,
Goodness born of love.
O Alma Mater, may we be
Forever true to thee.

Bishop England High School *Charleston, South Carolina*

DEDICATION

Gracious Goodness, Charleston!
a collection of Lowcountry delectables,
has been assembled with
great fun, enthusiasm and devotion.
It is presented
with love
to alumni, family, friends, and
the present and future students
of Bishop England High School

To our founder,
Monsignor "Doc" O'Brien,
we graciously dedicate this publication.

Angela R. Basha
Ann M. Stafford
Audrey M. Runey
Peggy Conway Joseph

Be it known to all, that the book known as ***Gracious Goodness, Charleston***, could never have made it to fruition without the generous time and talents of our dear friends on the following committees. We wish to thank them with our deepest appreciation.

The Recipe Contributors

The Testing Committee

The Typing Committee

And also to our Alumni and friends who have offered their expertise so generously in all phases of the cookbook; especially,

. . . To our cover artist, Virginia Fouché Bolton, and her *"Charleston Doorways"* for making our book complete. Mrs. Bolton is a very well-known local artist. She has received many awards, state, national and worldwide. Her studio in Charleston is filled with wonderful pieces of art that display a true extension of this loving and caring person. Mrs. Bolton is presently teaching art classes at Bishop England High School.

...To Sandy Logan, with LS3P Architects, for his beautiful Palladian doorway.

. . . To our artists, Pati Crosby Croffead and Angel Montgomery Allen for their wonderful contributions to our sectional dividers and the many hours they have given for our cause, and to Fred Downs for the use of his *"Bishop England High School"*.

. . . To our student artists, Wendy Boughamer, Hayden Ferri, Drew Levay, Brian Manning and Meg Westendorff for their contributions.

...To Suzie Johnson Basha who lovingly labored over our art ideas for the menu section.

. . . To Julia Terry Templeton, author of *"By Request - Only the Best"* for her endless assistance.

. . . To Coach Lavelle, for his undying support and patience.

. . . To the Freshmen Teachers, who sacrificed their workspace to piles of recipes, and

. . . To *all* who have assisted us without hesitation . . . *We Thank You!*

HISTORY

If only my walls could talk, oh, what tales they could tell . . .

When my eyes - or rather, my doors- opened on that day in 1915, I could see it was going to be a good life.

With my birth, Charleston finally had a Catholic school. My Father "Doc" O'Brien and Father May were so pleased. I was a dream come true. Wrapped in warmth and excitement, and "christened" Bishop England High School, I, along with the "B. E. Spirit," was welcomed into the world of education.

At an early age, I became quite famous for my strict discipline. The students seemed to want it, and the parents gave me such enthusiastic support. I look back now, and would you believe the boys sat on one side and the girls on the other, even during lunch periods and assemblies? And girls wearing make-up . . . NEVER . . . not under the watchful eye of Father O'Brien.

I began to grow very quickly, and in 1947 Father Manning came into my life. He was one of my graduates. Continuing Father O'Brien's philosophy, he thought I was ready for something called "Saturday school". Father Manning's love for me and my students touched many people. In fact, many of my teachers today were graduated during this era and still show a gleam in their eye when speaking of Monsignor Manning.

Father Croghan came to me at a time in my life when I was growing by leaps and bounds. My sister, Immaculate Conception School, even helped house some of my students. Father Croghan spent a lot of time with me. He also taught classes. Many alumni, after thirty-five years, can still recite the verb "to be" in Latin, after having written it twenty-five times for him.

I became older, and my sports program was wonderful. Then I met Father Robert Kelly. I don't think Father missed a game. You could always spot him in his long black cassock. I always thought he had my steps on the left side of the gym reserved. Even now, Father still shows up for an occasional Key Club basketball game.

Father Charles Kelley was only with me for a short time; but in this short time, he and I had a special relationship. I can see him now in the halls teasing my freshmen.

And speaking of freshmen . . . Monsignor Lawrence McInerny was once one of my freshmen. I see Father quite often now preparing for Mass. It's very impressive to see the many visiting priests. I was so proud to see him return as my Rector.

Not only do my graduates return to work with me, many of my students have sent me their children; and now I am watching their children's children in my halls. I guess I am like a parent now, pleased to see my "children" come home for a visit. All of them appear to be grateful for what they have received during their stay with me; and I feel so proud that many of them have made great contributions to our community.

Although a feeling of sadness overcomes me each year when I lose my seniors, I know that they'll come back to visit and that my feelings will change again in the fall when the enthusiasm of a new freshman class fills my halls.

I feel extremely lucky that, all through my long and illustrious lifetime, I have been protected, nourished and guided by such wise leaders as Monsignor O'Brien and Monsignor Manning, and today, Mr. Nick Theos, whose idea it is to protect me **in perpetuity** *. . . thus an endowment to ensure that I, Bishop England High School, will live forever!!!*

I cannot over look the efforts of . . .

Angela Rowland Basha
Peggy Conroy Joseph
Audrey Meyer Runey
and
Ann Montgomery Stafford

who saw the need for a continuing source of nourishment to keep the "B. E. Spirit" alive. Together, we share the dream that this book, **Gracious Goodness, Charleston!** *will be a source of pleasure and enjoyment for many generations to come.*

Bishop England High School

P. S. "May the saints smile at your success."
(An Irish Wish from County Cork.)

TABLE OF CONTENTS

Gift recipes scattered throughout the book are designated by this Charleston Gift Basket.

Gracious Entertaining

Parties

Bridal Luncheon
Helena Blanchard McKay

Charleston Cup Tailgate
Kay & Robbie Wolfe

Charleston Dining Elegantè
Mary & Bob Register

St. Patrick's Celebration
Pat & John McDougald

Supper Club Dinner Party
Kathy Hostetter Duffy

Sweet Girl Graduate
Julia Terry Templeton

Football Tailgate
Alberta Way Freeman

11

Gracious Entertaining

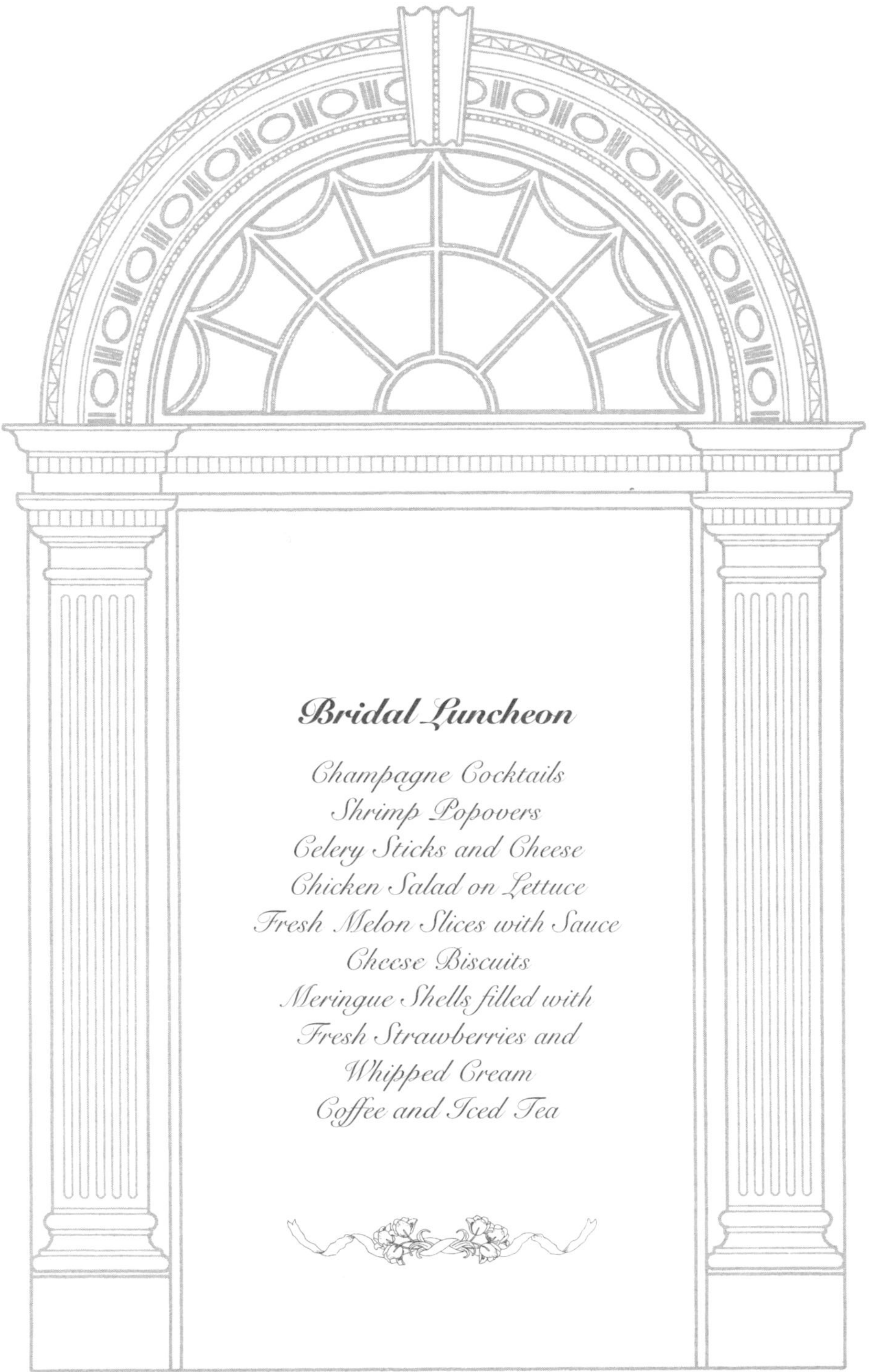

Bridal Luncheon

Champagne Cocktails
Shrimp Popovers
Celery Sticks and Cheese
Chicken Salad on Lettuce
Fresh Melon Slices with Sauce
Cheese Biscuits
Meringue Shells filled with
Fresh Strawberries and
Whipped Cream
Coffee and Iced Tea

Bridal Luncheon

Centerpiece—
Pink Roses & Baby's Breath
White Candles

For an added touch...have the florist fix your arrangements in a purchased crystal bowl and two smaller ones for your table. After the shower, give the larger arrangement to the bride-to-be and the smaller ones to the bride's Mother and the Mother of the groom.

Use white linens and your crystal and silver. Pink ribbon can be used for decoration.

Bride's corsage—Pink Sweetheart Roses

Purchase pretty note cards and give one to each guest. Ask them to write one or two sentences of good advice for a long and happy marriage and sign it. Collect and tie with a pretty pink ribbon and give to the bride-to-be.

Champagne Cocktail

1 tablespoon concentrated orange juice
Champagne, chilled

Put orange juice in bottom of a champagne glass. Then fill with chilled champagne.

Celery Sticks and Cheese

1 (8-ounce) package cream cheese
3 tablespoons mayonnaise
½ cup pecans, chopped
Havarti cheese
Parsley

Soften cream cheese to room temperature. Add mayonnaise and pecans. Mix until well blended. Set aside. Wash celery in cool water and cut into 3-inch sticks. Fill with cream cheese mixture. Place on crystal platter garnished with bite-sized cubes of Havarti cheese and parsley.

Shrimp Popovers

- 1 package crescent rolls
- ½ pound shrimp, cooked and chopped
- 1 teaspoon onion, grated
- 1 (8-ounce) package cream cheese, at room temperature
- ½ teaspoon lemon juice
- Dab horseradish
- Mayonnaise, as needed

Cut crescent rolls in halves. Mix shrimp, onion, cream cheese, lemon juice and horseradish. Add mayonnaise until right consistency. Spread mixture on rolls. Roll and seal. Bake at 350° until brown and puffy.

Melons and Sauce

- 3 honeydew melons
- 3 canteloupe melons
- 1 jar marshmallow creme
- 1 (8-ounce) package cream cheese, softened
- 1 teaspoon amaretto (more or less)

Mix marshmallow creme, cream cheese and amaretto.

Peel and slice melons, alternating slices on plate and topping with sauce.

Cheese Biscuits

- 2 cups all-purpose flour
- 4 teaspoons baking powder
- ½ teaspoon salt
- ½ cup shortening
- 1 cup sour cream
- 1 cup finely grated sharp cheese
- Sprinkle of cayenne pepper
- 1 to 2 tablespoons milk

Mix all ingredients except milk with fork. If mixture is too dry, add milk as needed. Roll and cut with biscuit cutter. Bake at 450° for 10 to 12 minutes.

Chicken Salad

- 6 chicken breasts
- 6 chicken thighs
- 1 cup celery, chopped
- 6 medium eggs, hard boiled
- 1 teaspoon mustard
- 1 teaspoon lemon juice
- Mayonnaise for desired consistency
- Salt and pepper to taste
- 1 cup walnuts, chopped
- Lettuce

Boil chicken in salted water, drain and cool. Remove skin and cut into chunks. Add all other ingredients, mix well and serve on bed of lettuce. For a delightful change, you can also add green seedless grapes, cut in half, or pineapple chunks.

Meringue Shells with Strawberries

- 6 egg whites, at room temperature
- ¼ teaspoon salt
- ¼ teaspoon cream of tartar
- 1 teaspoon vanilla
- 2 cups sugar
- ¾ cup finely chopped pecans (optional)
- Fresh strawberries
- 1 pint whipping cream (whipped and sweetened)

Beat egg whites until frothy. Slowly add sugar, salt and vanilla. Add pecans if desired. Line cookie sheet with brown paper bag. Drop by large spoonfuls on bag. Depress middle with back side of spoon. Preheat oven to 275°. Bake one hour, turn oven off. Leave oven door closed at least one hour or overnight. Peel off paper and serve filled with fresh hulled sweetened strawberries. Top with sweetened fresh whipped cream.

15

Gracious Entertaining

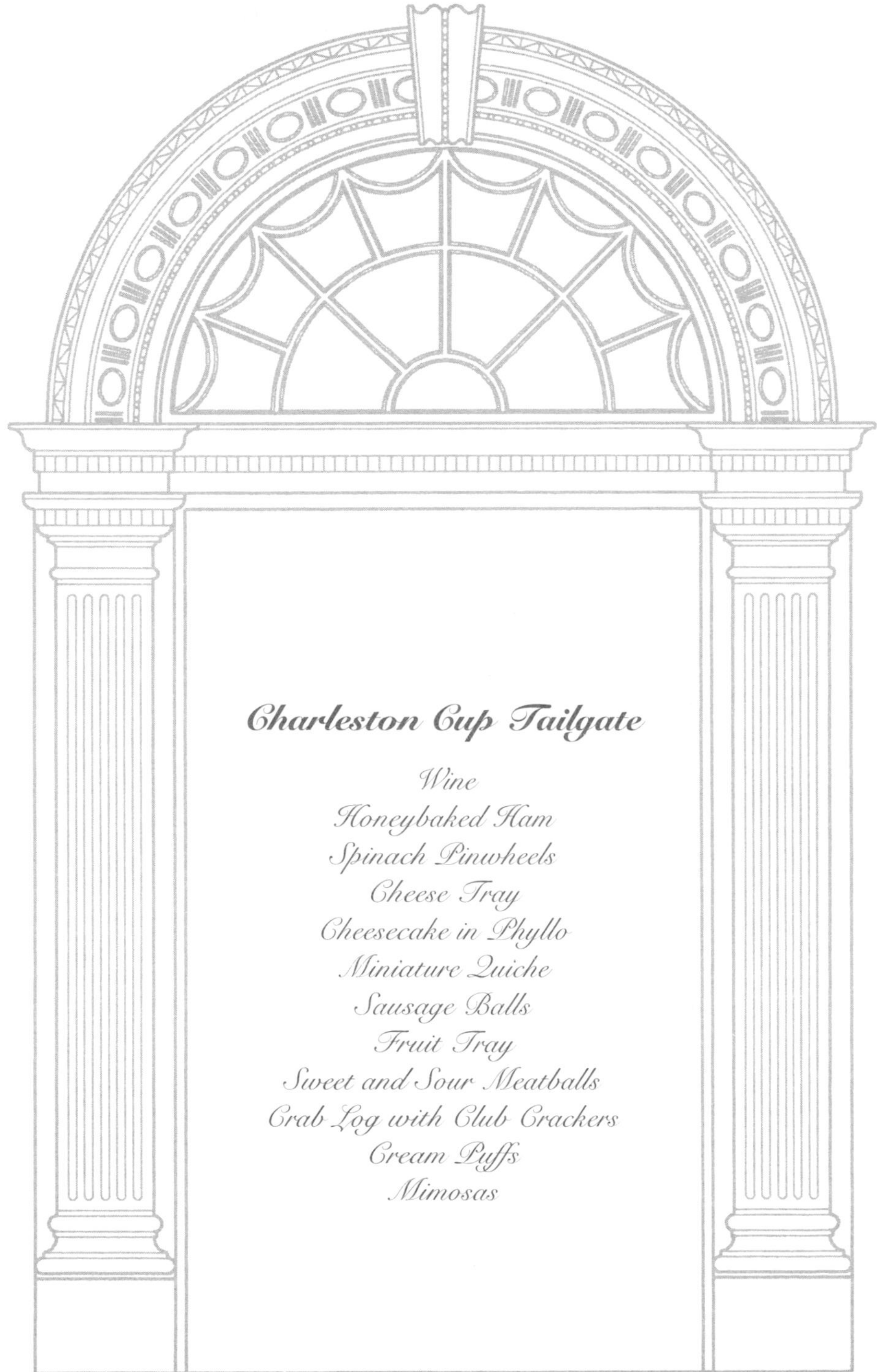

Charleston Cup Tailgate
Wine
Honeybaked Ham
Spinach Pinwheels
Cheese Tray
Cheesecake in Phyllo
Miniature Quiche
Sausage Balls
Fruit Tray
Sweet and Sour Meatballs
Crab Log with Club Crackers
Cream Puffs
Mimosas

Set Up and Presentation

With two infield parking spaces, we set up three tables in a horseshoe and skirted them with white linens. A beautiful arrangement of white and bright pink tea roses with greenery flanked by two candelabras served as our centerpiece. We used "silver" trays (plastic with silver coating that are disposable) to display our treats. We kept the meatballs and quiche piping hot with silver chafing dishes and Sterno. We used a third chafing dish to keep the ham from spoiling. By putting crushed ice in the liner and the ham in the inside tray, the ham stayed cool all day.

To make sure everything stayed fresh on a very warm day, we set out small portions and used a mini-van full of coolers with ice as our kitchen. As food began to dwindle, we replenished it from the supply kept in the van.

Our guests used small clear plastic disposable plates, forks, and knives for their treats and we served mimosas and wine in clear plastic champagne flutes and wine glasses. We used small white cocktail napkins and party toothpicks for the fruit, cheese and meatballs.

By following what we did as a guide and adding a bit of your own personality, you should be able to have a spectacular tailgate that friends will talk about for weeks!

Spinach Pinwheels

- **1 envelope Lipton vegetable soup mix**
- **1 (16-ounce) container sour cream**
- **½ cup mayonnaise**
- **1 (10-ounce) package frozen, chopped spinach, thawed and squeezed dry**
- **1 (8-ounce) can water chestnuts, drained and chopped**
- **1 loaf white bread, crusts trimmed**

In medium bowl, mix soup, sour cream, and mayonnaise. Stir in spinach and water chestnuts. Mix well and set in refrigerator.

Remove all crust from bread leaving yourself a perfect square. With a rolling pin, flatten each slice of bread. Spread a thin layer of spinach mixture on each slice. Roll it up, jelly roll style. Slice roll with a serrated knife about ½ inches. Arrange on platter and garnish. Serve chilled.

Cheesecake in Phyllo

- **1 package phyllo dough**
- **½ cup butter, melted**
- **2 (8-ounce) packages cream cheese, softened**
- **1 cup powdered sugar**
- **Fruit topping glaze**

Pastry Cups:
Separate phyllo dough into stacks of 3 sheets each. Using kitchen scissors, cut each stack into 4½-inch squares. Using handle of wooden spoon, press squares into cups of small muffin tins, leaving edges of dough extended above top of cup. Brush with melted butter and bake at 400° until golden brown. Remove from muffin tins and let cool. (Pastry cups will be very fragile!)

Filling:
Combine cream cheese and powdered sugar. Add more powdered sugar to taste. Mix with electric mixer until well blended. Spoon mixture into pastry cups and top with fruit topping. Garnish with fresh fruit and serve chilled.

Cheese Tray

Swiss cheese
Cheddar cheese
Gouda cheese
Jalapeño cheese

Cube the cheeses. Arrange cubes on a silver tray. Serve with Carr's table crackers and party toothpicks.

Miniature Quiche

Sam's Wholesale Club sells pre-made, pre-baked Quiche Florentine and Quiche Lorraine in packages of twenty-five for around $8 per package. All you have to do is bake them (to make the crust crispy and flaky) and serve. (Temperature instructions are on the package.)

Sausage Cheese Balls

12 ounces bulk sausage, hot or mild
1 pound sharp Cheddar cheese, shredded
2 cups buttermilk baking mix
Hot mustard and/or cocktail sauce, optional, for dipping

Mix uncooked sausage, cheese and biscuit mix until combined. Place foil on top of baking sheet. Make balls and place on top of foil. Bake at 325° for 15 to 20 minutes. Serve hot. Makes 3 dozen balls.

Fruit Tray

Fresh fruit, sliced

Arrange sliced, fresh seasonal fruit on sliver tray or glass dish and serve with powdered sugar and party toothpicks.

Sweet and Sour Meatballs

Sam's Wholesale Club sells pre-made, pre-cooked meatballs in seven pound packages. They have a wonderful flavor, but can be a "tad" greasy. I combat the grease by baking the meatballs on a cookie sheet and blotting them with paper towels. Cover with Sweet and Sour Sauce and serve warm.

Sweet and Sour Sauce:

- **⅓ cup sugar**
- **⅓ cup cider vinegar**
- **¼ cup ketchup**
- **2 tablespoons soy sauce**
- **2 tablespoons dry sherry**
- **2 tablespoons cornstarch**
- **½ cup pineapple juice**

Combine sugar, vinegar, ketchup, soy sauce, and sherry in a saucepan. Dissolve cornstarch in pineapple juice and add to sugar mixture. Bring mixture to a boil; cook one minute or until thickened, stirring constantly.

NOTE: Double recipe if using Sam's meatballs.

Crab Log with Club Crackers

- **3 (8-ounce) packages cream cheese, softened**
- **2 tablespoons bottled steak sauce**
- **¼ cup creamy salad dressing (like Miracle Whip)**
- **1 teaspoon garlic powder or 1 clove garlic**
- **1 small onion, finely chopped**
- **8 ounces crabmeat, chopped**
- **1 tablespoon chile powder**
- **Chopped fresh parsley**
- **3 cups chopped pecans**

Mix first six ingredients and chill until firm. Divide the mixture in half and mold into two logs, approximately 12 inches long. Wrap in wax paper and chill again until firm. Combine chile powder, chopped nuts, and chopped parsley—enough parsley to add a rich green color. Spread the mixture over your workspace, approximately 12 inches square. Remove your logs from the refrigerator and unwrap them. Roll the logs in the nut mixture, covering them completely. Use any leftover nut mixture to fill in the holes you may have. Garnish with decorative leaf lettuce and serve with club crackers.

Cream Puffs

Cream Puff Pastry:

- **⅔ cup water**
- **⅓ cup butter or margarine**
- **⅔ cup all-purpose flour**
- **⅛ teaspoon salt**
- **3 eggs**

Combine water and butter in medium saucepan; bring to a boil. Add flour and salt together, stirring vigorously over medium-high heat until mixture leaves sides of pan and forms a smooth ball. Remove from heat and cool four to five minutes.

Add eggs, one at a time, beating thoroughly with a wooden spoon after each addition; then beat until dough is smooth. Spoon mixture into decorating bag fitted with a No. 5 or 6B large fluted tip. Pipe mixture into 30 small balls on lightly greased baking sheets. (You can drop by teaspoon instead of decorating bag). Bake at 400° for 20 minutes or until puffed and golden brown. Cool away from drafts.

Cream Filling:

- **2 cups milk**
- **2 (3½-ounce) packages instant vanilla pudding**
- **2 pinches ground nutmeg**

Pour 2 cups cold milk into a bowl. Add pudding mixes. Mix with hand beater at lowest speed for 1 to 2 minutes or until well blended. Fold in 2 pinches of ground nutmeg. Spoon mixture into cake decorating bag fitted with a round tip No. 3. Insert the tip into the side of each puff and pipe in the filling, approximately the size of a Hershey's Kiss. Sprinkle with powdered sugar and serve chilled.

21
Gracious Entertaining

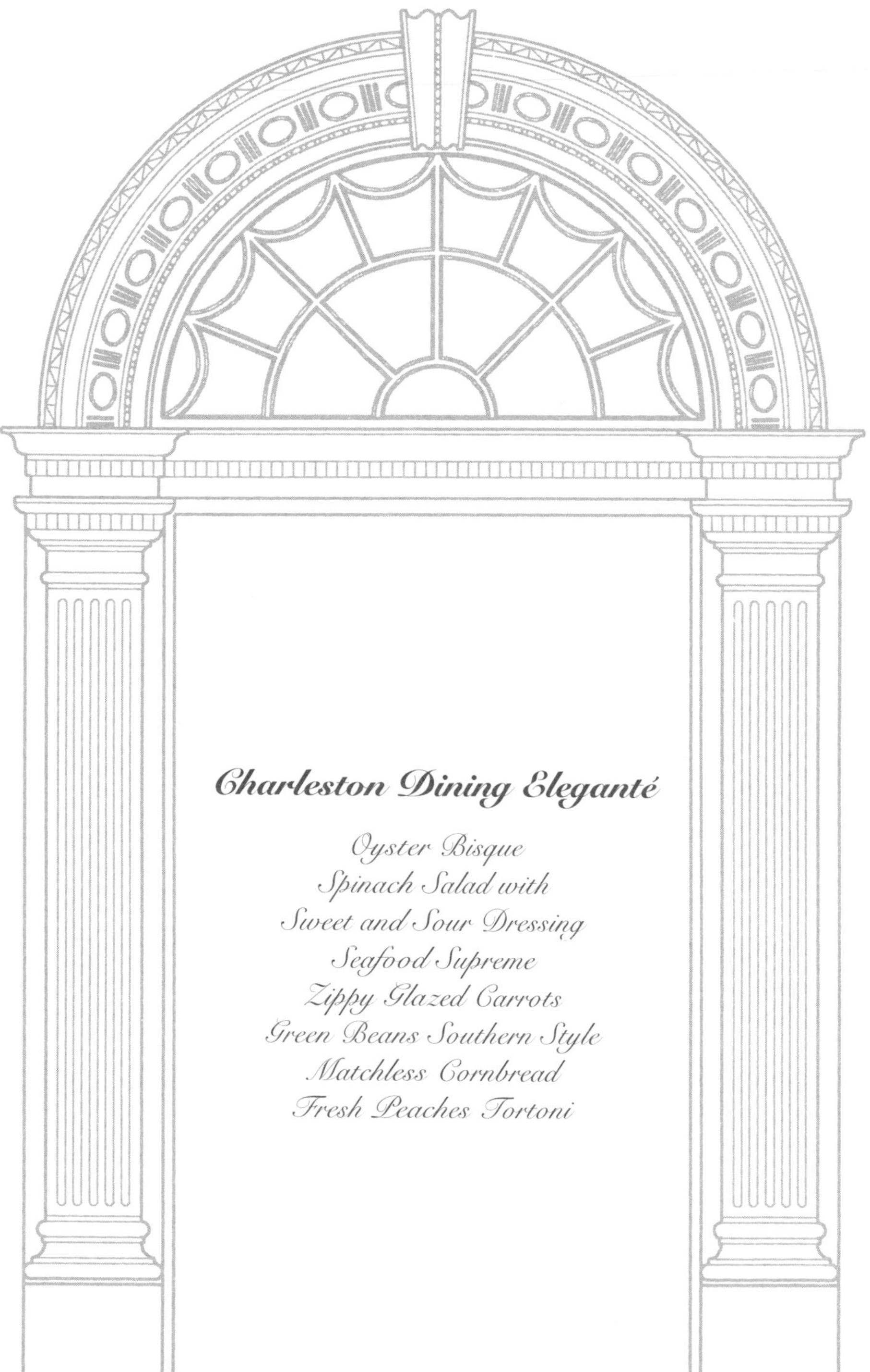

Charleston Dining Elegante

Oyster Bisque
Spinach Salad with
Sweet and Sour Dressing
Seafood Supreme
Zippy Glazed Carrots
Green Beans Southern Style
Matchless Cornbread
Fresh Peaches Tortoni

In Celebration of our wonderful location on the Seacoast of Charleston, SC, we present a Seafood Dinner Party for Eight.

For our table setting, we chose straw mats, representing sea oats on the beaches, using porcelain dinnerware with shell edging and silverware in a shell pattern. Wine goblets enhance the table setting as do the water goblets of fine crystal. Brass candlesticks with shrimp colored candles, a centerpiece of coral Gerber daisies, snapdragons and dried cattails add the finishing touches to our Seacoast setting.

Oyster Bisque

1 quart cooking oysters with liquid
4 tablespoons butter
4 cups milk
2 tablespoons butter
1 teaspoon salt
⅛ teaspoon pepper
1½ tablespoons flour
Sherry

In double boiler, heat 4 tablespoons butter and 1 quart cooking oysters with liquid. Set aside. Combine and scald in saucepan 3½ cups milk, 2 tablespoons butter, salt and pepper. Mix ½ cup milk and 1½ tablespoons flour. Add to saucepan. Stir and boil until it thickens. Then pour it over hot oysters. Serve in small compotes with a teaspoon of sherry in each bowl. Serves 8.

Spinach Salad

Fresh spinach
2 hard boiled eggs, sliced
4 scallions, chopped
1 pint fresh mushrooms, sliced
1 red bell pepper, sliced

Using fresh spinach washed thoroughly, tear up and mix with eggs, scallions, mushrooms and red bell pepper. Toss and mix with dressing IMMEDIATELY before serving.

Dressing for Salad:
½ pound bacon, fried and crumbled
½ cup sugar
1 cup mayonnaise
2 tablespoons vinegar

Mix all together before pouring over salad. Serves 8.

Seafood Supreme

1½ pounds shrimp
1½ pounds scallops
1 pound lobster meat
1 pound rock lobster
1 teaspoon salt
1 bay leaf
1 onion, sliced
1 stalk of celery
Black pepper to taste

Clean shrimp and rock lobster and boil for 5 minutes in water seasoned with above. Poach scallops gently in enough water to cover for 5 minutes and drain well. Cut up lobster meat and remove dark veins.

Sauce for Seafood:
¾ cup butter
9 tablespoons flour
1 teaspoon salt
Dash of pepper
3 cups milk
3 egg yolks
1 cup dry white wine
1 cup grated Swiss cheese
Breadcrumbs and cheese for topping

Melt butter and blend in flour, salt and pepper. Gradually add milk. Cook until smooth, stirring constantly. Add 6 tablespoons of this sauce to the egg yolks. Beat slightly. Add yolk mixture to the rest of the sauce and cook over low heat about 5 minutes. Add the white wine and cheese; stir until melted. Add mixed seafood, having cut up scallops and lobsters into bite-size pieces. Pour into large flat casserole. (9x11-inches). Sprinkle with dry breadcrumbs and additional cheese. Bake at 350° for approximately 20 minutes. Serves 8.

Southern Green Beans

3 slices bacon
4 cups water
2 pounds green beans
½ teaspoon sugar
Dash Tabasco sauce
1 teaspoon flour

Place bacon in large saucepan with water. Bring to boil—reduce heat, cover and simmer 30 minutes. Add washed green beans, sugar and Tabasco. Cook 2 hours. Mix in flour to slightly coat beans 15 minutes before serving. Serves 8.

Zippy Glazed Carrots

- 3 tablespoons butter
- 3 tablespoons prepared mustard
- 4 cups sliced carrots, cooked just tender and drained well (small whole carrots may be used)
- 1 tablespoon snipped parsley
- ½ cup brown sugar
- ½ teaspoon salt

Melt butter in skillet, stir in brown sugar, mustard and salt. Add cooked carrots—heat, stirring constantly, until nicely glazed—approximately 5 minutes. Sprinkle with fresh parsley. Serves 8.

Matchless Cornbread

- 1 small can whole kernel corn
- 1 small can creamed corn
- 1 (12-ounce) package cornbread mix
- ½ cup butter, softened
- 1 (8-ounce) container sour cream
- 2 eggs

Combine ingredients, place in greased oblong pan (9x11-inches). Bake at 450° for 30 to 35 minutes. Cut into squares and serve hot. Serves 8.

Fresh Peach Tortoni

- 1 quart vanilla ice cream
- 1 cup fresh peaches, sliced
- Rum to flavor
- 8 whole toasted almonds

Stir 1 quart vanilla ice cream until soft. Add 1 cup of peaches and enough rum to flavor. Spoon into 8 individual muffin pans. Freeze until nearly firm. Poke a whole toasted almond, point down, into each ice cream cup and freeze until firm. Serves 8.

25
Gracious Entertaining

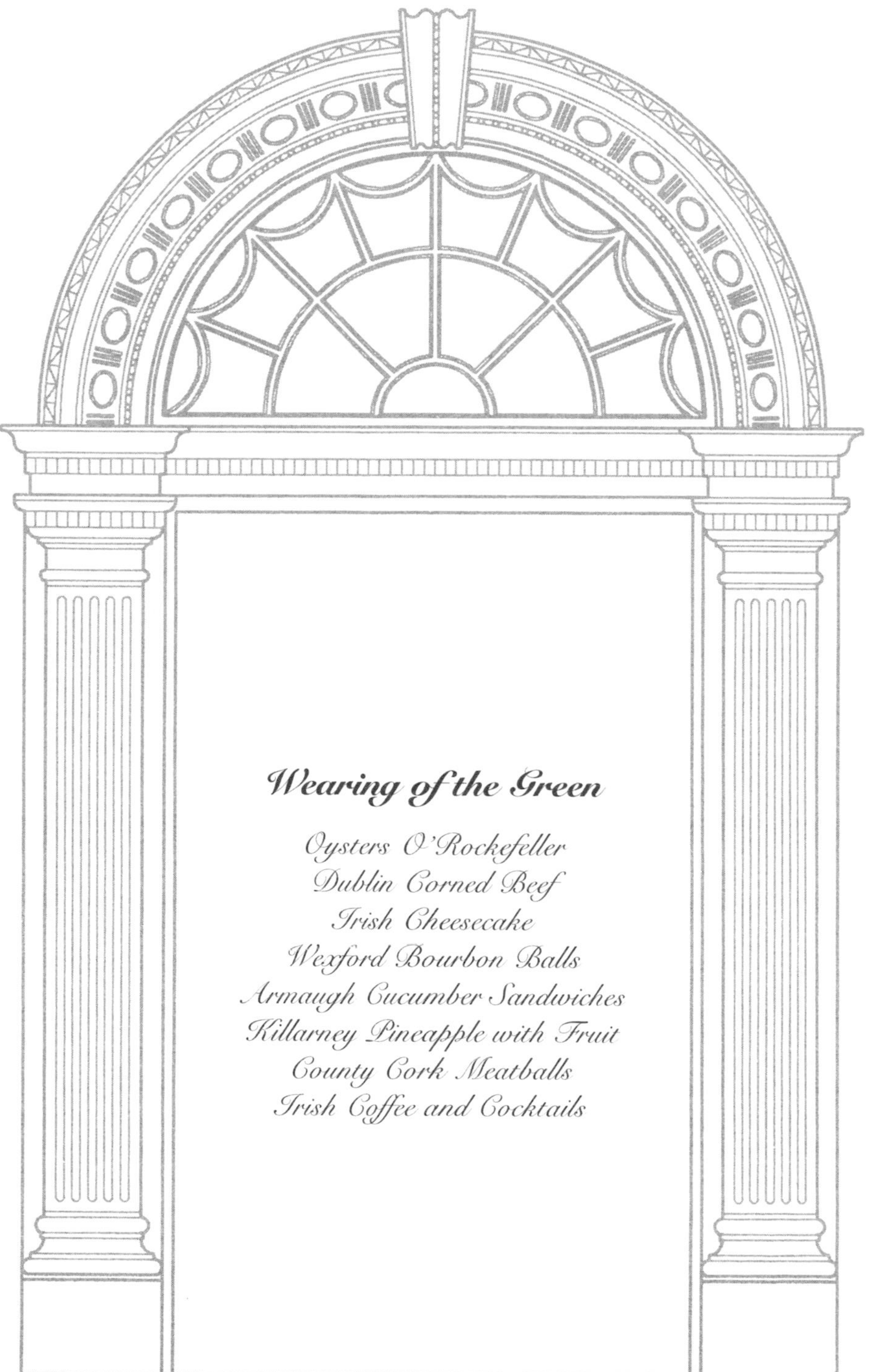

Wearing of the Green

Oysters O'Rockefeller
Dublin Corned Beef
Irish Cheesecake
Wexford Bourbon Balls
Armaugh Cucumber Sandwiches
Killarney Pineapple with Fruit
County Cork Meatballs
Irish Coffee and Cocktails

Begorra! Happy St. Patrick's Day

Re: Preparation for an Irish Cocktail Party
Decorations: The Irish flag is unfurled on the front of the house. It will fly about 4-5 days prior to March 17 and be removed the evening of March 17 (the day of the parade). The tables are covered with runners of the Irish flag—green, orange, and white—duplicating the colors of the flag except the runners have white fringe on both ends.

Various four-leaf clover plants are placed on tables.

Other decorations can include a miniature Irish harp on the cheese-cake, shamrocks or leprechauns on the tables and mantels.

If you have hurricane globes with candles, be certain to use green candles and have a small orange bow wrapped around each candle.

Have a basket at the door with the traditional Irish pins to hand out to guests so they will have these for the parade on the **"Grand Day"**—March 17.

Party Happenings: Besides socializing and enjoying the treats and grog, there are several happenings during the evening. More often than not, several of the Irish priests will be in attendance and they are usually called upon to give the traditional Irish toast to honor the patron saint of Ireland, St. Patrick. He usually prays for good weather for the parade and also for a reunited Ireland. After this, guests return to more merriment but listen attentively to the harpist, then later sing along with Irish songs. Sometime during the evening, people congregate around a map of Ireland that is usually displayed on a wall or on an easel and those with Irish heritage can choose a stick pin and place it on the county that their ancestors hailed from.

Upon leaving, Irish pins are distributed. Sometimes one of the Senior Irish citizens has crocheted the shamrocks. Others will add these to the adornment of pins from previous years and if a member of the family, father, uncle, brother, grandfather, has served on the parade committee, the women will be proudly wearing one of the special pins given to the parade committee members.

Let's party, Begorra!

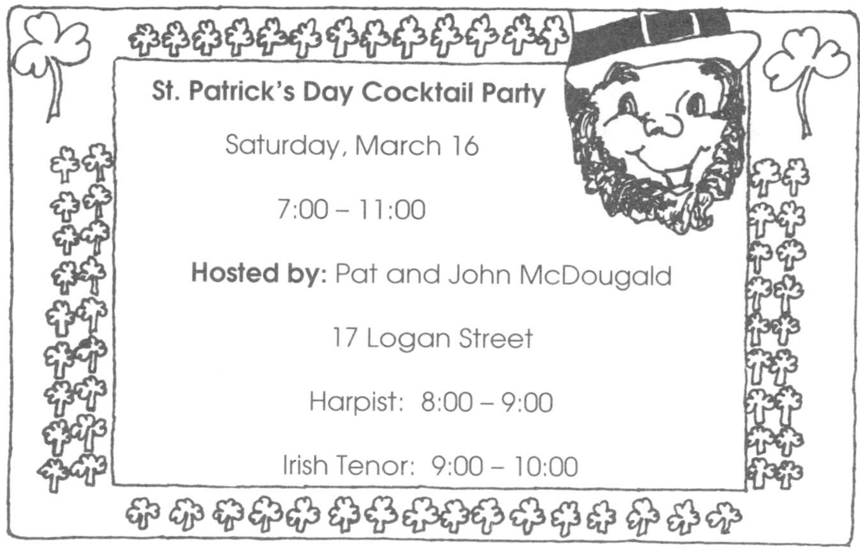

St. Patrick's Day Cocktail Party
Saturday, March 16
7:00 – 11:00
Hosted by: Pat and John McDougald
17 Logan Street
Harpist: 8:00 – 9:00
Irish Tenor: 9:00 – 10:00

County Cork Meatballs

- 2 pounds ground round
- 1 cup breadcrumbs
- 3 tablespoons onions, diced
- 1 egg
- 1 teaspoon salt
- 2 teaspoons pepper
- 1 tablespoon Worcestershire
- 1 teaspoon Escoffier Diable Sauce
- 3 packages prepared brown gravy mix
- 1 cup leftover gravy (beef or pork)

Combine all ingredients except gravy mix and gravy. Shape mixture into 1½-inch meatballs. Prepare gravy mix according to package; add leftover gravy. Add meatballs and cook until tender. Transfer to chafing dish and keep heated. Serve with fluted or feathered toothpicks.

A little red wine added to the gravy sauces adds a "bit" more flavor.

Armaugh Cucumber Sandwiches

Several loaves of soft white bread
Round cookie cutter
Mayonnaise
Cucumbers
Watercress, parsley, or fluffy ruffled lettuce

Use cookie cutter to cut round shapes of bread avoiding the crust. Spread a very thin layer of mayonnaise on each slice. Skin cucumbers and cut paper-thin. Put one to two slices between two pieces of bread. Garnish serving platter or tray with either watercress, parsley or fluffy ruffled lettuce.

Wexford Bourbon Balls

2½ cups vanilla wafer crumbs
1 cup pecans, finely chopped
⅓ cup bourbon
1 cup powdered sugar
3 tablespoons cocoa
2 tablespoons white corn syrup

Break wafers into blender, ¾ cup at a time; blend to crumbs. Blend pecans ½ cup at a time. Place in bowl and mix well. Put remaining ingredients in blender; cover and blend thoroughly for 10 seconds. Pour liquids over dry ingredients. Mix well. Roll into balls about one-inch in diameter; then roll in additional powdered sugar. Store in airtight container. Age 18 to 24 hours before serving. Makes 40 to 48 balls.

Dublin Corned Beef

4 to 5 pounds brisket
1 head green cabbage, (sliced or cubed)
1 medium onion, sliced
4 bay leaves
1 teaspoon cloves

Place brisket in large pot of cold water. Bring to a boil and simmer one hour. Drain, cover with fresh cold water. Add bay leaves, cloves, onion, and cabbage. Bring to a boil gradually and simmer gently until meat is tender. Slice thin and serve with party rye bread.

Oysters O'Rockefeller

- ½ package frozen, chopped spinach, drained
- 6 green onions
- 2 ribs celery
- ⅓ bunch parsley
- ⅓ head lettuce
- 8 tablespoons butter
- ¾ cup breadcrumbs
- 1 tablespoon Worcestershire sauce
- 1 teaspoon anchovy paste
- Dash hot sauce
- 1½ tablespoons absinthe
- ¼ teaspoon salt
- 3 dozen oysters (select)
- ¼ cup Parmesan cheese, grated

Place first 5 ingredients in blender and mince finely. Mix softened butter and ¼ cup breadcrumbs in large bowl. Add blended onion mixture. Stir. Add remaining ingredients with the exception of oysters, cheese, and remaining breadcrumbs. Mix thoroughly. Drain oysters and place on half shells. Set on pan of ice cream salt which has been heated for 20 minutes at 450°. Spread 2 tablespoons sauce over each oyster. Combine Parmesan cheese and remaining breadcrumbs and top each oyster with 1 teaspoon of cheese mixture. Bake at 450° for 25 minutes or until lightly browned. Serves 12.

Killarney Pineapple with Fruit

- 1 large pineapple, fresh
- 2 oranges, cubed
- 2 apples, cubed
- ¼ package coconut
- 2 peaches, skinned and quartered
- 1 small bunch green grapes, seedless
- ½ jar maraschino cherries with juice
- ¼ pound pecans
- Pineapple cubes

Cut a thin slice horizontally down length of a fresh large pineapple. Core pineapple. Cube all of the above fruits, except grapes. Place fruit in pineapple. Top with coconut, pecans and cherries.

Irish Cheesecake

- Butter
- ½ cup graham cracker crumbs
- 2 lemons
- 1 orange
- 1 (8-ounce) package cream cheese
- 1 teaspoon vanilla
- ½ cup heavy cream
- ¾ cup plus 2 tablespoons sugar
- 4 large eggs
- 2 tablespoons sour cream
- ¼ cup half and half
- Mandarin oranges and kiwi slices for garnish

Preheat oven to 375°. Generously butter a sheet pan. Sprinkle with crumbs, shake excess crumbs away. Grate lemons and orange. Set grated rind aside. In electric mixing bowl, beat cream cheese, grated rinds and vanilla. Beating constantly on moderate speed, gradually add heavy cream and sugar. (Avoid high speed). Add eggs one at a time, beating well after each addition. Add sour cream and half and half. Mix well. Pour mixture into pan and smooth surface. Bake in oven 40 minutes or until center does not quiver when pan is shaken. Let stand on rack until cool.

Decorate top to resemble the Irish flag. Use the kiwi fruit slices on ⅓, leave the center plain and the last ⅓, decorate with well-drained orange slices. Serves 15 to 20.

This is very colorful for the "Grand Day".

Gracious Entertaining

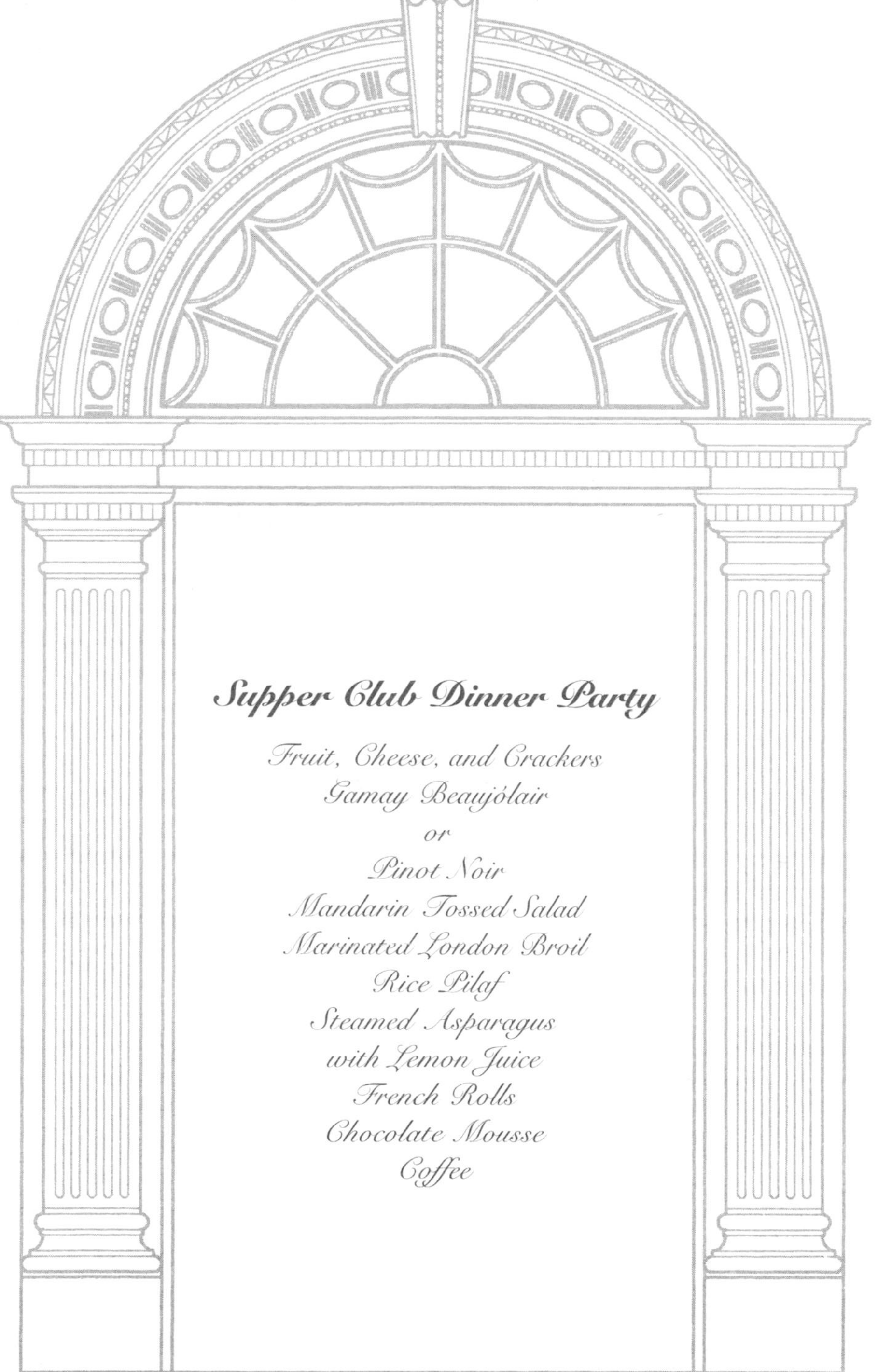

Supper Club Dinner Party

Fruit, Cheese, and Crackers
Gamay Beaujólair
or
Pinot Noir
Mandarin Tossed Salad
Marinated London Broil
Rice Pilaf
Steamed Asparagus
with Lemon Juice
French Rolls
Chocolate Mousse
Coffee

Supper Clubs are quite popular in the Lowcountry. It is a wonderful excuse for friends to get together on a regular basis. It's the time to try out that new recipe and share the latest family happenings. Here's a menu to get you started.

The man of the house can take charge of the grilled London Broil. While the male guests are overseeing the grill, the ladies can help toss the salad. The fruit and cheese tray along with the other dishes can be made ahead so you can enjoy your guests.

Mandarin Tossed Salad

1 head lettuce, torn
1 cup chopped celery
6 green onions, chopped
3 tablespoons chopped fresh parsley
2 (11-ounce) cans mandarin oranges, drained
½ cup slivered almonds, toasted

Dressing:
½ cup vegetable oil
¼ cup tarragon wine vinegar
¼ cup sugar
½ teaspoon salt
¼ teaspoon pepper

Combine dressing ingredients in a jar. Cover tightly and shake vigorously. Chill. Shake again before serving and pour over tossed salad. Serves 6.

Marinated London Broil

1 (3-pound) London Broil cut
1½ teaspoons dry mustard
¾ teaspoon ground ginger
⅛ teaspoon ground pepper
⅛ teaspoon garlic powder
6 tablespoons soy sauce
3 tablespoons lemon juice
3 tablespoons oil

Combine mustard, ginger, pepper, and garlic powder. Mix soy sauce, lemon juice, and oil and add to seasonings. Allow meat to marinate for at least 4 hours. Grill to desired degree of doneness and depending on thickness of meat, usually 12 minutes per side. Before serving, slice thin across the grain. Serves 6.

Rice Pilaf

½ cup butter or margarine
1 large onion, sliced
1 cup sliced mushrooms
¼ cup chopped green pepper
1 cup uncoooked rice
Dash thyme leaves
2 cups chicken broth

Sauté onions in ¼ cup butter. Add mushrooms and green pepper. Cook, then remove from pan. Heat remaining butter. Add rice and brown slightly, stir over low heat. Stir in vegetables and thyme. Heat broth to boiling. Stir in rice. Put in 1-quart casserole. Cover and bake at 350° for 30 minutes. Serves 6.

Chocolate Mousse

1 (6-ounce) package semisweet chocolate chips
5 tablespoons boiling water
4 eggs, separated
2 tablespoons dark rum

Put the chocolate pieces into the container of an electric blender and blend on high speed for 10 seconds. Scrape sides and then add water and blend 10 seconds. Add the egg yolks and rum and blend three seconds or until smooth. Fold the chocolate mixture into stiffly beaten egg whites. Spoon the dessert into individual serving dishes and chill one hour before serving. Serves 6.

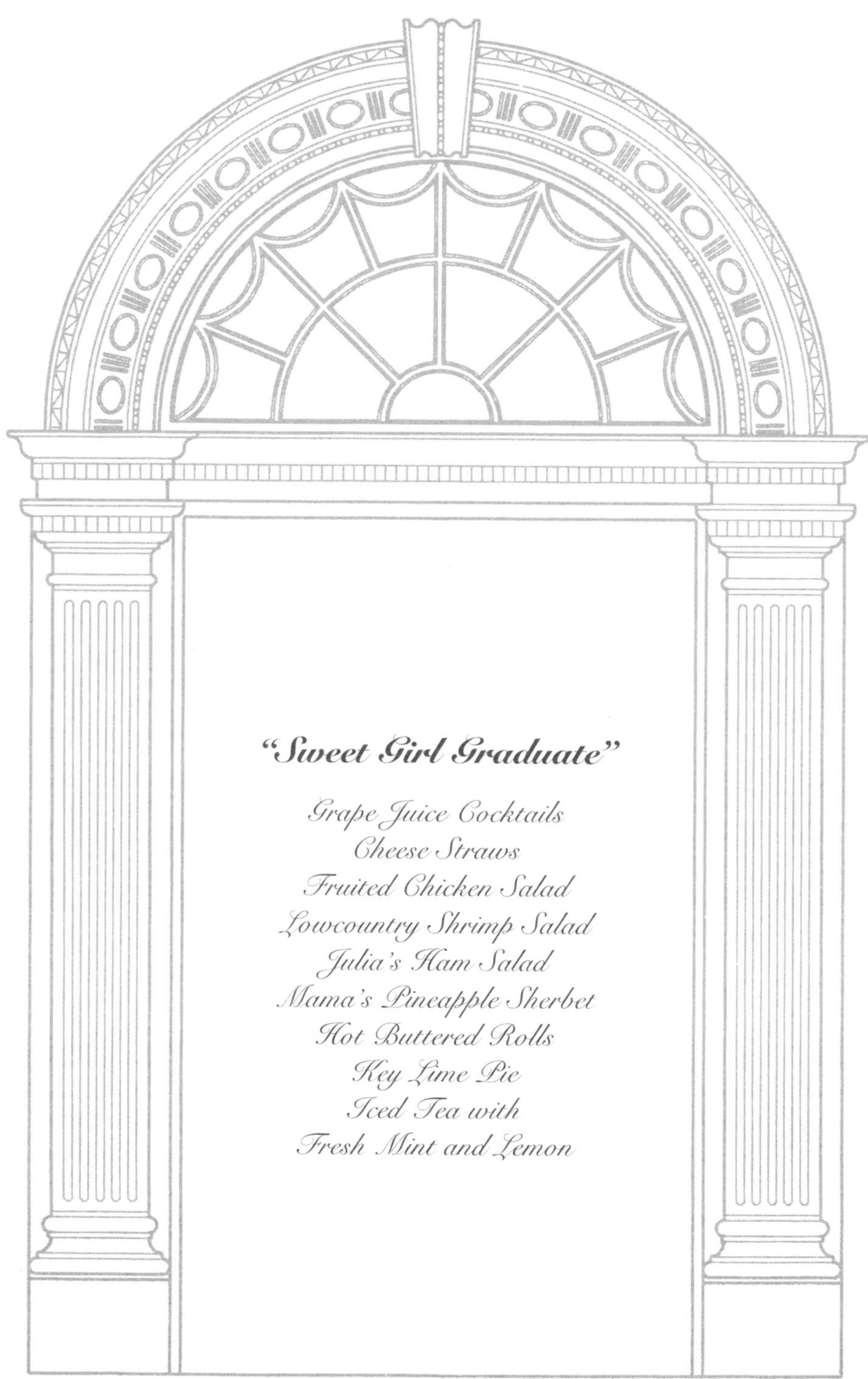

"Sweet Girl Graduate"

Grape Juice Cocktails
Cheese Straws
Fruited Chicken Salad
Lowcountry Shrimp Salad
Julia's Ham Salad
Mama's Pineapple Sherbet
Hot Buttered Rolls
Key Lime Pie
Iced Tea with
Fresh Mint and Lemon

Gracious Entertaining

Celebrate the "Sweet Girl Graduate"

High school graduation is always an important event in our lives—for the graduates, parents and relatives. It usually comes in the spring when nature is at its showiest best, and everything and everyone seems fresh, young and full of anticipation! It's this feeling that I wanted to project as I planned a special memory for a special young friend.

The graduation theme starts with the invitations. It was a Bishop England graduation, so I used white cards with bright green ink for the border and print. Mine were written in calligraphy by a friend; however, there are many clever invitations in your favorite card shop.

The party was to be a seated luncheon, using my finest china, sliver, crystal and linens. The color scheme was built around the school colors. The bright green and white was a perfect "spring" color.

The white linen napkins were tied with green and white satin ribbons. The centerpiece for each table was a relatively small basket of white daisies with green centers and greenery from my yard. I also made a corsage of daisies, greens and a mini-diploma for the honoree.

The "placecards" were white index cards rolled and tied with narrow green and white ribbons which appeared to be mini-diplomas. These were also used on picks in the flower arrangements throughout the house (including the powder room).

My front doors were also decorated with "diplomas" made of poster board rolled up and tied with wide green and white bows.

You will note the menu chosen could be easily done in advance so I, too, could enjoy the party.

Arriving guests were invited to the family room for pre-lunch drinks and appetizers. Sparkling white grape juice is served in champagne glasses with green cherries on a toothpick. Trays of cheese straws were garnished with a tiny bouquet of daisies tied with green and white ribbons.

The salads were served in a separate scallop shell (or oyster shell). The three shells were placed on a bed of lettuce so they wouldn't rattle on the plate. In the center of each plate, I put a stemmed sherbet glass filled with one scoop of lime sherbet and one of pineapple (green and white). The hot pre-buttered rolls were served in baskets.

The Key Lime Pie (green and white) was put into individual dessert size tart shells so that I did not have the last minute pie-cutting to worry about. Coffee was offered with dessert although my younger guests declined. I may skip coffee next time.

A special touch can be added by marking each guest's place with a small address book wrapped in the theme colors, a tiny basket filled with nuts, mints or potpourri, or a small bouquet...the cost of the gift is determined by the number of guests and your budget. Obviously it is not necessary to gift the guests, but will add to the occasion and the memory.

Cheese Straws

2½ cups butter or margarine
2 (12-ounce) packages Kraft sharp cheese, grated
6 cups all-purpose flour, sifted
3 teaspoons baking powder
1 teaspoon red pepper, or to taste
4 to 6 tablespoons ice water
¼ teaspoon salt

Cream butter and cheese. Add flour, baking powder and red pepper. Mix smoothly until it forms a firm dough. Run through a cookie cutter (star tube) the length of your baking sheet. Using a wet knife, cut dough in 2-inch lengths. Bake at 350° until crisp. Sprinkle with salt while hot. Let cool before putting in a can. Makes 6 dozen.

Fruited Chicken Salad

- **2 quarts coarsely cut cooked chicken, approximately 4 to 6 pounds**
- **1 pound fresh seedless green or red grapes**
- **2 cups finely chopped celery**
- **4 green onions, finely chopped, tops included**
- **3 cups toasted slivered almonds, divided**
- **3 cups mayonnaise**
- **2 tablespoons lemon juice**
- **1 tablespoon curry powder**
- **1 (20-ounce) can pineapple chunks**

Cut cooked chicken into bite-size pieces. Wash grapes and dry on paper towel; cut each grape into quarters. Put the cut chicken pieces into a large mixing bowl and add to it the celery, quartered grapes, onion, and 2 cups toasted almonds. Mix well. In another bowl, blend mayonnaise with lemon juice and curry powder. Combine mayonnaise mixture with chicken mixture, adding some pineapple juice to make the salad the consistence you prefer. Chill for several hours in a large glass or stainless steel bowl. Place a generous serving on a crisp lettuce leaf, sprinkle each mound with remaining almonds and garnish with pineapple chunks. Makes 12 servings.

NOTE: If serving in scallop shells, do not use lettuce leaves and fold pineapple chunks (cut small or pineapple tidbits) into the salad mixture as with grapes.

Lowcountry Shrimp Salad

- **½ cup sour cream**
- **¼ teaspoon salt**
- **⅛ teaspoon mace**
- **1 tablespoon fresh lemon juice**
- **1 tablespoon Miracle Whip Salad Dressing**
- **2 hard-boiled eggs, finely chopped**
- **1 pound medium shrimp, cooked, shelled and deveined**

Mix all ingredients together except the shrimp and chill for several hours. Add the shrimp, cut into large chunks or left whole. Refrigerate again for at least an hour. May be made as much as a day ahead of serving. Serves 4 on lettuce leaves; 6 servings in scallop shells.

Julia's Ham Salad

- **4 cups ground baked ham**
- **4 tablespoons Miracle Whip, or more**
- **¾ cup chopped sweet pickle relish**
- **½ cup sweet pickle juice**
- **1 teaspoon Worcestershire sauce**
- **1 teaspoon prepared horseradish mustard**
- **1 teaspoon prepared mustard**
- **1 (8-ounce) package cream cheese**

Mix all ingredients together in large mixing bowl. Add more sweet pickles and more Miracle Whip according to taste and consistency. Refrigerate for several hours in tightly covered container. Serve either as sandwich spread or as filling for a hollowed out tomato on bed of lettuce.

You can form into a ball and serve with party size pumpernickel or rye bread for a party. Serves 8 to 10.

Mama's Pineapple Sherbet

- **3 small cans frozen lemonade**
- **1 large can (20-ounce) crushed pineapple**
- **½ gallon whole or skim milk (not cream)**

Mix all ingredients together and pour into freezer can. Freeze according to your ice cream freezer's directions. Remove dasher and pack. Leave to set for about two hours and it will be ready to serve. Or remove from freezer can and place in air-tight container. The resulting sherbet will be more like an "ice" than a creamy sherbet. Makes 1 slight gallon.

NOTE: This recipe as given results in a VERY tart sherbet. You may add granulated sugar to the mixture before freezing if you want a sweeter taste. Frozen LIMEADE may be substituted.

Key Lime Pie

1 (8-inch) pie plate lined with your favorite pastry, cooked and cooled
1 (14-ounce) can Eagle Brand milk (no substitute)
½ cup fresh Key lime juice (may use bottled Key lime juice which is available in most gourmet sections of the grocery store or at specialty shops)
Several drops green food coloring (optional)
Butter cookies, crushed in food processor (optional)
Whipped cream

Blend lime juice and Eagle Brand milk with wire whisk, adding food coloring if desired. Pour into prepared crust. Refrigerate, covered with plastic wrap. Before serving, sprinkle top of pie with cookie crumbs and a dollop of whipped cream. Serves 8.

NOTE: This can be made in demitasse cups or champagne glasses, using the crushed cookies in the bottom of the glass. Pour the pie filling into the glass and top with whipped cream. Remember that this is a VERY rich dessert, so only small portions are needed.

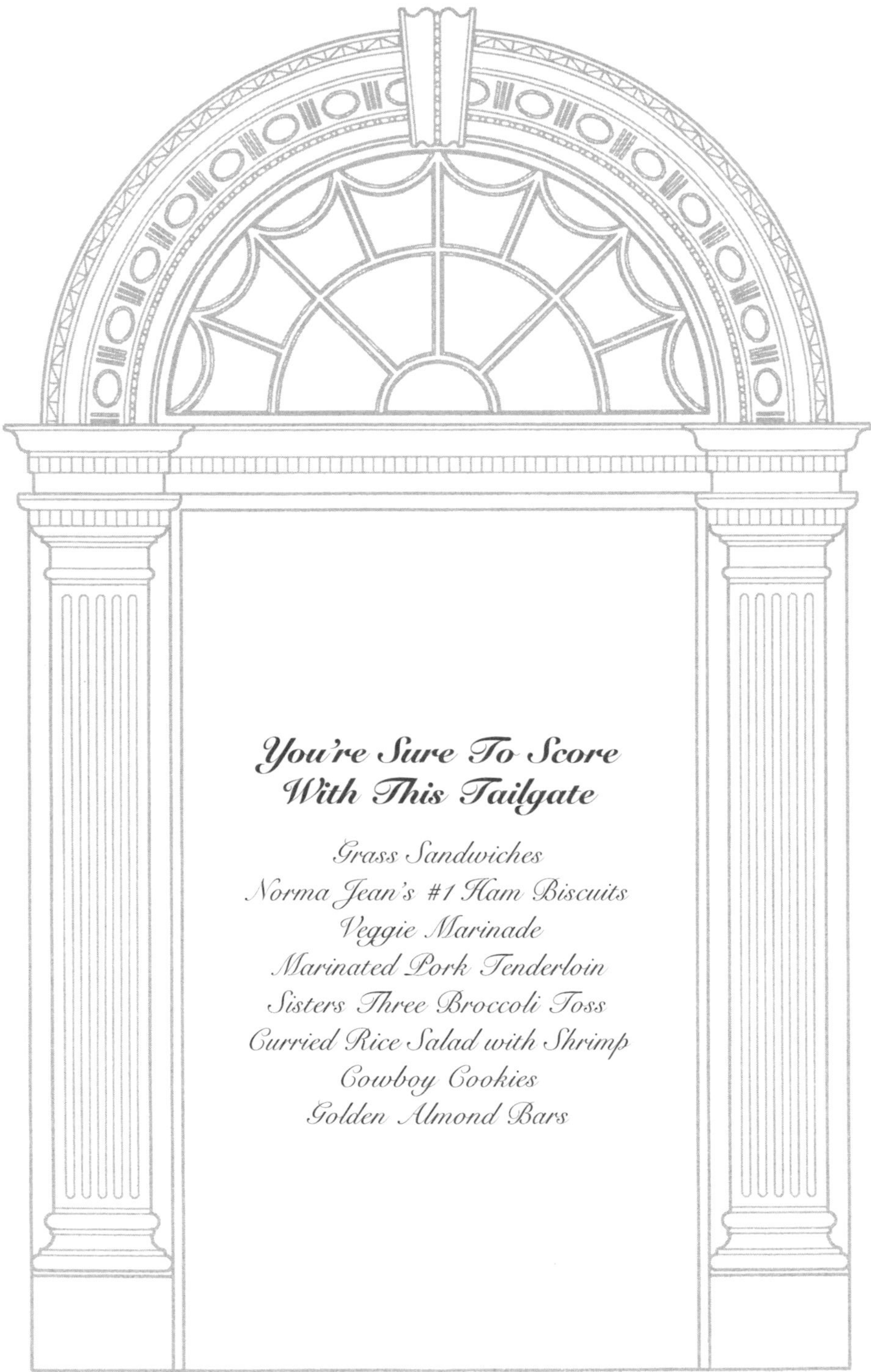

You're Sure To Score With This Tailgate

Grass Sandwiches
Norma Jean's #1 Ham Biscuits
Veggie Marinade
Marinated Pork Tenderloin
Sisters Three Broccoli Toss
Curried Rice Salad with Shrimp
Cowboy Cookies
Golden Almond Bars

This ticket entitles you to attend the

Pre-Game Tailgate Party

Saturday, the 12th, Noon

"Berta and Robbie Freeman"

Field E
Space 12

It's football season once again...

Time to head to Carolina, Clemson or the Citadel for a super Tailgate party. Here's a simple check list to follow so you don't forget a thing:

1) Card table with cloth in school colors. (Chairs optional).

2) Paper plates, napkins, cups and plastic ware also in school colors. (Paper makes clean-up much easier).

3) Arrangement for table. (Could be Pom Poms of your school colors.)

4) Cooler full of drinks and a bottle of champagne or wine for the table. (Looks very chic).

5) Lots of food. You will probably have to share. After all, your tailgate will be the talk of the parking lot.

6) Trash bags and Wet Ones for a fast clean-up.

7) Have fun!

Grass Sandwiches

- 1 package Knorr vegetable soup mix
- 1 (10-ounce) package chopped frozen spinach
- 1½ cups sour cream
- 1 cup mayonnaise
- 1 loaf wheat bread

Squeeze thawed spinach dry and set aside. Blend together the soup mix, sour cream and mayonnaise. Stir in spinach and cover and chill. Make sandwiches on wheat bread.

Very good!

Norma Jean's #1 Ham Biscuits

- 5 packages of "Heat 'N Serve Golden Crust Rolls"
- 1 cup margarine
- 1 teaspoon Worcestershire sauce
- 2 teaspoons mustard
- 1 medium onion, grated
- 3 teaspoons poppy seeds
- 3 ounces shredded Swiss cheese
- 2 pounds ham (thinly sliced from "Deli"), shredded

Melt butter and add all other ingredients. Mix well. Refrigerate mixture for 30 minutes and then stuff rolls. Bake at 350° for 15 to 20 minutes. Before serving, slice rolls in half across the width. Makes 8 unsliced or 16 sliced.

These are great for serving at parties and have always been raved about!

Veggie Marinade

- 1 cup cider vinegar
- 1½ cups Mazola oil
- 1 teaspoon salt
- 1 teaspoon garlic salt
- 1 teaspoon coarse pepper
- 1 tablespoon oregano
- 1 tablespoon dill weed
- 1 teaspoon Accent

Cut vegetables (such as mushrooms, onions, peppers, and cherry tomatoes). Marinate at least 24 hours. Makes 1½ cups.

Marinated Pork Tenderloin

2 pork tenderloins
1 cup olive oil
1 cup soy sauce
1 tablespoon brown sugar
1 package dry Italian dressing
1 tablespoon tarragon vinegar

Mix all ingredients and put in Ziplock bag with two 2½-pound pork tenderloins. Marinate for 2 to 3 days. Cook on grill for 6 minutes on each side. Put back in marinade until you slice it. After slicing, put back in marinade until you serve at room temperature. Each tenderloin should make 20 slices.

Sisters Three Broccoli Toss

1 bunch broccoli
6 slices bacon
½ cup golden raisins
½ cup toasted almonds
1 small red onion
1 can mandarin oranges
1 cup "Versatile Dressing"

Cut broccoli into small pieces. Fry bacon until crisp, drain and set aside. Cut onions into rings. Drain and refrigerate oranges. Three hours before serving, toss broccoli, raisins and oranges with dressing. Before serving, add chopped bacon and almonds; garnish with onion rings. Serves 6 to 8.

Versatile Dressing

1½ cups sugar
1 tablespoon dry mustard
½ teaspoon ginger
½ teaspoon salt
1½ cups salad vinegar
1¾ cups Mazola oil
1 tablespoon grated onion

Beat oil with vinegar and add dry ingredients and onion. Beat well until blended. Makes 4 cups.

Curried Rice Salad with Shrimp

- 1⅓ cups raw rice
- 1 (10-ounce) box frozen English peas, cooked
- ¼ cup French dressing
- ¾ cup mayonnaise
- 1 tablespoon minced onion
- ¾ teaspoon curry powder
- ½ teaspoon salt
- ⅛ teaspoon pepper
- ½ teaspoon dry mustard
- 1 cup celery, diced
- 1 pound cooked, peeled shrimp

Cook rice in water and salt according to rice directions. Mix rice, peas and other ingredients. Refrigerate until ready to serve. Best made a day ahead. Serves 6 to 8.

Cowboy Cookies

- 2 cups all-purpose flour
- 2 teaspoons baking soda
- ½ teaspoon salt
- ½ teaspoon baking powder
- ¾ cup shortening
- 1 cup granulated sugar
- 1 cup brown sugar
- 2 eggs
- 2 cups rolled oats
- ½ teaspoon vanilla
- 1 (12-ounce) package chocolate chips

Preheat oven to 350°. Sift flour, soda, salt and baking powder together and set aside. Blend shortening and sugars together. Add eggs and beat until fluffy. Add flour mixture and mix well. Add oats, vanilla, and chocolate chips. Bake at 350° for 15 minutes. Makes 22 large cookies.

Golden Almond Bars

- 1 package yellow cake mix
- ⅓ cup margarine or butter, softened
- 1 cup ground almonds
- 1 cup powdered sugar
- 1 teaspoon almond extract
- 4 egg whites
- ½ cup chopped almonds

Preheat oven to 350°. In large bowl, mix cake mix and margarine at low speed until crumbly. Reserve ½ cup crumbs for top. Press crumbs into bottom of greased 13x9-inch pan. In same large bowl, beat ground almonds, powdered sugar, almond extract and egg whites on highest speed for 4 minutes. Pour over crumbs. Combine ½ cup reserved crumbs and chopped almonds and sprinkle on top. Bake at 350° for 20 to 30 minutes. Makes 36 bars.

Gracious Entertaining

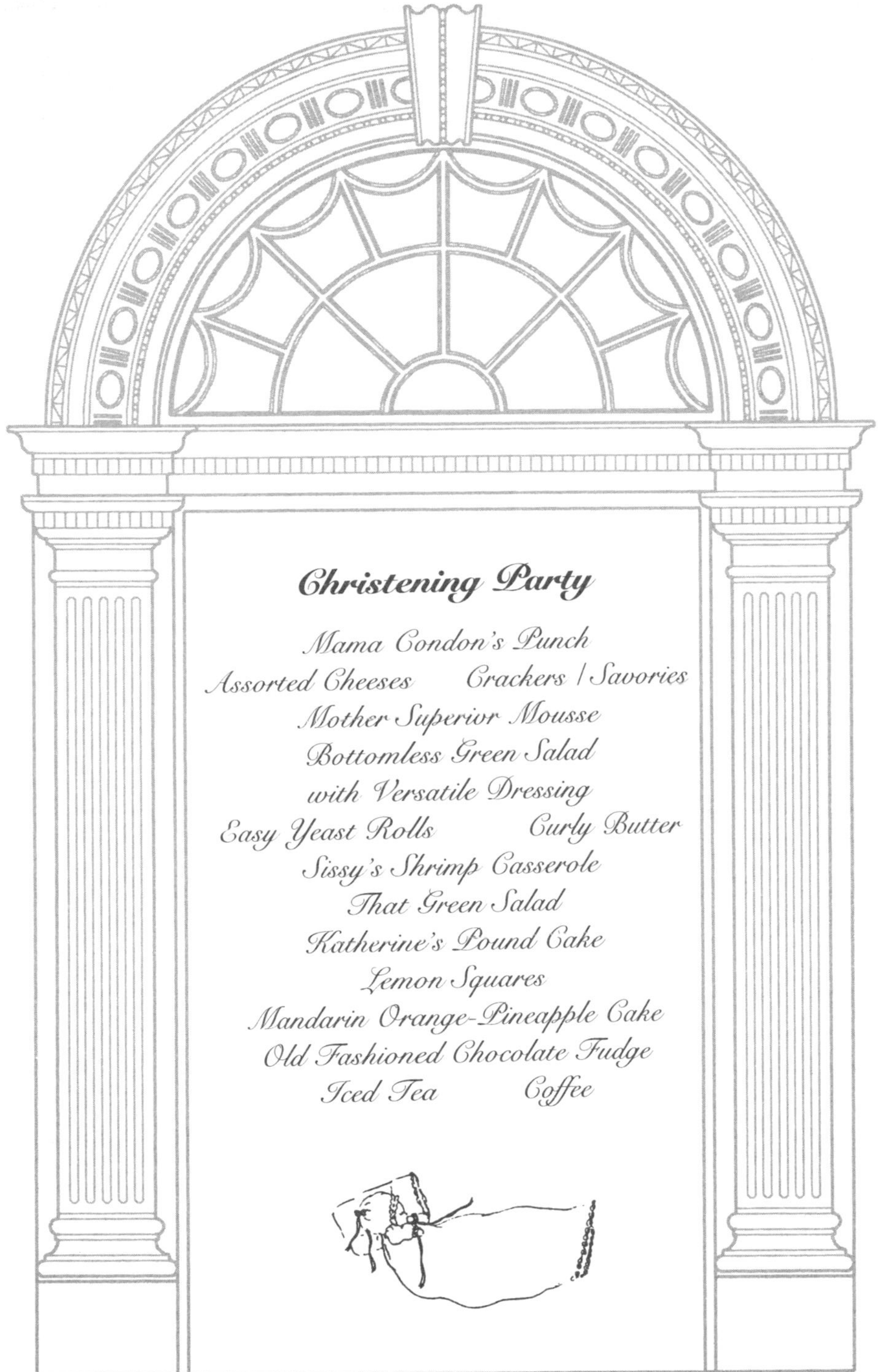

Christening Party

Mama Condon's Punch
Assorted Cheeses   Crackers / Savories
Mother Superior Mousse
Bottomless Green Salad
with Versatile Dressing
Easy Yeast Rolls   Curly Butter
Sissy's Shrimp Casserole
That Green Salad
Katherine's Pound Cake
Lemon Squares
Mandarin Orange-Pineapple Cake
Old Fashioned Chocolate Fudge
Iced Tea   Coffee

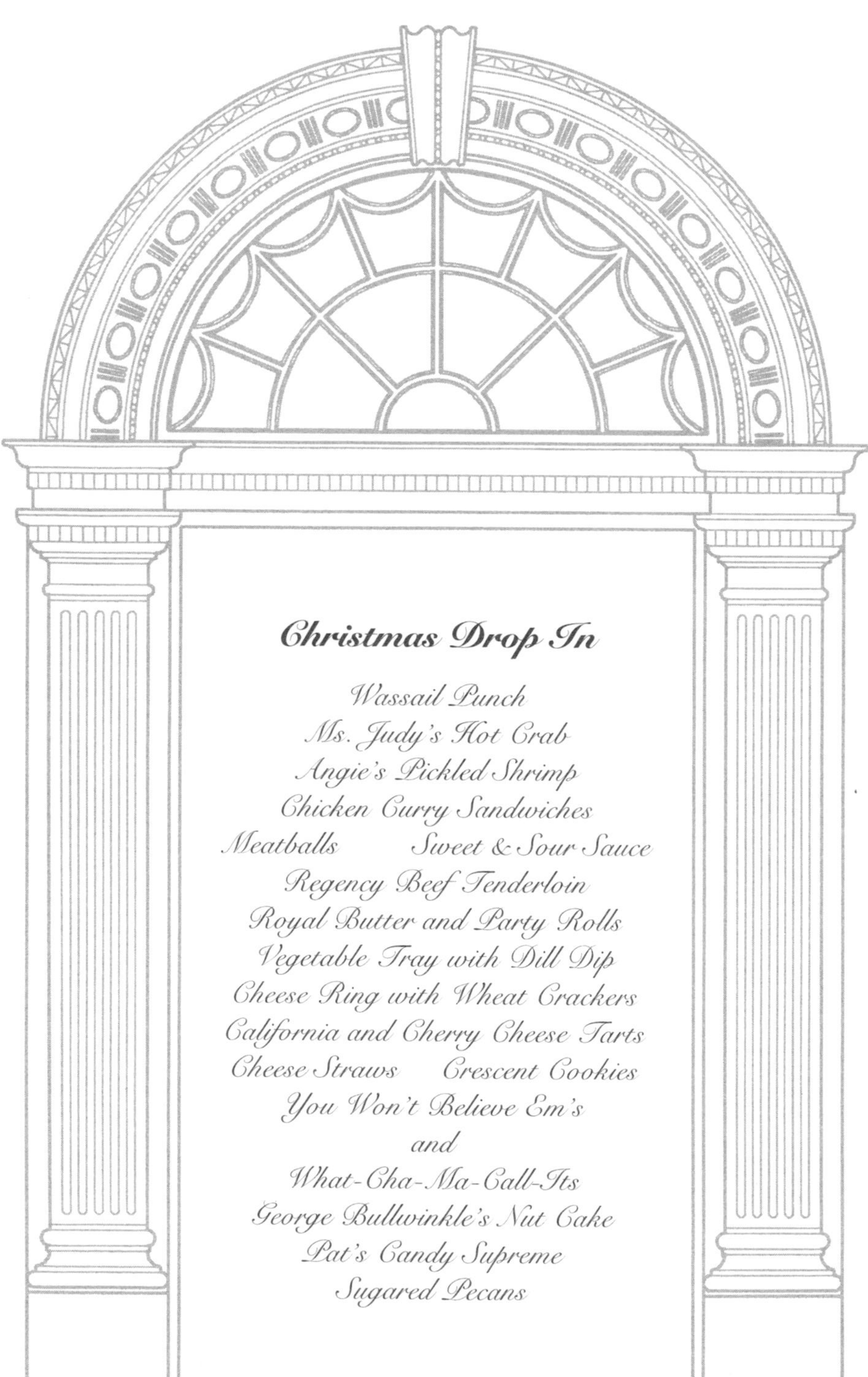

Christmas Drop In

Wassail Punch
Ms. Judy's Hot Crab
Angie's Pickled Shrimp
Chicken Curry Sandwiches
Meatballs   Sweet & Sour Sauce
Regency Beef Tenderloin
Royal Butter and Party Rolls
Vegetable Tray with Dill Dip
Cheese Ring with Wheat Crackers
California and Cherry Cheese Tarts
Cheese Straws   Crescent Cookies
You Won't Believe Em's
and
What-Cha-Ma-Call-Its
George Bullwinkle's Nut Cake
Pat's Candy Supreme
Sugared Pecans

Gracious Entertaining

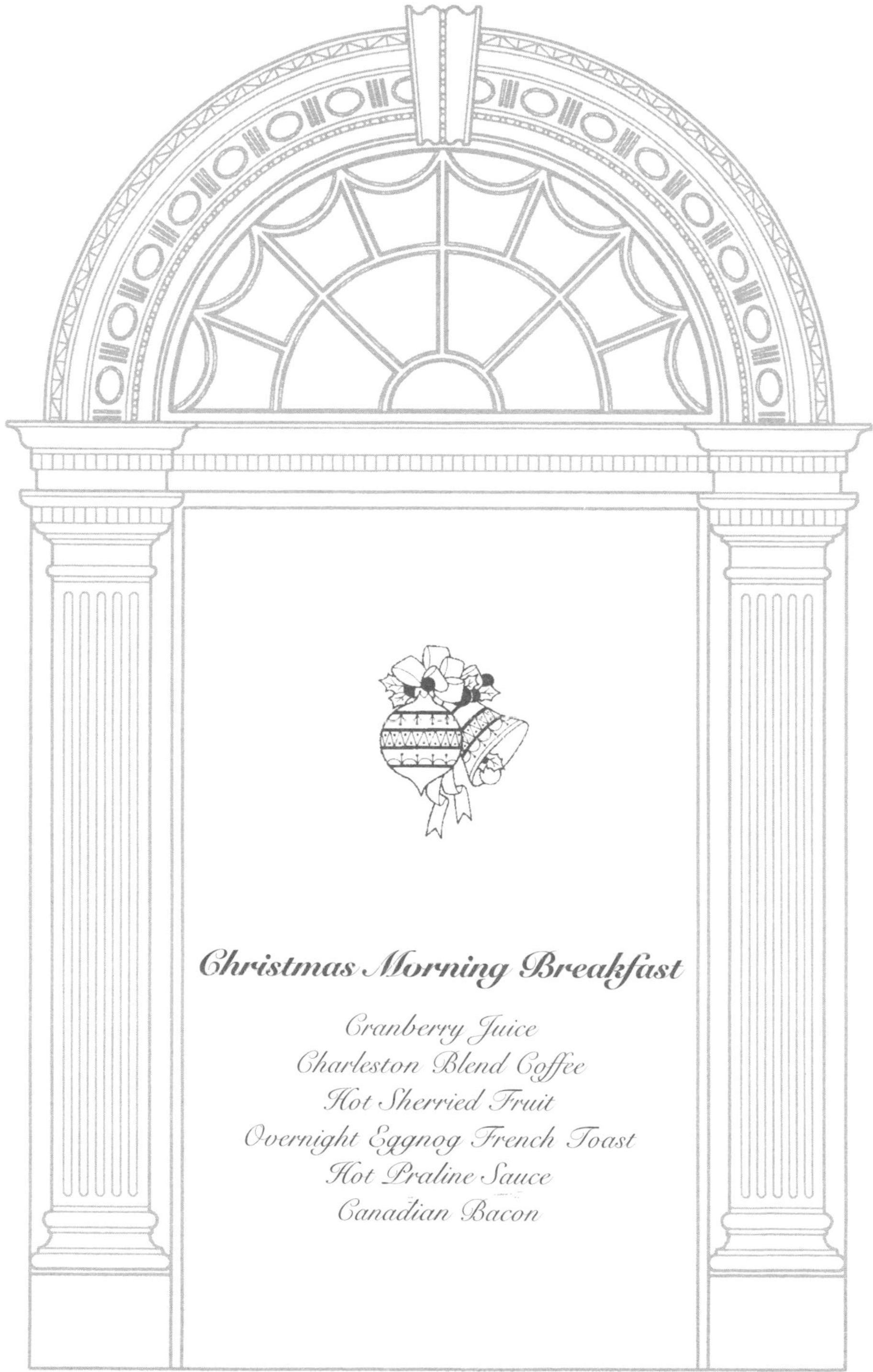

Christmas Morning Breakfast

Cranberry Juice
Charleston Blend Coffee
Hot Sherried Fruit
Overnight Eggnog French Toast
Hot Praline Sauce
Canadian Bacon

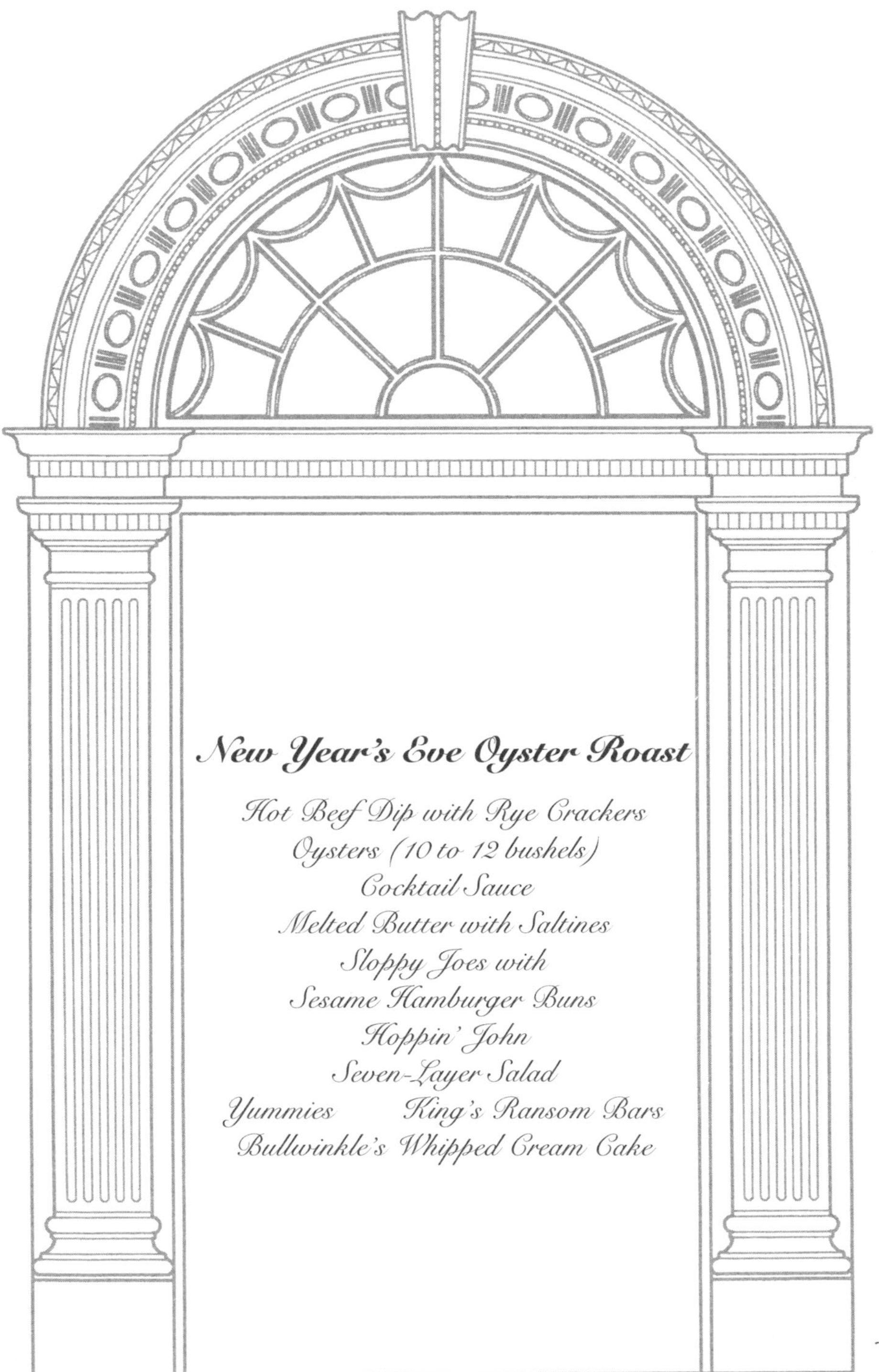

New Year's Eve Oyster Roast

Hot Beef Dip with Rye Crackers
Oysters (10 to 12 bushels)
Cocktail Sauce
Melted Butter with Saltines
Sloppy Joes with
Sesame Hamburger Buns
Hoppin' John
Seven-Layer Salad
Yummies *King's Ransom Bars*
Bullwinkle's Whipped Cream Cake

Gracious Entertaining

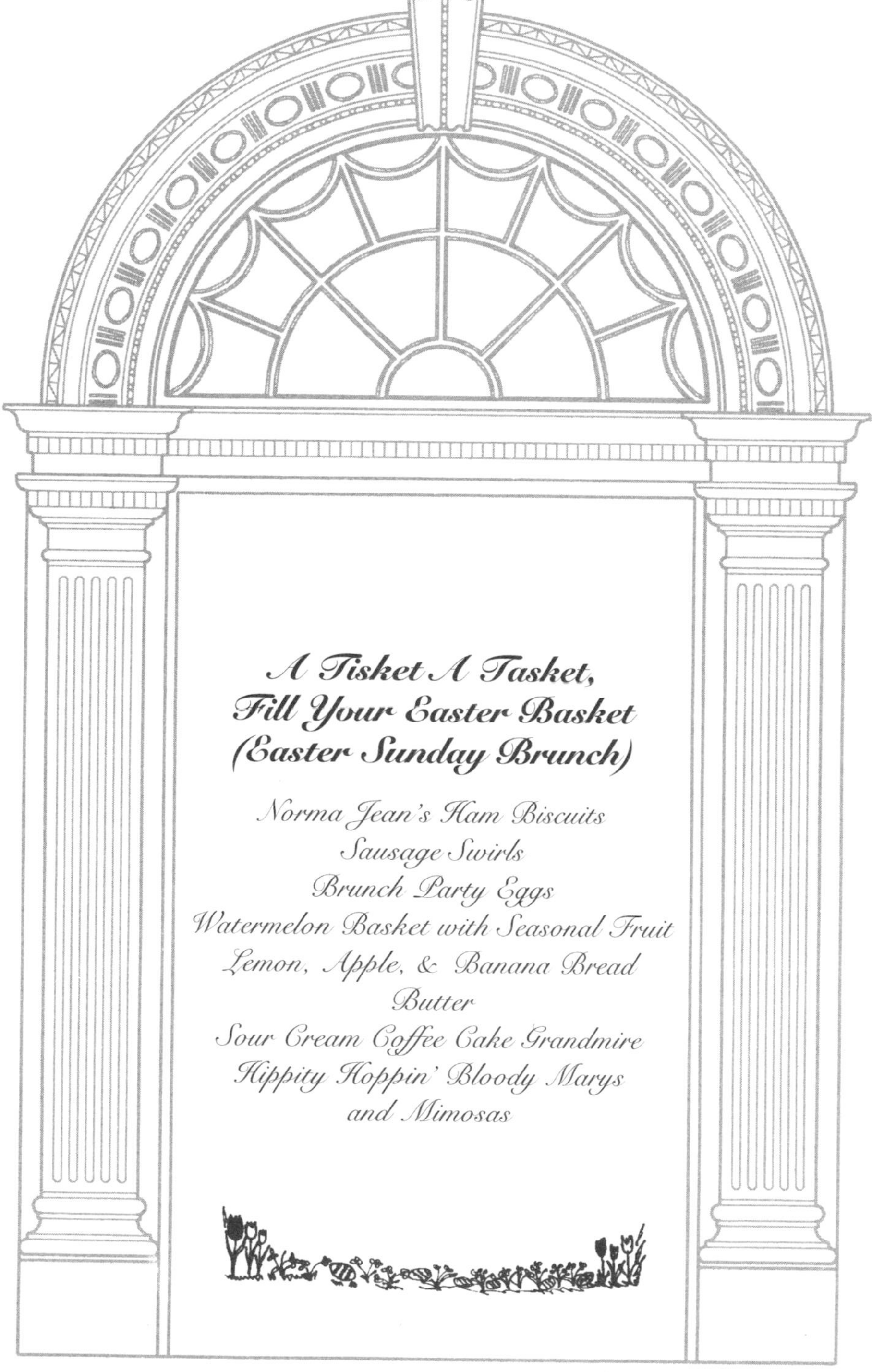

A Tisket A Tasket, Fill Your Easter Basket (Easter Sunday Brunch)

Norma Jean's Ham Biscuits
Sausage Swirls
Brunch Party Eggs
Watermelon Basket with Seasonal Fruit
Lemon, Apple, & Banana Bread
Butter
Sour Cream Coffee Cake Grandmire
Hippity Hoppin' Bloody Marys and Mimosas

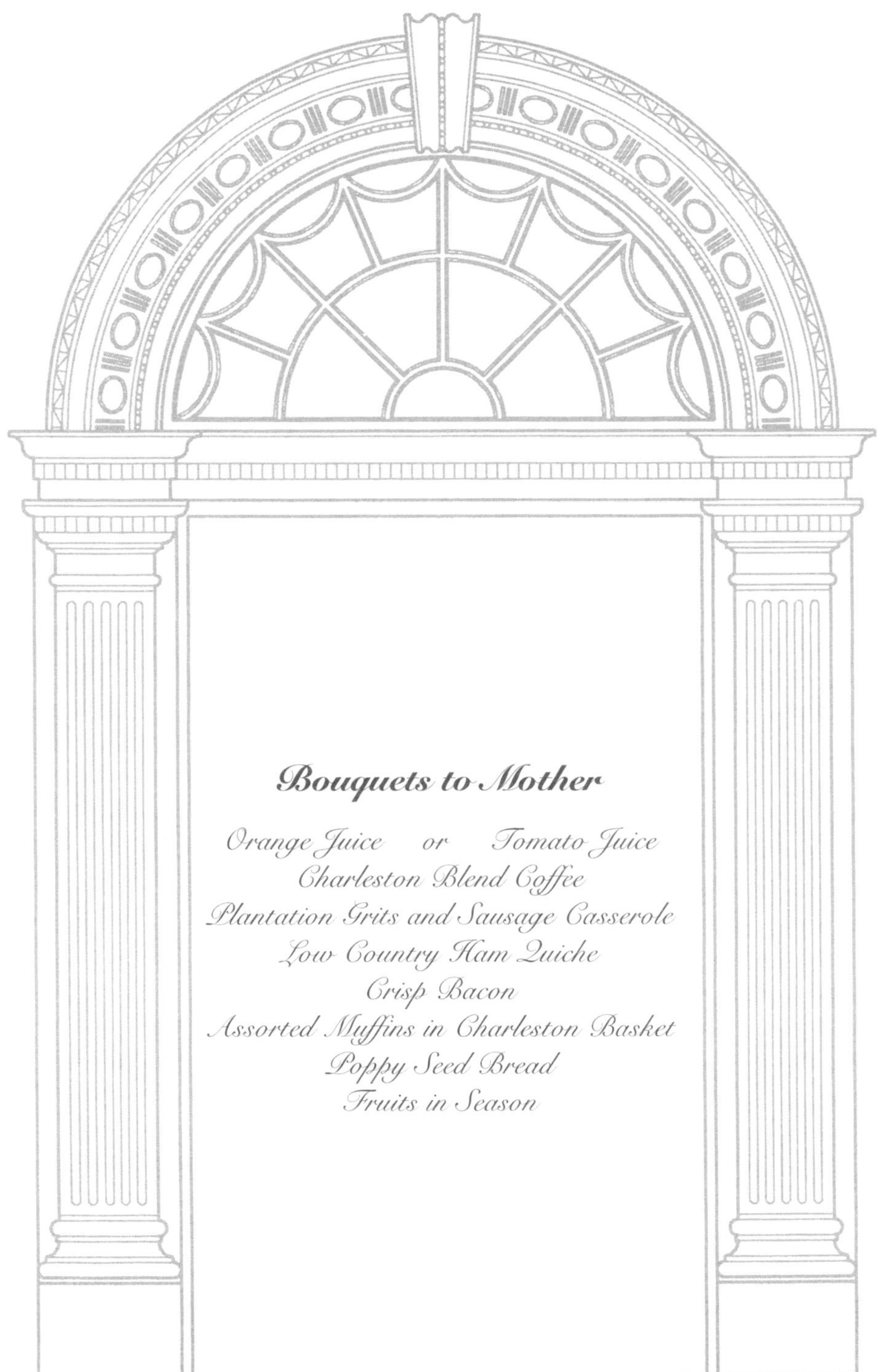

Bouquets to Mother

Orange Juice or Tomato Juice
Charleston Blend Coffee
Plantation Grits and Sausage Casserole
Low Country Ham Quiche
Crisp Bacon
Assorted Muffins in Charleston Basket
Poppy Seed Bread
Fruits in Season

Gracious Entertaining

Fiesta Olé

Margaritas Coronas
Stuffed Mushrooms
Lt. Baker's Party Dip
Basket of Large Fritos
Kit's Nachos Con Carne Quiche Olé
Jalapeño Cheese Crackers
Miniature Spinach Cornbread Muffins
Mary Ann's Pralines
Kahlúa Angel Food Cake
Hazel Nut Coffee

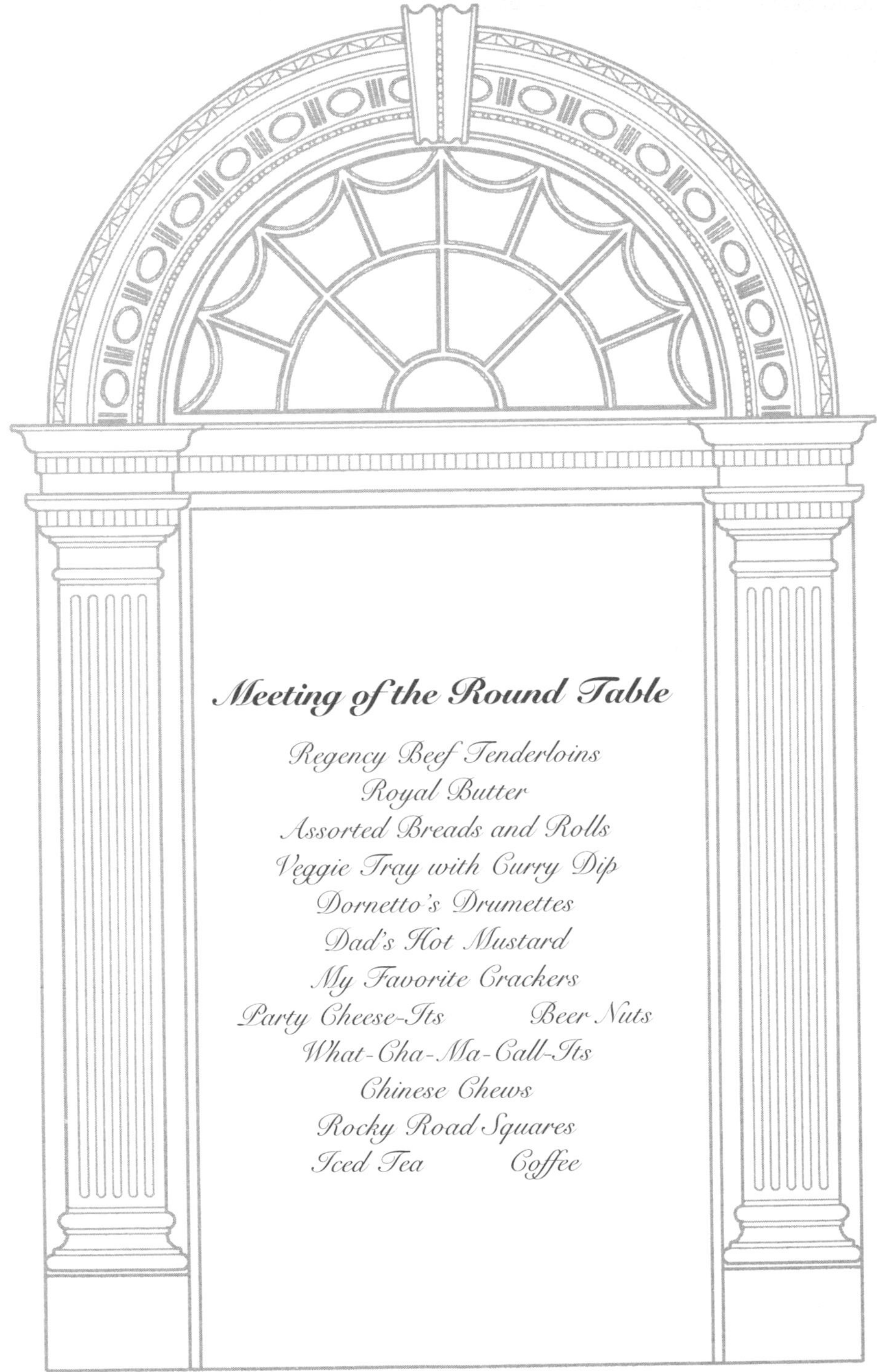

Meeting of the Round Table

Regency Beef Tenderloins
Royal Butter
Assorted Breads and Rolls
Veggie Tray with Curry Dip
Dornetto's Drumettes
Dad's Hot Mustard
My Favorite Crackers
Party Cheese-Its *Beer Nuts*
What-Cha-Ma-Call-Its
Chinese Chews
Rocky Road Squares
Iced Tea *Coffee*

Gracious Entertaining

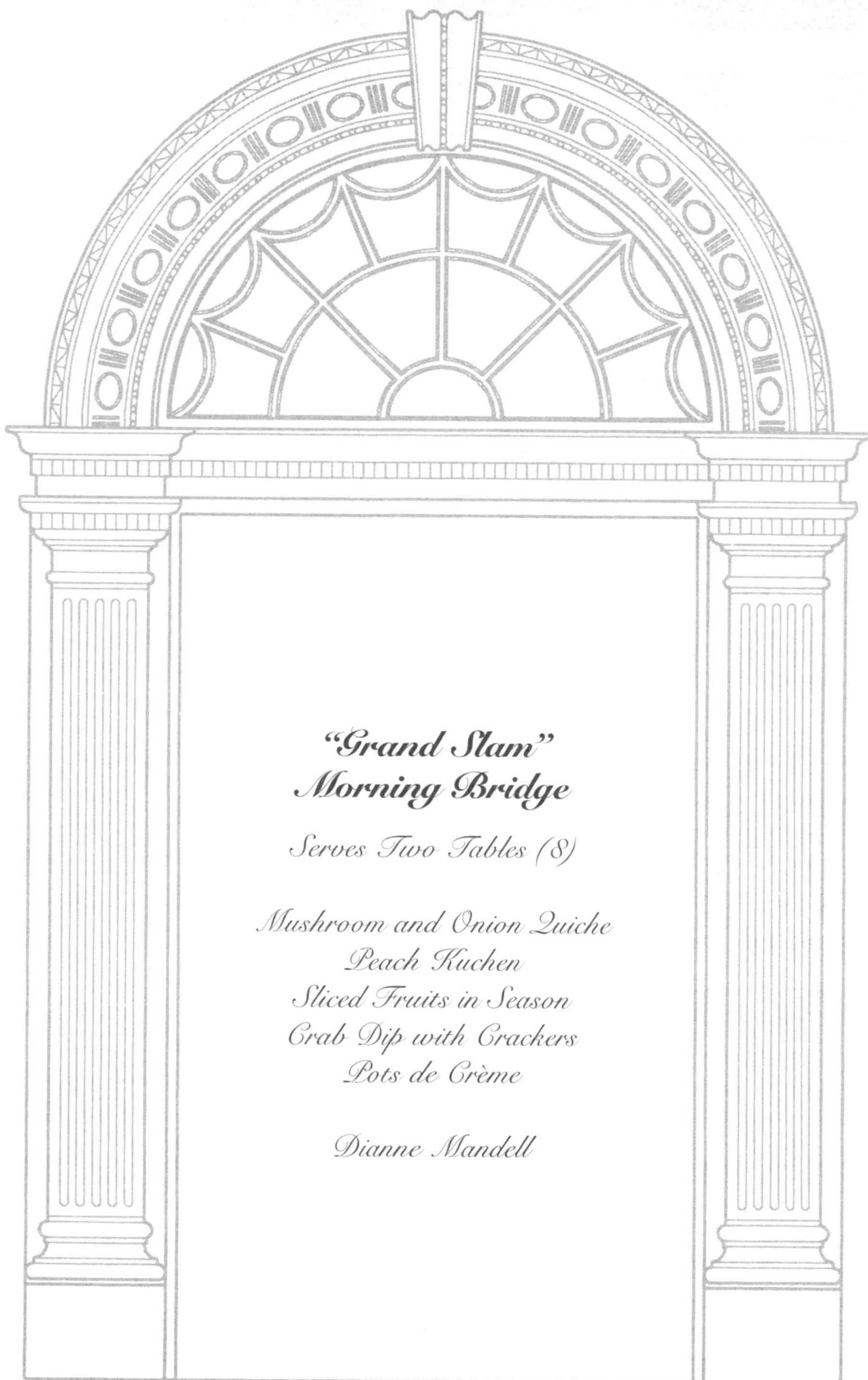

"Grand Slam" Morning Bridge

Serves Two Tables (8)

Mushroom and Onion Quiche
Peach Kuchen
Sliced Fruits in Season
Crab Dip with Crackers
Pots de Crème

Dianne Mandell

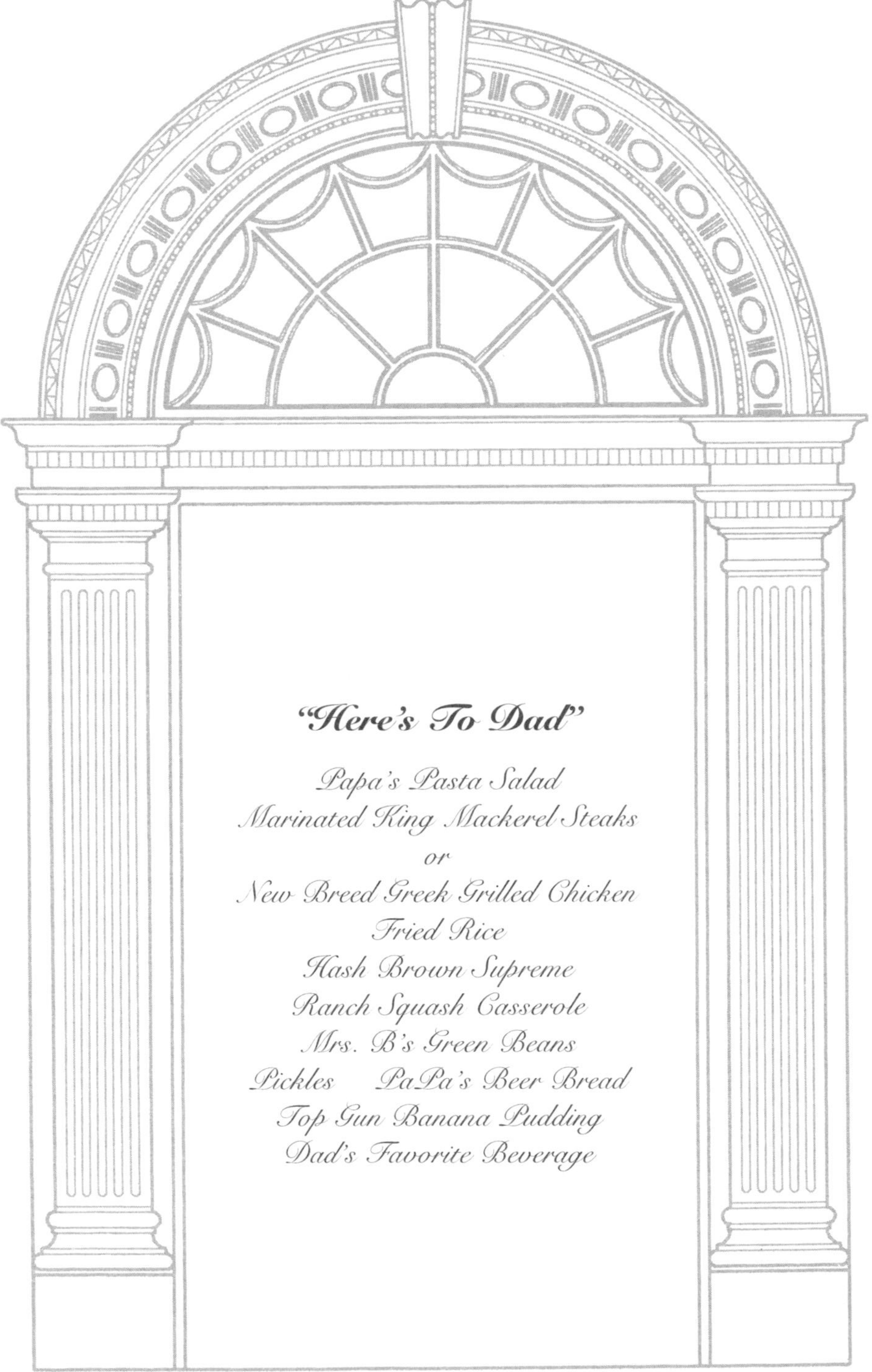

"Here's To Dad"

Papa's Pasta Salad
Marinated King Mackerel Steaks
or
New Breed Greek Grilled Chicken
Fried Rice
Hash Brown Supreme
Ranch Squash Casserole
Mrs. B's Green Beans
Pickles PaPa's Beer Bread
Top Gun Banana Pudding
Dad's Favorite Beverage

Gracious Entertaining

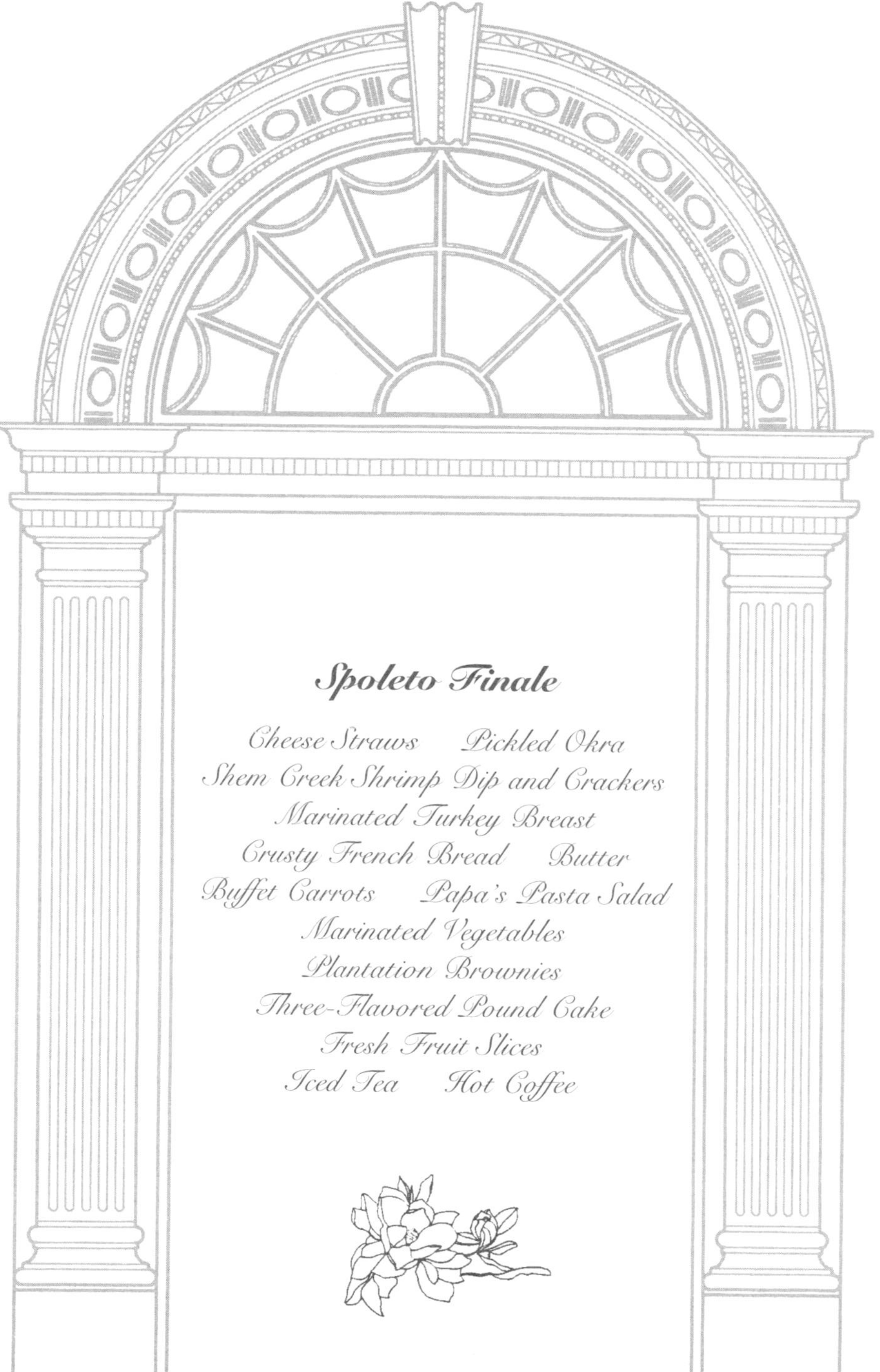

Spoleto Finale

Cheese Straws   Pickled Okra
Shem Creek Shrimp Dip and Crackers
Marinated Turkey Breast
Crusty French Bread   Butter
Buffet Carrots   Papa's Pasta Salad
Marinated Vegetables
Plantation Brownies
Three-Flavored Pound Cake
Fresh Fruit Slices
Iced Tea   Hot Coffee

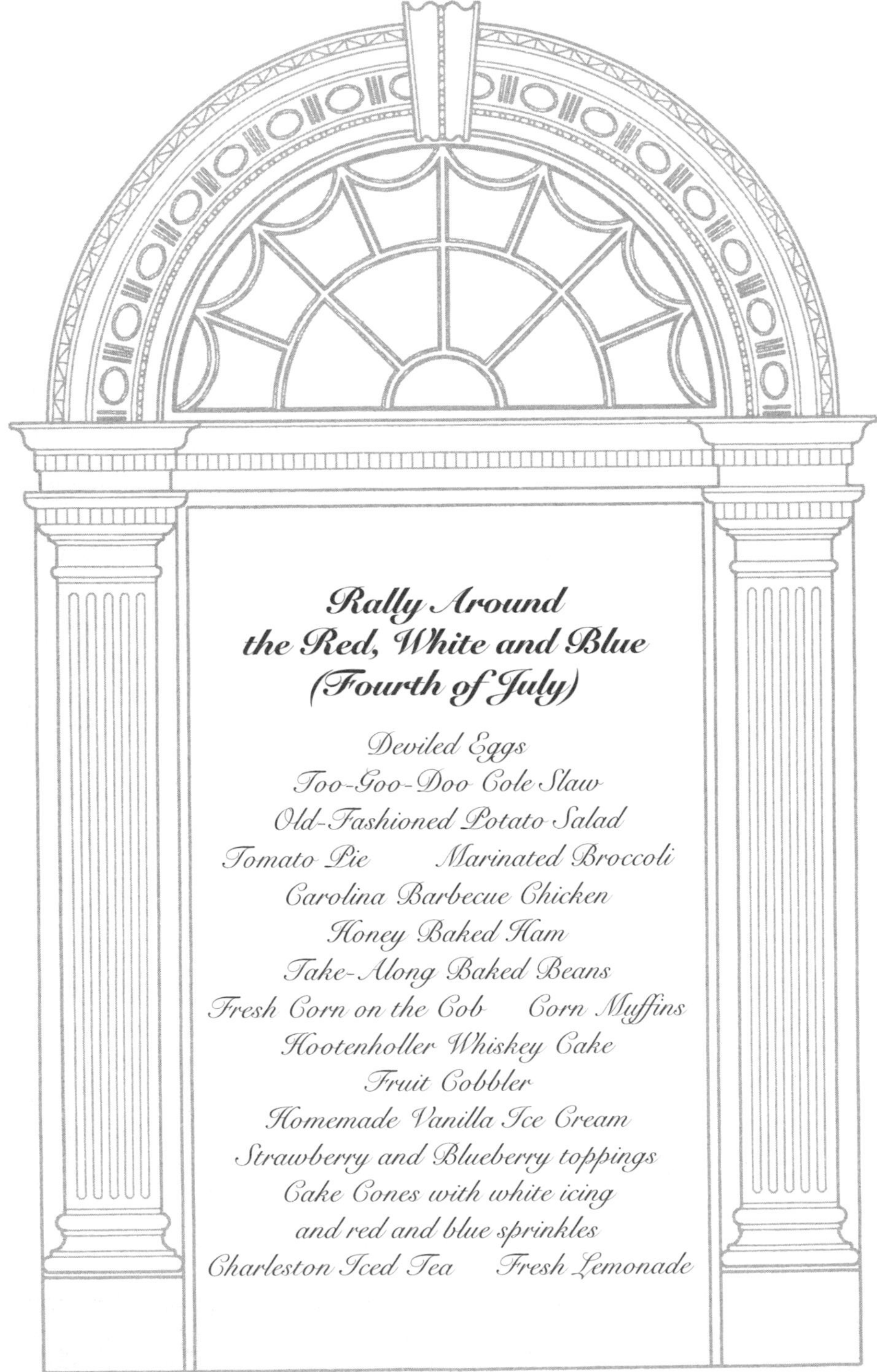

Rally Around the Red, White and Blue (Fourth of July)

Deviled Eggs
Too-Goo-Doo Cole Slaw
Old-Fashioned Potato Salad
Tomato Pie   Marinated Broccoli
Carolina Barbecue Chicken
Honey Baked Ham
Take-Along Baked Beans
Fresh Corn on the Cob   Corn Muffins
Hootenholler Whiskey Cake
Fruit Cobbler
Homemade Vanilla Ice Cream
Strawberry and Blueberry toppings
Cake Cones with white icing and red and blue sprinkles
Charleston Iced Tea   Fresh Lemonade

Gracious Entertaining

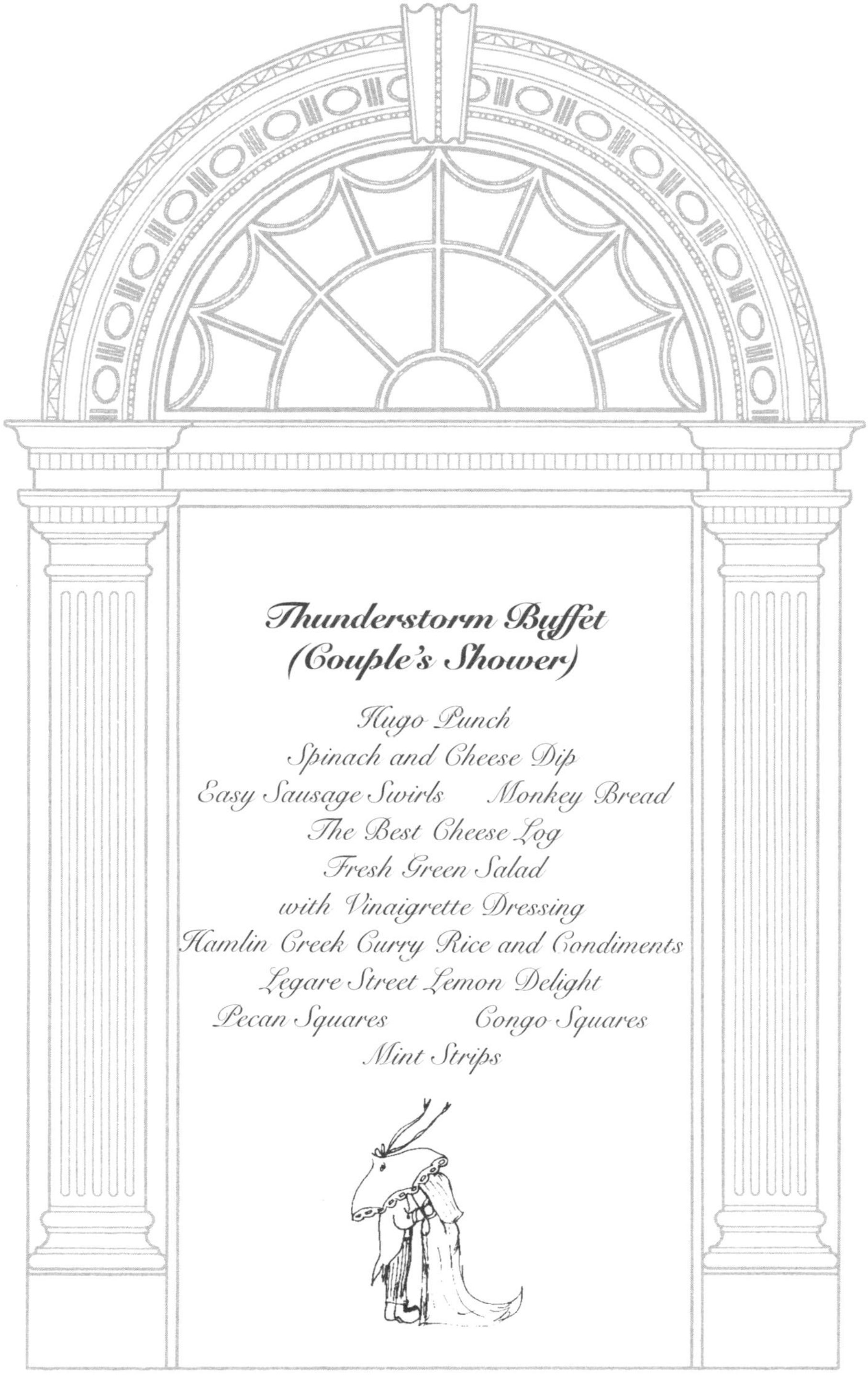

Thunderstorm Buffet (Couple's Shower)

Hugo Punch
Spinach and Cheese Dip
Easy Sausage Swirls   Monkey Bread
The Best Cheese Log
Fresh Green Salad
with Vinaigrette Dressing
Hamlin Creek Curry Rice and Condiments
Legare Street Lemon Delight
Pecan Squares   Congo Squares
Mint Strips

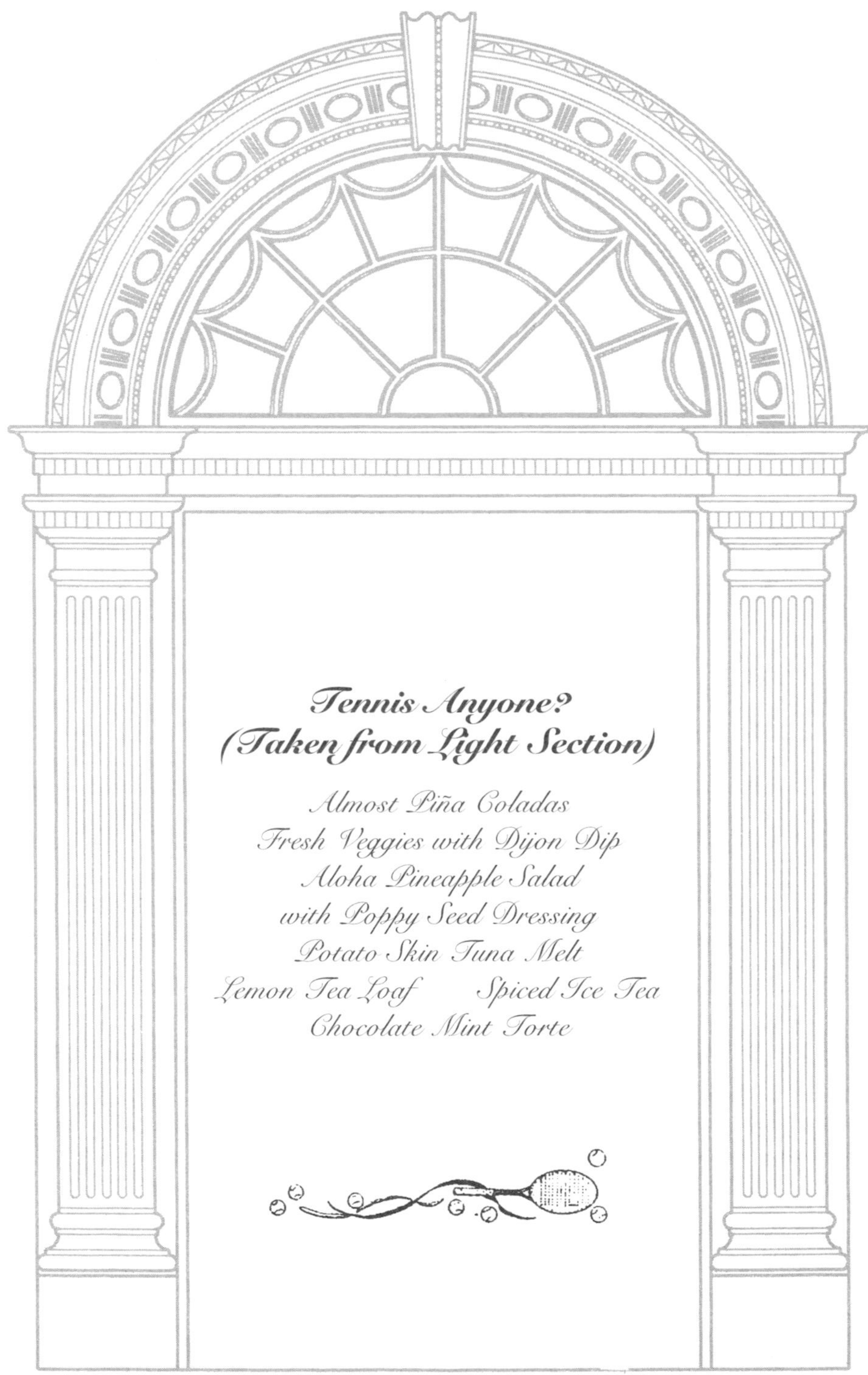

Tennis Anyone?
(Taken from Light Section)

Almost Piña Coladas
Fresh Veggies with Dijon Dip
Aloha Pineapple Salad
with Poppy Seed Dressing
Potato Skin Tuna Melt
Lemon Tea Loaf *Spiced Ice Tea*
Chocolate Mint Torte

Gracious Entertaining

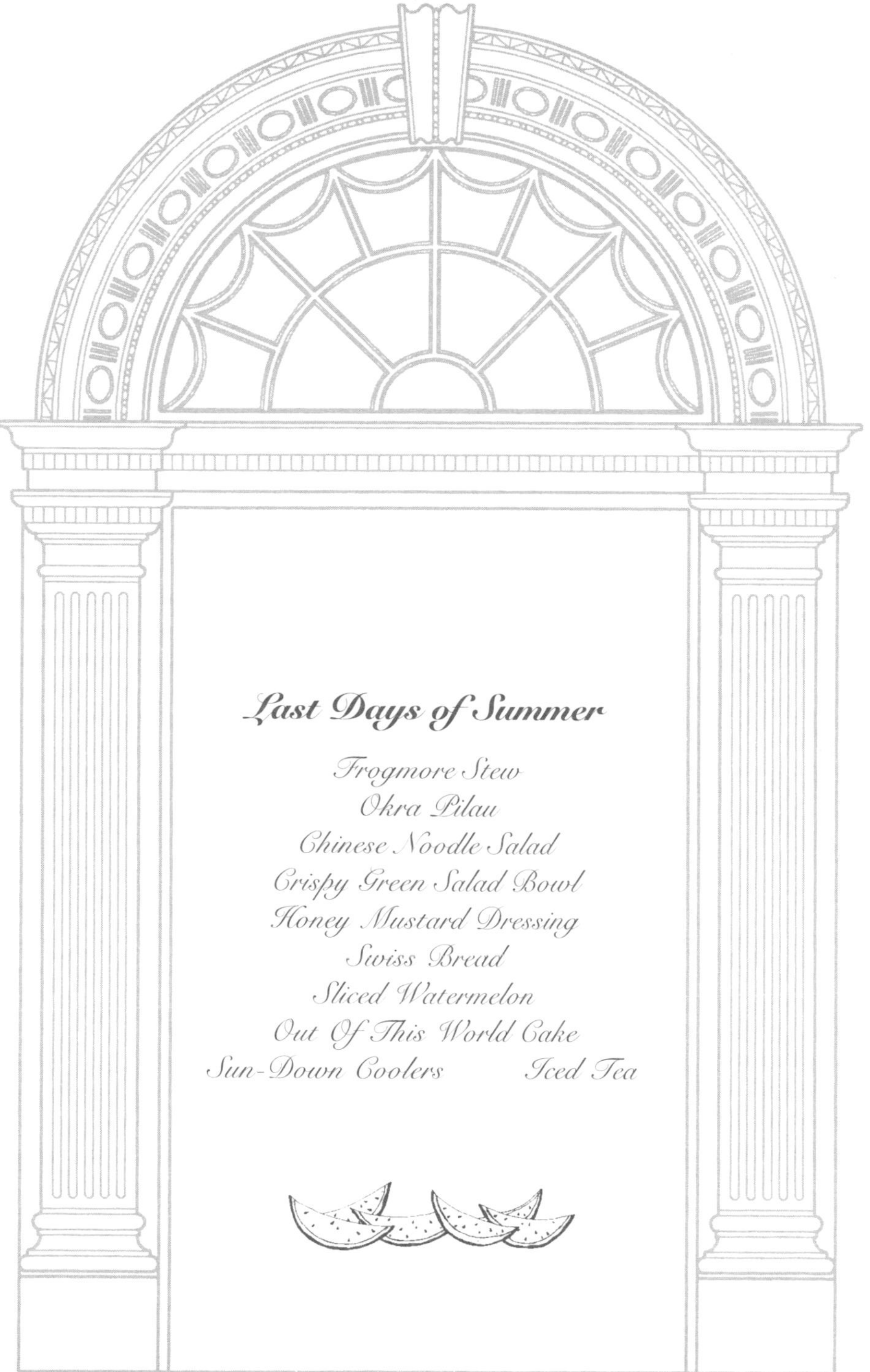

Last Days of Summer

Frogmore Stew
Okra Pilau
Chinese Noodle Salad
Crispy Green Salad Bowl
Honey Mustard Dressing
Swiss Bread
Sliced Watermelon
Out Of This World Cake
Sun-Down Coolers *Iced Tea*

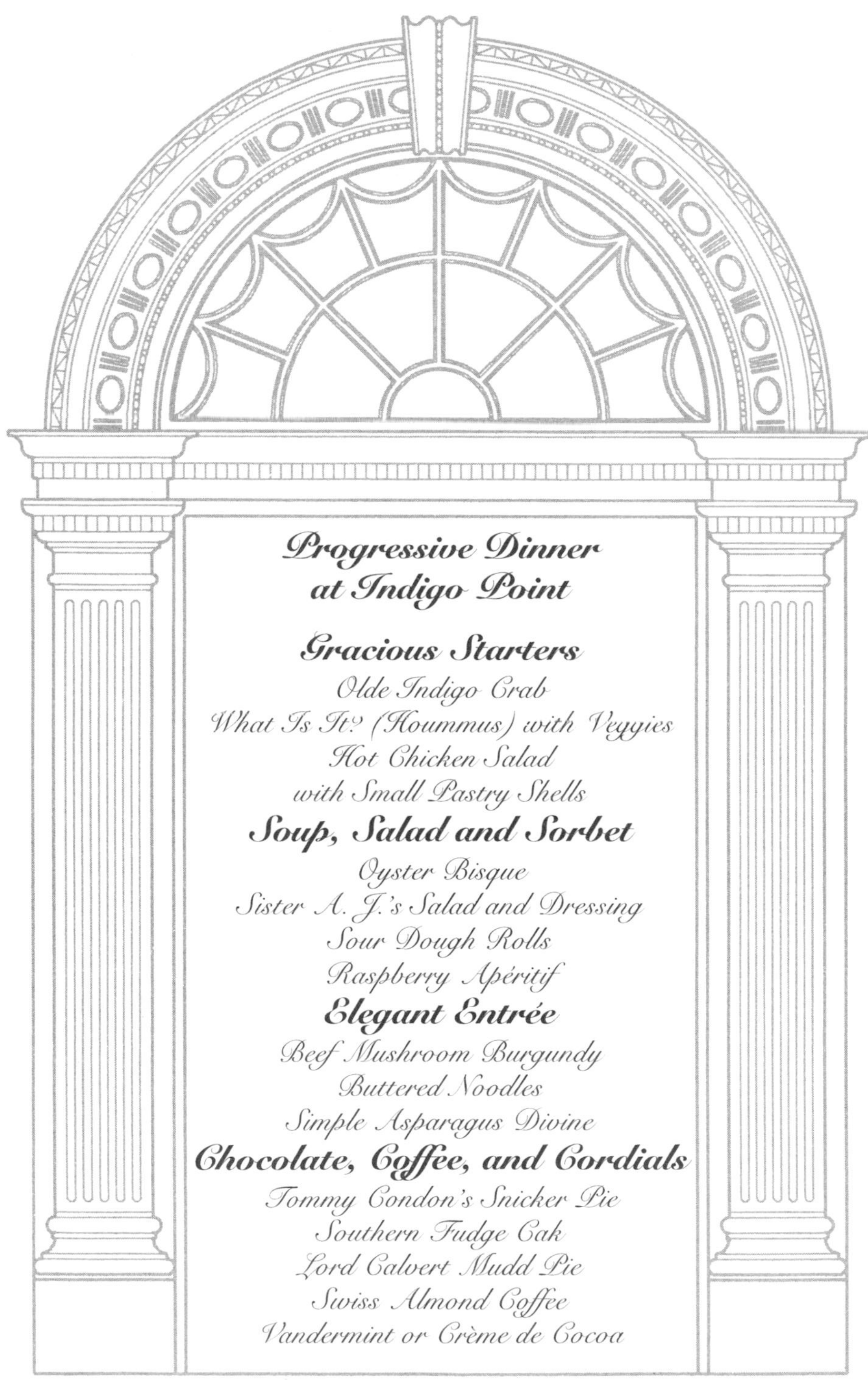

Progressive Dinner at Indigo Point

Gracious Starters

Olde Indigo Crab
What Is It? (Hoummus) with Veggies
Hot Chicken Salad with Small Pastry Shells

Soup, Salad and Sorbet

Oyster Bisque
Sister A. J.'s Salad and Dressing
Sour Dough Rolls
Raspberry Apéritif

Elegant Entrée

Beef Mushroom Burgundy
Buttered Noodles
Simple Asparagus Divine

Chocolate, Coffee, and Cordials

Tommy Condon's Snicker Pie
Southern Fudge Cak
Lord Calvert Mudd Pie
Swiss Almond Coffee
Vandermint or Crème de Cocoa

Gracious Beginnings

Appetizers

Charleston Coffee Punch

4 quarts strong coffee
1 quart half and half
1 quart coffee ice cream
1 quart vanilla ice cream
5 teaspoons vanilla flavoring
5 tablespoons sugar
1 pint whipping cream - whipped

Chill or freeze coffee with sugar. Place in punch bowl 1-2 hours before serving. Just before serving, chop ½ of ice cream and place the other half solid in the bowl. Add vanilla flavoring and half and half. Float whipped cream on top of punch. Serves 20.

Famous at auxiliary meetings.

Dr. Runey's Pain Killer

1 part dark rum
1 part pineapple juice
2 parts orange juice
1 part cream of coconut
Nutmeg

Mix and serve over crushed ice or blenderize until frothy. Sprinkle with nutmeg.

Guaranteed to help you watch the clouds roll by.

Hamby's Champagne Punch

2 (33.8) bottles ginger ale chilled
1 (6-ounce) can frozen lemonade
12 maraschino cherries
1 (12-ounce) can frozen orange juice
1 (25.4) bottle dry champagne, chilled

Mix together in punch bowl. Makes 18 cups.

Garnish with fresh strawberry ice ring.

Eggnog Noel

- **6 tablespoons sugar**
- **¼ teaspoon salt**
- **6 eggs**
- **1 quart whole milk divided in half**
- **1 teaspoon vanilla**
- **bourbon or rum to taste**
- **1 pint whipping cream**
- **ground nutmeg**

In large saucepan, mix sugar, salt, and eggs. Beat with mixer. Add 2 cups milk and stir well. Cook over low heat, stirring constantly, until mixture is thick enough to coat a metal spoon (160°). Remove from heat. Add remaining 2 cups milk and vanilla and mix well. Cover and chill thoroughly several hours or overnight. Just before serving add bourbon or rum to taste. Beat whipping cream until thick. Pour Eggnog into punch cups and top with whipping cream. If desired, sprinkle with a dash of nutmeg. Makes 12 (½ cup) servings.

A special part of a family Christmas tradition.

Hugo Punch

- **3½ cups dry white wine, chilled**
- **½ cup Triple Sec**
- **¼ cup sugar**
- **1 (10-ounce) bottle club soda, chilled**
- **Lemon, lime and orange slices**

Pour wine, Triple Sec and sugar in punch bowl. When ready to serve, add club soda and garnish with sliced fruit. Serves 8.

Mama Condon's Punch

- **2 large cans frozen orange juice**
- **2 large cans frozen lemonade (not pink)**
- **2 large cans pineapple juice**
- **1 cup Lipton tea (3 tea bags in one cup of hot water)**
- **1½ quarts ginger ale**
- **3 large packages frozen strawberries**

Pour all ingredients in punch bowl that has an ice ring in it. (frozen block of ice). You can also freeze some strawberries in a Jello mold filled with water to use as an ice ring. Makes 40 punch cup servings.

We fix this all the time for bridal showers and christenings. Very, very good!!!

Dill Dip

1 cup mayonnaise
1 cup sour cream
1 teaspoon Spice Island Beaumond
1 teaspoon Spice Island dill weed (or use fresh, chop fine)
1 tablespoon dried minced onion (if using fresh, chop fine)
1 tablespoon dried parsley (if using fresh, chop fine)

Mix all ingredients together well and chill in covered container for at least 24 hours so all flavors can blend. Serve with raw vegetables. Makes 2 cups.

What Is This Dip? (Hoummus)

1 (16-ounce) can garbanzos (chick peas), drained
1 clove garlic
½ teaspoon salt
2 tablespoons tahini (sesame seed mix)
¼ cup lemon juice
Olive oil

Mix all ingredients in food processor until smooth and soft. Pour into a dish and sprinkle with olive oil (or paprika). Decorate with parsley and green onions. Serve with pita bread. Makes 2 cups.

This is a favorite dish of our Lebanese community in Charleston. It is sure to be a conversation piece.

Italian Vegetable Dip

1 package dry Italian salad dressing mix
½ cup mayonnaise
½ cup sour cream
1 tablespoon lemon juice

Place all ingredients in blender and mix well. Serve with colorful vegetables or apple slices. Makes 1 cup.

Delicious and very easy!

Curry Dip

- 1 cup mayonnaise
- 1 tablespoon Worcestershire sauce
- 1 teaspoon curry (or to taste)
- 1 tablespoon prepared horseradish
- 1 lemon, juiced

Blend together and serve as a dip for raw vegetables. Makes 1 cup.

Spinach and Cheese Dip

- 1 package Knorr vegetable soup and recipe mix
- 2 cups sour cream
- ½ cup mayonnaise
- 1 (10-ounce) package frozen chopped spinach, thawed
- 2 cups Swiss cheese, shredded
- 1 (8-ounce) can water chestnuts, chopped

Blend soup mix, sour cream and mayonnaise. Drain and stir in spinach, cheese and chestnuts. Cover and chill 2 hours. Makes 5 cups.

Very colorful served in hollowed out purple cabbage or brown round loaf of bread.

Fruit Dip

- 1 (3-ounce) package vanilla instant pudding
- 2 cups milk
- 1 (8-ounce) sour cream
- ⅛ cup orange liqueur
- ½ teaspoon orange zest (the outer rind of the orange obtained by grating the fruit without any of the bitter white)
- Fresh fruit - especially bananas, apples and grapes

Mix milk with pudding, blend in sour cream, liqueur and orange rind. Chill. Makes 3 cups.

Serve with fresh fruit for a summer dip.

Dipsidoodle Crab

- **1 (6½-ounce) can crabmeat**
- **1 (3-ounce) package cream cheese**
- **¼ cup Miracle Whip Horseradish (cream style), to taste**
- **2 tablespoons ketchup**
- **1 teaspoon Worcestershire sauce**
- **4 ounces grated Cheddar cheese**

Drain crabmeat. Soften cream cheese in Miracle Whip. Add crabmeat, horseradish, ketchup, Worcestershire sauce, and grated cheese to the softened cream cheese. Serve with crackers of your choice. Serves 8 to 10.

My Favorite Crab

- **1¼ cups Hellman's mayonnaise**
- **1½ cups crabmeat**
- **¾ cup shredded sharp Cheddar cheese**
- **1½ teaspoons horseradish**
- **4 tablespoons French dressing**

Mix all ingredients together. Serve on your favorite crackers. Serves 6.

This is a copy of the old Trawler's recipe.

Shem Creek Shrimp Dip

- **1 (3-ounce) package cream cheese**
- **1 cup sour cream**
- **2 teaspoons lemon juice**
- **1 package Italian salad dressing mix (dry)**
- **½ to 1 cup boiled shrimp, cooked, deveined and chopped**

Blend all ingredients well and serve with crackers. Serves 6.

Shrimp Dip

- **1 cup of shrimp, (cooked, cleaned and chopped)**
- **½ cup of mayonnaise**
- **1 (8-ounce) package cream cheese**
- **½ cup Cheddar cheese, grated**
- **¼ teaspoon Worcestershire sauce**
- **¼ teaspoon garlic salt**

Combine soft cream cheese and mix all other ingredients. Refrigerate. Serves 8.

VARIATION: Substitute 8 ounces of crab for shrimp.

Sombrero Dip

- **3 medium ripe avocados**
- **2 tablespoons lemon juice**
- **½ teaspoon salt**
- **¼ teaspoon black pepper**
- **1 cup sour cream**
- **½ cup Hellman's mayonnaise**
- **1 package taco seasoning mix**
- **2 (10½-ounce) cans bean dip OR equivalent cans of refried beans with peppers**
- **Large round tortilla chips**
- **1 large bunch green onions, chopped (1 cup)**
- **3 medium size tomatoes, chopped**
- **2 (3½-ounce) cans chopped, ripe olives**
- **1 (12-ounce) package grated sharp Cheddar cheese**

Prepare this in a round pie pan. and the final product will resemble a decorated Mexican Sombrero ... hence the name.

Peel, pit and mash avocados with lemon juice, salt and pepper in large bowl. Combine sour cream, mayonnaise and taco seasoning in another bowl. Spread bean dip in large, shallow pie pan or dish. Top with avocado mixture, layer with sour cream/taco seasoning mixture. Now sprinkle with chopped tomatoes, olives, onions and cheese, making a circle around the dish with each item. Serve with tortilla chips. Leftovers make delicious burritos. Serves 6 to 10.

Renee's Onion Dip

- **3 cups Cheddar cheese, grated**
- **2 cups mayonnaise**
- **1 cup finely chopped onion**
- **3 to 4 slices bacon, cooked and crumbled**

Combine cheese, mayonnaise and onion. Spread into a small casserole dish or pie plate. Bake at 350° for 20 minutes. Garnish with bacon before serving. Serve with crackers, etc.

Lt. Baker's Party Dip

- **1 (16-ounce) block Velveeta cheese**
- **½ pound sausage**
- **1 (10-ounce) can Ro-tel tomatoes, drained (Mexican food section)**
- **Crock pot**

Melt cheese in double boiler or microwave. Brown sausage in frying pan and drain. Mix all ingredients in crock pot. Serve with corn chips.

A guaranteed hit!! Monsignor McInerny's favorite.

Hot Beef Dip

- **1 (8-ounce) package cream cheese, softened**
- **2 tablespoons milk**
- **1 (3-ounce) package dried beef, chopped fine**
- **½ cup green pepper, chopped**
- **2 tablespoons dried onion flakes**
- **½ teaspoon garlic salt**
- **½ cup sour cream**
- **1 cup pecans, chopped**

To cream cheese, blend in other ingredients. Place in 8 or 9-inch pie plate that has been sprayed lightly with Pam. Top this mixture with 1 cup of pecans which have been heated in 2 tablespoons butter and salt. Bake at 350° for 25 minutes. Serve hot or cold—best warm. Serves 10.

Good with Ritz crackers, hot veggies or bread sticks.

Kit's Nachos Con Carne

- 1½ to 2 pounds lean ground meat
- 1 (8-ounce) can jalapeño relish (Old El Paso)
- 1 (8-ounce) jar of taco sauce
- 1 pint of sour cream
- 1 medium block of Cheddar cheese, grated
- Jalapeño peppers (optional)
- Black olives (optional)
- 1 medium can of refried beans
- 1 bag of tortilla chips

Preheat oven to 375° degrees. Line a 13x9-inch pan with aluminum foil. Place a generous portion of chips in bottom of pan. Brown ground meat and drain. Add relish, beans and taco sauce and simmer for about 8 to 10 minutes. Spoon meat mixture over chips. Top with dollops of sour cream. Sprinkle with grated Cheddar cheese according to your taste. Garnish with jalapeño peppers and black olives and bake uncovered for 10 minutes. Serves 12 to 18.

Saturday Night Special.

Kathy's Crab Spread

- 1 can tomato soup
- 1 (8-ounce) package cream cheese
- 2 tablespoons unflavored gelatin
- 1 onion, chopped
- 1 cup celery, chopped
- 1 pound crabmeat
- 2 tablespoons horseradish
- 1 tablespoon Worcestershire sauce
- 1 cup mayonnaise
- Salt and pepper to taste

Empty soup into saucepan and add cream cheese. Stir over low heat until cream cheese melts. Dissolve the gelatin in ¼ cup warm water and add to soup and cream cheese. Remove from stove and add onions, celery, horseradish, Worcestershire sauce, and mayonnaise. Stir until well blended and add crabmeat. Season with salt and pepper. Spray 1-quart mold with Pam. Fill mold with mixture and chill several hours. Place on platter and serve with crackers. Serves 8.

Pretty!

Mother Superior Mousse

2 tablespoons Knox gelatin
¼ cup cold water
1 can cream of mushroom soup
1 cup Hellman's mayonnaise
1 cup crabmeat, cooked
6 ounces cream cheese
1 cup celery, finely chopped
1 small onion, grated
Pinch of salt

Soften the gelatin in water over a double boiler. Stir in soup and mayonnaise. Add crabmeat and other ingredients. Pour into oiled mold. Chill 12 hours. To unmold, immerse mold in hot water up to rim. Count to 8 and then invert on serving dish. Serve with Triscuits. Serves 12.

Salmon Party Log

1 (15½-ounce) can salmon
1 (8-ounce) package cream cheese, softened
1 tablespoon lemon juice
2 teaspoons onion, grated
1 teaspoon prepared horseradish
¼ teaspoon salt
¼ teaspoon liquid smoke
1 cup chopped pecans
3 tablespoons snipped parsley

Drain and flake salmon removing skin and bones. Combine salmon with next 6 ingredients and mix thoroughly. Chill several hours. Combine pecans and parsley. Shape salmon mixture in 8x2-inch log, roll in nut mixture on wax paper and chill well. Serve with crackers. Serves 6 to 8.

You can also line an empty Cool Whip dish with Saran Wrap, firmly pack the dish with the loaf, chill and invert onto platter when firmed.

Sonya's Shrimp Butter

7 ounces shrimp, cooked and chopped
1 tablespoon minced onion
Juice of 1 lemon
1 (8-ounce) package of cream cheese, softened
1½ sticks butter (no substitute)
Salt to taste
4 tablespoons mayonnaise

All ingredients should be at room temperature before you begin. Put all ingredients except shrimp into a bowl and beat well. Stir in chopped shrimp and mix. Shape into a mound or mold into some desired shape. Chill thoroughly (at least several hours). Serve with rye toast crackers. This freezes well. It is also good served on hot grits. Makes 3 cups.

This recipe is a shrimp lover's dream! It's the tastiest shrimp butter we've ever eaten and is a Charleston specialty. Do give it a try.

Chicken Liver Pâté

¼ cup green onion, finely minced
2 pounds chicken livers
¼ cup butter, melted
⅔ cup brandy
½ cup whipping cream
¾ teaspoon salt
¼ teaspoon pepper
¼ teaspoon allspice
¼ teaspoon thyme
1 cup butter, melted

Sauté onions and livers in ¼ cup butter until liver is done. Place in blender container. Pour brandy into small saucepan, and simmer on low until 6 tablespoons. Add brandy, whipping cream, and seasonings to livers in blender. Blend until smooth and add butter to mixture and blend well. Spoon pâté into lightly oiled 5 cup mold. Makes 5 cups.

Cheese Ring

- **1 pound Cheddar cheese, grated**
- **1 cup pecans, chopped**
- **¾ cup mayonnaise**
- **1 medium onion, grated**
- **1 clove garlic, pressed**
- **½ teaspoon Tabasco**
- **1 cup strawberry preserves**

Combine all ingredients except preserves, and mix well. Mold into ring. Fill center with strawberry preserves. Serve with crackers (wheat crackers are good). Serves 25.

Not only easy, but pretty as well.

Coach Hanna's "We're No. 1" Cheese Ball

- **11 green cherries**
- **2 (8-ounce) packages cream cheese, softened**
- **2 cups pecans, chopped**
- **1 cup crushed pineapple, drained and almost dry**

Mix 10 chopped green cherries, pecans (1 cup), and pineapple with cream cheese. Shape into a ball. Roll in remaining pecans. Place on tray and place remaining green cherry on top. Surround with parsley. Serve with crackers. Serves 24.

Chutney Cheese Spread

- **1 (8-ounce) package cream cheese**
- **¼ cup chutney**
- **¼ teaspoon dry mustard**
- **1 tablespoon curry powder**
- **Pineapple half**
- **Toasted slivered almonds**

Blend all ingredients except almonds and pineapple. Chill at least 4 hours. Cut pineapple horizontally, including green top. Scoop out carefully and fill with mixture. Top with toasted almonds. Serve with ginger snaps, tea biscuits, or apple slices. Serves 12.

Looks very pretty.

Olde Indigo Crab

- 1 stick softened margarine
- 1 jar Kraft Olde English Cheese Spread (or equivalent sharp Cheddar cheese spread)
- ½ teaspoon salt
- ½ teaspoon seasoned salt
- 6½ ounces crab, rinsed well
- 1½ tablespoons mayonnaise
- 6 English muffins

Mix first 6 ingredients together and spread on each half of split English muffins. Freeze halves on cookie sheet, then stack in plastic bag until ready to use. When ready to serve, thaw the amount needed and cut each half into 6 small triangles and broil. Serve hot. Makes 72 pieces.

Whiz Bang Snaps and Cheese Spread

- 1 (16-ounce) container cream cheese
- 1 large box dates, chopped
- 1 teaspoon vanilla
- ½ cup pecans, finely chopped
- 1 box gingersnaps

Combine cream cheese, dates and vanilla. Form into ball and roll in pecans. Serve on gingersnaps. May be frozen. Serves 10.

Savories

- ½ pound Cheddar cheese, grated
- 8 slices fried bacon (crisp), chopped
- 2 small green onions, chopped
- 1 teaspoon dry mustard
- 2 teaspoons mayonnaise
- Melba rounds

Mix all ingredients well, and spread on toast rounds. Broil until golden brown. Makes 24 toast rounds.

Scallops 'N Bacon

1 pound scallops
¼ cup melted margarine
2 tablespoons lemon juice
½ teaspoon salt
Dash white pepper
Sliced bacon
Paprika

Rinse scallops in cold water. Combine margarine, lemon juice, salt and pepper and pour over scallops; let stand 30 minutes in refrigerator, turning once. Drain scallops; set aside. Cut bacon slices in half and partially cook until the slices ruffle, but are flexible. Drain on paper towel. Wrap each scallop with a partially cooked piece of bacon and hold in place with a tooth pick. Place bacon-wrapped scallops on a broiler pan, and sprinkle tops with paprika. Preheat the broiler and broil 6 inches from the heat 5 minutes; turn and sprinkle with paprika and broil another 5 to 8 minutes until bacon is crisp and brown.

Makes 18 to 24 pieces.

Little Pizzas

1 pound hot sausage
1 pound hamburger meat
1 pound Velveeta cheese
1 teaspoon basil
1 teaspoon oregano
½ teaspoon garlic powder
1½ tablespoons dry parsley
Party rye sandwich bread

Brown sausage and meat in fry pan with no oil. Add basil, oregano, garlic powder and parsley, stir well. Melt cheese into meat mixture and mix well over heat. Remove from heat and mound on party rye. Place on cookie sheet and freeze. When pizzas are frozen, remove and put in plastic freezer bags until ready to serve. To serve, heat at 350° for 8 to 10 minutes or until hot.

For after school snacks, try spreading mixture on half of English muffins. Freeze as above. Children can remove them from the freezer and pop them in the microwave a few seconds.

Chicken Bites

- ¼ pound cream cheese
- 2 tablespoons mayonnaise
- 1 cup cooked chicken breast, coarsely ground
- 1 cup blanched almonds, chopped fine
- 1 tablespoon chutney (your choice)
- ½ teaspoon salt
- 1 teaspoon curry powder

Mix above ingredients. Roll into 36 balls and then roll in finely chopped coconut. Makes 36 pieces.

Attractive mounted on parsley-covered cone for Christmas.

Shrimp Secrets

- 2 (3-ounce each) packages cream cheese, softened
- 1½ teaspoons prepared mustard
- 1 tablespoon grated onion
- 1 tablespoon lemon juice
- Dash cayenne pepper
- Dash of salt
- 1 (4½-ounce) can shrimp
- ⅔ cup chopped nuts

Blend cream cheese, mustard, onion, lemon juice, salt and pepper. Rinse shrimp and drain thoroughly. Break shrimp into pieces and stir into cheese mixture. Chill thoroughly. Form into ½ inch balls and roll in chopped nuts just prior to serving. Makes 3 dozen.

Chicken Curry Sandwiches

- 1¾ cups finely chopped cooked chicken
- ¼ cup mayonnaise
- ¼ cup plain yogurt
- ½ cup teaspoon curry powder
- Salt and pepper to taste
- Cinnamon raisin bread
- Sliced almonds to garnish

Combine chicken, mayonnaise, yogurt, curry powder, salt and pepper to taste.

Trim crusts from thinly sliced cinnamon raisin bread into circles, rectangles, or other desired shapes. Spread with chicken curry topping. Place on damp cloth and refrigerate, covered, until serving time.

Easy Sausage Swirls

2 cans (8-ounces each) crescent dinner rolls
2 tablespoons hot or mild mustard
1 pound hot pork sausage (or 2 packages ham slices)

Separate rolls into 4 rectangles and spread with mustard. Spread with thin layer of sausage (or ham). Roll and chill until ready to serve. Thinly slice each roll (10 swirls to a roll) and place on ungreased pan. Bake at 400° degrees for 18-20 minutes. Serve hot. Makes 20 pieces.

These swirls go in a whirl!

Ms. Judy's Hot Crab

2 (8-ounce) packages of cream cheese
⅓ cup mayonnaise
3 tablespoons Sauterne
4 teaspoons powdered sugar
½ teaspoon salt
¾ teaspoon garlic powder
½ teaspoon onion juice
1 pound crab, picked

Combine cream cheese and mayonnaise. Slowly melt over low heat. Add remaining ingredients. Keep warm over double boiler or small crock pot. Serve in chafing dish with Bremner wafers. Serves 8 to 10.

"Your guests will be delighted with this heavenly crab."

Bull's Island Hot Crab

1 (8-ounce) package cream cheese, softened
1 cup sour cream
1 small onion chopped finely
1 tablespoon horseradish
Dash of Tabasco sauce
Dash of salt
Dash of white pepper
1 teaspoon dried shallots
1 teaspoon dill
8 to 12 ounces crabmeat
Parmesan cheese

Combine all ingredients except Parmesan cheese. Place in oven-proof serving dish. Sprinkle with Parmesan cheese and bake at 350° for 20 to 30 minutes until lightly browned on top. Serve with toast rounds or water crackers. Serves 12.

Becky's Party Shrimp

- 2 pounds shrimp, cleaned and cooked
- ½ cup butter or margarine
- 1 cup green pepper, chopped
- 1 cup onions, chopped
- 1 cup tomatoes, chopped
- 1 (8-ounce) container sour cream
- 2 (8-ounce) packages cream cheese

Sauté green pepper and onions in butter. Over low heat, melt cream cheese. Add sour cream, butter, pepper, onions, tomatoes and shrimp. Pour in chafing dish.

Serve with crackers. Garnish with different colored grapes on a tray under the chafing dish. Serves 12 to 16.

Easy and delicious.

Party Chicken Salad

- 3 cups chicken, cooked and chopped
- 2 (10-ounce) cans undiluted cream of chicken soup
- 2 cups celery, diced
- 4 teaspoons minced onions
- 1 cup blanched, slivered almonds
- 1 cup sliced water chestnuts, drained
- 1 teaspoon salt
- 1 teaspoon hot sauce
- 1 tablespoon fresh lemon juice
- 1 cup mayonnaise
- 5 hard cooked eggs, chopped
- 2 cups breadcrumbs (can use melba rounds)

Mix first 10 ingredients together and put half of this mixture into buttered 9x11-inch casserole dish or chafing dish. Sprinkle chopped eggs on top. Put remaining chicken mixture on top of eggs.

Preheat oven to 350°. Put breadcrumbs on top of casserole and bake approximately 35 minutes until bubbly and brown.

Serve in small pastry shells.

Seafood Calhoun

- 1 pound crabmeat
- 1 pound shrimp, cooked and deveined
- ¼ cup butter or margarine
- 4 tablespoons flour
- 1 cup half and half
- 4 tablespoons sherry
- 1 cup sharp grated cheese
- Salt and pepper

Make cream sauce with the butter, flour, cream, salt and pepper. Remove from fire and add crab and sherry. Pour into buttered 1¼- to 2-quart casserole dish. Top with grated cheese. Cook at 350° until cheese melts over seafood. Do not overcook. Serves 6 to 8.

This recipe is a favorite for cocktail parties. Use with plain crackers or pastry shells and serve in chafing dish. Also can be served as main dish or in individual oven proof dishes.

Hot Broccoli Dip

- 1 package chopped broccoli
- 1 (6-ounce) garlic cheese log
- 1 medium onion, chopped
- 1 tablespoon butter
- ¼ teaspoon Tabasco sauce
- 1 teaspoon Worcestershire sauce
- 1 small can of sliced mushrooms
- 1 teaspoon Accent
- 1 small package sliced almonds

Cook and drain broccoli and set aside. Pat broccoli with paper towel.

Cook onion in butter until transparent and add all other ingredients except the broccoli. Stir over medium heat to blend well. Last of all add broccoli.

Serve with large Fritos. Serves 8 to 10.

Real nice for a party in the cold months.

Logan Street Artichoke Dip

- **2 cans of artichoke hearts (in brine, NOT marinade)**
- **3 large cloves of garlic (you may increase or decrease this amount depending on your tolerance for garlic or fear of vampires)**
- **½ cup of mayonnaise**
- **1½ cups of cream cheese, soft**
- **Juice of one large lemon**
- **1 cup of grated Parmesan or Romano cheese**
- **1 cup of whole wheat breadcrumbs**

Preheat oven to 375°. Combine finely chopped artichoke hearts and minced or pressed garlic. In a separate bowl, mix the mayonnaise, cream cheese, lemon juice and ½ cup of the grated cheese. Combine the mayonnaise-cheese and the artichoke-garlic mixtures and put in an oven-proof serving dish. Top with the remaining ½ cup grated cheese and the breadcrumbs. Bake at 375° for ½ hour until lightly browned and bubbly.

Serve with crackers, bread sticks or vegetables.

VARIATION: Substitute 4-ounces blue cheese for cream cheese, and serve with pita chips.

Clam Puffs

- **⅓ cup mayonnaise**
- **½ teaspoon grated horseradish**
- **¼ teaspoon salt**
- **¼ teaspoon garlic powder**
- **½ cup drained minced clams**
- **1 egg white**
- **Melba toast or tiny tart shells**

Mix mayonnaise, grated horseradish, salt, garlic powder and clams. Beat egg white until stiff and glistening, not dry. Fold the egg white into the clam mixture, gently, so as not to break down the egg whites. Pile into tiny tart shells, already baked, or on tiny Melba toast triangles and slide under broiler at high heat. Watch them carefully and pull them out as soon as they are nicely browned. Makes 12 pieces.

Corinne's Gougere Puffs

- **1 cup milk**
- **8 tablespoons sweet butter**
- **1 teaspoon salt**
- **1 cup sifted unbleached all-purpose flour**
- **5 eggs**
- **1½ cups grated Parmesan cheese (or ½ Parmesan and ½ Gruyère)**
- **OPTIONAL: ½ cup grated Parmesan for topping**

Preheat oven to 375°. Combine milk, butter and salt in a saucepan and bring to a boil. Remove pan from heat and add the flour ALL AT ONCE. Whisk vigorously and then return the pan to medium heat and cook. Stir constantly until the batter has thickened and is pulling away from the sides and bottom of the pan. Remove from pan and stir in 4 eggs, one at a time. Stir in the cheese.

Lightly butter baking sheet. Drop mixture by rounded tablespoons on baking sheet about 1-inch apart.

Beat remaining egg and brush the tops of the puffs. You can sprinkle with the additional Parmesan.

Reduce oven to 350° and bake for 15 to 20 minutes or until puffs are well browned. Serve while hot. Makes 24 pieces.

This recipe is different and delicious. Great with your favorite wine and fruit.

Dornetto's Drumettes

- **40 drumettes or wings**
- **1 (8-ounce) bottle of French dressing**
- **1 (8-ounce) bottle of apricot jam**
- **1 package of Lipton dry onion soup**

Combine the three above ingredients and mix well. Place 40 chicken drumettes or chicken wings in a glass dish. Spread mixture over *meat or chicken. (*Can substitute spare ribs for chicken). Bake covered for 3 hours at 275° Serves 20.

VARIATION: In place of drumettes, use cocktail-size sausage links.

Chicken Fingers

- **6 chicken breasts (boned)**
- **1½ cups buttermilk**
- **2 tablespoons lemon juice**
- **2 teaspoons Worcestershire sauce**
- **1 teaspoon soy sauce**
- **1 teaspoon paprika**
- **1 tablespoon Greek seasoning**
- **1 teaspoon salt**
- **1 teaspoon pepper**
- **2 cloves garlic (minced)**
- **4 cups soft breadcrumbs**
- **½ cup sesame seed**
- **¼ cup melted margarine**
- **¼ cup vegetable oil**

Cut chicken in ½-inch strips. Combine buttermilk, lemon juice, Worcestershire, soy sauce, paprika, Greek seasoning, salt, pepper and garlic in bowl. Add chicken and mix until chicken is well coated. Cover and refrigerate overnight. Drain chicken thoroughly. Combine breadcrumbs and sesame seed; mix well. Add chicken and toss to coat. Place chicken in 2 greased 13x9x2-inch baking dishes. Combine margarine and oil. Brush over chicken. Bake at 350° for 35 to 40 minutes. Serve with Plum Sauce.

Plum Sauce:

- **1½ cups red plum jam (or currant jelly)**
- **1½ tablespoons prepared mustard**
- **1½ tablespoons horseradish**
- **1½ teaspoons lemon juice**

Combine all ingredients in small saucepan, mixing well. Place over low heat, stirring until just warm. Serves 12.

Talk about "finger-lickin' good"...

Crab Balls

- **¼ pound saltines, crumbled**
- **1 pound crabmeat**
- **1 small onion, grated**
- **½ bell pepper, finely chopped**
- **1 tablespoon of prepared mustard**
- **½ cup margarine**
- **1 egg**
- **Salt and pepper (to taste)**

Mix all of the ingredients together and make small, flat balls. Flour the balls and fry in hot vegetable oil until slightly brown. Makes 16 small balls.

Meatballs with Sweet and Sour Sauce

- 1 pound ground chuck
- 2 tablespoons all-purpose flour
- 1 egg
- 1 teaspoon salt
- 3 tablespoons minced onion
- Pepper to taste
- 1 teaspoon Worcestershire sauce
- Vegetable oil

Mix all ingredients except oil, and form little meat balls. Brown in small amount vegetable oil and drain on paper towels. Makes approximately 30 meatballs. (For a large group, quadruple the recipe.)

Put meatballs in Sweet and Sour Sauce (recipe follows).

Sweet and Sour Sauce:

- 1 teaspoon vegetable oil
- 1 cup pineapple juice
- 1 tablespoon cornstarch
- 1 tablespoon soy sauce
- 3 tablespoons vinegar
- 6 tablespoons water
- ½ cup granulated sugar
- 2 tablespoons molasses
- 4 pineapple slices, diced, or small can pineapple chunks
- 1 green pepper, diced

Mix all ingredients together in quart pan on medium heat, stirring constantly. Put meatballs in sauce 30 minutes before serving and add pineapple pieces and green pepper. Heat over low heat. Makes 2 cups.

Buffalo Wings

- 24 chicken wings or drumettes
- 1 (1-ounce) envelope ranch salad dressing mix
- ⅓ cup margarine, melted
- ¼ cup hot pepper sauce
- 3 tablespoons vinegar
- ½ teaspoon paprika

Dredge chicken in salad dressing mix. Dip in mixture of margarine, pepper sauce and vinegar. Lay chicken in baking pans lined with aluminum foil. Sprinkle with ½ of the paprika. Bake at 400° for 25 to 30 minutes. Turn. Sprinkle with remaining paprika and bake at 450° for 20 to 25 minutes, or until brown. Serves 8.

Stuffed Mushrooms

- 12 large mushroom caps
- 2 to 3 tablespoons melted butter
- Salt and pepper to taste

Preheat oven to 375°. Brush caps with butter and place hollow side up. Sprinkle lightly with salt and pepper. Set aside.

Stuffing:

- 3 tablespoons onion, finely minced
- 2 tablespoons butter or margarine
- 1 tablespoon corn oil
- 3 tablespoons green onion, minced
- Mushroom stems, finely minced
- ¼ cup Madeira
- 3 tablespoons fine dry breadcrumbs
- ¼ cup Swiss cheese, finely grated
- ¼ cup Parmesan cheese
- 4 tablespoons parsley, minced
- ½ teaspoon tarragon
- Salt and pepper
- 2 to 3 tablespoons whipping cream

Sauté onions 3 to 4 minutes without browning. Add green onions and mushrooms pieces and sauté 6 to 8 minutes (until pieces begin to separate). Add Madeira and boil down rapidly. Remove from heat and mix all ingredients except cream. Add cream, 1 tablespoon at a time. Blend just enough to keep stiff enough to hold shape in spoon. Fill caps with stuffing. Dip stuffed caps in 3 tablespoons grated Swiss cheese, and put a little melted butter on each. Bake in upper third of oven 15 or 20 minutes until stuffing is slightly brown. May be frozen and reheated for serving. Makes 12 pieces.

Simply the Best Chocolate Fondue

- 1 can prepared chocolate frosting
- Fresh strawberries
- Fresh pineapple chunks
- Angel Food cake chunks

Open can of frosting and place this open can in a saucepan. Add about 3-inches of water to pan. Place on medium heat until frosting melts. Stir occasionally until thoroughly melted. Pour into fondue pot. Serve with fresh fruit and cake bits. Makes 1½ cups.

Old Fashioned Pickled Shrimp

5 pounds shrimp, boiled and peeled and deveined
2 large onions, sliced
1 pint vegetable oil
1 bottle capers with juice
1 teaspoon powdered sugar
1 teaspoon prepared mustard
1 dash paprika
1 pint vinegar
2 tablespoons lemon juice
1 dash cayenne
Toothpicks

Layer shrimp and onions in a deep flat pan or large gift jars. Combine remaining ingredients and pour over shrimp and onions. Cover. Place in refrigerator 24 hours. Before serving, stir several times. Serves 12.

No one can ever get enough.

Party Cheese-Its

1 cup vegetable oil
1 package original ranch style dressing (dry)
3 teaspoons lemon pepper
3 teaspoons dill weed
¼ teaspoon garlic powder
1 (14 to 16-ounce) package Cheese-It crackers

Mix together first 5 ingredients. Mix this with the Cheese-Its and toss until all crackers are well coated. This does very well in a large ziplock bag turned up and down a few times. Tastes better if made the day before serving. Also delicious made with oysterettes. Makes 2 cups.

Makes a great gift in a pretty tin. Use your imagination, using mixture of other mini-crackers.

Raspberry Apéritif

1 (10-ounce) package frozen raspberries
3 ounces orange liqueur
1 bottle champagne, chilled

Purée and strain raspberries. Save juice and discard seeds. Chill thoroughly. Add liqueur and champagne. Freeze. Serve in chilled, stemmed glasses. Serves 4 to 6.

To make punch, add 1 bottle ginger ale.

Stuffed Grape Leaves

- 1 (15-ounce) jar vine grape leaves
- 1 cup raw rice, washed
- 1 pound lamb shoulder ground (or round steak)
- 1 teaspoon pepper (more or less to taste)
- 3 lemons (juice from 3 lemons)
- 1 teaspoon salt (more or less to taste)

Place grape leaves on tray or waxed paper and set aside. Mix rice, meat, and spices together; blend well. Take 1 grape leaf at a time and place 1 tablespoon of filling across leaf and fold sides away from you. Arrange stuffed leaves in pot and alternate the direction with each row. Sprinkle salt on tops. Cover with a resistant plate. Cover with water to cover top of plate. (You may also add lemon juice on top of plate.) Cook, covered, on medium heat for about 40 minutes, or until rice is done. Leban (yogurt) is served with this dish. Makes 36 pieces.

Angie's Pickled Shrimp

- 2 pounds shrimp (cooked and deveined)
- 1 large firm onion, sliced in rings
- 1 cup catsup
- ½ cup Wesson oil
- 2 tablespoons prepared mustard
- 1 cup vinegar
- 1 tablespoon sugar
- 1 tablespoon Worcestershire sauce
- 1 teaspoon celery seed
- Dash of red pepper
- Dash of dill
- Dash garlic powder
- Salt and pepper to taste
- 3 bay leaves
- Toothpicks

Layer shrimp and onions in jar. Mix other ingredients in blender and pour over shrimp and onions. Top with 3 bay leaves. Let sit in refrigerator. Will keep at least a week. Serve with crackers. Serves 6 to 8.

SOUPS & STEWS

Soups & Stews

Chili Con Carne

- 1½ pounds ground beef
- ½ pound ground pork
- 4 tablespoons chili powder
- 2 teaspoons cumin
- 3 teaspoons paprika
- 1½ teaspoons salt
- 1 teaspoon garlic powder
- Cayenne to taste
- 1 (28-ounce) can tomatoes
- 1 (10-ounce) can of tomatoes and peppers
- 1 cup water
- Flour or cornstarch to thicken

Brown meat and cook for 15 minutes. Add cumin and mix into the meat. Then add the salt, garlic powder and paprika to meat mixture. Put chili powder, water, tomatoes and peppers in a blender or food processor. This may have to be done in two batches depending on the blender size. Add this to the meat mixture. Simmer for 30 minutes. Thicken the broth with the water and flour (or cornstarch). Chili beans may be added if desired. Serves 6 to 8.

Sib's Chili

- 3 pounds ground beef
- 2 (28-ounce) cans tomatoes
- 2 cans tomato soup
- 3 cans hot chili beans (use 2 cans with juice, drain third can and just use beans)
- 4 onions, chopped
- 1 tablespoon Worcestershire sauce
- 1 teaspoon garlic salt
- ½ teaspoon pepper
- 2 bay leaves
- 2 teaspoons chili powder
- ¼ teaspoon thyme
- 1 teaspoon oregano
- 4 tablespoon parsley

Brown beef with salt, pepper and Worcestershire. Drain well. Add all other ingredients and cook for several hours over medium low heat. If too thick, add more tomatoes or tomato sauce. Serves 6 to 8.

Auntie's Chicken Soup

- 3½ to 4 pound chicken fryer, skinned (or 6 skinless chicken breasts)
- 2½ quarts water for broth
- 2 medium onions, chopped
- ½ cup celery, chopped
- 1 can garbanzo beans (remove outer coating)
- ¼ cup Acini pipe #44 pasta (Ronzoni)
- Salt and pepper to taste
- Dash of thyme

Boil chicken (skinless) in large pot until tender (about 45 minutes). Remove chicken from pot. Let cool and debone. Strain broth if needed, then add onions, celery, garbanzo beans and pasta. Salt and pepper to taste. Place on slow boil for about 30 minutes. Add boned chicken. Boil 1 cup extra pasta and drain—add to chicken soup if desired when serving. Serves 4 to 6.

Corn Cheese Soup

- 6 or 8 slices of bacon
- 1 small onion, thinly sliced
- 1 (17-ounce) can cream corn
- 2 cups cooked potatoes, cubed
- ⅔ cup evaporated milk
- 2⅓ cups hot water
- 1½ teaspoons salt
- ¼ teaspoon garlic salt
- 1 cup Swiss or American cheese, cubed

Fry bacon until crisp. In 4 tablespoons of bacon drippings, add onions and cook slowly until limp. Add corn, potatoes, milk, hot water, salt, and garlic salt. Boil for 2 minutes then simmer about 15 minutes. Put cheese in soup bowl and add soup. Top with crumbled bacon. Serve with garlic bread and salad. Serves 4 to 5.

Cream of Broccoli Soup

- 2 (16-ounce) boxes of frozen broccoli
- 1 cup chicken broth
- 4 cups water
- 2 teaspoons nutmeg
- 4 cups milk
- 4 tablespoons all-purpose flour
- 1 cup grated cheese

Put broccoli in pot with 4 cups water and simmer until broccoli is soft. Chop with knife while in pot. Add chicken broth and 4 cups milk. Sprinkle flour and nutmeg into soup and stir until thick. Serve with grated cheese and hot rolls. Serves 4 to 6.

Crab Soup

- ½ cup butter
- 4 ribs celery, chopped fine or grated
- 1 pound crab meat
- ½ cup flour
- 1 teaspoon dry mustard
- 1 teaspoon Worcestershire sauce
- 4 cups half and half
- 8 cups milk
- ½ cup sherry wine
- Salt and pepper to taste

Sauté celery in butter for about 3 minutes. Add crab and continue over medium heat for an additional 5 minutes. Combine flour, 2 cups milk, mustard and Worcestershire sauce and add to crab mixture. Add remaining milk and half and half. Cook over medium heat stirring often until soup begins to boil. Simmer for 5 minutes. Add sherry, salt and pepper and let stand before serving. Additional sherry may be added to each serving if desired. Serves 10 to 12.

Easy Onion Soup

- 3 large onions (about 2 pounds), thinly sliced
- ¼ cup butter or margarine, melted
- 5 cups boiling water
- 1 tablespoon chicken bouillon granules
- 2 teaspoons beef bouillon granules
- ½ teaspoon salt
- Dash of pepper
- 1 tablespoon sugar (optional)
- ½ teaspoon browning and seasoning sauce
- 6 (¾-inch-thick) slices French bread, toasted
- 6 (4x⅛-inch) slices Swiss cheese

Separate onions into rings, and sauté in butter in a Dutch oven until tender. Add water to onions. Combine bouillon granules, salt, pepper, and sugar, if desired; add to onions. Stir in browning and seasoning sauce. Bring to a boil; reduce heat, and simmer, uncovered, 1 hour.

Place 6 ovenproof individual serving bowls on a baking sheet. Place 1 slice of bread in each bowl; ladle soup over bread. Top each with 1 slice cheese; broil 6 inches from the heat until cheese melts. Serves 6.

Dried Bean Soup

1 pound dry beans (northern, lima, black, black-eye)
1 meaty ham bone
½ teaspoon salt
6 peppercorns
1 bay leaf
1 medium onion, chopped
½ cup celery, diced
1 carrot, peeled and grated
Salt and pepper to taste

Wash beans, add cold water and soak overnight. Do not drain. Add ham bone, salt, peppercorns and bay leaf. Cover pot and simmer 3 hours. Add onion, celery, and carrot. Remove the ham bone and mash the beans slightly, using potato masher. Cut the ham from the bone and add to the soup. Add salt and pepper to taste. Serves 6 to 8.

Delicious on a cold winter night.

Gazpacho

4 large tomatoes, quartered
1 medium onion, quartered
2 cloves garlic
1 green pepper, coarsely chopped
1 cucumber, peeled and coarsely chopped
3 tablespoons olive oil
¼ cup white vinegar
1 cup tomato juice
1 teaspoon salt
Croutons

Blend together in a large bowl: tomatoes, onion, garlic, green pepper, cucumber, olive oil, vinegar, tomato juice and salt. CHILL!

Croutons:
Before serving, either make your own croutons from 1 to 2 slices of bread or bagels, whatever is on hand. (Cut into cubes and toast under broiler or sauté in 1 teaspoon olive oil and ¼ teaspoon of garlic until crisp).

Garnish with croutons and serve cold. Serves 4 to 8.

Jean's Lentil Soup

1 medium onion, diced
1 tablespoon vegetable oil
1 bay leaf
1 (1 pound 13-ounce) can tomato purée
½ teaspoon baking soda
2 cups lentils
1 cup shaped pasta or noodles, cooked
1 teaspoon garlic powder
Grated Parmesan cheese

Brown onion in oil with bay leaf. Add purée and 2 cans of water along with baking soda. Let this come to a boil and simmer for ½ hour. Wash lentils and put in the tomato mixture. Add enough water to make a large pot of soup. Salt and pepper along with garlic powder is added next. Let cook for 2 to 2½ hours. Just before lentils are finished cooking, cook your pasta in another pot until done. Drain and add to your lentils. Serve with grated cheese.

Pasta Fijole

½ cup DeVinci Acini DeRepe #44 (or any very tiny pasta)
1 pound extra lean ground beef
1 large onion, chopped
4 ribs celery, chopped
2 large carrots, thinly sliced
1 (28-ounce) can tomatoes with juice, chopped
1 (15-ounce) can chick peas, drained
1 (15-ounce) can black beans, drained
1 (15-ounce) can pinto beans, drained
½ teaspoon garlic powder
1 tablespoon Italian seasoning
28 ounces water (use tomato can)

Cook, drain, and rinse pasta. Chill in refrigerator. Put all other ingredients in large pot and simmer for at least one hour, or until carrots and onions are tender. Add cooked pasta. Sprinkle with Parmesan or Romano cheese when served if desired. Serves 4 to 6.

Okra Soup

- **2 (28-ounce) cans of peeled tomatoes**
- **2 quarts of water**
- **2 medium sized onions (white or yellow), chopped**
- **Several pieces of beef bone (neck or shank)**
- **2½ pounds of stew beef**
- **1 pound of ham**
- **2 teaspoons of sugar**
- **2½ pounds of fresh okra, cut thinly**
- **2 medium sized bell peppers**
- **2 packages of frozen butter beans or about 1 quart of fresh**
- **1 (16-ounce) can of shoe peg corn (or fresh white if available) drained**
- **2 pints of rice gruel**

Place the tomatoes, water, onions, beef bone, stew beef, ham, and sugar in a large soup pot (at least 8-quart). Cook for about 2 hours.

Cook the okra and the bell peppers in a small amount of oil in a frying pan (do not brown the okra), then add immediately to the tomato mixture.

Add the butter beans and cook for about 1 hour at a slow boil until the okra and the butter beans are soft and tender. Add the corn and simmer for about ½ hour. Add one to two pints of rice gruel to thin and enrich the soup. Salt and pepper to taste. Makes 4½ to 5½ quarts.

(NOTE: The rice gruel is made by boiling about a cup of rice in about 2 quarts of water. The water left over is the gruel.)

It goes without saying that fresh vegetables will always enhance the flavor of this soup.

Quick She Crab Soup

- **1 can cream of mushroom soup**
- **1 can cream of celery soup**
- **1 pound crab meat**
- **Salt and pepper to taste**
- **1 can whole milk**

Combine the two cans of soup in pot and add the crab meat. Add milk to consistency you wish and simmer on top of stove for about 10 minutes. Serve in bowl with sherry on top, if desired, and buttered croutons on top. Serves 6.

Delicious! Fast and easy!

Sullivan's Island Okra Soup

- 2 tablespoons oil
- ½ green pepper, chopped
- 1 large onion, chopped
- 1 medium button garlic, minced
- Dusting of celery salt and black pepper
- 1 can lima beans
- 1 can whole kernel corn
- 1 large can tomatoes, cored and chopped
- 1 small can tomato sauce
- 1 package frozen okra (fresh if available), chopped
- 1 quart water
- Salt to taste
- Lemon juice to taste
- Tabasco sauce to taste
- Worcestershire sauce to taste
- Parsley to taste
- Basil to taste
- Cinnamon to taste
- ½ to 1 pound of shrimp
- 3 cups rice, cooked

In a large pot combine first 5 ingredients. Sauté 5 to 10 minutes. Add the next 13 ingredients and simmer. In separate pot, put shrimp in boiling water for 1 to 2 minutes (no longer). Remove with slotted spoon reserving hot water. Put shrimp under cold water then peel and put aside. Put shells back in hot water and boil 15 minutes to make liquor, which you then strain into big pot with all other ingredients. Bring to a boil, then simmer for 3 to 5 hours. While bringing to boil, stir constantly to prevent scorching and sticking. You may want to add a little more water. Serve over a dollop of rice and a good handful of shrimp. Serves about 6.

Ingredients 12 to 19 better light than heavy. You can always add spice - can't take out!

Pawley's Island Clam Chowder

- 3 quarts clams
- 2 large onions, chopped fine
- 2 large potatoes
- 6 ribs celery
- ⅓ cup flour
- 2 teaspoons salt
- 4 to 5 tablespoons bacon drippings
- 1 quart water
- 1 tablespoon Worcestershire
- 3 tablespoons catsup
- Tabasco to taste

Chop onions, potatoes, celery and clams. In dutch oven or large pot, add bacon drippings, stir in flour. Add chopped vegetables and water. Add seasonings, cover and bring to boil over medium heat until vegetables are tender. Makes a generous amount depending on whether you serve the chowder in cups or soup bowls. Serves 6 to 8.

Uncle George's Soup

- 4 medium onions, chopped
- 6 cloves garlic, finely chopped
- 4 tablespoons oil
- 2 pounds Kielbasa or smoked sausages, cut into ½" slices
- 2 pounds cabbage, shredded and chopped
- 2 or 3 medium potatoes, diced
- 6 (10½-ounce) cans beef consommé with gelatin added
- 2 (1-pound) cans light red kidney beans, undrained
- ⅔ cup vinegar
- 1 (14-ounce) bottle ketchup
- 2 to 3 jalapeño peppers (optional)

Sauté onions and garlic in oil in large 8-quart pot. Add smoked sausage and simmer for 10 to 15 minutes.Add all other ingredients. Bring to a boil and then simmer for 30 minutes. Yield 24 cups.

Very good on a cold football afternoon.

Split Pea Soup

1 pound dried split peas
2 to 3 ham hocks
3 carrots
2 onions
3 ribs celery
2 beef bouillon cubes

Pre-soak peas. Put ham hocks and split peas in 6 to 8-quart pot and fill with water to about 2 inches from top. Bring to boil and simmer for about 1½ hours. Meanwhile chop the vegetables. Put in sauce pan with 2 beef bouillon cubes and water from ham hocks. Cook until tender, then process in blender until smooth and add to soup pot. Cook until thickened a little and add seasoning to taste. Take out the ham hocks. Cut off the meat and return it to soup. Makes 6 quarts.

This keeps thickening each time you cook it.

Veggie Cheese Soup

½ cup water
1 (10-ounce) package frozen corn
¼ cup onion, chopped
2 cans cream of potato soup
2 cups milk
1 cup Cheddar cheese, grated
½ cup provolone cheese, shredded
1 cup broccoli, chopped
2 tablespoons butter
¼ cup carrots, shredded
⅛ teaspoon pepper
1 pinch tarragon (optional)

In 4-quart pot combine water, butter, carrots, onion and pepper. Cover and simmer on medium for 10 minutes. Add soup, broccoli, milk and cheese. Stir until cheese melts. Simmer on low for 20 to 30 minutes stirring occasionally to keep cheese from sticking. Serves 6 to 8.

DO NOT FREEZE.

Turkey Soup

- 1 turkey carcass with some meat left on it
- 2 quarts of water
- 4 ribs of celery with leaves, chopped
- 2 medium onions, chopped
- 6 carrots, peeled and sliced
- Salt and pepper to taste
- 4 potatoes, cubed

Place turkey bones in large soup pot with water, celery, onion and carrots. Bring to a boil. Skim foam off top. Cover and simmer for 2 to 3 hours. Strain off broth. Remove turkey meat from bones and add to broth. Add vegetables. Cook on simmer another 45 minutes. Serves 4 to 6.

Delicious soup for the weekend after Thanksgiving.

Baked Oyster Stew

- 2 cups fresh oysters with juice
- 3 tablespoons margarine
- ½ teaspoon Worcestershire sauce
- 3 tablespoons all-purpose flour
- 2½ cups milk
- ½ teaspoon pepper
- Salt (depending on oysters)*
- 1 small box saltine crackers
- 1 scant cup medium sharp cheese, grated

Melt butter in saucepan, mix with Worcestershire and flour to make paste. Add milk and pepper and mix with whisk. *NOTE: You will not need salt if you have salty oysters. Heat over medium heat stirring constantly until thickened. Add oysters and juice, remove from heat, cover and set aside. Line 2-quart casserole dish with saltine crackers, pour ½ of stew over crackers, make another layer of saltines, and add remaining stew. Top with grated cheese. Cover with plastic wrap and refrigerate until ready to serve. Heat in oven 350° for 20 to 25 minutes or until cheese melts. Do not overcook the oysters. Spoon into heated mugs and serve with extra saltines. Makes 4 cups.

Great on cold night, sitting by the fire.

Brunswick Stew

- 1 large chicken
- ½ pound fatback, cut into small pieces
- 2 large onions, chopped
- ½ gallon canned tomatoes
- 6 large potatoes
- 2 cans butter beans
- 2 cans cream corn
- Salt to taste
- Tabasco to taste
- 2 tablespoons Worcestershire
- 1 tablespoon sherry

Cook chicken until tender. Debone and cut into small pieces. Reserve 1 quart or more of stock. Fry fatback. Brown onions in fat. Put pork, onions, stock and tomatoes in large pot. Add potatoes and mash as they cook. When almost done add butter beans and corn. Add chicken and season highly with all the above seasonings. If fresh vegetables are available this makes a big difference. Makes 8 quarts.

This stew freezes nicely.

Buff's Fish Stew

- 3 pounds of fish fillets
- Lemon
- Water
- Salt and pepper
- 4 to 6 slices of bacon, crumbled
- 3 to 4 medium potatoes, diced
- 3 carrots, sliced
- 1 green bell pepper, diced
- 2 onions, chopped
- 1 (14-ounce) bottle of catsup
- 2 to 4 cans of fish stock
- Worcestershire sauce to taste
- ¼ teaspoon cayenne pepper
- 1 tablespoon vinegar
- 2 ribs of celery, chopped

Simmer the fish fillet about 30 minutes in enough water to cover fish. Add lemon, salt and pepper. Strain and reserve the liquid. Fry the bacon in a large pot, remove and drain. In the same pot sauté onions until soft. Add potatoes, carrots and celery. Stir well. Add rest of ingredients except fish along with two cans of stock and stir well. Add fish and simmer at least 2 hours. Add more stock from time to time depending on desired consistency Serves 6 to 8.

Drunken Beef Stew

- 4 pounds lean beef, cut into ½-inch chunks
- 2 pounds large onions, sliced thickly
- ½ cup flour
- ½ cup oil
- 6 garlic cloves, crushed fine
- 3 tablespoons dark brown sugar
- ¼ cup red wine vinegar
- ½ cup chopped parsley
- 2 small bay leaves
- 2 teaspoons thyme
- 1 tablespoon salt
- Freshly ground black pepper
- 2 (10½-ounce) cans beef broth
- 3 cups beer
- ½ cup chopped parsley for garnish

Preheat oven to 325°. Dredge beef with flour and brown in hot oil in skillet. Put browned meat in large casserole. Set aside. Put onions and garlic in skillet with oil and lightly brown them; add to casserole with meat. Combine sugar, 2 tablespoons vinegar, parsley, bay leaves, thyme, salt and pepper; stir several times. Pour off any remaining oil in skillet. Put broth in skillet and heat over low heat, stirring to loosen all remaining browned bits. Pour over meat mixture in casserole. Add the beer and cover casserole and bake 2 hours. Take casserole out of oven and put on medium heat on stove top. Stir in remaining 2 tablespoons of vinegar and cook for 5 minutes. Serve over cooked noodles or rice. Garnish with remaining ½ cup chopped parsley. Serves 6 to 8.

This is a different but very good stew . . . Men love it!

Stay A Bed Stew

- 3 pounds stew beef
- 1 cup carrots, diced
- 2 large potatoes, diced
- 2 onions, chopped
- 1 package frozen green peas
- 3 bay leaves
- 1 can (large) tomato sauce
- 1 can cream of celery or cream of mushroom soup
- Salt, pepper, and Accent to taste

Combine above ingredients. Stir well. Bake covered for 5 hours at 275°. Serves 6 to 8.

Adaptable to crock pot.

Fred Waring's Beef Stew

2 pounds beef rump, chuck, round or stew meat
2 medium size onions, sliced
3 tablespoons oil
3 cups hot water
1 bay leaf
3 teaspoons salt
1½ teaspoons caraway seeds
¼ cup vinegar
1 medium-sized red cabbage, cut in wedges
½ cup broken gingersnaps
1 package egg noodles, cooked according to directions

Cut beef in 2-inch cubes. Brown beef and sliced onions in oil in a heavy saucepan or Dutch oven. Add water, bay leaf, salt, pepper and caraway seeds. Cover tightly and cook slowly for 1½ hours. Add vinegar to stew, place cabbage wedges on top, and cover and cook until tender, 45 minutes to an hour longer. Soak gingersnaps in ¼ cup warm water. Lift out cabbage and meat; add gingersnaps to liquid, bring to boil, stir for gravy. Add meat to gravy, reheat. Serve on a bed of buttered egg noodles. Surround with red cabbage wedges. Serves 6.

Fun - unusual recipe!

Frogmore Stew

4 inch linked smoked sausage, sliced
¾ pound shrimp in the shell
1 ear corn
1 small new potato
4 crab claws
Crab boil seasoning (about 2 teaspoons per quart of water)

Fill pot with just enough water to cover all ingredients. Add crab boil, potato and sausage. Cover, reduce heat and simmer for 20 minutes. Add corn and crab claws and cook for 10 minutes. Add shrimp and cook for 3 minutes or until done. Drain. Serve on cookie sheets or on table covered with newspaper. Serve with beer and rolls. **Serves 1.**

NOTE: Adjust cooking time if cooking large quantities. Shrimp are done when large shrimp are opaque all the way through when cut in half.

The ultimate casual and fun dish. You can serve it for a party of 4 to 100 and they'll love it.

Old Lyme Beef Stew

2½ pounds boneless chuck
2 tablespoons vegetable oil
1 medium onion, chopped
1 clove garlic
1 tablespoon salt
½ teaspoon pepper
1 teaspoon sugar
1 teaspoon soy sauce
1 tablespoon vinegar
2 beef bouillon cubes
1 tablespoon lemon juice
½ teaspoon paprika
1 large bay leaf
1 teaspoon Italian seasoning
Dash of allspice
2 to 3 cups water
6 medium potatoes, cubed
6 carrots
1 pound small onions, peeled
1 package frozen green peas
2 to 3 tablespoons all-purpose flour
⅓ cup cold water

Cook beef in oil over medium heat about 20 minutes. Brown evenly. Add all seasonings and water, cover and simmer about 1½ hours, stirring occasionally. Remove bay leaf, add potatoes, carrots and onions, simmer until done. Add peas. Mix ½ cup cold water with flour and mix well, pour into stew and stir until thickened. Simmer about 5 to 8 minutes. Serves 4 to 6.

Serve over rice with crusty French bread.

Fred's Chicken Bog

4 skinned chicken breasts (floured)
2 tablespoons olive oil
1 large chopped onion
1 green pepper, chopped
½ pound smoked ham
1 large link kielbasa sausage, cut into slices then quartered
Pepper
¼ teaspoon chili powder
3 cloves of chopped garlic
⅛ teaspoon ground cloves
1 bay leaf
2 cups rice
4 cups chicken stock

Lightly flour chicken and cook in olive oil until well browned and remove. Add onions. green pepper, ham, sausage, garlic and cook until onions and green pepper are soft. Meanwhile debone chicken. Transfer all ingredients to a large stock pot and bring to a boil. Reduce heat and cook at least 30 minutes but it's better after about an hour. Serves 6 to 8.

SALADS & SALAD DRESSINGS

Salads & Salad Dressings

Hawaiian Chicken Salad

- **1 medium-size fresh pineapple**
- **3 cups cooked chicken, diced**
- **2 cups cold, cooked long-grain and wild rice mix**
- **¾ cup chopped celery**
- **⅓ cup chopped red pepper**
- **2 tablespoons chopped scallions**
- **½ cup vegetable oil**
- **¼ cup wine vinegar**
- **2 tablespoons Dijon-style mustard**
- **⅛ teaspoon ginger**
- **⅓ cup sliced almonds, toasted**

In season when whole pineapple is not available, substitute canned pineapple cubes in the salad.

Cut pineapple in half lengthwise, slicing through top. Scoop out pineapple; dice and set aside. In medium non-metal bowl, combine chicken, rice, 1 cup of the diced pineapple, celery, red pepper and scallions; set aside.

In small bowl, using wire whisk beat oil, vinegar, mustard and ginger until smooth. Stir into chicken mixture until well coated. Cover and chill for several hours to blend flavors. To serve, gently toss chicken salad with almonds, serve in pineapple shell. Serves 6.

The Best Chicken Salad

- **4 cups chicken, cubed**
- **1 cup celery, chopped fine**
- **1⅓ cups mayonnaise**
- **2 tablespoons Durkee's sandwich and salad sauce**
- **2 teaspoons lemon juice**
- **½ teaspoon black pepper**
- **Salt to taste (if desired)**

Boil chicken and then cube and measure. Combine all the ingredients. Let stand for several hours before serving.

Serving Suggestion: Add 1 cup grapes (cut in half) and 1 cup pecans. Serves 4 to 6.

The Durkee's sandwich and salad sauce is what makes the difference.

Hot Chicken Salad

- 3 cups cooked chicken, diced
- 2 cups celery, sliced
- ½ cups slivered almonds, toasted
- ½ cups water chestnuts, sliced
- ¼ cup pimento, chopped
- 1 cup mayonnaise
- ½ cup sour cream
- 3 tablespoon lemon juice
- 2 tablespoon onion, grated
- ½ teaspoon salt
- ¼ teaspoon pepper
- 1 cup Chinese noodles or French fried onion rings
- ½ cup grated Cheddar cheese

Mix chicken, celery, almonds, water chestnuts and pimento. In separate bowl, blend mayonnaise, sour cream, lemon juice, onion, salt and pepper. Mix with chicken mixture. Pour into buttered 2-quart casserole. Top with noodles and cheese. Bake at 350° for 30 minutes. Serves 6.

A Friend-In-Need Salad

- 2 (3-ounce) packages orange Jello
- 2 (6-ounce) cans mandarin oranges, drained
- 1 small can frozen orange juice
- 1 (16-ounce) can crushed pineapple and juice
- 1 (3-ounce) package instant lemon pudding
- ½ pint whipping cream

In a 1½ quart mixing bowl or an 11x7-inch oblong dish, dissolve orange Jello with 2 cups boiling water. Add frozen orange juice and stir till juice dissolves. Add mandarin oranges and add pineapple along with its juice. Set in refrigerator to congeal. When set, add topping.

Topping:
Fix whipped cream to taste. Mix lemon pudding with 1 cup of milk. Combine whipped cream with pudding. Spread on top of congealed salad. Serve cold as a salad or as a dessert. Serves 8 to 10.

Apricot Cheese Delight

- 1 (17-ounce) can apricots
- 1 large can crushed pineapple
- 1 large package orange Jello
- 2 cups hot water
- ½ cup apricot juice
- ½ cup pineapple juice
- 2 cups miniature marshmallows
- 1 or 2 large bananas, mashed

Drain fruit, keeping juices separate. Mash the apricots and bananas and set aside. Dissolve the gelatin in hot water, and add juices. Put in refrigerator. When it begins to set, add fruit and marshmallows. Pour into flat dish. When firm, top with the following topping:

- ½ cup sugar
- 2 heaping teaspoons flour
- 1 egg, beaten
- 2 tablespoons margarine
- ½ cup pineapple juice
- ½ cup apricot juice
- 1 cup whipped cream or Cool Whip
- ¾ cup Cheddar cheese, grated

Combine flour and sugar; blend in egg and butter, and add juices. Cook over low heat, stirring well. Let cool. Fold in whipped cream and spread on congealed salad. Sprinkle with cheese and chill. Cut into squares and serve on lettuce leaves. Serves 6 to 8.

Cranberry Crush

- 2 small packages lemon Jello
- 1 (16-ounce) can crushed pineapple (reserve juice)
- 1 (16-ounce) can cranberry sauce
- 7 ounces ginger ale
- ½ cup pecans
- 1 tablespoon butter
- 1 (12-ounce) container frozen whipped topping
- 1 (8-ounce) package cream cheese

Drain pineapple, add enough water to juice to make one cup. Bring juice mixture to boil, add Jello and dissolve. Add pineapple, cranberry sauce, and ginger ale. Chill in 13x9-inch dish until firm.

Bake ½ cup pecans and butter at 350° for 10 minutes. Set aside.

Mix whipped topping and cream cheese and spread on top of firm Jello. Garnish with toasted pecans. Serves 8 to 12.

Berry-Berry Salad

- **2 cans whole cranberry sauce**
- **2 cups boiling water**
- **1 large package strawberry Jello**
- **1 package Knox gelatin**
- **2 tablespoons lemon juice**
- **½ teaspoon salt**
- **2 whole apples, chopped**
- **1 cup celery, chopped**
- **1 cup pecans, chopped**
- **1 cup mayonnaise**

Over medium heat melt the whole cranberry sauce. Drain the liquid in a large bowl setting the berries aside for later use. Add the water, Jello and gelatin to the berry juice stirring until dissolved. Add lemon juice and salt, chilling until mixture mounds on a spoon. Now add the mayonnaise and beat until smooth. Fold in cranberries, celery, apples and nuts. Pour into a glass baking dish 9x13-inch (or a 2-quart ring) sprayed with Pam.

To unmold, use a knife to loosen the edges. DO NOT dip the mold in hot water. Serves 8 to 12.

Congealed Grape Salad Delight

- **2 small boxes grape Jello**
- **2 cups hot water**
- **¾ cup cold water**
- **1 (20-ounce) can crushed pineapple with juice**
- **1 large can blueberry pie filling**

Dissolve Jello with 2 cups of hot water and add the cold water. Blend in the pineapple in its own juice, along with the blueberry pie filling. Pour into a 9x13-inch dish and refrigerate until completely set.

Topping:

- **1 (8-ounce) package cream cheese**
- **1 (8-ounce) carton sour cream**
- **½ cup powdered sugar**
- **1 teaspoon vanilla**

To make topping, beat cream cheese, vanilla, sour cream and sugar, and spread on top. May decorate with chopped pecans and cherries if desired. May make 1 or 2 days ahead. Cover with Saran Wrap to keep fresh. Serves 10 to 12.

Cranberry Salad

Salad:

1 pound washed fresh cranberries
1 cup celery, chopped
2 cups sugar
1 cup pecans, chopped
1 (3-ounce) package orange Jello

Mix Jello with ½ cup water. Refrigerate until almost set. Cook cranberries with sugar and ½ cup water. Boil and stir 1 minute. Set aside to cool. Combine Jello, celery, nuts and cranberries. Pour in Jello mold. Refrigerate.

Topping:

½ pint whipping cream (shake well)
1 (3-ounce) package cream cheese, softened
1 cup mini marshmallows

Pour whipping cream in a deep bowl which has been refrigerated. Add marshmallows, set aside for 15 minutes. Whip slightly. Add softened cream cheese. Beat until stiff. Serve on the side. Serves 4 to 6.

Strawberry Pretzel Salad

2⅔ cups broken pretzels (about 6-ounces)
¾ cup melted butter
1 cup sugar
8 ounces cream cheese, softened
1 package Dream Whip
2 (3-ounce) packages strawberry Jello
2 cups boiling water
2 (10-ounce) packages of frozen strawberries, thawed

Combine pretzels and butter. Spread in 9x13x2-inch baking dish. Bake at 350° for 10 minutes. Cool. Cream together sugar and cream cheese. Prepare Dream Whip according to package directions. Mix Dream Whip and cheese mixtures. Layer over pretzel mixture. Refrigerate several hours. Dissolve Jello in water. Stir in strawberries. Let cool. Pour over cheese layer and refrigerate. Cut into squares. Serves 8 to 12.

Ribbon Salad

First Layer:
- 2 (3-ounce) packages lime Jello
- 2 cups hot water
- 2 cups cold water
- 2 cups crushed pineapple, drained
- ½ cup nuts

Second Layer:
- 1 (3-ounce) package lemon Jello
- 1 cup hot water
- ½ cup small marshmallows
- 1 (8-ounce) package cream cheese
- ½ cup mayonnaise
- 1 cup pineapple juice
- 1 cup pineapple, drained
- 1 cup heavy cream

Third Layer:
- 2 packages cherry Jello
- 2 cups hot water
- 2 cans whole cranberry sauce

Dissolve lime Jello in hot water. Add cold water. Add pineapple and nuts. Pour this mixture into salad mold or trifle bowl and leave until congealed. Then dissolve lemon Jello in hot water. Whip the cream, and add marshmallows, mayonnaise, cream cheese, pineapple juice, and pineapple. Pour this mixture onto first layer and let set until congealed. Dissolve cherry Jello in hot water and add cranberry sauce. Pour this mixture on second layer. When congealed, cut into squares. This is a colorful salad with green, yellow, and red layers. Serves 10 to 12.

Pistachio Salad

- 1 (20-ounce) can crushed pineapple and juice
- 2 small or 1 large container Cool Whip
- 2 cups tiny marshmallows
- 2 (3-ounce) boxes pistachio instant pudding
- 1 cup chopped pecans

Mix pudding and pineapple with juice. Add marshmallows and nuts. Fold in the topping. Spoon into large crystal bowl or into individual serving size crystal or glass containers, if you want to use as a dessert. This makes a really pretty addition to your table. Serves 4 to 6.

Strawberry Soufflé Salad

1 (10-ounce) package frozen sliced strawberries, thawed
1 (3-ounce) package strawberry flavored gelatin
1 cup boiling water
2 tablespoons lemon juice
¼ cup mayonnaise
¼ cup chopped walnuts
1 (20-ounce) can pineapple, sliced

Drain berries, reserving syrup. Add water to syrup to make ¾ cup. Dissolve gelatin and ¼ teaspoon salt in boiling water. Add reserved syrup and lemon juice. Beat in mayonnaise. Chill till partially set. Whip with electric mixer till fluffy. Fold in berries and nuts. Pour into individual molds (or use a Jello mold). Chill until set. Unmold on lettuce-lined platter atop pineapple. Serve with additional mayonnaise, if desired. Serves 6 to 8.

This has always been a favorite at Christmas time. Very festive looking and delicious!

Enrica Delight (Frozen Fruit Salad)

2 (18-ounce) cans fruit cocktail, drained
2½ cups miniature marshmallows
½ cup chopped nuts
2 (8-ounce) packages cream cheese, softened
¾ cup sugar
2 tablespoons lemon juice
2 cups sour cream
⅓ cup cherries
2 drops red food coloring

Cream cheese, sour cream, sugar, food coloring and lemon juice, Fold in well-drained fruit, cherries, nuts and marshmallows. Place in 8x8-inch aluminum pan or glass dish. Cover and place in freezer. Take out a few minutes before serving and cut into squares. This is very tasty and the food coloring adds a soft pink touch to this delicate salad. Serves 8.

Those to whom I have served this salad have always expressed their enthusiasm over this.

Frozen Mint Salad

- **1 (8½-ounce) can crushed pineapple**
- **1 (20-ounce) can crushed pineapple**
- **1 (3-ounce) package lime Jello**
- **3 cups mini marshmallows**
- **1 cup crushed buttermints**
- **1 (9-ounce) Cool Whip**
- **24 cupcake liners (foil)**

In large bowl combine both cans of undrained pineapple, dry Jello, marshmallows and mints. Cover and refrigerate 3 hours. Fold in Cool Whip and spoon mixture into 24 cupcake liners in muffin tins. Cover and freeze overnight. Peel off paper and serve on lettuce leaf. Makes 24 muffins.

Great for summer family gathering or for after school snack.

Chinese Noodle Salad

- **2 packages chicken flavored Ramen noodles crumbled**
- **¼ cup butter**
- **1 package slivered almonds**
- **2 tablespoons sesame seeds**
- **1 medium head cabbage, cut fine**
- **1 onion, diced**

Brown noodles, almonds and sesame seeds in butter. Let cool. Mix cabbage, onion and noodle mixture.

Dressing:

- **¼ cup vinegar**
- **¼ to ½ cup sugar**
- **¾ cup vegetable oil**
- **2 tablespoons soy sauce**

Mix dressing ingredients together and pour over cabbage mixture. Serves 6 to 8.

Italian Salad Bowl

- ½ medium head lettuce, torn into bite-sized pieces
- ½ head romaine lettuce, torn into bite-sized pieces
- 2 cups raw zucchini, thinly sliced
- ½ cup radishes, sliced
- ½ cup fresh mushrooms, sliced
- 3 green onions, sliced
- Italian or wine vinegar dressing
- ½ cup blue cheese, crumbled

In large bowl combine lettuce, romaine, zucchini, radishes, mushrooms and sliced green onions. Season to taste. Toss lightly with dressing and sprinkle top with crumbled blue cheese. Serves 6.

Mandarin Orange Salad

Salad:

- 1 or more types of lettuce
- Sliced fresh mushrooms
- 1 (11-ounce) can of mandarin oranges, drained
- 1 red onion, sliced thin

Combine lettuce, mushrooms, onions and drained orange slices.

Dressing:

- ½ cup sugar
- ⅔ cup oil
- 1 teaspoon prepared mustard
- ¼ cup vinegar
- 1 teaspoon salt

Mix, in a medium bowl, sugar, oil, mustard, vinegar and salt. Cover. Pour over salad ingredients just before serving. Serves 4 to 6.

Salata

- 1 small head lettuce
- 2 sprigs celery, including tops
- 2 green onions, chopped
- 1 small cucumber, sliced
- 1 tomato, sliced
- 1 small green pepper, cut in strips
- Feta cheese cut in 6 cubes or crumbled
- Anchovy fillets
- Calamata black olives
- Dressing (recipe follows)

Break lettuce in small pieces. Place in salad bowl with celery, onions, cucumber, tomato and green pepper. Pour only enough dressing over vegetables to coat each piece lightly.

Garnish with cubes of Feta cheese, anchovy fillets and Calamata olives. Serves 4 to 6.

Dressing:

- ⅔ cup olive oil
- ⅓ cup wine vinegar
- 1 teaspoon salt
- ¼ teaspoon pepper
- 1 clove garlic, crushed (optional)
- 1 teaspoon oregano

Combine ingredients in jar; cover and shake well before using. Makes 1 cup.

That Green Salad

- 1 large package lime Jello
- 1 cup hot water
- 1 cup evaporated milk
- 1 cup fruit cocktail, drained
- 1 cup cottage cheese
- ½ cup chopped pecans
- ½ cup mayonnaise

Mix Jello and hot water, cool. Stir in cream and add remaining ingredients and put in a 9x13-inch dish. Chill. Serve in squares on lettuce. Serves 10 to 12.

Seven Layer Salad

- 1 head iceberg lettuce, broken into small pieces
- ½ cup celery, chopped
- ½ cup onion, chopped or use rings of sweet Bermuda onion
- ½ cup bell pepper, chopped
- 1 package frozen garden peas, uncooked
- ½ pint sour cream blended with ½ pint mayonnaise and 2 tablespoons of white sugar
- 4 ounces sharp Cheddar or Swiss cheese (or a mixture of both) grated
- 1 pound bacon, fried crisp, drained, chopped

Into a salad bowl with a rather flat bottom, layer ingredients in order given. The sour cream mixture should be spread over the entire surface when you come to it in the list. Then sprinkle the cheese over entire surface of sour cream mixture; likewise over the cheese sprinkle the chopped bacon.

Cover and refrigerate overnight. Lettuce will be crisp and the "dressing" flavors will permeate the salad. Serves 6 to 8.

VARIATION: Mix 1 pint mayonnaise, thinned with lemon juice to taste, 2 tablespoons sugar and ½ cup Parmesan cheese instead of sour cream mixture; omit the other cheeses and the bacon. This is tasty and has considerably fewer calories. Use sugar substitute if preferred.

OPTIONAL: Use LeSeur peas instead of frozen peas.

Italian Pasta Salad

¾ cup vegetable oil
⅓ cup wine vinegar
¼ cup Dijon-style mustard
2 tablespoons heavy cream
1 teaspoon Italian seasoning
1 clove garlic, coarsely chopped
1 pound tortellini, cooked and cooled
2 cups tomatoes, chopped and seeded
2 cups broccoli flowerettes, blanched
2 tablespoons scallions, chopped

In blender or food processor container, combine oil, vinegar, mustard, heavy cream, Italian seasoning and garlic; blend until smooth. Set aside.

In large non-metal bowl, combine tortellini, broccoli, tomatoes and scallions. Gently toss with dressing.

Cover; refrigerate for several hours to blend flavors. Serves 8.

Papa's Pasta Salad

4 (16-ounce) packages shell macaroni, cooked
7 pounds shrimp, cleaned, shelled and boiled in salt water
1 pound Havarti cheese with caraway
1½ cups celery, chopped
¼ cup onion, chopped
1 large green pepper, chopped
Tarragon dressing

Marinate shrimp in dressing with onion overnight. Combine with other ingredients at least 12 hours ahead. Season to taste. **Serves 40.**

Tarragon Dressing:
⅓ cup olive oil
⅔ cup tarragon vinegar
3 tablespoons Dijon mustard
1 teaspoon dill weed
½ teaspoon salt
¼ teaspoon pepper

This is truly better the second day.

Pasta Salad with Chicken and Basil

- **2 cups well flavored chicken broth**
- **3 large chicken breast halves (boned and skinned makes it easier)**
- **½ pound bacon - cut in ½" cubes (fried until crisp)**
- **½ cup cherry tomatoes, cubed**
- **4 ounces mozzarella cheese, cubed**
- **3 cups cooked pasta (Rotini, Zita, etc.)**
- **½ cup fresh basil leaves**
- **Salt and freshly ground pepper**
- **2 teaspoon salt-free seasoning**
- **1 teaspoon Dijon-style mustard**
- **3 tablespoons red wine vinegar**
- **½ cup olive oil**
- **½ cup sour cream**

Bring chicken broth to a boil. Simmer chicken breasts until just cooked through. Remove the chicken from the broth and cool. Cut or break into bit-sized pieces. Toss together the chicken, bacon, tomatoes, mozzarella, pasta and basil.

In a small bowl, beat together salt, salt-free seasoning, pepper, mustard and vinegar. Beat in the oil and then the sour cream. Toss with the chicken vegetable mixture. Chill 2 hours or overnight. Serves 6.

Charleston Crabmeat Salad

- **1 pound back fin crab**
- **1 cup celery, diced**
- **⅓ cup mayonnaise**
- **1 tablespoon lemon juice**
- **½ teaspoon salt**
- **1 dash white pepper**
- **Few drops of Tabasco sauce**
- **¼ teaspoon Worcestershire sauce**
- **2 tablespoons French dressing**
- **Lettuce**

Pick crab meat and discard shells. Combine crabmeat with celery. Mix remaining ingredients except lettuce. Mix gently. Serve on lettuce. Serves 4.

Cindy's Almond Tuna Salad

- ¾ cup mayonnaise
- 1 tablespoon lemon juice
- ½ teaspoon garlic salt
- 1 package frozen green peas
- 1 cup celery, chopped
- ½ (5-ounce) can chow mein noodles
- 1 teaspoon soy sauce
- 1 large can white albacore tuna fish
- 2 green onions, chopped
- 1 (3-ounce) package slivered almonds, toasted

Mix the mayonnaise, soy sauce, lemon juice and the garlic salt. Steam the peas and let cool. Add the tuna to the soy sauce mixture. Gradually add the peas and the celery. Refrigerate overnight. Just before serving, add the almonds and noodles. Serves 4.

You may substitute boiled shrimp for the tuna.

Cold Island Crab

- 1 can claw crab meat
- 1 can white crab meat
- 1 tablespoon lemon juice
- 1 green onion, chopped
- 1 large bunch parsley, chopped
- 2 ribs celery, chopped
- ½ large green pepper, chopped
- 12 ounces soft cream cheese
- 1 teaspoon mace
- 1 teaspoon thyme
- 1 teaspoon coarse ground pepper
- ½ teaspoon garlic salt
- ¼ teaspoon salt
- 1 tablespoon capers

Mix the first 3 ingredients and set aside. Combine the next five ingredients and stir until the cream cheese if soft and green. Gently fold in the crab meat and season with the mace, thyme, pepper, garlic salt and regular salt. Last of all, add the capers. It should be very light. For added crunchiness, add more finely chopped celery and pepper.

Serves 8 to 10.

Seabrook Seafood Salad

- **2 to 3 pounds medium shrimp, boiled, peeled, deveined and cut into bite-size pieces**
- **½ pound crab meat (you can use canned crab)**
- **6 boiled eggs, chopped**
- **Celery, chopped**
- **Sweet pickles**
- **1 small jar pimentos**
- **Salt**
- **Pepper**
- **Onion powder**
- **Garlic Powder**
- **1 tablespoon mustard**
- **Mayonnaise to taste and consistency**
- **3 to 4 boiled potatoes, cooked, peeled and diced (optional)**

Combine all ingredients, but make sure you add the mayonnaise last. Make the salad 6 to 8 hours before serving. Serves 4 to 6.

Serve on a platter with a bed of lettuce surrounded by pickled crab apples and sprinkled with paprika for color.

Yonges Island Shrimp Salad

- **1 pound shrimp, cooked, then peeled, deveined, and chopped**
- **1 cup celery, finely chopped**
- **2 hard boiled eggs, finely chopped**
- **¼ cup bell pepper, finely chopped**
- **1 tablespoon onion, finely chopped**
- **½ cup mayonnaise**
- **Salt and pepper to taste**

Mix all of the above ingredients thoroughly and serve on lettuce leaves. Serves 4.

Old Fashioned Russian Dressing

- **1 cup mayonnaise**
- **1 cup chili sauce**
- **½ teaspoon Worcestershire sauce**
- **1 hard cooked egg, chopped**
- **1 teaspoon chives, chopped**
- **1 teaspoon caviar (optional)**

Blend ingredients together. Chill. Serve with shrimp, crab or tossed salad greens. Makes 1 to 1½ cups.

Creamy Roquefort Dressing

- **½ cup mayonnaise**
- **⅓ cup Roquefort cheese, crumbled**
- **¼ teaspoon crushed garlic**
- **1 tablespoon half and half**
- **½ teaspoon Worcestershire sauce**
- **⅛ teaspoon salt**
- **Dash white pepper**

Mix mayonnaise, cheese and garlic - leave lumpy. Beat in cream, Worcestershire sauce and salt and pepper. Makes 1¼ cups.

Honey Mustard Dressing

- **½ cup vinegar**
- **¼ cup sugar**
- **¼ cup honey**
- **1 teaspoon dry mustard**
- **1 teaspoon paprika**
- **1 teaspoon celery seed**
- **1 teaspoon celery salt**
- **1 teaspoon onion juice**
- **1 cup vegetable oil**

Mix the vinegar, sugar, honey, mustard and paprika together. Boil 3 minutes and cool. Add the celery seed, celery salt, onion juice and vegetable oil and beat or shake vigorously. Serve with any fresh or frozen fruit salad. If kept under refrigeration, shake well before using. Makes 1 to 2 cups.

Vinaigrette Dressing

- **1 pinch salt**
- **1 dash of pepper**
- **1 teaspoon French style mustard**
- **1 tablespoon red wine vinegar**
- **2 tablespoons olive oil**

Mix salt, pepper and mustard. Add vinegar and mix well. Add olive oil a small amount at a time, mixing well. (You must mix these ingredients in order given.) Makes ¼ cup.

You'll want to mix up a bottle at a time and keep it on hand for your favorite salad. Just shake well before using.

Big Joe's Veggies

4 stalks fresh broccoli (cut off the flowerets into bite-size pieces)
8 large mushrooms, sliced
1 medium green pepper, chopped
1 small head cauliflower, cut into flowerets
2 cups celery, chopped

Marinade:
1 cup sugar (some use only ¾ cup)
2 teaspoons dry mustard
1 teaspoon salt
1½ cups vegetable oil
1 small onion, grated
½ cup vinegar
2 teaspoons poppy seeds

Combine the first 5 ingredients and toss lightly. Combine remaining ingredients, mix well and pour over the vegetables. Chill at least 3 hours or overnight. Stir every couple of hours. Serves 8 to 10.

Broccoli Salad

1 bunch broccoli tops, cut into bite-size pieces
4 spring onions
½ cup raisins
8 to 10 slices cooked crisp bacon
1 cup chopped pecans

Dressing:
1 cup mayonnaise
½ cup sugar
2 teaspoons vinegar

Mix all salad ingredients together. Mix dressing, and chill for at least 1 hour before adding to broccoli mixture. Toss.

VARIATION: Add ½ cup shredded Cheddar cheese or purple onion slices.

The best broccoli salad you'll ever taste.

Old Fashioned Potato Salad

2 pounds large new potatoes, peeled and cut into bite-size pieces
1 tablespoon vinegar
1 cup celery, chopped
1 medium onion, grated
¼ cup parsley, chopped (optional)
1½ teaspoons salt
¼ teaspoon pepper
1 to 1½ cups mayonnaise
3 hard boiled eggs, chopped

Cook potatoes in lightly salted water. Eggs may be added carefully to the same pot and cooked at the same time. Cook potatoes until tender, not soft. Drain and rinse with cold water. (To prevent discoloration of potatoes, spread some of the mayonnaise over them). Peel eggs and chop. When potatoes have cooled slightly, add celery, onion, parsley and chopped eggs. Add remaining mayonnaise and gently toss. Season with salt and pepper to taste. Try to make early in the day or the day before so seasonings have time to blend and salad to chill. Serves 4 to 6.

VARIATION: Add 1 pound cooked shrimp.

Buffet Carrots

- 2 pounds carrots, sliced
- 3 small onions, sliced
- 1 green pepper, diced
- ¾ cup sugar
- ¼ cup vinegar
- 1 teaspoon salt
- Dash of pepper
- 1 teaspoon Worcestershire sauce
- 1 (10½-ounce) can tomato soup
- ¼ teaspoon prepared mustard

Cook carrots and drain. Make a sauce of sautéed onion and green pepper, spices and tomato soup. Pour over carrots. Refrigerate overnight or all day. Serve at room temperature. May also be served warm as a side dish. Canned carrots may also be used. Serves 6 to 8.

When you need color on your table, it's the perfect addition.

Tabouli Salad

- 1 cup fine Bulgur wheat
- 1 cup cold water
- ½ cup green onion, finely diced
- 2 bunches parsley, chopped (stems removed)
- 1 small head of lettuce torn into small pieces
- 1 cup chopped fresh mint leaves or 2 tablespoons dried
- 4 tomatoes, diced
- ½ cup fresh lemon juice
- ½ cup olive oil
- Salt and pepper to taste

Soak wheat in water for 30 minutes. Squeeze dry by pressing between palms. Mix onions, parsley, mint, tomatoes and lettuce. Add wheat, lemon juice, olive oil, salt and pepper and mix well. Let stand ½ hour before serving to bring out flavors. Serves 6.

This is a family favorite.

Too Goo Doo Cole Slaw

- **1 medium cabbage**
- **1 medium green pepper**
- **1 medium onion**
- **1 cup sugar**
- **1 cup vinegar**
- **1 teaspoon salt**
- **1 teaspoon celery seed**
- **1 teaspoon dry mustard**
- **¾ cup salad oil**

Shred cabbage, green pepper, and onion. Put in layers in bowl. DO NOT MIX. Cover with layer of sugar. Boil other ingredients and pour over layers. Cover lightly and refrigerate for 4 hours. Mix before serving. Serves 6.

Sister A.J.'s Salad and Dressing

Salad:

- **1 small head lettuce**
- **Spinach leaves**
- **Purple onion rings**
- **Sunflower seeds**

Dressing:

- **⅓ cup sugar**
- **1 teaspoon dry mustard**
- **½ teaspoon onion salt**
- **½ teaspoon celery seed**
- **⅓ cup white vinegar**
- **¾ cup Crisco oil**

Mix together thoroughly and chill 1 hour before using. Pour over salad. Serves 4.

The sunflower seeds are a delightful surprise in this salad.

BREADS

Breads

Apple Kuchen

- **1 cup all-purpose flour**
- **1 teaspoon baking powder**
- **¼ teaspoon salt**
- **1 tablespoon sugar**
- **1 tablespoon butter**
- **1 egg**
- **3 apples, peeled, cored and sliced as for pie**
- **½ cup milk (about)**
- **1 teaspoon cinnamon (or more to taste)**
- **¼ to ⅓ cup sugar**

Sift flour, baking powder, salt and 1 tablespoon sugar. Cut in butter. Beat egg and add enough milk to make 1 cup (egg and milk together). Add to flour mixture and stir until smooth. Place in 9-inch buttered round or square pan. Arrange sliced apples on top of batter. Sprinkle with cinnamon and sugar, dot with butter. Bake in 450° oven 15-20 minutes, or until browned. Serves 6 to 8.

HINT: I used Macintosh apples because of the taste and also they cook quickly for such a short baking time.

Cheese Danish

- **2 cans crescent rolls**
- **2 (8-ounce) packages cream cheese, softened**
- **¾ cup sugar**
- **1 teaspoon vanilla**
- **Juice of one lemon or one small can crushed pineapple, drained**
- **1 egg white**

Roll out one can of crescent rolls in bottom of greased 9x13-inch pan. Mix softened cream cheese, sugar and vanilla. Spread cheese mixture on crescent rolls, then pineapple. Top with second can of crescent rolls. Brush with egg white. Bake at 350° for 30 minutes. Serves 12.

Easy and delicious, great for brunch or breakfast.

Apricot Prune Coffee Cake

¾ cup dried apricots, chopped coarsely
¾ cup dried prunes, chopped coarsely
2 tablespoons flour
3 cups all-purpose flour
1½ teaspoons baking powder
¾ teaspoon baking soda
¼ teaspoon salt
¾ cup margarine, softened
1½ cups sugar
4 eggs
1½ teaspoons vanilla
1 cup sour cream
2 tablespoons slivered almonds

Streusel Mixture:
½ cup light brown sugar
2 tablespoons butter
2 tablespoons flour
1 teaspoon cinnamon

Preheat oven to 350°.

Mix streusel topping in a small bowl and set aside. Grease and flour 10-inch tube pan.

In a small bowl combine flour, salt, soda, and baking powder. Set aside.

In a large bowl cream the butter and sugar well. Gradually add eggs—one at a time. Beat until light and fluffy. Add vanilla. Alternately beat in flour (3 cups) and the sour cream until all blended. Gently fold in apricots and prunes—which have been coated with 2 tablespoons of flour. Spoon one-third of batter into prepared pan. Sprinkle with one third streusel mixture. Repeat layers twice. Sprinkle slivered almonds on top.

Bake 55 to 60 minutes until center comes out clean with toothpick. Let cool on wire rack 20 minutes before removing from pan.

Easy Breakfast Loaves

- **1 cup pecans, chopped**
- **1 package frozen rolls**
- **¾ cup brown sugar**
- **1 (3½-ounce) package vanilla pudding (not instant)**
- **1 teaspoon cinnamon**
- **4 tablespoons butter or margarine**

Spray two loaf pans with non-stick spray. Sprinkle bottom of pans with pecans. Line rolls close together in pans. Mix sugar, pudding and cinnamon together and sprinkle over rolls. Dot with butter. Cover with foil and let stand overnight to rise. Bake at 350° for 30 to 40 minutes Serves 8 to 10.

Sour Cream Coffee Cake Grandmere

- **½ cup butter**
- **1 cup sugar**
- **2 eggs**
- **2 cups all-purpose flour**
- **1 teaspoon baking soda**
- **1 teaspoon baking powder**
- **½ teaspoon salt**
- **1 cup sour cream**
- **1 teaspoon vanilla**

Topping:

- **⅓ cup brown sugar**
- **¼ cup granulated sugar**
- **1 teaspoon cinnamon**
- **¼ cup pecans, finely chopped**

Cream butter and sugar together until light. Add eggs, one at a time, then add dry ingredients, alternating with sour cream. stir in vanilla. Pour half of batter into a well-buttered and floured 13x9-inch pan. Cover with half of topping, then pour remaining batter and top with remaining topping. Bake in 325° oven for 40 minutes. (You may want to substitute 1 teaspoon almond flavoring for vanilla for a change). Serves 10 to 12.

Great for Christmas breakfast!

Peach Bread

- 3½ cups chopped fresh peaches
- ½ cup sugar
- 2¼ cups plain flour
- 1 teaspoon baking powder
- 1 teaspoon baking soda
- ½ teaspoon salt
- 1 teaspoon cinnamon
- 2 eggs
- 1 cup sugar
- ½ cup oil
- 1 teaspoon vanilla
- 1 cup chopped pecans

Heat peaches and ½ cup sugar just until sugar dissolves and peaches tender. Do Not Cook. Cool. Sift together flour, baking powder, baking soda, salt and cinnamon. Set aside. Beat eggs and add remaining one cup sugar, oil and vanilla. Mix well. Add peach mixture and stir. Add sifted ingredients and mix well. Stir in pecans. Bake in two 9x5x3 loaf pans at 350 degrees for about 50 minutes.

Great with cream cheese. Or make it a dessert - cover a slice with chopped fresh peaches, a spoon of whipped cream (or vanilla ice cream) and top with chopped pecans.

Apple Muffins

- 1¾ cups plain flour
- ½ cup sugar
- ½ teaspoon salt
- ½ teaspoon baking soda
- ½ teaspoon ground cinnamon
- 1½ cups apple, finely chopped and peeled
- 1 (8-ounce) carton sour cream
- ½ cup vegetable oil
- 1 egg
- ½ cup chopped pecans
- 1 teaspoon vanilla extract

Combine flour, sugar, salt, soda, cinnamon and apple in large mixing bowl. Combine sour cream, oil, egg, pecans and vanilla. Add to dry ingredients, stirring just until moistened. Spoon batter into greased or paper lined muffin pans, filling ¾ full. Bake at 350° for 25 minutes or until lightly browned. Remove from pan and cool slightly on wire racks. Serve warm. Makes 1½ dozen.

Delicious with honey butter!

Blueberry Muffin Cake

- ½ cup margarine
- 1 cup sugar
- 2 eggs
- 1½ cups of sifted all-purpose flour
- 1 teaspoon baking powder
- ½ teaspoon salt (optional)
- ⅓ cup milk
- 1 teaspoon vanilla
- 1½ cups blueberries, floured

Cream the margarine with sugar until fluffy; add eggs and beat well. Sift flour, baking powder and salt together. Add flour mixture to creamed mixture, alternately with milk. Mix extremely well—the longer you beat, the better the cake will be! Fold in vanilla and floured blueberries. Pour batter into well-greased 8-inch square pan. Sprinkle with granulated sugar. Bake at 350° for 35 to 40 minutes. Serves 4 to 6.

Pumpkin Apple Streusel Muffins

- 2½ cups all-purpose flour
- 2 cups sugar
- 1 tablespoon pumpkin pie spice
- 1 teaspoon baking soda
- ½ teaspoon salt
- 2 eggs, slightly beaten
- 1 cup Libby's solid pack pumpkin
- ½ cup vegetable oil
- 2 cups apples, peeled and finely chopped
- Streusel topping

In large bowl, combine flour, sugar, spice, soda and salt. Set aside. In medium bowl. combine eggs, pumpkin and oil. Add liquid ingredients to dry ingredients, stir until just moistened. Stir in apples. Spoon batter into a greased or paper lined muffin cups, filling ¾ full. Sprinkle streusel topping over batter. Bake in preheated 350° oven for 35 to 40 minutes or until toothpick comes out clean.

Streusel Topping:

- 2 tablespoons all-purpose flour
- ¼ cup sugar
- ½ teaspoon cinnamon
- 4 teaspoons butter

Mix flour, sugar and cinnamon. Cut in butter until mixture is crumbly. Serves 12 large, 24 medium.

Christmas Cran-Orange Muffins

- 1 egg
- 1 cup milk
- 1 cup cranberries, cut in halves
- ½ cup orange juice
- ¼ cup vegetable oil
- 2 cups all-purpose flour
- ¼ cup sugar
- 3 tablespoons orange peel, grated
- 3 teaspoons baking powder
- 1 teaspoon salt
- ½ cup chopped nuts
- 3 tablespoons butter, melted
- ½ cup sugar
- 1 teaspoon cinnamon

Preheat oven to 350°. Grease bottom only of 12 medium muffin tins. Beat egg. Stir in milk, cranberries, juice and oil. Stir in remaining ingredients just until flour is moistened. (Batter will be lumpy) Fill muffin cups ⅔ full. Bake until golden brown about 20 to 25 minutes. Combine sugar and cinnamon. Set aside. When muffins have finished baking, remove from oven and brush tops with melted butter and sprinkle with cinnamon-sugar mixture. Remove from pan and place on wire rack to cool. (Cup-cake liners work well.) Serves 12.

Double Oat Muffins

- 2 cups Quaker oat bran, uncooked
- ⅓ cup brown sugar
- ¼ cup all-purpose flour
- ¼ teaspoon nutmeg
- 1 cup buttermilk
- 2 eggs (or egg substitute)
- 1½ teaspoons vanilla
- 3 tablespoons vegetable oil
- ¼ cup Quaker Quick oats
- 1 tablespoon brown sugar

Heat oven to 400°. Line 12 muffins cups with paper liners. Combine oat bran, ⅓ cup brown sugar, flour and nutmeg. Set aside. In small bowl mix milk, eggs, oil and vanilla. Add to flour mixture just until moistened. Fill cups ¾ full. Combine oats and remaining brown sugar and sprinkle evenly over batter. Bake 20 to 22 minutes until golden brown. Makes 12 muffins.

A healthful grain muffin perfect for breakfast or as a snack.

Bake As You Please Bran Muffins

- **3 cups boiling water**
- **5 teaspoons baking soda**
- **1 cup shortening**
- **2 cups sugar**
- **4 eggs**
- **1 quart buttermilk**
- **5 cups all-purpose flour**
- **1 tablespoon salt**
- **2 cups bran cereal flakes**
- **4 cups all-bran cereal**
- **1½ cups raisins (optional)**

Mix the soda in boiling water and set aside to let cool. Cream shortening and sugar. Add eggs and all other following ingredients. Last of all add the soda and water. Mix in large bowl and let stand in refrigerator overnight. Stir well. Fill greased muffin tins approximately ½ full and bake at 400° for 15 to 20 minutes. Makes 4 to 5 dozen.

The batter will keep nicely in your refrigerator 3 to 4 weeks.

Sweet Potato Muffins

- **½ cup butter**
- **1¼ cups sugar**
- **2 eggs**
- **1¼ cups canned sweet potatoes, mashed**
- **1½ cups all-purpose flour**
- **2 teaspoons baking powder**
- **¼ teaspoon salt**
- **1 teaspoon cinnamon**
- **¼ teaspoon nutmeg**
- **1 cup milk**
- **¼ cup pecans, chopped**
- **¼ cup raisins, chopped**

Preheat oven 400°. Grease 1½-inch muffin tin. Cream the butter and sugar. Add the eggs and mix well. Blend in the sweet potatoes. Sift the flour with the baking powder, salt, cinnamon and nutmeg. Add alternately with the milk. Do not over-mix. Fold in the nuts and raisins. Fill the greased tins ⅔ full. Bake at 400° for 20 to 35 minutes. Makes 12 large muffins.

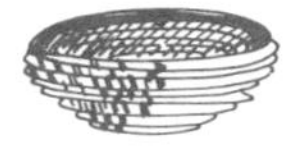

Rose Marie's Blueberry Muffins

- 2 cups Bisquick buttermilk baking mix
- ¾ cup sugar
- ½ teaspoon cinnamon
- 1 cup sour cream
- 2 eggs, unbeaten
- 1 cup blueberries, drained well

Preheat oven to 425°. Combine Bisquick, sugar and cinnamon. Make a large indention in the mix and put in sour cream and eggs. Beat by hand with a fork until ingredients are combined. Fold in blueberries. Pour into greased medium muffin pans. Bake at 425° until golden or approximately 20 to 25 minutes. Makes 12 large muffins.

Wonderful anytime!

Banana Nut Bread

- 2 cups all-purpose flour
- 1 teaspoon soda
- ½ teaspoon salt
- ½ cup butter
- ¾ cup sugar
- 2 eggs
- 1 teaspoon lemon juice
- 2 cups bananas, mashed (about 4 average ripe)
- 1 cup walnuts, chopped

Cream sugar, butter. Add eggs, lemon juice, flour, soda, and salt. Add bananas and nuts. Bake in greased loaf pan for 50 minutes at 350°. May bake in small loaf pans for 25 to 30 minutes. Use your judgement.

Carrot Nut Loaf

- 1½ cups all-purpose flour
- 1 teaspoon soda
- ½ teaspoon salt
- 1 teaspoon ground cinnamon
- ¾ cup vegetable oil
- 2 eggs
- 1 cup sugar
- 1 cup carrots, grated
- 1 cup pecans, chopped

Combine first 4 ingredients in a small mixing bowl; set aside. Combine oil, eggs, and sugar in large mixing bowl. Beat at medium speed for 1 minute. Add dry ingredients; mix at low speed just until blended. Fold in carrots and pecans. (Batter will be stiff.) Spoon batter into a greased and floured 9x5x3-inch loaf pan. Bake at 350° for 1 hour and 25 minutes. Cool bread in pan 10 minutes; then turn out on wire rack. Cool completely. Serves 6 to 8.

Cranberry Bread

- **1½ cups fresh cranberries**
- **2 cups all-purpose flour**
- **1 cup sugar**
- **1½ teaspoons baking powder**
- **½ teaspoon soda**
- **1 teaspoon salt**
- **¼ cup butter or margarine**
- **1 egg, beaten**
- **1 teaspoon orange rind, grated**
- **¾ cup orange juice**
- **1½ cups golden raisins**

Wash cranberries, drain, and grind coarsely in food grinder or blender. Set aside. Combine flour, sugar, baking powder, soda, and salt in a large mixing bowl; cut in butter with a pastry blender until mixture resembles coarse crumbs. Add egg, orange rind, and juice; stir in raisins and cranberries; spoon into a greased and floured 9x5x3-inch loaf pan. Bake at 350° for 1 hour.

This makes a special treat for a Christmas brunch.

Date Nut Bread

- **1 pound package chopped dates**
- **1½ cups boiling water**
- **2 teaspoons soda**
- **2½ tablespoons butter**
- **1¾ cups sugar**
- **1 egg**
- **2¾ cups all-purpose flour**
- **1 cup chopped nuts (pecans or walnuts)**
- **1½ teaspoons vanilla**

Add soda to boiling water and pour over dates. Let this mixture stand. Cream butter and sugar, then add egg. Strain water from date mixture INTO batter. Add flour and beat well. Add dates, nuts, and vanilla. Mix well. Pour into two greased loaf pans. Bake at 350° for one hour. Makes 2 loaves.

My husband loves to put peanut butter on his slice of date nut bread. He says it really is delicious! Try it, you might like it!!
The bread keeps very well wrapped in foil and placed in refrigerator or freezer. Also, this is a wonderful Christmas gift. You can bake these in small aluminum loaf pans. Approximately 30 minutes. Check for doneness by putting a knife down the center of the loaf. If it comes out clean then it is done. I personally like for my "knife" to come out with a tiny bit of batter on it. That way I know it is nice and moist.

Fresh Apple Bread

- **1 cup sugar**
- **½ cup shortening**
- **2 eggs**
- **2 cups all-purpose flour**
- **1 teaspoon soda**
- **½ teaspoon salt**
- **1½ tablespoons buttermilk**
- **½ teaspoon vanilla**
- **1 cup pecans, chopped**
- **1 tablespoon all-purpose flour**
- **1 cup apple, peeled and grated**
- **1½ tablespoons sugar**
- **½ teaspoon ground cinnamon**

Combine 1 cup sugar and shortening; cream until light and fluffy. Add eggs, one at a time, beating well after each addition. Combine 2 cups flour, soda, and salt and set aside. Combine buttermilk and vanilla. Add dry ingredients to creamed mixture alternately with buttermilk mixture, beating well after each addition. Combine pecans and 1 tablespoon flour and stir until all pecans are coated. Stir pecans and apple into batter. Pour batter into greased and floured 9x5x3-inch loaf pan. Combine 1½ tablespoons sugar and cinnamon and mix well; sprinkle evenly over batter. Bake at 350° for 1 hour. Serves 6 to 8.

Lemon Bread

- **½ cup shortening (butter)**
- **1 cup sugar**
- **2 eggs, beaten**
- **1⅔ cups all-purpose flour**
- **1 teaspoon baking powder**
- **½ teaspoon salt**
- **½ cup milk**
- **½ cup nuts (optional)**
- **Peel of one lemon, grated**

Preheat oven to 350°. Cream shortening with sugar. Add eggs. Sift flour with baking powder and salt. Alternately add flour and milk to shortening mixture. Add lemon peel and nuts. Grease and flour one 5x9-inch loaf pan. Bake for one hour.

Topping:

- **¼ cup sugar (powdered)**
- **Juice of one lemon**

Mix together sugar and lemon juice and pour over hot bread. Makes 1 loaf.

Peanut Butter Bread

2 tablespoons butter or margarine, melted
¼ cup firmly packed brown sugar
¼ cup chopped roasted peanuts
1 tablespoon water
1 egg
1 cup firmly packed brown sugar
2 tablespoons peanut butter
2 tablespoons butter or margarine, melted
1 cup buttermilk
2 cups all-purpose flour
1 teaspoon baking powder
½ teaspoon baking soda
½ teaspoon salt

Grease bottom and sides of an 8½x4½x2½-inch loafpan. Pour 2 tablespoons butter in pan. Sprinkle ¼ cup sugar and peanuts evenly over bottom of pan. Sprinkle water over mixture.

Beat egg at medium speed of an electric mixer. Add 1 cup sugar, and beat well. Add peanut butter and 2 tablespoons butter, mixing well. Add buttermilk, mixing until blended. Combine flour and next 3 ingredients; add to creamed mixture, mixing well. Spoon into prepared pan. Bake at 350° for 50 minutes or until a wooden pick inserted in center comes out clean. Cool in pan 10 minutes; remove from pan, and let cool on a wire rack. Makes 1 loaf.

Zucchini Bread

3 eggs
2 cups sugar
1 cup oil
1 teaspoon vanilla
1 teaspoon salt
1 cup nuts, chopped
2 cups zucchini, grated
2 cups all-purpose flour
1½ teaspoons cinnamon
2 teaspoons soda
¼ teaspoon baking powder

Preheat oven to 350°. Grease and flour 2 loaf pans. Mix all ingredients well and pour ½ the mixture into each pan. Bake for 1 hour. Serves 8 to 10.

Easy to prepare and delicious with any meal or by itself.

Poppy Seed Bread

Bread:

- **3 cups all-purpose flour**
- **2½ cups sugar**
- **1½ teaspoons salt**
- **1½ teaspoons baking powder**
- **2 tablespoons poppy seeds**
- **3 eggs, beaten**
- **1½ cups milk**
- **1⅛ cups oil**
- **1½ teaspoons vanilla**
- **1½ teaspoons almond extract**
- **1½ teaspoons butter flavoring**

Sift flour and add dry ingredients. Beat eggs with milk, oil and flavoring. Combine all ingredients and pour into 2 large or 3 small loaf pans that have been greased. Bake in 325° or 350° oven for 1 hour. Cool in pans for 10 minutes.

Glaze:

- **½ cup sugar**
- **¼ cup orange juice**
- **½ teaspoon vanilla**
- **½ teaspoon almond extract**
- **½ teaspoon butter flavoring**

Prick top of loaves with fork or tooth pick. Pour or spoon over bread. Serves 10 to 12.

Good enough to be a dessert.

Easy Yeast Rolls

- **½ cup margarine**
- **¼ cup sugar**
- **Pinch of salt**
- **½ cup boiling water**
- **1 egg**
- **1 package dry yeast**
- **½ cup lukewarm water**
- **3 cups all-purpose flour**

Combine sugar, salt, margarine and boiling water (margarine should be completely melted). Beat egg lightly. Dissolve yeast in lukewarm water. When the first mixture is cool, fold in the egg, yeast and water along with 3 cups flour. Let stand overnight in refrigerator. This will keep up to 3 days in the refrigerator. Roll out onto floured board 2 to 3 hours before cooking. Cut with biscuit cutter. Brush with melted margarine and fold. Place close together in greased pan, and brush tops with melted margarine. Let rise 2 to 3 hours. Bake at 400° for about 10 to 12 minutes or until brown. Makes 12-18 rolls.

Easy and delicious. This can be made the day before.

Strawberry Bread

3 cups all-purpose flour
2 cups sugar
3 teaspoons cinnamon
1 teaspoon salt
1 teaspoon baking soda
1¼ cups salad oil (Wesson or Crisco is what I use)
4 eggs, beaten
2 (10-ounce) packages frozen strawberries, thawed and cut into bite-size pieces
1 cup pecans, chopped

Grease and flour two regular size loaf pans and preheat oven to 350°. Mix all dry ingredients (you do not have to sift anything). Add oil, beaten eggs and strawberries, including the juice. Make sure everything is mixed well. Pour into pans and bake for 1 to 1¼ hours. (You can tell when done by checking with a toothpick). I always check after 45 minutes. Do not overcook. Let cool completely in pan before removing. This makes two loaves and can be made in advance and frozen. Makes two loaves.

This is good for a breakfast bread served with coffee or a dessert served with fresh strawberries and whipped cream or Cool Whip on top.

Dilly Bread

1 package active dry yeast
¼ cup warm water
1 cup cream style cottage cheese (heated to lukewarm)
1 teaspoon onion, minced
1 tablespoon butter
2 tablespoons sugar
1 teaspoon salt
¼ teaspoon baking soda
¼ teaspoon dill seed
1 egg
2¼ to 2½ cups all-purpose flour

Soften yeast in water, and let stand 10 minutes. In a bowl, put cottage cheese, butter, sugar, salt, onion, dill seed, egg, and softened yeast. Blend well and add flour gradually, beating well. Cover and let rise in warm place until double, (about 1 hour). Stir dough down and turn into a well-greased pan (or a 2-quart round casserole dish). Let rise in a warm place until light (about 30 to 40 minutes). Bake at 350° for 35 to 40 minutes until golden. Serves 10 to 12.

A great place for bread to rise is on top of television set if it is on.

Cinnamon Rolls

4¼ cups unsifted all-purpose flour
⅓ cup sugar
1 teaspoon salt
2 packages active dry yeast
¾ cup milk
½ cup water
1 stick butter
2 eggs

Combine 1 cup flour, ⅓ cup sugar, salt, and undissolved yeast. Heat milk, water and ½ cup butter over low heat to 120°. Add to dry ingredients and beat 2 minutes at medium speed; add ½ cup flour and eggs; beat at high speed for 2 minutes. Add enough flour to make a stiff batter. Do not add all flour at one time. Cover tightly and refrigerate 2 hours or up to 2 days. Roll dough to 16x8-inch rectangle.

Topping:
3 tablespoons butter, melted
1 cup sugar
1 tablespoon cinnamon

Combine the melted butter, sugar and cinnamon and spread over the dough. Carefully roll up lengthwise and pinch seam closed. Cut in one-inch slices and place on greased cookie sheet. Allow to rise until double in size (about 45 minutes). Bake at 375° for 20 to 25 minutes. Frost with confectioners' icing if desired. Serves 24.

Create your own specialty. Try sprinkling your favorite fruit and fiber cereal on dough before rolling.

Feather Rolls

5 cups all-purpose flour
1 package active dry yeast
½ cup potatoes, cooked and mashed
⅓ cup cooking oil
¼ cup sugar
1 teaspoon salt

In a mixer bowl combine 2 cups of the flour and the yeast. Combine potatoes, oil, sugar, salt, and 1½ cups warm water (110°). Add to dry ingredients; beat at low speed with electric mixer for ½ minute, scraping sides of bowl constantly. Beat 3 minutes at high speed. By hand, stir in remaining flour. Cover; refrigerate for at least 2 hours or up to 3 days. Punch down; turn out on lightly floured surface. Cover; let rest 10 minutes. With lightly floured hands, shape into 24 buns. Place in greased 13x9x2-inch baking pan. Cover; let rise till almost double (40 minutes). Bake at 400° till done, 16 to 20 minutes. Makes 24.

Flower Pot Bread

½ cup milk
3 tablespoons butter
1½ cups water
5½ cups all-purpose flour
3 tablespoons sugar
2 teaspoons salt
1 package dry yeast

Combine milk, butter and water. Heat until warm. In a large bowl combine 2 cups flour, sugar, salt and dry yeast, mix well. Gradually add warm milk to flour mixture - beat well. Add 1 cup of flour and continue to beat. Add rest of flour to form soft dough. If more flour is needed, add small amounts at a time. Turn out on floured board and knead until smooth. Place in greased bowl, cover, place out of draft (in cold oven) and allow to rise about 1 hour until it has doubled in size. Punch down and turn out again on floured surface. Separate into 6 or 8 pieces. Roll out to small rectangles 4x6-inch. Fold under and push into **greased** 3-inch flower pots. Let double in size and bake at 400° for 25 to 30 minutes. Remove from pot and cool. Before serving put the bread in pots. Makes six to eight 3-inch pots of bread.

Sally Lunn Bread

3½ to 4 cups unsifted all-purpose flour, divided
⅓ cup sugar
1 teaspoon salt
1 package dry yeast
½ cup milk
½ cup water
½ cup softened margarine
3 eggs (room temperature)

Combine 1¼ cups flour, sugar, salt and yeast in a large bowl; mix thoroughly. Combine milk, water and margarine over low heat until warm. (Margarine does not need to melt). Gradually add liquid to dry ingredients and beat about 2 minutes, scraping bowl occasionally. Add eggs and 1 cup flour or enough to make thick batter. Cover and let rise in warm place, free from drafts, until doubled in bulk (about one hour). Stir batter down and beat well for 1 minute. Spoon into a well-greased 9-inch tube pan. Cover and let rise until doubled in bulk once again. Bake at 325° for 45 to 50 minutes. Remove from pan and place on wire rack. Serves 10 to 12.

Sourdough Bread Basic Starter

2½ cups warm water
½ cup sugar
1 package dry yeast
1 cup bread flour
2 cups instant potatoes
1 teaspoon salt

Add sugar to warm water, stir. Sprinkle package of yeast on top of water, let sit a few minutes. If the yeast is good, it will fall to the bottom of bowl and then begin to rise as if to boil. After the yeast is dissolved, add flour, potatoes and salt and stir until smooth. Store in one-gallon container with lid in a warm draft-free place three to four days, stirring two or three times a day. (Cover during night, uncover during day). Then store in refrigerator three to five days. Remove the basic starter from the refrigerator, mix well and divide into three one-quart jars and add starter food to each jar. Punch a hole in jar tops.

Starter Food:
¾ cup sugar
3 tablespoons instant potatoes
1 cup warm water

Mix starter food ingredients and add to basic starter. Let stand out of refrigerator eight to ten hours with lid on until bubbly (make sure lid has a hole in top). Take one cup starter to make bread and return rest to the refrigerator three to five days and feed again. The starter must be fed every 3 to 5 days and 1 cup must always be removed after feeding. If you do not make bread, remove the cup and give it away to a friend. You'll find that someone is always waiting for it. The first time you feed a new starter, the one cup you remove should be thrown away. A starter will make better bread after you feed it the second time.

Sourdough Bread

- **½ cup sugar**
- **½ cup corn oil**
- **1 tablespoon salt**
- **1 cup sour dough bread basic starter**
- **1½ cups warm water**
- **6 cups unsifted bread flour**

At night, mix all ingredients in a large bowl, making a stiff batter. Transfer batter into a greased bowl. Oil top of batter and set in oven overnight.

The next morning, punch dough down and knead thoroughly on a floured board. Divide into 3 parts and put in greased loaf pans. Brush tops with oil. Let rise 4 to 5 hours or until just rounded over top of pans. Bake on bottom rack at 350° for 40 to 45 minutes. Remove and brush with butter. Cool on rack. Wrap well. Makes 3 loaves.

Monkey Bread:
Makes 2 tube pans instead of dividing dough in 3 parts after rising overnight, divide dough in 2 parts and roll to about ⅓-inch thick, cut with biscuit cutter, then dip in ½ cup melted butter. Arrange pieces around tube pan. Let rise 4 to 5 hours or until just rounded over top of pans. Bake on bottom rack at 400° for 20 minutes. Reduce heat to 350° and bake 20 to 25 minutes. Serve hot and pull apart.

Benne Beer Bread

- **1 (12-ounce) can of beer**
- **¼ cup maple syrup**
- **3 tablespoons Benne seeds (or caraway seeds)**
- **2 cups whole wheat flour**
- **1 cup unbleached flour**
- **4 tablespoons baking powder**
- **1 teaspoon salt**

Preheat oven to 350° and grease loaf pans. In a large bowl combine flours, salt and baking powder—Mix well.

In small pan combine beer, maple syrup and benne seeds (caraway) Heat until warm. Pour warm mixture into dry ingredients. Stir rapidly and pour into well greased loaf pans. Bake for 30 minutes.

Alice O'Neill's Irish Soda Bread

Sift:

3½ cups all-purpose flour
3½ teaspoons baking powder
½ teaspoon baking soda
1 teaspoon salt
2 tablespoons sugar
½ cup shortening
1 egg
2 cups buttermilk
2 teaspoons caraway seeds (optional)
1 cup raisins

In large bowl combine dry ingredients.

Cut into mixture ½ cup shortening until mixture is quite fine. Add 2 teaspoons caraway seeds (optional) and 1 cup raisins (optional. Beat 1 egg with 1 cup buttermilk add another cup of buttermilk. Gradually add liquid to flour mixture until it is the consistence of biscuit dough (you won't use all the liquid). Turn onto floured board, knead quickly and shape into round. Place in greased and floured cast iron frying pan. Cut a cross on the top for a blessing on the bread. Bake at 450° for 10 minutes then lower heat to 350° and bake for 50 minutes more -1 hour total. Make sure to preheat oven to 450°. Serves 6 to 8.

NOTE: This is delicious hot, but cuts better the next day. In Ireland you are served yesterday's bread.

Straight from Ireland, we believe this would have been a favorite of Bishop John England.

Swiss Bread

- **8 ounces Swiss cheese, grated**
- **1 cup butter**
- **½ teaspoon garlic salt**
- **½ teaspoon celery seed**
- **½ teaspoon parsley**
- **1 long soft crust French bread (not Pepperidge Farm)**

Mix above ingredients together. Cut crust off bread, except for bottom. Cut bread in slices almost to bottom crust. Spread half the cheese mixture between slices. Frost the rest of the loaf with the cheese. Place loaf in a boat of foil, and cover the top with foil. Bake at 400° for 15 minutes. Uncover the loaf and continue baking for 10 to 15 minutes until crusty and brown. Make several and freeze. Allow to thaw and come to room temperature before baking. Bake on cookie sheet. Serves 8.

Your friends will want to steal this recipe!

Broccoli/Spinach Cornbread

- **1 (10-ounce) package frozen broccoli, thawed and chopped**
- **1 large onion, finely chopped**
- **6 ounces cottage cheese**
- **½ cup butter, melted**
- **1 teaspoon salt**
- **4 eggs, beaten**
- **1 box Jiffy cornbread mix**

Combine broccoli, onion, cottage cheese, butter, salt and eggs. Mix well and add cornbread mix. Pour into greased 9x13-inch casserole and bake at 400° for 25 minutes.

VARIATION: Instead of broccoli, add 1 package frozen spinach, thawed and drained. Mix same as above and bake in greased muffin tins at 400° for 20 minutes. Serves 12.

How can something so easy get so many compliments?

Trevor Tom's Shrimp Puppies

2 cups shrimp, cooked and chopped
2 (6-ounce) packages jalapeño cornbread mix
1 (7-ounce) can cream style corn
¼ cup green onions, chopped
1 jalapeño pepper, finely chopped
Oil for frying

Chop or shred shrimp in a food processor or with a knife. Combine all ingredients except oil in a large bowl. Heat oil to 365°. Drop mixture by heaping teaspoonfuls into hot oil. Fry until golden brown. Remove from oil and drain on absorbent paper. Makes 5 dozen.

Papa's Beer Bread

2 cups self-rising flour
3 tablespoons sugar
1 (12-ounce) can of beer, warm
1 tablespoon butter, melted

Combine flour, sugar and beer; stir just until all ingredients are moistened. Pour into a greased loaf pan. Bake at 375° for 30 to 35 minutes. Brush with melted butter. Remove bread from pan and cool. Serves 6 to 8.

Garlic Bread Twists

Nonstick spray coating
1 (10-ounce) package refrigerated pizza dough
1 egg white
1 tablespoon water
¼ teaspoon garlic powder
Grated Parmesan cheese, sesame seed or poppy seed

Coat baking sheet with nonstick spray. Remove pizza dough from package but do not unroll. Cut dough roll crosswise into 12 slices. Unroll each slice, cut in half and twist. Place on baking sheet. In a small bowl, mix egg white, water and garlic powder and brush onto dough. Sprinkle with Parmesan, sesame seed or poppy seed. Bake at 375° for 12 to 15 minutes until golden brown. Makes 24.

Entrées / Casseroles

Entrées/Casseroles

B.E.'s Lunchroom Mezzetti

- 2 tablespoons margarine
- 1½ pounds ground chuck
- ½ pound bulk sausage
- 1 can tomato soup
- 1 can cream of mushroom soup
- 1 medium onion, diced
- 1 green pepper, diced
- ¼ teaspoon curry
- ¼ teaspoon oregano
- ¼ teaspoon red pepper
- ¼ teaspoon thyme
- 1 (8-ounce) mozzarella cheese, shredded
- 1 (8-ounce) Cheddar cheese, shredded
- 1 (8-ounce) package egg noodles, cooked according to directions

Cook noodles and drain. Sauté meats in 1 tablespoon melted margarine and drain. Sauté onion and green pepper in 1 tablespoon margarine and add to the meat mixture. Combine spices and soups to meat mixture along with the cooked noodles. Add ½ of the cheeses to the mixture and place in a greased 13x9-inch casserole dish. Sprinkle with remainder of cheeses. Bake at 350° for 30 minutes or till bubbly. Serves 6 to 8.

Great to make ahead and freeze. Good to serve a crowd.

Beef & Vegetable Chow Mein Casserole

- 1¼ pounds ground beef
- 1 small onion, chopped
- 1 (10¾-ounce) can cream of mushroom soup, undiluted
- 1 (10-ounce) can chicken and rice soup, undiluted
- 1 (10-ounce) package frozen mixed vegetables
- 1 cup celery, chopped
- 1 (3-ounce) can chow mein noodles, divided

Brown beef and onion in large skillet stirring to crumble. Drain well. Stir in remaining ingredients, reserving half of chow mein noodles. Spoon mixture into lightly greased 2-quart baking dish. Bake at 350° for 30 minutes or until bubbly. Sprinkle remaining noodles over casserole before serving. Serves 6.

Very easy to put together, even little children love it.

Coach Cantey's Shepherd Pie

1½ to 2 pounds ground beef
1 medium onion, chopped
1 can sliced carrots and peas
Mashed potatoes
Mild Cheddar cheese, grated
Salt to taste
Pepper (optional)

Fry ground beef mixed with onion, salt and pepper until done. Drain grease. Add peas and carrots. Let simmer for about 5 minutes. Fix mashed potatoes, approximately 2 cups (fresh or instant). Spread meat mixture into a 2-quart casserole dish and cover with mashed potatoes, top with grated cheese. Heat in microwave or 350° in conventional oven, just long enough for cheese to melt. Serves 4.

This is a very quick and easy recipe, a meal in itself.

South of the Border Dinner

1½ pounds ground beef
2 tablespoons salad oil
1 medium onion, chopped
1 medium bell pepper, chopped
1 (15-ounce) can tomato purée
4 tablespoons chili powder
1½ teaspoons salt
1 box cornbread mix (about 8-9 ounces)

Cook ground beef until brown stirring so it will be broken up. Drain and put beef aside. Put 2 tablespoons salad oil in 10-inch skillet and cook onion and bell pepper until soft. Add purée, chili powder, and salt. Cook until mixture is heated and add cooked beef. Pour mixture into a 9x9-inch baking pan or Pyrex dish. Mix cornbread according to package directions. Spread cornbread on top of mixture. Bake at 400° until cornbread is lightly browned. Loosen side of pan with knife and invert onto platter. Serve hot. Serves 6.

Husband's Delight

1 (8-ounce) package thin egg noodles
1½ pounds ground round
1 medium onion, chopped fine
2 small cans tomato sauce
1 (8-ounce) package cream cheese
1 (8-ounce) carton sour cream
1 large package of grated Cheddar cheese

Cook noodles and set aside. Brown onion and meat together. In a bowl, combine tomato sauce, softened cream cheese, and sour cream. Put half the noodles in a greased 2-quart casserole. Add all of the creamed mixture, then the rest of noodles. Place the meat mixture on top of this and sprinkle with the grated cheese. Bake at 375° for 30 to 40 minutes. Serves 4.

Stuffed Bell Peppers

½ cup onion, chopped
¼ cup celery, chopped
Salt and pepper to taste
1 pound ground beef
1½ teaspoons Worcestershire sauce
4 bell peppers
1 cup cooked rice
1 (15-ounce) can tomato sauce
Shredded Cheddar cheese

Sauté onion, celery, meat and Worcestershire sauce. Add salt and pepper to taste. Drain excess fat. Remove tops and seeds from peppers; cook in boiling water for about 5 minutes; drain. Add rice and ½ the tomato sauce to the meat mixture; stir thoroughly. Spoon meat mixture into peppers; stand peppers in baking dish. Add about ½-inch water to baking dish. Spoon remaining tomato sauce over stuffed peppers. Bake at 350° for 25 minutes, uncovered. Garnish peppers with grated Cheddar cheese and bake an additional 5 minutes. Serves 4.

Chicken Chestnut Casserole

1 (6-ounce) box long grain and wild rice
2 2½-pound fryers or 10-12 chicken breasts, cooked, boned, and chopped
1 (10¾-ounce) can condensed cream of celery soup
1 onion, minced
1 (2-ounce) jar pimientos
2 cups mayonnaise
1 (8-ounce) can water chestnuts, sliced thin
2 (16-ounce) cans French-style green beans, drained
Paprika
Grated Parmesan cheese

Cook rice as directed on box. Add all ingredients except paprika and cheese and mix thoroughly. Pour into greased shallow 3-quart baking dish. Sprinkle with paprika and Parmesan cheese. Bake at 350° until bubbly, about 30 to 40 minutes. Serves 12.

Great for a crowd - make early and when company comes, heat and eat!

Mary's Chicken Casserole

2 cups chicken broth
½ cup butter
½ cup flour
1 teaspoon salt
2 cups milk
4 cups cooked spaghetti
4 cups cooked chicken, diced
1 (8-ounce) can mushrooms
½ cup sliced almonds
1 tablespoon onion, grated
½ cup breadcrumbs
½ cup stuffed olives, sliced
1 cup cheese, grated

Cook chicken and reserve 2 cups broth. Put chicken in broth in a 2-quart saucepan. Add butter. Mix flour and salt with milk and stir into chicken stock. Continue stirring and cook over low heat until thickened. Add all of the remaining ingredients except breadcrumbs, olives and cheese. Pour into 2-quart casserole. Top with breadcrumbs, grated cheese and olives and bake for 30 minutes in a 350° oven. Serves 6 to 8.

Serve with buttered carrots and Sister A.J.'s Favorite Salad.

Nancy's Chicken Casserole

- **2 to 3 cups chicken, cooked, skinned, deboned and cut up**
- **2 cups celery, chopped**
- **1 cup mayonnaise**
- **2 tablespoons onion, chopped**
- **1½ tablespoons lemon juice**
- **1 can water chestnuts**
- **3 boiled eggs, chopped**
- **Pepperidge Farm herb stuffing**
- **Salt and pepper to taste**
- **Cream of chicken soup, as desired**

Mix chicken, celery, onion, mayonnaise, water chestnuts, seasonings, eggs and lemon juice. Put in 13x9-inch casserole dish and top with cream of chicken soup. Put stuffing on top. Bake at 350° for 30 minutes.

VARIATION: This could also be layered beginning and ending with a layer of the stuffing. Serves 6.

Eggplant Parmesan Casserole

- **1 large eggplant, peeled and sliced**
- **½ cup milk**
- **1 egg, beaten**
- **½ cup flour**
- **1 pound ground beef**
- **1 onion, chopped**
- **1 green pepper, chopped**
- **Salt and pepper to taste**
- **2 (15-ounce) cans of tomato sauce**
- **1 (8-ounce) package of mozzarella cheese**
- **½ cup grated Parmesan cheese**
- **1 teaspoon Italian seasoning**
- **Vegetable oil**

Peel and slice eggplant. Dip slices in egg and milk and dredge with flour, salt and pepper. In large skillet, heat oil and brown egg plant slices on both sides. Drain on brown paper bag. Rinse skillet and sauté ground beef, onion, and green pepper until tender, and drain. Add tomato sauce, salt, pepper, and Italian seasoning. In a greased 8x11-inch casserole place alternating layers of eggplant, cheese, and beef mixture. Top with Parmesan cheese and bake uncovered at 350° for 45 minutes or until bubbly. Serves 4 to 6.

Crabmeat Casserole

- 1 pound fresh clean crabmeat
- 1 medium onion
- 6 slices whole wheat bread
- 1 cup mayonnaise
- 2 tablespoons prepared mustard
- 1 (5-ounce) can evaporated milk
- Salt and pepper to taste
- ⅓ stick margarine

Break bread into small pieces. Chop onion. Combine all ingredients and stir until well blended. Do this a couple of hours before cooking to enhance flavor. Melt margarine in 12x7½x2-inch casserole dish before adding mixture. Bake in oven at 350° for 45 minutes. Serves 4.

This casserole is delicious served with tossed salad and baked potato.

Shrimp Supreme

- 6 slices of bacon
- 2 medium onions, chopped
- 2 cans cream of mushroom soup
- 1 (13-ounce) can evaporated milk
- 1 small package Uncle Ben's wild rice
- 2 pounds shrimp, peeled and deveined
- 1 small package Pepperidge Farm bread dressing
- ½ cup margarine, melted

Fry bacon until crisp. Remove and crumble bacon, set aside for topping. Sauté onions in bacon drippings until translucent. Add soup, milk, rice, and shrimp. Pour into large casserole dish. Mix bacon, margarine and dressing and sprinkle on top. Cover with foil and bake 50 minutes at 350°. Serves 4 to 6.

Wonderful company dish, serve with steamed broccoli, and hot rolls.

Sissy's Shrimp Casserole

- 2 cups raw rice
- 2 to 3 pounds shrimp, cooked, shelled and deveined
- 1 large bell pepper
- 1 large onion
- 1 (4-ounce) can sliced mushrooms, drained
- 1 (16-ounce) bottle 1000 Island dressing
- 6 to 8 slices of raw bacon

Cook rice, set aside. Chop onion and bell pepper and sauté in a small amount of grease until cooked. Combine cooked rice, shrimp, onion and bell pepper and the can of mushrooms in a large rectangular greased 9x13-inch casserole. Stir in bottle of 1000 Island dressing. Cover with strips of raw bacon. Cook at 350° for 1 hour uncovered. Fluff with fork. Serves 8.

This is truly delicious. Serve with 7-layer salad and rolls.

Limehouse Street Casserole

- 2 pounds shrimp, peeled and cooked
- 1 tablespoon lemon juice
- 2 tablespoons salad oil
- ¼ cup green pepper, chopped and cooked
- ¼ cup onion, chopped and cooked
- 1 to 2 cups cooked rice
- ⅛ teaspoon pepper
- ⅛ teaspoon mace
- ¾ can tomato soup
- ½ cup half and half cream
- ½ cup sherry

Sauté green pepper and onion with 2 tablespoons salad oil. Mix all ingredients in a large baking dish and bake at 350° till bubbly. Almonds and paprika can be sprinkled on top. Use a 13x9-inch pan. Serves 6 to 8.

Deviled Seafood Casserole

- 1 cup mayonnaise
- 2 pounds raw shrimp, peeled
- 1 (6-ounce) can crabmeat or ½ pound fresh crab
- 1 medium onion, chopped
- 1 small green pepper, chopped
- 1 cup celery, chopped
- Dash of Worcestershire sauce
- ⅛ teaspoon pepper
- ½ teaspoon salt
- 1 cup buttered cracker or bread crumbs

Mix all above ingredients (except crumbs) and place in buttered casserole dish. Top with the crumbs. Bake for ½ hour. Serves 4 to 6.

Very good and very easy.

Tradd Street Shrimp

- 2 to 3 pounds cooked shrimp
- 1 box Uncle Ben's white and wild rice, cooked
- 1 cup Cheddar cheese, grated
- 1 cup Swiss cheese, grated
- 1 can mushroom soup
- 1 cup green pepper, chopped
- 1 cup onion, chopped
- 1 cup celery, chopped
- 6 tablespoons butter
- 4 lemons, sliced very thin
- Salt and pepper

Mix first five ingredients together. Sauté peppers, onions and celery in butter. Add to shrimp mixture and put in a 13x9-inch greased casserole. Season to taste with salt and pepper. Cover the top completely with lemon slices. Sprinkle with a bit more pepper. Cover with foil. Bake at 375° for 30 minutes until heated through. Serves 6 to 8.

A Charleston favorite.

Why Worry - Shrimp Curry

- **1½ cups rice, cooked as directed**
- **1 small onion, grated**
- **1½ cups butter**
- **1 teaspoon curry**
- **1 teaspoon white pepper**
- **1 teaspoon Beau Monde**
- **1 teaspoon celery salt**
- **2½ pounds shrimp, cleaned and cooked**
- **½ cup slivered almonds**
- **¾ cup golden raisins**
- **6 pieces bacon, cooked and crumbled**

Sauté onion in butter until tender and add seasonings. Stir shrimp in butter sauce over medium-low heat for 3 to 4 minutes. Remove from heat stirring in cooked rice, almonds and raisins. Place in casserole and bake at 350° for 20 minutes. Before serving, top with bacon. Serves 8.

ADDITIONAL CONDIMENTS: chopped eggs, chutney, chopped onion, coconut, etc.

Serves eight and freezes great!

Team Spirit Casserole

- **½ pound cooked crabmeat**
- **1 (16-ounce) package cream cheese**
- **½ cup soft butter**
- **6 tablespoons basil**
- **6 tablespoons dried parsley**
- **1½ teaspoons garlic powder**
- **1 cup Parmesan cheese**
- **4 (6 ½-ounce) cans chopped clams, keep juice**
- **1 cup slivered almonds**
- **1 teaspoon pepper**
- **1 cup sour cream**
- **1 cup mushrooms**
- **1 pound cooked shrimp, peeled and deveined**
- **1 box spaghetti (family size)**

Cook spaghetti. Heat cream cheese, butter in double boiler until smooth. Add spices. Blend in Parmesan cheese. Stir in drained clams and 1 cup of clam juice. Heat in double boiler until warm. Add sour cream, mushrooms, crab and cooked shrimp. Serve sauce over spaghetti and sprinkle with slivered almonds. Serves 8 to 10.

Curried Tuna

- **1 cup tuna**
- **1 cup cooked rice**
- **3 hard boiled eggs, chopped**
- **1 can mushroom soup**
- **½ soup can of milk**
- **1 teaspoon curry powder**
- **1 onion, chopped**
- **2 teaspoons butter**
- **1 cup nuts, chopped and toasted**

Sauté onion in a little butter (do not brown). Add soup and milk and heat. Add curry powder and mix well. Place a layer of rice in a 9x9-inch baking dish. Add a layer of chopped egg, and then a layer of tuna. Place half of soup mixture over tuna. Repeat layers. Cover top of casserole with chopped, toasted nuts. Bake at 350° for 30 minutes. Serves 4.

Creekside Casserole

- **1 pound crabmeat (pick out shells)**
- **1 pound shrimp, cooked and shelled**
- **3 hard cooked eggs, chopped**
- **1 can water chestnuts, chopped**
- **3 cups Pepperidge Farm herb dressing (not cornbread)**
- **1 stick butter or margarine (less, if you like)**
- **Seafood seasoning to taste**
- **1 pint half and half (I use whole milk)**
- **1 cup mayonnaise**

Mix Pepperidge Farm dressing with melted butter. Reserve one cup. Mix remaining two cups with other ingredients. Put in greased casserole. Top with remaining cup of dressing. Bake in 350° oven until bubbly. Serves 6.

Delicious.

Savory Sausage Casserole

1 pound pork sausage
1 cup uncooked rice
2 (2-ounce) packages dehydrated chicken noodle soup
¼ cup onion, finely chopped
1 cup celery, sliced
2½ cups water
1 tablespoon soy sauce
1 cup blanched almonds or 1 can water chestnuts, drained (optional)

Brown sausage, pouring off any excess fat and then remove from heat. Mix together in a 2-quart casserole the sausage, rice, soup, onions and celery. Refrigerate. When ready to bake, mix the soy sauce with water and add this to the casserole. Cover and bake at 350° for 1 hour. Serves 6.

Bobbie's Crab & Shrimp Bake

1 cup green pepper, chopped
2 cups celery, chopped
½ onion, chopped
4 cups shrimp, cooked
2½ cups crab
1 teaspoon salt
Dash pepper
2 teaspoons Worcestershire sauce
½ teaspoon thyme
3 cups herb stuffing

Mix all ingredients with your hands and place gently (DO NOT PACK) in lightly greased 13x9-inch baking dish. Bake at 350° for 30 to 45 minutes uncovered. Serves 6 to 8.

This freezes well.

Three Cheese Tuna Casserole

- 1 (10-ounce) package egg noodles
- 1 onion, chopped
- 1 green pepper, chopped
- 2 tablespoons margarine
- 1 can cream of celery soup
- 1 can cream of mushroom soup
- 1 soup can of milk
- 1 (3-ounce) jar mushrooms, sliced
- ¼ teaspoon pepper
- 1 (8-ounce) container cottage cheese
- 1 (8-ounce) package Cheddar cheese
- 1 small can Parmesan cheese
- 3 (6-ounce) cans white tuna (Variation: 3 cups chicken)

Cook noodles according to package directions and rinse with cold water and drain.

In a saucepan:
Sauté onions and green peppers in 2 tablespoons of margarine. Add soups, milk and mushrooms (drained) and pepper. Open tuna, rinse and drain. Layer into a 13x9-inch greased casserole: half the noodles, half the sauce, 1½ cans of tuna, ½ the cottage cheese and ½ the Cheddar cheese. Repeat layers (noodles, sauce, tuna, cheeses) and top with Parmesan cheese. Cover and bake at 350° for 35 to 45 minutes. Remove cover for last ten minutes and continue to bake until soft brown crust appears. Serves 6 to 8.

Tuna Noodle Casserole

- 1 (8-ounce) box sea shell noodles, cooked
- 2 (7-ounce) cans tuna, drained
- 1 (8-ounce) package sour cream
- ½ cup milk
- 1½ teaspoons salt
- ¼ teaspoon pepper
- 1 cup bread crumbs
- ¼ cup Parmesan cheese
- 2 tablespoons melted butter
- 1 can cream of celery soup
- Paprika

Combine cooked noodles, tuna, sour cream, milk, salt and pepper and add can of cream of celery soup. Pour into casserole dish. Melt butter and add to cheese and drop over casserole. Sprinkle with bread crumbs and paprika on top. Bake at 350° for 35 to 40 minutes until bubbly. Serves 6.

ENTRÉES / MEAT

Entrées/Meat

Coach Lavelle's Favorite Meat Loaf

1 pound ground beef
1 pound ground pork
1 cup carrots, shredded
2 cups saltines, coarsely ground
1 cup sour cream
¼ cup onion, chopped
1 teaspoon salt
1 teaspoon pepper

Combine all ingredients and shape into loaf. Place in loaf pan and bake at 350° for 1½ hours. Let cool for 10 minutes and remove from pan. Serve with mushroom sauce.

Mushroom Sauce:
1 beef bouillon cube
½ cup drippings from meat loaf
½ cup hot water
½ cup sour cream
1 tablespoon flour
1 (3-ounce) can broiled mushrooms, undrained

Dissolve bouillon cube in drippings from meat loaf and water. Combine with sour cream, flour and mushrooms. Heat until boiling. Serves 4 to 6.

The sauce is great with mashed potatoes.

Basic Beef Mixture

This **basic beef mixture** will be the secret ingredient that you will need to make a complete dish out of the next three beef recipes. This is wonderful for the working mother or for someone who likes to entertain at the last moment. Keep rice and noodles handy in the pantry. Definitely a winter favorite!

2 pounds round steak, cut into ¾-inch cubes (about 4 cups) (this meat is easier to cut if partially frozen)
2 tablespoons oil
½ cup onion, chopped
¾ cup water
4 beef bouillon cubes

In a large skillet brown meat in hot oil. Add onion and sauté. Add water, bouillon. Cover tightly and simmer 45 to 60 minutes until tender. Put into 2 pint-size zip lock freezer bags and freeze. No seasonings added to this mixture. Makes 4 cups.

Beef Stew

2 cups basic beef mixture
1½ cups water
4 cups frozen stew vegetables
Salt and pepper
1½ cups water
1 bay leaf

Combine all ingredients and bring to a boil. Cover and simmer 30 minutes. Thicken if desired with 2 tablespoons flour and ¼ cup water. Serves 4.

VARIATION: Canned carrots and potatoes, frozen peas and fresh celery and onion may be used. Cook same amount of time.

Beef-Mushroom Burgundy

- 2 cups Basic Beef Mixture
- 1 medium onion, sliced
- 1 or 2 (4-ounce) cans mushrooms, drained
- 1 cup water
- ½ red wine or water
- ½ teaspoon thyme
- 2 tablespoons flour, combined with ¼ cup water
- Salt and pepper to taste

Combine first six ingredients, cover and simmer for 30 minutes. Add flour mixture and stir until thickened. Season and serve over buttered noodles or rice. Serves 4.

Pepper Steak

- 1 tablespoon oil
- 1 large green pepper, cut into thin strips
- 1 large onion, sliced
- 2 cups Basic Beef Mixture
- ¼ cup soy sauce
- 2 tablespoons cornstarch
- 1 teaspoon sugar
- 1 large tomato, cut into thin wedges (optional)

In large skillet, stir fry pepper and onion in hot oil for 2 minutes. Add beef and water. Simmer uncovered 15 minutes if beef is frozen or 5 minutes if thawed. Blend soy sauce, cornstarch and sugar together before adding to beef mixture. Cook and stir until clear and thickened. Add tomatoes. Serve with rice. Serves 4.

For a Chinese flare add 1 teaspoon ginger and 2 tablespoons sherry.

Fajitas

Marinade:

- **½ cup Italian salad dressing**
- **½ cup salsa**
- **2 tablespoons soy sauce**
- **1 tablespoon oil**
- **1 small onion , cut into rings**
- **1 medium bell pepper, cut into strips**

- **1½ pounds sliced beef, pork, chicken or 1 pound peeled raw shrimp**
- **8 flour tortillas,**
- **Sour cream**
- **Guacamole (optional)**

Cut steak or pork into thin strips. Marinate at least 3 hours. Drain meat or shrimp on paper towels before cooking. Sauté until meat is cooked. Drain juices from pan. Heat the flour tortillas until warm. To eat, place the meat or shrimp mixture in center of tortilla and garnish with sour cream or guacamole if desired. Serves 4 to 6.

Delicious!

Monsignor Manning's Special (Salisbury Steak)

- **1½ pounds ground chuck**
- **1 can onion soup**
- **½ cup dry bread crumbs**
- **1 egg, beaten**
- **¼ teaspoon salt**
- **½ teaspoon MSG**

Mix meat and ½ can onion soup. Mix in bread crumbs, egg, salt, pepper and M.S.G. and shape into oval patties. Brown on all sides, remove from pan and set aside.

Sauce:

- **1 tablespoon flour**
- **¼ cup catsup**
- **½ cup water**
- **1 teaspoon Worcestershire**
- **½ teaspoon dry mustard**

Combine all ingredients together and rest of onion soup and simmer 10 minutes. Return patties to pan until ready to serve. Serves 4 to 6.

Marinated Flank Steaks

- 2 (1-1½ pound) flank steaks
- ½ cup vegetable oil
- ¼ cup teriyaki sauce or soy sauce
- 1 tablespoon onion, minced
- 3 tablespoons honey
- ½ teaspoon garlic powder
- ½ teaspoon ground ginger

Using a fork, prick both sides of meat and put in large shallow dish. Combine all other ingredients and pour over meat. Cover and marinate 24 hours in refrigerator. Turn every now and then. Grill steaks over hot coals 4 to 5 minutes on each side. Slice across grain into thin slices. Serves 4 to 6.

NOTE: This meat is very tender and tasty when fixed this way. Serve with baked potatoes, cooked on grill and hearty tossed salad.

Super summertime meal.

Regency Beef Tenderloin with Royal Butter

- 1 whole beef tenderloin, trimmed
- 1 cup soy sauce
- 2 tablespoons Dijon mustard
- 3 tablespoons brown sugar
- ⅔ cup vegetable oil
- 1 tablespoon vinegar
- 1 teaspoon garlic powder
- 1 green onion, chopped

Combine all ingredients and mix well. Spread marinade on meat. Cover with plastic wrap. Let stand overnight in refrigerator. Preheat oven to 400°. Place in roasting pan lined with foil. Insert meat thermometer and bake 40 to 55 minutes or until done. (rare = 140 degrees and medium = 160 degrees). Baste with marinade three times during the first 15 minutes of baking time. Slice thick for Sunday dinner, or slice thinner for an appetizer and serve with party rolls and Royal Butter. Serve ½ pound per person.

Royal Butter:

- ½ cup butter, softened
- 1 (8-ounce) package cream cheese, softened
- ¼ cup mayonnaise
- ¼ cup prepared horseradish, drained

Combine all ingredients and whip until fluffy. Serve at room temperature. Makes 2 cups.

Carré D' Agneau À La Provence (Rack of Lamb Provence-style) with Mint Sauce

1 rack of lamb (7 to 8 ribs)
1 teaspoon chopped garlic
1 tablespoons chopped parsley
1 teaspoon dried rosemary
3 tablespoons olive oil
1 teaspoon lemon juice
1 teaspoon salt
1 teaspoon black pepper
1 cup fresh breadcrumbs
2 tablespoons Dijon mustard

Select a well-trimmed rack, leaving just a thin layer of surface fat, with chine bone removed and top of rib bones frenched (fat removed). Roast, fat side down, on the bottom rack of a 425° oven for 15 minutes. Remove from the oven.

While the lamb is cooking, put together in a mortar and pestle (or food processor) the garlic, parsley, rosemary, olive oil, lemon juice, salt, and pepper. Grind into a paste, and mix with the breadcrumbs.

Spread the mustard on the fat side of the lamb and pack the breadcrumb mixture evenly on top. Roast for 15 minutes, or until a meat thermometer reaches 140° and the breadcrumbs are browned.

Remove the meat to a serving platter and let it rest in the oven, with the heat turned off, for 15 minutes before carving. Slice off each chop between the bones. (Serve immediately with Fresh Mint Sauce). Serves 2 to 3.

Domestic lamb is tastier and more tender than the New Zealand variety, but at a premium price. For this dish, the extra expense is justified.

Fresh Mint Sauce

½ cup white vinegar
¾ cup sugar
¼ cup puréed shallots (use food processor)
2 teaspoons cornstarch diluted in 1 tablespoon water
½ cup minced fresh mint leaves (measured loosely packed)

Robert's of Charleston, Inc.

Slowly heat and mix the vinegar and sugar until dissolved, about 3 minutes. Add the shallots and bring to a boil. Add the cornstarch mixture and simmer, uncovered, for 1 minute.

Chop the mint in a food processor with 2 tablespoons water until fine. Add to the hot mixture. Do not cook the mint, or it will lose its bright green color. Set aside to cool.

This will keep indefinitely covered in the refrigerator. Makes 1 cup.

No cook should be without a superb mint sauce to add zest to roast lamb or lamb chops. It may be somewhat more unexpected to team it with tiny boiled new potatoes or peas, but it is a sensation here too.

St. Patrick's Day Delight

4 to 5 pound corned beef brisket
Cold water to cover
½ bay leaf
5 whole peppercorns
¼ teaspoon basil
¼ teaspoon thyme
¼ teaspoon parsley
8 whole carrots, scraped and cut in half
10 small onions, peeled
8 medium potatoes, peeled
1 green cabbage, cored and cut in wedges

Place beef in a deep kettle and cover with cold water adding the spices but **no salt**. Bring water to a boil. Skim off fat. Cover and simmer 3 to 4 hours. Add all the vegetables **but the cabbage** and continue to cook for 20 minutes. Add the cabbage and cook until all vegetables are tender (about 30 minutes). Place beef on platter, surround with vegetables. Serves 4 to 6.

Andouille Barbeque Over Rice Pilaf

Rice Pilaf:

- **2 cups raw rice**
- **1 pound bacon, diced**
- **½ large green bell pepper, diced**
- **½ large red bell pepper, diced**
- **½ large yellow onion, diced**
- **1 cup chicken broth**

Cook rice as per instructions. Sauté diced bacon till crisp, drain and reserve drippings. Add bell peppers and onion. Sauté until tender. Do not brown. Add chicken broth, reduce over medium heat by ½. Stir into cooked white rice. Add two tablespoons bacon drippings and mix well.

Andouille Barbeque

(NOTE: Ingredients are proper amounts for one person)

- **2 tablespoons butter or margarine**
- **3 ounces white or dark boneless and skinless chicken, cut in strips**
- **4 ounces Andouille sausage cut in ¼-inch wheels. (use only authentic Cajun Andouille for best results)**
- **3 ounces peeled shrimp**
- **¼ cup barbecue sauce (your favorite)**

In skillet over medium high heat, melt butter. When sizzling hot, add chicken and Andouille and sauté until sausage is brown and crusted. Add shrimp and cook until opaque. Pour in barbeque sauce and heat until sauce is bubbling.

NOTE: Since Andouille sausage is traditionally spicy, be careful not to add other spices.

To serve: Spoon over rice pilaf.

Sloppy Joes

Serves 5:
- 2½ cups ground beef
- ¾ cup catsup
- 1 large onion, chopped
- 2 tablespoons sugar
- 2 tablespoons prepared mustard
- 1 teaspoon salt
- 2 teaspoons vinegar
- ¼ teaspoon pepper

Serves 50:
- 12 pounds ground beef
- 2 large bottles catsup
- 4 large onions, chopped
- 1 cup sugar
- 1 cup prepared mustard
- 2 tablespoons salt
- ½ cup vinegar
- 1 tablespoon pepper

Brown onions and meat and drain. Add all other ingredients and simmer for 2 hours. Spoon on toasted sesame seed hamburger buns.

Chinese Oven Fried Pork Chops

- 1 egg
- 3 tablespoons soy sauce
- 1 tablespoon water
- ⅛ teaspoon ground ginger
- ½ teaspoon garlic powder
- Breadcrumbs
- 4 to 6 lean pork chops
- Pam cooking spray

Spray cookie sheet with Pam. Beat together first five ingredients. Dip and coat both sides of chops in egg mixture. Press each chop coating both sides in breadcrumbs. Place onto cookie sheet. Bake at 350° for 30 minutes, turn and bake 20 minutes longer. Serves 4 to 6.

Sweet & Sour Pork Chops

- 4 pork chops
- ¼ cup soy sauce
- ¼ cup ketchup
- ½ cup apple jelly

Trim fat from pork chops and place in casserole dish. Mix sauce, ketchup and jelly. Pour over chops. Bake at 325° for 45 minutes or until meat is tender. Serves 2 to 4.

So easy and so good.

Gingered Ham Slice

- 1 fully cooked center cut ham 1-inch thick
- ½ cup ginger ale
- ¼ cup brown sugar
- 1½ teaspoons wine vinegar
- ¼ teaspoon ground ginger
- ½ cup orange juice
- 1 tablespoon salad oil
- 1 teaspoon dry mustard
- ⅛ teaspoon ground cloves

Slash fat edge of ham. Combine remaining ingredients; pour over ham in shallow dish. Refrigerate overnight or let stand at room temperature 2 hours, spooning marinade over ham several times. Grill ham slice over low coals about 15 minutes on each side, brushing frequently with marinade over ham. Serves 4 to 5.

Wonderful change for outdoor cooking. Real Rich!

Low Country Veal

- 1 pound veal scallops
- 4 tablespoons butter
- 12 peeled shrimp
- 12 scallops
- Sherry wine
- 1 cup heavy cream
- Salt and pepper

Cut veal into serving sized pieces, pound veal until thin, coat veal pieces with flour. Sauté lightly in butter on both sides. Remove from pan, add shrimp and scallops to the same pan and sauté until shrimp turns pink. Return veal pieces to pan with seafood and ¼ cup sherry. Let wine reduce. Add heavy cream. Let cook until thickened over heat. Add pinch of salt and pepper. Serves 4.

Nana's Apricot Orange Pork Chops

6 to 8 center cut pork chops
3 tablespoons flour
Salt and pepper to taste
1 cup orange juice
½ cup brown sugar
1 small can apricots
Vegetable oil

Place flour and salt and pepper in brown paper bag. Put pork chops (one at a time) in bag and shake. Set on piece of wax paper until all chops are floured. In a large skillet or electric frying pan, put enough vegetable oil just to cover bottom lightly. When oil is hot, add chops one at a time, and brown on each side. Drain. Add orange juice and brown sugar to pork chops and turn heat to low (with lid slightly tilted to let out steam) and cook 45 minutes to 1 hour on simmer. After 30 minutes, add apricots on top of pork chops. Serve on platter with apricot on top of each chop. Serves 6 to 8.

Pork Roast with Sauce

1 (4-5 pound) pork loin
2 tablespoons dry mustard
2 teaspoons thyme
1 teaspoon salt
½ teaspoon pepper
1 cup sherry
Dash garlic powder
¾ tablespoon soy sauce
2 cloves garlic
2 teaspoons ground ginger

Place meat in shallow dish and rub well with mixture of dry mustard and thyme. Punch holes in meat about 4 inches apart and fill with salt, pepper and garlic powder. Combine sherry, soy sauce, garlic cloves and ginger. Pour over meat and let stand 3 or 4 hours at room temperature. Place meat on rack in shallow roasting pan. Bake uncovered for 2½ to 3 hours. Serve with currant sauce.

Currant Sauce:

1 jar currant jelly
1 tablespoon soy sauce
2 tablespoons sherry

Melt jelly and add other ingredients. Pour over warm pork roast. Serves 4 to 6.

Beef Teriyaki

- **1½ pounds boneless sirloin steak**
- **¼ cup teriyaki sauce**
- **¼ cup water**
- **2 tablespoons brown sugar**
- **2 tablespoons Worcestershire sauce**
- **½ teaspoon fresh garlic, minced**
- **1 tablespoon vegetable oil**
- **1½ cups carrots, sliced**
- **1½ cups celery, sliced**
- **1 cup onions, chopped**
- **1 tablespoon vegetable oil**
- **1 tablespoon cornstarch**
- **1 cup rice, cooked**

Partially freeze steak (it makes it easy to slice thinly). Slice steak across grain. Combine next five ingredients in large bowl, add meat and marinade in refrigerator 4 to 6 hours. Pour 1 tablespoon oil in top part of wok, coating sides. Heat at medium heat for 2 minutes, then add vegetables and stir-fry about 4 minutes. Remove from wok. Pour in another 1 tablespoon oil into wok. Drain meat from marinade and place in wok; stir-fry until brown. Combine cornstarch and remaining marinade and stir well. Stir into beef, and cook, stirring constantly. Combine vegetables and rice and place on serving plate and top with meat. Serves 2 to 4.

Never reuse marinades.

ENTRÉES / POULTRY

Entrées/Poultry

Apricot Chicken

6 boned chicken breasts, halved
½ cup orange juice concentrate
¼ cup apple juice
½ cup brown sugar
8 ounces orange or grapefruit marmalade
3 cups dried apricots
3 cups currants

Wash chicken and place in large pan. In mixing bowl, combine orange juice concentrate, apple juice, brown sugar and marmalade. Mix well and pour over chicken. Bake 30 minutes at 350°, then add apricots and currants and bake for an additional 30 minutes. Serve hot over rice, or drain and serve dry. When serving, place chicken in center of dish and place apricots around the chicken, and add parsley. Serves 4 to 6.

Elegant for entertaining!

Chicken Cacciatora

3 pounds chicken, cut up
3 tablespoons shortening
2 medium onions, sliced thinly
2 cloves garlic, minced
1 (1-pound) can tomatoes
1 (8-ounce) can tomato sauce
⅓ cup green pepper, minced
1 teaspoon salt
¼ teaspoon black pepper
¼ teaspoon cayenne pepper
1 teaspoon ground oregano
½ teaspoon crushed basil
½ teaspoon celery salt
1 bay leaf
¼ cup Chianti wine

Brown chicken pieces. Layer onion in slow cooker. Put chicken on top of onion and add remaining ingredients. Cover and cook on low heat 6 to 8 hours (or 3 to 4 hours on high). Discard bay leaf. Serve chicken pieces with sauce over buttered spaghetti. Serves 6 to 8.

Great for buffet supper!

Carolina Bar-B-Que Chicken

- **1 chicken, cut up**
- **1 cup apple cider vinegar**
- **4 tablespoons margarine**
- **2½ tablespoons flour**
- **1 to 2 teaspoons red pepper flakes, crushed**

Cook chicken covered about 1 hour at 350°. In saucepan, melt margarine and stir in flour until mixed. Remove chicken from oven and pour all juices from chicken into margarine mixture. Stir over medium heat until thickened. Add vinegar and red pepper. Pour over chicken, return to oven until browned about 10 to 15 minutes. Serves 4.

Delicious! An old family recipe.

Chicken Marengo María

- **8 chicken breasts or thighs (boneless very good)**
- **1 tablespoon olive oil**
- **1 large onion, sliced**
- **1 large bell pepper, sliced**
- **1 (4-ounce) can sliced mushrooms**
- **½ cup white raisins**
- **1 (7½-ounce) can tomatoes, cut-up**
- **¼ cup dry red wine**
- **1 clove garlic, minced**
- **3 beef bouillon cubes**
- **1 tablespoon sugar (or 2 packages Sweet 'n' Low)**
- **1 tablespoon cornstarch combined with ⅓ cup water**

Remove skin from chicken. Season lightly with salt and pepper and brown in hot oil (more oil may be needed). Place chicken in a flat baking dish. Sauté onions, pepper, and garlic in oil used for chicken. Add tomatoes, mushrooms, wine, raisins and bouillon cubes. Cook for 5 minutes. Add cornstarch, cook and stir until bubbly for 3 to 4 minutes. Pour sauce over chicken and cover with foil. Bake 1 hour at 375°. Makes an excellent sauce for rice or pasta if tomatoes are chopped in small pieces. Serves 8.

Company dinner with a new flair.

Chicken Divan À La Crites

- **3 cups cooked chicken breasts**
- **1 large bunch fresh broccoli or 2 (10-ounce) packages**
- **2 tablespoons butter**
- **Salt and pepper**
- **1 can mushroom soup**
- **½ cup cream**
- **½ cup white wine**
- **1 cup grated cheese**
- **1 teaspoon lemon juice**
- **½ cup mayonnaise**
- **Parmesan cheese**

Butter large casserole. Layer chicken and broccoli. Dot with butter and sprinkle with salt and pepper. In saucepan, heat soup and cream, add wine, cheese and lemon juice. Stir until cheese is melted. Add mayonnaise and pour over chicken and broccoli. Sprinkle with Parmesan. Bake at 350° for about 25 minutes or until bubbly. May be prepared ahead of time. Serves 6.

Chicken Picata

- **1 (6-ounce) chicken breast**
- **Flour (for dredging)**
- **Olive oil**
- **1 ounce tomatoes, diced**
- **2 medium mushrooms, sliced**
- **½ ounce scallions, chopped**
- **½ ounce capers**
- **6 ounces chicken stock**
- **4 ounces white wine**
- **1 ounce butter and flour (mixed cold)**
- **4 ounces cooked linguini**

Dredge chicken in flour. Add olive oil to sauté pan. Add chicken and sauté until golden brown on both sides. Add white wine and reduce by half. Add vegetables and chicken stock, simmer until hot. Add butter and flour mixture. Simmer for 3 to 5 minutes or until chicken is thoroughly cooked and sauce is thickened. Place chicken breast on hot linguini and top with remaining sauce. (This dish is also popular with veal replacing the chicken.) Serve with a seasonal vegetable medley on a side plate. **Serves 1**.

Chicken Parmesan

- **4 chicken breasts, boned**
- **½ cup Italian breadcrumbs**
- **¼ cup Parmesan cheese**
- **Salt and pepper to taste**
- **1 egg beaten with 1 tablespoon water**
- **2 tablespoons vegetable oil**
- **4 ounces shredded mozzarella cheese**
- **1 (8-ounce) can tomato sauce**
- **1 tablespoon crushed oregano or Italian seasoning**

Mix breadcrumbs, Parmesan cheese, salt and pepper. Dip chicken in beaten egg and dredge in crumb mixture. Heat oil in skillet. Sauté chicken 2 minutes on each side. Place chicken in a single layer in casserole dish. Sprinkle with mozzarella cheese. Pour tomato sauce over chicken and sprinkle with oregano. Bake at 350° for 35 minutes.

VARIATION: This is easily adapted to Veal Parmesan by using veal cutlets in place of the chicken breasts.

Honey French Chicken

- **6 chicken breast pieces, skinned and boned**
- **¼ cup corn oil**
- **¼ cup honey**
- **¼ cup cider vinegar**
- **¼ cup chili sauce**
- **½ (1⅜-ounce) envelope dry onion soup mix**
- **¼ teaspoon salt**
- **2 teaspoons Worcestershire sauce**

In a jar, place oil, honey, vinegar, chili sauce, soup mix, Worcestershire sauce, salt and pepper. Shake well. Place chicken in single layer in large shallow pan. Pour sauce over chicken. Bake uncovered at 350° about 40 minutes or until fork tender. Serves 4.

I serve this with wild rice mix - cooked according to directions, of course.

Couturier's Party Chicken

8 boneless chicken breasts
8 bacon slices
4 ounces chipped beef
1 can mushroom soup
1 cup sour cream
Paprika

Wrap each chicken breast in bacon. Cover the bottom of a greased 8x12-inch baking dish with chipped beef. Arrange chicken on top. Blend soup and sour cream and pour over chicken. Sprinkle with paprika. Bake uncovered at 275° for 3 hours. Serves 6 to 8.

This chicken deserves your fine china and cloth napkins.

Gingered Chicken Stir-Fry

1 to 2 pounds boneless chicken
1 (11-ounce) can mandarin oranges
1 teaspoon fresh ginger or 1½ teaspoons ground ginger
1 tablespoon cooking oil or peanut oil
¼ pound snow peas or 1 (16-ounce) package frozen snow peas
¼ cup Oriental stir-fry sauce

Drain oranges, reserve ½ cup liquid. Cook ginger in hot oil. Add chicken to ginger and stir-fry 3 minutes. Add snow peas, reserved syrup and stir fry sauce. Heat to boiling and stir constantly. Reduce heat, cover and cook 2 minutes. Top with orange sections. Serve over rice. Serves 4.

No Peek Chicken

1 box Uncle Ben's wild rice with herbs
1 can cream of mushroom soup
1 can cream of celery soup
1 can cold water
1 teaspoon parsley
6 to 8 pieces of chicken, skinned
1 package Lipton onion soup mix

Lightly grease casserole. Mix first five ingredients, spread in casserole and place chicken on top. Sprinkle chicken with onion soup mix. Seal with foil and bake at 350° for 2½ hours. Serves 6 to 8.

"Don't Peek".

Individual Chicken Pies

Crust:

2 cups sifted all-purpose flour
1 teaspoon salt
⅔ cup shortening
5 to 7 tablespoons cold water

Combine salt to sifted flour. Add shortening, ⅓ cup at a time. Cut shortening into flour until mixture starts to form small beads. Add water. Divide into 2 equal balls and roll out. Cut to fit 6 small oven-proof dishes. Bake on ungreased cooked sheet at 400° for 10 to 12 minutes.

Filling:

½ cup onion, chopped
6 tablespoons butter or margarine
½ cup all-purpose flour
1 teaspoon salt
3 cups chicken broth
3 cups cooked chicken, cubed
1 (10-ounce) package frozen mixed vegetables, cooked and drained

Cook onion in butter until tender. Blend in flour and salt. Add broth all at one time. Cook and stir until thick and bubbly. Add all remaining ingredients. Heat until bubbly. Pour into 6 individual casseroles. This may also be baked in a 13x9-inch pan. Place pastry on top. Serves 6 to 8.

This is great for a covered dish supper.

Honolulu Chicken

1 chicken, cut up
¼ cup flour
¼ teaspoon salt
Dash pepper
Cooking oil
1 (10-ounce) jar peach preserves
½ cup barbecue sauce
½ cup chopped onions
2 tablespoons soy sauce
1 (6-ounce) can water chestnuts, sliced and drained
1 green pepper, cut in strips

Coat chicken with seasoned flour. Brown in oil. Drain off oil. Combine preserves, barbecue sauce, onions and soy sauce. Pour over chicken. Cover and simmer 45 minutes. Add water chestnuts and green pepper. Simmer 10 to 15 more minutes. Serve over rice. Serves 4.

La Brasca's Chicken Chop Suey

¼ pound boned chicken, chopped
2 cups celery, chopped
2 cups onion, chopped
½ teaspoon salt
Pinch black pepper
½ teaspoon Accent
½ teaspoon soy sauce
¼ teaspoon thick black molasses
½ teaspoon cornstarch
1 tablespoon Wesson oil

Mix chopped celery and onions together, boil, drain off water and set aside. Put 1 tablespoon Wesson oil in saucepan. When oil is hot put chicken, celery and onions and other ingredients into pot, adding 1 cup water. Cover and cook until done. After food is cooked, dissolve ½ teaspoon cornstarch in a little water and pour over all ingredients. Mix well and steam for five minutes and then serve. Serves 1.

Curried Orange Chicken

1 chicken (quartered or pieces)
1 cup orange marmalade
1 tablespoon curry powder
1 teaspoon salt
½ cup warm water

Grease a 9x13x2-inch baking pan. Combine marmalade, curry powder, salt and warm water. Place chicken cut side down in pan. Spoon marmalade sauce over the chicken and bake **uncovered** at 350° for 45 minutes. Spoon sauce over chicken several times while cooking. If sauce begins to stick, add ¼ cup water to pan. To serve - remove chicken and spoon off any fat from the sauce. Serves 4.

This can be served with buttered noodles. I like it with wild rice. Very good - very easy.

Microwave Chicken Parmesan

- 2 (8-ounce) cans tomato sauce
- 1 teaspoon Italian seasoning
- ¼ teaspoon garlic powder
- 1 cup corn flake crumbs
- ¼ cup grated Parmesan cheese
- 1 teaspoon dried parsley flakes
- 1½ to 2 pounds of split boneless, skinless chicken breasts
- 1 egg beaten or 1 egg substitute
- ½ cup shredded mozzarella cheese
- Grated Parmesan cheese

Mix tomato sauce, Italian seasoning and garlic powder in small casserole, cover and microwave at high for 2 minutes. Stir. Reduce power to medium and cook 5 minutes. Set sauce aside. Mix corn flake crumbs, ¼ cup Parmesan cheese and parsley flakes. Dip chicken breasts in beaten egg, then in crumb mixture. Place in rectangular 9x12-inch baking dish or a 10x10-inch square dish. Cover with wax paper. Microwave med-high until chicken is tender, 9 to 14 minutes, rearranging after half the cooking time. Do not turn over. Pour sauce over chicken. Sprinkle mozzarella over chicken breasts. Sprinkle with Parmesan. Microwave at med.-high until mozzarella melts and sauce is hot, 2 to 5¼ minutes.

NOTE: Good served with spaghetti noodles as a side dish. You can double the amount of sauce to serve over pasta or use a prepared sauce such as Ragu. Serves 4 to 6.

Marinated Chicken Breast on Grill

- 1½ cups oil
- ¾ cup soy sauce
- ¼ cup lemon juice (or pineapple juice)
- ¼ cup white wine
- 1 teaspoon garlic salt
- 1 teaspoon ginger
- 1 teaspoon seasoned salt
- 8 to 12 boneless chicken breasts

Combine all ingredients. Place 8 to 12 boneless chicken breasts and marinade in a 13x9-inch pan and refrigerate overnight. Pat chicken with paper towels. Cook on grill about 10 to 12 minutes until tender. Serves 6 to 8.

New Breed Greek Chicken (Grilled)

4 leg quarters or breast quarters
Garlic powder
Salt
Pepper
Oregano
½ cup butter or margarine
⅓ cup lemon juice

Clean chicken, pat dry. Lightly sprinkle both sides with garlic powder, salt, pepper and oregano. Cover bottom of a grill with charcoal. When the coals are "ash" white, put chicken on rack bone side down for 15 to 18 minutes. Turn chicken over and cook 10 to 12 minutes. Keep a cup of water handy to keep coals from flaming up. In a small pot, melt butter, add lemon juice, 1 tablespoon garlic powder, pepper and oregano. When chicken is done, remove from grill and baste with butter-lemon mixture and serve. Serves 4.

The man who prepares this chicken gets all bragging rights.

Poppy Seed Chicken

1 can cream of chicken soup
8 ounces sour cream
6 to 8 chicken breasts, cooked
½ cup butter, melted
1 stack Ritz crackers, crushed
2 tablespoons poppy seed

Cook chicken and cut into cubes. Mix soup, sour cream and chicken. Pour in a 13x9-inch Pyrex dish. Toss butter, crackers and poppy seed in small fry pan and sprinkle over chicken mixture. Bake at 350° for 30 minutes. Serves 6.

To serve 8 to 10 and be more economical, use 8 to 10 chicken breasts, double the soup and sour cream and add ½ cup chicken broth and 1 package shell pasta which has been cooked according to directions. The topping of butter, crackers and poppy seed remain the same. Bake at 350° for about 45 minutes.

A wonderful dish to take to a friend-in-need.

St. Clair's Chicken Pilaf

- **4 to 6 chicken breasts**
- **1½ cups long-grain rice**
- **1 teaspoon seasoned salt**
- **2 tablespoons margarine**
- **1 large onion, diced**
- **1 cup pine nuts**
- **¾ teaspoon salt**
- **½ teaspoon pepper**
- **¾ teaspoon cinnamon**
- **3¾ cups chicken broth**

Place chicken breasts in a dutch oven. Cover chicken with cold water and add seasoned salt. Bring to boil, cover, and cook on medium-low heat about 30 minutes until chicken is tender. Remove chicken from pot, reserving the broth. Debone the chicken and cut into medium to large size pieces. Wash out dutch oven and continue to use. Heat 2 tablespoons of margarine and sauté onion. When onion is clear add pine nuts and raw rice. Sauté until pine nuts begin to get golden and rice clears. Add chicken, broth, salt, pepper and cinnamon. Bring to a boil, reduce heat to low and cook 30 to 40 minutes until broth is absorbed. Stir occasionally. Serve with sautéed vegetables. Serves 6.

Swiss Chicken

- **10 chicken half-breasts, boned and skinned**
- **10 slices Swiss cheese**
- **1 (10¾-ounce) can cream of chicken or cream of mushroom soup**
- **¼ cup dry white wine**
- **½ cup butter or margarine, melted**
- **3 cups prepared herb stuffing mix**

Place chicken breasts in a greased 9½x15-inch pan. Top each breast with a slice of cheese. Dilute soup with 10¾-ounces water and wine. Mix well and pour over chicken. Toss butter with stuffing mix and sprinkle over chicken. Bake for 2 hours at 300°. If baking at a later time, put stuffing mix on just before baking. Serves 10.

Great for working wives - easy.

Glazed Cornish Hens

4 Cornish hens, split in half
½ cup butter, melted
½ cup orange juice
¾ cup apricot nectar
1 cup brown sugar
Lawry's salt

Place Cornish hens skin side up in shallow roasting pan. Sprinkle with Lawry's salt. Roast in oven 350° for about 20 minutes. Combine butter, orange juice, nectar and brown sugar over low heat. Brush glaze over Cornish hens. Bake an additional 25 to 30 minutes. Basting with glaze frequently. Serve with wild rice sprinkled with cashews. Serves 8.

Elegant dining with friends or smaller number hens for intimate dinner for two!

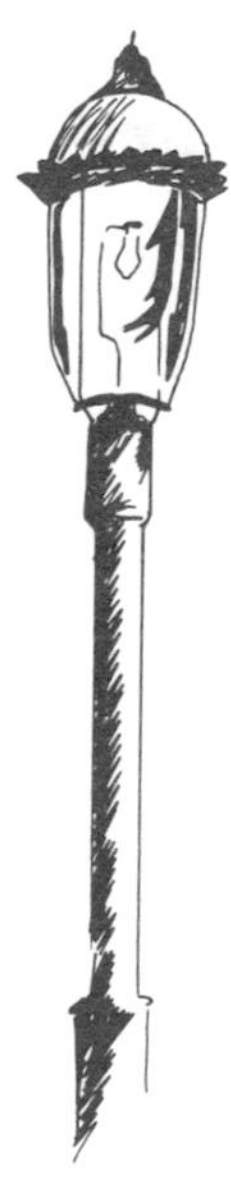

Marinated Turkey Breast

2 small cans pineapple juice
⅔ cup soy sauce
4 tablespoons cooking oil
2 teaspoons ground ginger
1 teaspoon dry mustard
½ teaspoon garlic powder

Mix all above listed ingredients in large container. (I use Tupperware cake cover). Remove skin from turkey breast which has been thawed or is fresh. Marinate turkey 12 to 24 hours in refrigerator. Wrap turkey tightly in foil. Preheat oven to 500°. Bake turkey for 1 hour. After 1 hour, turn off oven. Do not open door. Let turkey remain in oven 2 to 3 hours.

Turkey will easily pull or fall off bone. Wonderful for sandwiches for parties of tailgating.

The Perfect Turkey

1 turkey
Vegetable oil
Salt and pepper
Poultry seasoning
1 "V" roasting rack

Remove all giblets from the turkey. Wash well with cold water. Pat dry. Rub with salt and vegetable oil inside and out. Sprinkle with pepper and poultry seasoning. Place on "V" rack **breast side down** in shallow roasting pan uncovered. Bake at 325° as follows:

12-14 pounds 14-16 minutes per pound
16-20 pounds 13-14 minutes per pound

If you have a meat thermometer, the internal temperature should be 180°.

This will be the juiciest white meat you have ever eaten.

Entrées / Seafood & Game

Entrées/Seafood & Game

Seafood À La Carter

- ¾ cup butter
- 1 cup celery, chopped
- 1 cup onion, finely chopped
- 1 pound fresh mushrooms, sliced
- ½ teaspoon dry mustard
- ½ teaspoon white pepper (or black)
- Dash red pepper
- 1 to 2 teaspoons regular or crazy salt
- ½ cup Argo corn starch
- 1 quart half and half cream
- 8 ounces sour cream
- 1 cup whole milk
- 2 cans mushroom soup
- 4 to 5 pounds mediums shrimp, cooked and deveined
- 2 cups pimento, chopped
- 1 tablespoon Worcestershire sauce
- Sherry to taste
- Small bay leaf
- Dash of rosemary

In heavy large saucepan, melt butter. Add celery, onion and mushrooms. Cook until soft. Add dry mustard, salt, pepper and cornstarch, stirring constantly until thickened. Remove from heat. Gradually add cream, sour cream, milk and soup. Stir until well blended. Return to heat. Stirring constantly, boil for 3 minutes. Add shrimp, pimentos, Worcestershire, sherry, bay leaf, and rosemary. Remove from heat and serve on toast or in patty shells. Serves 12.

Deviled Crab

- 1 pound fresh crab
- 1 onion
- 1 bell pepper
- 2 celery sticks
- 1 cup crushed saltine crackers
- 1 egg, beaten
- ½ cup butter
- Mayonnaise
- Evaporated milk
- Salt and pepper
- Worcestershire sauce
- Hot sauce
- French dressing
- Prepared mustard

Sauté onion, bell pepper and celery in butter. Add crackers, crab and egg. Add mayonnaise until gummy consistency. Add milk for desired moistness. Salt, pepper, Worcestershire, hot sauce, French dressing and mustard to taste. Bake at 400° for approximately 30 minutes. Makes 10 crabs.

The more crab used the better!

Seafood Botticelli (Three Graces)

- 1 cup butter
- 2 cups all-purpose flour
- 1 large red onion, chopped
- 3 celery stalks, chopped
- 1 bunch scallions and tops, chopped
- 2 cloves garlic, chopped
- 1 tablespoon sweet basil
- ½ tablespoon tarragon
- 1 tablespoon thyme
- 1 teaspoon Tabasco
- 1 pint sour cream
- ½ pint heavy cream
- 2 cups seafood stock
- ½ cup white wine
- ½ pound mushrooms, sliced
- 2 teaspoons salt
- 1 pound peeled shrimp
- 1 pound crawfish or scallops
- 1 pint stewing oysters

In large pot, melt butter. Add flour, stirring until the mixture is a light brown color. Turn down heat and add onions, celery, scallions and garlic. Add seasonings. Simmer for 10 minutes. Add sour cream and heavy cream, stock and wine. Simmer 10 to 15 minutes. Drain oysters (or scallops) but do not rinse. Add the oysters, crawfish (or scallops), shrimp and mushrooms and salt. Simmer for 10 minutes. (Before you add the seafood, the mixture may be thick. Usually the water in the seafood will provide the correct consistency.)

May serve over pasta, or on rice. Good French bread and a nice dry white wine are excellent accompaniments as is a salad with a vinaigrette dressing. Serves 4 to 6.

Big Daddy's Trout Almondine

- 4 to 6 trout fillets, skinned
- 1 cup milk
- 1 egg
- 1 teaspoon almond extract
- 2 tubes saltine crackers, crumbled fine
- ½ cup slivered almonds

Soak fillets in milk, egg and almond extract for 1 to 2 hours. Drain fillets but DO NOT wipe away any excess. Put fillets in cracker crumbs and mash down hard so crackers stick well to fish. Fry in hot grease until done. Sprinkle slivered almonds on top of each fillet before serving. Serves 4.

This wonderful recipe was from the old Robertson's Cafeteria.

Sherried Seafood

- 2 cups oysters
- 5 tablespoons margarine, melted and divided
- 1 cup mushrooms, sliced
- 4 cups shrimp, cooked, peeled and deveined
- 1 cup cooked chicken, chopped
- 2 (10¾-ounce) cans cream of mushroom soup
- 1 tablespoon onion, grated
- ½ teaspoon pepper
- 1 teaspoon salt
- 1 tablespoon parsley, finely chopped
- 2 tablespoons sherry
- ¼ teaspoon cayenne pepper
- Hot cooked rice

Sauté oysters in 3 tablespoons margarine until edges curl; drain and set aside. Sauté mushrooms in remaining 2 tablespoons margarine; drain. Combine all ingredients except rice; simmer over low heat 5 minutes, stirring occasionally. Transfer to a chafing dish set on low heat. Serve over rice. Serves 8 to 10.

Can be made a day ahead, very convenient to serve.

Dotty's Deviled Crab

- 1 cup crabmeat
- 2 cups soft breadcrumbs
- 1 cup mayonnaise
- 1½ to 2 teaspoons onion, chopped
- 3 hard boiled eggs, chopped
- 2 teaspoons Worcestershire sauce
- Salt and pepper to taste

Add all ingredients and mix well. Put in buttered casserole or cleaned crab shells. Sprinkle with buttered breadcrumbs. Bake at 400° for 15 to 20 minutes. Serves 4.

Father Knows Best Crab Cakes

- 1 cup Town House crackers, crumbled
- ¼ cup mayonnaise
- 2 teaspoons prepared mustard
- 1 pound back fin crabmeat, cleaned and picked out of shells

Mix in large bowl. Shape into cakes. Sauté 3 to 5 minutes in a small amount of vegetable oil. Serves 4.

Buddy's Stuffed Baked Flounder

- 1 3 to 5 pound dressed fresh flounder
- 1 pound crabmeat (lump or back fin)
- 1 pound medium shrimp, shelled, deveined and cut in thirds
- 2 tablespoons olive oil
- 1 small ham hock or pork shank
- 1 medium bell pepper, chopped
- 1 tablespoon pimientos, chopped
- 2 ribs celery (optional)
- 2 tablespoons onion, chopped
- 1 tablespoon flour
- 1 cup milk
- 1 tablespoon lemon juice
- 1 tablespoon margarine
- 1 tablespoon Worcestershire sauce
- 1 tablespoon hot mustard
- ½ teaspoon salt
- ½ teaspoon pepper
- Dash cayenne pepper
- 1 egg, beaten
- 1 tablespoon parsley
- 1 cup herb stuffing mix
- 1 cup wine (white, sweet)

Place olive oil and ham hock in deep skillet on simmer heat. Add chopped bell pepper, pimientos, celery and onion. Cover and allow to simmer until tender. Remove ham hock and blend in flour. Add milk gradually and cook until thick, stirring constantly. Add lemon juice, margarine, Worcestershire, mustard, salt and pepper. Stir a little of this hot sauce into the egg, then add egg mixture to sauce, stirring constantly. Add parsley, crabmeat and shrimp and continue stirring. Add margarine and stuffing mix and stir to desired consistency. Remove from heat and allow to set while preparing flounder.

Line baking pan or dish with foil and grease lightly to prevent sticking. Stuff flounder, place in dish. Pour wine into pan and baste fish. Cover pan with foil and place in preheated oven at 350°. Cook 20 to 25 minutes; baste fish at least twice while cooking. Garnish with lemon wedges. Serves 4 to 6.

If your flounder is not quite so large and you're lucky enough to have some deviled shrimp and crab left over, place in washed crab shells or individual baking dishes and bake along with fish.

Truly a fish fit for a king.

Flounder Florentine

- 2 (10-ounce) packages frozen chopped spinach
- 4 tablespoons onion, chopped
- 1 teaspoon salt
- ½ teaspoon pepper
- 2 tablespoons butter
- 1½ tablespoons all-purpose flour
- 1 cup milk
- 4 tablespoons dry vermouth
- 1 pound flounder fillets, cut in serving pieces
- 1 cup grated cheese

Cook and drain spinach. Place the spinach in a greased shallow casserole and sprinkle with onion and other seasonings. Melt butter in a saucepan and stir in flour and milk until thickened. Add the vermouth. Place fillets on spinach and top with white sauce. Sprinkle with cheese and bake at 350° for 45 minutes. Serves 4 to 6.

For 2 pounds of fish, use 3 packages of spinach. Also use 1½ times the recipe for the white sauce, cheese and vermouth.

Grouper is an excellent choice for a different fish.

Grouper Alla Giardinere

- 6 pounds grouper, cut into serving size pieces
- 2 tablespoons olive oil
- 1 cup celery, chopped
- 1 cup green onion, chopped
- 1 large red pepper
- 1 large green pepper
- ½ cup sweet onion, chopped
- 1 tablespoon parsley
- 1 teaspoon basil
- ½ teaspoon garlic salt
- ¼ teaspoon pepper
- Paprika
- Grated Parmesan
- Knorr seasoning
- ¾ to 1 cup mayonnaise
- 2 tablespoons lemon juice

Sauté vegetables in oil until tender and add parsley, salt, basil and pepper. Place in bottom of shallow casserole (4-quart or a round dish). Combine mayonnaise and lemon juice. Roll grouper in this mixture and place on top of vegetables. Sprinkle with paprika, Parmesan and Knorr all-purpose seasoning. Bake at 375° uncovered approximately 40 minutes, depending on the thickness of the fish. Serves 8.

Grilled Dolphin

2 pounds skinless dolphin
½ cup melted margarine
½ cup vegetable oil
2 tablespoons soy sauce
1 tablespoon Worcestershire sauce
1½ tablespoons lemon juice
Pepper to taste

Cut tile fish into serving pieces. In a 1-quart bowl, combine all other ingredients. Place fish in a well-greased hinged wire grill about 4 inches from hot coals. Cook approximately 7 minutes per side. Baste frequently with sauce. Remove to warm dish when fish flakes easily when tested with a fork. Serves 4.

Can be used with most deep-sea fish.

Swordfish Dijon

4 swordfish steaks
⅓ cup soy sauce
¼ cup lemon juice
½ cup vegetable oil
1 clove garlic, crushed
2 teaspoons Dijon mustard
½ cup parsley

Combine all ingredients for marinade. Place swordfish in shallow dish. Pour marinade over fish. Refrigerate 4 to 6 hours. Remove fish from marinade and pat dry with paper towel. Place fish in fish rack. Grill or broil till flaky. Serves 4.

Grouper Henry

2 ounces clarified butter
⅓ green pepper, cut in thin strips
⅓ red pepper, cut in thin strips
¼ red onion, cut in thin strips
6 ounces of fresh grouper, cut in ½-inch strips

Sauté above items together and add the following:

½ teaspoon of tarragon
1 ounce of white wine
Juice of ½ fresh lemon
Salt and pepper to taste

Serves 1.

Marinated King Mackerel Steaks

King mackerel steaks, ¾ to 1-inch thick
⅓ cup teriyaki sauce
⅓ cup lemon juice
⅓ cup olive oil
Medium onion, cut in rings
Bell pepper

Cut fish in ¾ to 1-inch steaks and marinate in mixture of teriyaki sauce, lemon juice, and olive oil for two hours. Cut medium onion and bell pepper into rings. Just before you put the fish on the grill, press ring of onion and pepper into the fish on the side you are going to put toward the fire. Grill on a low fire until the meat is white and flaky and baste constantly with the marinade. This is also ideal for wahoo. Serves 1 person.

Fit for a king!

Poached Salmon

1½ cups white wine
1 lemon, sliced
1 teaspoon dried dill
¼ teaspoon pepper
4 (1-inch) salmon steaks
½ cup water
1 onion
4 sprigs of parsley

Combine all ingredients, except the salmon steaks in a skillet. Bring to a boil, reduce heat, simmer 10 minutes. Add salmon steaks. Cover and simmer 8 to 10 minutes or until fish is flaky.

Dill Sauce:
1½ cups water
1 chicken bouillon cube
2 tablespoons butter
2½ tablespoons flour
1 teaspoon dill
1 teaspoon onion powder
1 teaspoon parsley
1 teaspoon tarragon
¼ cup sour cream

Combine boiling water and bouillon, set aside. Melt butter in saucepan, add flour and stir until smooth. Cook one minute. Add bouillon mixture and seasonings, gradually add sour cream. Spoon onto cooked fish and serve. Serves 4.

A luxurious meal!

Salmon Loaf with Shrimp Sauce

- **2 (1-pound) cans salmon**
- **¼ cup onion, finely minced**
- **¼ cup parsley, chopped**
- **¼ cup lemon juice**
- **½ teaspoon salt**
- **½ teaspoon pepper**
- **½ teaspoon thyme**
- **2 cups coarse cracker crumbs**
- **½ cup milk**
- **4 eggs, well beaten**
- **¼ cup butter, melted**

Drain salmon - save liquid. Flake salmon into bowl, add onion, parsley, lemon juice, seasonings and cracker crumbs. Mix lightly. Add salmon liquid and enough milk to make 1 cup. Add eggs and melted butter. Mix lightly. Spoon into a greased 2-quart loaf pan (or quiche pan), bake at 350° approximately 1 hour or until loaf is set.

Shrimp Sauce:

- **1 can cream of shrimp soup**
- **1¼ cups milk**

Heat soup according to label, add milk, stir until smooth. Pour over loaf. Serves 6.

Excellent with grits for a light but filling supper.

Shrimp Fried Rice

- **2 cups cooked rice, cold**
- **4 ribs celery**
- **2 onions**
- **1 large bell pepper**
- **½ cup butter**
- **1 to 2 pounds shrimp**
- **3 to 4 tablespoons soy sauce**
- **3 tablespoons Worcestershire sauce**
- **Garlic, minced**
- **Salt and pepper**
- **Hot sauce (optional)**

Cook rice the day before if possible. Sauté chopped celery, onion and bell pepper in butter until soft. Add shrimp and stir until pink. On low heat add rice (crumbled), soy sauce, and Worcestershire sauce; add minced garlic, salt and pepper and hot sauce to taste. Stir well. Serves 6 to 8.

The more shrimp the better! Also tastes great cold.

Shrimp with Cashew Nuts

- ⅔ pound of shrimp
- ½ cup cashew nuts
- 10 slices ginger
- 1 egg white
- 1 tablespoon cornstarch
- ½ teaspoon salt
- 4 tablespoons oil

Seasoning Sauce:

- 1 tablespoon wine
- ¼ teaspoon salt
- 1 teaspoon pure sesame oil

Clean shrimp and pat dry. Mix this with egg white, cornstarch and salt. Soak for at least 1 hour. Fry the cashew nuts in 2 tablespoons warm oil, or until brown (about 3 minutes over a low heat). Remove, drain and set aside to cool. Heat the same oil again. Pour in shrimp and fry until done. Remove shrimp and drain oil from pan. Wipe out pan. With another 2 tablespoons oil, fry the green onions and ginger slices. Add shrimp and the seasoning sauce quickly. Stir until thoroughly mixed over high heat. Turn off heat and add the cashews and serve over rice. Serves 2 to 3.

Recipe does not call for soy sauce, but it can be used.

Deep Dish Shrimp Pie

- 3 slices bacon
- 1 bell pepper, chopped fine
- 1 large onion, chopped fine
- 1 clove garlic, chopped fine
- 1 cup milk
- 2 bay leaves
- ½ can whole kernel corn, drained or corn scraped from 2 fresh ears
- ½ cup celery, chopped fine
- 1 pinch sage
- 1 pound raw shrimp, peeled and deveined
- Salt and pepper to taste
- 1 two-crust pie shell (deep dish)

Fry bacon until crisp and remove from pan. Cook bell pepper, onion and garlic until onions are soft. Add milk, bay leaves, corn, celery, sage, shrimp and cook until moisture is gone. If shrimp draws too much water, you can drain off a bit rather than overcook the shrimp. Add salt, pepper and crumbled bacon. Put in uncooked pie shell. Prick top of top shell. Bake at 350° about 20 to 25 minutes or until crust is lightly browned. Serves 6 to 8.

Cajun Shrimp

- **1 to 2 cups butter or margarine**
- **1 to 2 cups olive oil**
- **¾ cup Worcestershire sauce**
- **6 tablespoons black pepper**
- **3 lemons, sliced**
- **2 teaspoons Tabasco**
- **1 tablespoon Italian seasoning**
- **3 cloves garlic, minced**
- **1 teaspoon paprika**
- **4 teaspoons salt**
- **8 pounds jumbo shrimp, raw, headed, unpeeled**

Heat butter and olive oil in 2-quart saucepan. Add Worcestershire, pepper, lemons, Tabasco, Italian seasoning, garlic, paprika and salt. Mix thoroughly. Simmer for 5 to 7 minutes. Divide shrimp between 2 dutch ovens and pour heated sauce over each. Cook over medium heat for 6 to 8 minutes or until shrimp begin to turn pink. Place dutch ovens in 450° oven and bake, uncovered for 10 minutes, turning shrimp once. Serve in a soup bowl with French bread on the side for dipping in the sauce. Serves 8 to 10.

This is messy, fun, and delicious. Definitely not to be served on your fine linen tablecloths.

Clark's Point Shrimp Pie

- **1 pound creek shrimp, cooked and peeled (about 2 cups)**
- **1 cup onion, sliced**
- **2 tablespoons oil**
- **1 can condensed cream of celery soup**
- **1 (4-ounce) can mushrooms, drained**
- **1 teaspoon Worcestershire sauce**
- **Dash black pepper**
- **2 cups mashed, seasoned potatoes**
- **½ teaspoon parsley**
- **Paprika**

Sauté onion in oil until tender. Combine with soup, mushrooms, Worcestershire sauce, pepper. Add shrimp. Pour mixture into buttered pie pan. Add parsley to mashed potatoes. Make a border topping on pie with mashed potatoes. Sprinkle with paprika. Bake at 450° for 15 to 20 minutes, or until lightly browned and bubbly. Serves 4.

This does not require many shrimp. Great for when children go seining!

Hamlin Creek Curry

- **15 pounds shrimp, shelled, cleaned and boiled in salt water**
- **2 cups butter**
- **½ cup all-purpose flour**
- **2 cups onion, chopped**
- **6 green onions, chopped**
- **3 cloves garlic, minced**
- **¾ cup celery, chopped**
- **1½ teaspoons salt**
- **4 tablespoons curry powder**
- **5 cups chicken broth**
- **6 cups half and half**
- **1 cup heavy cream**
- **8 tablespoons Madeira**

Melt butter and sauté vegetables. Stir in flour, salt and curry. Slowly add warm broth, half and half and cream. Simmer over low heat for 30 minutes. Add shrimp and Madeira and heat thoroughly. Serve with hot rice and curry condiments.

HINT: Also great for a brunch when served with grits, eggs, tomatoes and fruit.

This recipe is for a crowd of 35 to 40 people.

Creole Shrimp

- **4 slices bacon**
- **½ cup onions, chopped**
- **½ cup celery, chopped**
- **½ cup bell pepper, chopped**
- **2 cups stewed tomatoes**
- **½ cup chili sauce**
- **½ cup ketchup**
- **1 teaspoon Worcestershire sauce**
- **¼ teaspoon black pepper**
- **4 shakes Tabasco sauce**
- **1 teaspoon salt**
- **1½ pounds shrimp, cooked and peeled**

Fry bacon and remove from pan. Put onion, celery and bell pepper in the bacon fat and brown lightly. Add tomatoes, ketchup, chili sauce, Worcestershire sauce, black pepper, Tabasco and salt. Cook slowly until thick, stirring occasionally. Remove from heat and add shrimp 30 minutes before serving. Break the fried bacon in small pieces and add last. Serve over fluffy white rice. Serves 4 to 6.

Shrimp Thermidor

- **1 cup of white rice**
- **6 tablespoons butter**
- **1½ pounds shrimp, peeled**
- **½ cup celery**
- **¼ cup flour**
- **1 cup half and half**
- **1 teaspoon seasoning salt**
- **Dash of pepper**
- **½ cup Cheddar cheese, shredded**

Thirty minutes before serving, preheat oven at 450°. Prepare rice as directed. In 10-inch skillet over medium-high heat, cook shrimp, celery and butter for 3 minutes. Reduce heat to medium, stir in flour until blended, gradually stir in cream, seasoning salt, and pepper. Cook until thick. Put cooked rice in 2½-quart greased casserole; spoon in shrimp and sauce over rice. Sprinkle on the Cheddar cheese and cook for approximately 5 minutes. Serves 6.

McClellanville Oysters

- **1 pint oysters, drained**
- **Dash of Tabasco**
- **½ cup chopped celery**
- **2 cups crumbled Ritz crackers**
- **½ cup butter, melted**

Add Tabasco to oysters. Line the bottom of a 1-quart casserole with oysters. Then a layer of celery, cracker crumbs and melted butter. Repeat, ending with crackers on top. Set oven at 350° and bake for 30 minutes. Serves 4.

Scampi Scallops

- **2 pounds scallops or shrimp, shelled and deveined**
- **½ cup butter**
- **½ cup olive oil**
- **1 tablespoon lemon juice**
- **¼ cup shallots**
- **1 tablespoon garlic, chopped**
- **1 teaspoon salt**
- **Pepper to taste**
- **4 tablespoons parsley, finely chopped**
- **Lemon quarters**

Preheat broiler. Use a pan large enough to hold scallops in one layer. Melt butter and stir in olive oil, lemon juice, shallots, garlic, salt and pepper. Add scallops and coat completely with butter mixture. Broil 3 or 4 inches from heat for 5 minutes. Turn scallops and broil 4 to 10 minutes longer. Sprinkle with parsley. Serves 4.

Louie's Jumpin' Jambalaya

- 1 pound smoked sausage, thinly sliced
- 3 tablespoons olive oil
- ⅔ cup green pepper, chopped
- 2 cloves garlic, minced
- 1 cup celery, chopped
- ¾ cup fresh parsley, chopped
- 2 (16-ounce) cans tomatoes
- 2 cups chicken broth
- 1 cup green onions, chopped
- 1 teaspoon thyme
- 2 bay leaves
- 2 teaspoons oregano
- 1 tablespoon Creole seasoning
- ¼ teaspoon cayenne pepper
- ¼ teaspoon freshly ground pepper
- 2 cups uncooked long-grain converted rice, washed
- 3 pounds medium raw shrimp, peeled and washed

In a 4-quart heavy pot, sauté sausage until firm and remove with slotted spoon. Add olive oil to drippings and sauté green pepper, garlic, parsley and celery for 5 minutes. Chop tomatoes and reserve the liquid. Add tomatoes, tomato liquid, chicken broth and green onion to the pot. Stir in all the spices. Add the rice which has been washed and rinsed 3 times. Add the sausage and cook for 30 minutes, covered over low heat. Stir occasionally so that rice does not stick. After most of the liquid has been absorbed by the rice, add the shrimp and cook until they turn pink. Transfer mixture to an oblong casserole dish and bake at 350° for approximately 25 minutes. Serves 6 to 8.

Ted's Seafood Seasoning

- ½ cup salt
- ½ cup paprika
- ¼ cup black pepper
- ¼ cup garlic powder
- 4 tablespoons onion powder
- 2 tablespoons cayenne
- 3 tablespoons basil
- 2 tablespoons thyme
- 2 tablespoons oregano
- 1 tablespoon tarragon

Mix the spices and herbs together and store in a tightly sealed container.

This seasoning is similar to that used at Commander's Palace in New Orleans. You can use it to prepare "blackened" fish, or you can sprinkle it on virtually any seafood you want to broil, sauté, fry or bake.

Sesame Shrimp

- 2 tablespoons sesame seeds
- 1 clove garlic, minced
- 1 green pepper, chopped
- 5 green onions, chopped (green and white parts)
- 1 pint fresh mushrooms, washed and sliced
- 1 pound fresh shrimp, peeled and deveined
- Vegetable oil for cooking
- 1 tablespoon soy sauce
- ½ cup stir-fry sauce

Use large skillet or wok pan. Put in enough vegetable oil to lightly cover bottom of pan. Heat oil and add the sesame seeds and minced garlic. Cook on medium heat, stirring until lightly browned. Add the green pepper, onions and mushrooms; cook until tender, stirring constantly. Add the soy sauce and stir-fry sauce, and blend well. Add the shrimp and cook on low heat until shrimp are pink (about 5 minutes). Serve over cooked rice. Serves 2 to 3.

VARIATION: Steak strips or chicken strips can be used instead of shrimp.

Shrimp Chop Suey

- 4 slices of bacon
- 2½ cups onions, chopped
- 1 cup celery, sliced
- 2 cups water
- ¼ cup flour mixed with ¾ cup water
- 1 can Chinese noodles
- 1 tablespoon salt
- ½ teaspoon pepper
- 2 tablespoons Chinese brown gravy sauce
- 4 tablespoons sugar
- 2 cans Chinese bean sprouts
- 2 quarts shrimp, cooked and cleaned

Brown bacon in dutch oven, remove and crumble. Sauté onions and celery in bacon drippings until translucent. Add bacon, 2 cups water, salt, pepper, sugar, and brown gravy sauce. Bring to a boil and add flour and water mixture. Boil until thick and add cooked shrimp. Remove from heat. Just before serving, reheat and add 2 cans bean sprouts (drained). DO NOT COOK. Serve over cooked rice topped with crispy noodles. Serves 8 to 10.

Pesce Al Vescovo
Bishop David Thompson's Favorite

- **2 pounds fillet of flounder**
- **1 tablespoon olive oil**
- **1 teaspoon mayonnaise**
- **1 teaspoon Dijon mustard**
- **Salt and pepper**

Place flounder on tray. Pour or brush olive oil on both sides and sprinkle with salt and pepper on both sides. Mix mayonnaise and mustard together and spread on top of flounder. Broil for about four minutes. Serves 4.

Delicious!

Shrimply Delicious

- **7 tablespoons butter**
- **½ pound fresh mushrooms, sliced**
- **1½ pounds shrimp**
- **1 (19-ounce) can artichoke hearts, drained**
- **4½ tablespoons flour**
- **¾ cup milk**
- **¾ cup whipping cream**
- **¼ cup dry sherry**
- **Salt and white pepper to taste**
- **1 tablespoon Worcestershire sauce**
- **1 cup Parmesan cheese, freshly grated**
- **Paprika**
- **½ cup fresh parsley, finely chopped**

Boil, shell and devein shrimp. Set aside to cool. Melt 2½ tablespoons of butter and sauté mushrooms approximately 6 minutes. Set aside.

In 2-quart buttered casserole, make one layer each of artichoke hearts, shrimp and mushrooms.

Melt 4½ tablespoons of butter in heavy saucepan over low heat. Stirring with wire whisk, add flour until well blended and smooth. Add milk, then cream - whisk constantly until mixture thickens. Remove from heat, add salt, pepper and then Worcestershire sauce and sherry - blending all well. Pour mixture over layered ingredients. Sprinkle with cheese and paprika. Bake at 375° for 20 to 30 minutes. Allow to rest 5 minutes before serving. Garnish with extra sprinkling of paprika and chopped fresh parsley. May be served over saffron rice or white rice cooked in chicken broth. Serves 4 to 6.

An excellent company dish that may be prepared in advance.

Lobster Tails À La Scampi

8 lobster tails
4 garlic cloves
2 teaspoons salt
¼ teaspoon pepper
¼ cup parsley
1 cup vegetable oil
⅓ cup lemon juice

Fish out frozen lobster tails. Defrost. Clip along each edge of underside membrane close to shell with scissors. Pull off thin undershell. Combine all ingredients in a shallow bowl. Roll lobster tails in sauce. Place in shallow pan in single layer (shell side up). Broil 5 minutes exactly. Turn. Baste with remainder of sauce. Broil an additional 5 minutes. Serve immediately. Serves 4.

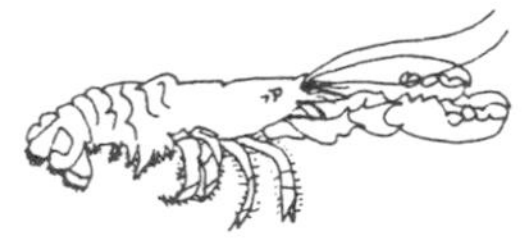

Magic Venison Meatballs

1 pound ground venison
2 tablespoons evaporated milk
1 teaspoon salt
3 tablespoons vegetable oil
2 teaspoons lemon juice
1 (16-ounce) can jellied cranberry sauce
½ package taco seasoning mix

Combine ground meat, milk, and salt. Mix well and form in balls about ¾-inch. Brown slowly over medium heat. Remove meat balls and drain. Combine cranberry sauce, taco mix and lemon juice and cook over low heat until mixture is smooth. Stir constantly while cooking. Add meatballs and simmer 15 to 20 minutes. Serve warm. Serves 8 to 10.

Venison Roast

1 (6-pound) venison roast
1 cup water
2 beef bouillon cubes
1 tablespoon salt
¼ teaspoon red pepper
½ cup flour
2 tablespoons bacon drippings

Marinade:
½ teaspoon thyme
1 teaspoon black pepper
1½ teaspoons garlic powder
1 teaspoon orange bits
½ teaspoon dry mustard
2 tablespoons olive oil
¾ cup red wine
1 medium onion sliced
5 cloves
2 bay leaves

Remove all fat from venison and wash well, place in heavy plastic bag. Put plastic bag in as small container as possible. Mix marinade and pour over meat. Marinate meat overnight or at least 6 to 8 hours in refrigerator, turning bag occasionally to distribute marinade.

Melt bouillon cubes in water, set aside. Mix salt, red pepper and flour on cookie sheet.

Remove meat from marinade and pat dry. Set marinade aside. Heat bacon drippings in large heavy dutch oven. Roll meat in flour mixture and brown on all sides. Add bouillon mixture, cover and place in oven at 350° for 35 to 40 minutes per pound. Baste with left over marinade every 30 minutes. When done, remove meat.

Gravy:
½ cup water
2 tablespoons current jelly
3 tablespoons flour

Mix water, jelly and flour till well blended. Place dutch oven on top burner. At medium-high heat bring drippings from meat to boil. Slowly add jelly and flour mixture stirring with whisk to prevent lumping. Cook until thickened. Serves 6 to 8.

The gravy is so good that you simply have to cook rice.

Father George's Quail Supreme

8 quail, cleaned and split down the back
¾ cup all-purpose flour
1 teaspoon salt
½ teaspoon pepper
½ cup butter
½ cup onion, chopped
½ cup mushrooms, chopped
½ cup dry white wine
¼ cup dry sherry
Dash of salt and pepper
8 slices French bread, toasted

Spread quail open and pat dry. Combine flour, salt and pepper. Dredge quail and set aside. Melt 2 tablespoons butter in skillet; add onions and mushrooms and sauté 4 minutes. Remove from pan and set aside. Melt ¼ cup butter in skillet and brown quail on all sides. Remove quail and place in 13x9x2-inch pan. Add wine to drippings in skillet and bring to a boil, scraping sides and bottom of skillet. Pour over quail and bake at 350° for 30 minutes. Combine onion mixture and 2 tablespoons butter, sherry and dash of salt. Spread over toasted bread and broil until bubbly. Place quail on toast slice and serve with plum sauce.

Plum Sauce:
1 cup red plum jam
Grated rind of 1 lemon
Grated rind of 1 orange
2 tablespoons lemon juice
½ cup orange juice
1 tablespoon cornstarch
½ teaspoon dry mustard

In a small saucepan place plum jam. Dissolve the cornstarch in juices - stir well. Add juice to pan. Stir over medium heat until all ingredients are thickened and warm. Serve over quail. Serves 4 to 6.

Lemon-Butter Sauce

¼ cup butter, melted
2 teaspoons boiling water
¼ teaspoon salt
Dash white pepper
1 tablespoon lemon juice

Mix all ingredients and cook over medium heat for 10 minutes. Makes about ½ cup.

Great sauce for seafood.

ACCOMPANIMENTS

Accompaniments

Hot Sherried Fruit

1 (1¼-pound) can sliced pineapple, half and drain
1 (16-ounce) can pears, drained
1 (16-ounce) cling peaches, drained
1 (15-ounce) jar red sliced apple rings, drained
½ cup butter
2 tablespoons flour
½ cup sugar
1 cup sherry (cream or pale dry)—may use Sauterne

Arrange fruit in large casserole. Heat last four ingredients until thick, stirring constantly. Pour over fruit and cover. Let stand overnight. When ready to serve, heat at 350° for 15 to 20 minutes. May want to use smaller can of fruit for smaller portions. Serves 8 to 10.

The sauce is delicious! Wonderful for holiday meals. You can use the fruits of your choice.

Coleen's Potato Casserole

8 medium potatoes
½ cup milk
¼ cup margarine or butter
Garlic powder to taste
Salt and pepper to taste
4 ounces mozzarella cheese, grated
4 ounces Cheddar cheese, grated
½ cup Parmesan cheese
Green onions, chopped (optional)
Bacon bits (optional
Ham, cut up (optional)

Preheat oven to 350°. Cut, cook, drain and mash potatoes. Add milk, butter, garlic powder, salt, pepper and cheeses. Mix well. Place in 2-quart casserole. Sprinkle top of casserole with Parmesan cheese. Bake at 350° until lightly browned. Serves 6 to 8.

Children love this. It can be made and kept in the refrigerator to be reheated at another time.

Pineapple-Cheese Casserole

- **2 (15½-ounce) cans chunk pineapple, save the juice**
- **1 cup sugar**
- **⅓ cup flour**
- **2 cups Cheddar cheese**
- **½ cup butter, melted**
- **1 stack of Ritz crackers**

Mix the juice, sugar and flour together and then add the pineapple. Put in a 9x12-inch casserole dish and sprinkle cheese on top. Sauté crushed Ritz crackers in melted butter and then sprinkle on top of cheese. Bake at 350° for 30 minutes. Serves 6 to 8.

This is great with ham—a delightful surprise.

Potatoes O'Ryan

- **6 medium potatoes, peeled, cubed and boiled**
- **1 medium onion, chopped**
- **3 tablespoons butter or margarine**
- **1 teaspoon paprika**
- **1 teaspoon seasoned salt**
- **½ teaspoon seasoned pepper**

Put the margarine in a large skillet on medium heat. Add onions and cook until clear (not brown). Add the potatoes, and the seasonings, and cook on medium heat until potatoes are golden on one side, then turn and cook on other side. Serves 4 to 6.

Delicious and so easy!!!

"Hoorah" Yams

- **6 red Delicious apples, sliced**
- **1½ cups chopped pecans**
- **1½ cups brown sugar**
- **1 teaspoon cinnamon**
- **2 (28-ounce) cans of yams, drained**
- **1 small bag miniature marshmallows (to cover)**
- **1 cup raisins**

Combine sliced apples, raisins, pecans, brown sugar and cinnamon. Alternate yams and above combination in layers. Bake at 325° for 40 to 50 minutes. Sprinkle with marshmallows. Broil until marshmallows are slightly brown. Serves 8 to 10.

Hash Brown Supreme

- **1 (2-pound) package frozen hash brown potatoes**
- **1 (10¾-ounce) can cream of chicken soup**
- **2 cups sour cream**
- **1 teaspoon salt**
- **½ teaspoon pepper**
- **1 medium onion, finely chopped**
- **¼ cup butter, melted**
- **2 cups New York sharp Cheddar cheese, grated**
- **2 cups corn flakes, crushed**
- **¼ cup butter, melted**

Combine first seven ingredients and pack in a 13x9x2-inch ungreased baking dish. Sprinkle top with grated cheese and crushed corn flakes, then dribble melted butter over top. Bake uncovered at 350° for 45 minutes. Serves 8 to 10.

Wonderful! Serves a crowd and easy to make.

Micro-Potatoes Parmesan

- **2 tablespoons butter or margarine**
- **2 medium potatoes, unpeeled, sliced ¼-inch thick**
- **⅓ cup onion, chopped**
- **1 clove garlic, minced**
- **½ cup green pepper (1-inch chunks)**
- **¼ teaspoon salt**
- **⅛ teaspoon pepper**
- **¼ cup grated Parmesan cheese**
- **Paprika**
- **Chopped parsley**

Melt butter in a shallow 9-inch dish in microwave. Add potatoes, onion, garlic and toss. Cover loosely with plastic wrap and place in microwave on full power for 5 minutes. Stir in green pepper, salt, and pepper—toss, cover and microwave on full power for 3 minutes. Gently mix in cheese. Toss and dust with paprika. Microwave on full power, uncovered, for 3 minutes. Let rest 2 minutes. Sprinkle with parsley. Serves 2.

Cheesy Crab-Stuffed Potatoes

- **4 medium baking potatoes**
- **Vegetable oil**
- **1 cup (4-ounces) shredded sharp Cheddar cheese**
- **½ cup butter or margarine, melted**
- **½ cup half and half**
- **¼ cup diced onion**
- **½ teaspoon salt**
- **¼ teaspoon ground red pepper**
- **1 (6-ounce) can crabmeat, drained, flaked, and chopped**
- **Paprika**

Scrub potatoes thoroughly, and rub skins with oil. Bake at 400° for 1 hour or until done.

Allow potatoes to cool to touch. Cut potatoes in half lengthwise; carefully scoop out pulp, leaving shells intact. Spoon pulp into a mixing bowl. Add remaining ingredients, except paprika; mash with a potato masher. Stuff shells with potato mixture; sprinkle lightly with paprika. Bake at 425° for 15 to 20 minutes. Serves 8.

Potatoes Supreme

- **8 medium potatoes**
- **½ cup butter**
- **2 cups evaporated milk**
- **1 teaspoon salt**
- **½ pound Velveeta cheese**
- **1 cup sour cream**
- **8 strips of fried bacon**

Boil potatoes in the skins. Cool overnight in refrigerator. Remove skins and grate potatoes in 2-quart casserole. Heat butter, salt, milk, and cheese in pan until cheese melts. Mix into potatoes. Bake at 350° for 35 minutes. Remove potatoes from oven and top with sour cream and crumbled bacon. Bake another 5 minutes and serve. Serves 8.

This is excellent served with marinated steak or eye of the round roast with spinach salad and French rolls.

Semi-Greek Potatoes

4 baking potatoes, scrubbed
1½ cups onion, chopped
2 cups spring onion tops, chopped
½ cup olive oil
2 teaspoons garlic, finely chopped
1 can beef bouillon
2 cups water from potatoes
Flour to dust potatoes
¼ cup seafood seasoning
4 teaspoons paprika
1 teaspoon curry powder (optional)
Salt to taste

Boil potatoes until half way cooked. In skillet, sauté onions in oil and garlic. Remove potatoes from pot and reserve two cups water. Slice potatoes and dust with seasoning salt and flour. Add the bouillon, paprika and curry to the sautéed onions and bring to a simmer. Add potatoes and stir gently. Cook for ten minutes and then add the two cups of reserved water. Let simmer for about 45 minutes stirring frequently. Serves 4.

MeMe's Sweet Potato Soufflé

12 medium sweet potatoes
½ cup soft margarine
6 eggs
2 cups milk
1 cup sugar
1 teaspoon cinnamon
1 teaspoon nutmeg
3 teaspoons vanilla extract
1 cup small marshmallows for mixture
1 cup small marshmallows for topping

Cook potatoes until soft, peel and sieve to remove strings. Add ½ cup of soft margarine to potatoes. Mix well. In another bowl add 6 well beaten eggs to 2 cups milk, then add sugar, cinnamon, nutmeg and vanilla extract. Stir this well into sweet potato mixture. Taste and add more spices if desired. Now add 1 cup small marshmallows to mixture and stir well (electric mixer can be used). Pour into baking dish approximately 12x3-inches deep. Cook approximately 30 to 45 minutes at 350°. Add marshmallows to top last 10 minutes of cooking (just brown). Add more milk if mixture is not good and creamy. Serves 10.

Stuffed Sweet Potatoes

- **6 medium sweet potatoes**
- **½ cup orange juice**
- **3 tablespoons margarine**
- **1 (8-ounce) can crushed pineapple**
- **⅓ cup firmly packed brown sugar**
- **½ cup chopped pecans**
- **2 tablespoons all-purpose flour**
- **2 tablespoons margarine**
- **Salt to taste**

Wash potatoes and bake at 375° for 1 hour or until done. Allow potatoes to cool to touch. Cut a 1-inch lengthwise strip from top of each potato; carefully scoop out pulp, leaving shell intact. Combine potato, orange juice, butter and salt in medium bowl. Beat at medium speed until fluffy. Stir in pineapple. Stuff shells with potato mixture. Combine pecans, flour and margarine to make a streusel and sprinkle over top of potatoes. Bake at 375° for 12 minutes. Serves 6.

For novelty idea, try using hollowed orange shell made from oranges, cut in half instead of potato shells.

Sweet Potatoes at 130 Broad

- **4½ cups sweet potatoes, mashed**
- **½ cup sugar**
- **3 eggs, slightly beaten**
- **¾ cup margarine, melted**
- **1½ teaspoons vanilla**
- **¾ cup milk**

Boil sweet potatoes until done; cool, peel and mash. Add next five ingredients and mix well. Pour into greased 13x8x2-inch casserole.

Topping:

- **1½ cups light brown sugar**
- **½ cup all-purpose flour**
- **6 tablespoons butter, melted**
- **1½ cups pecans, chopped**

Mix together brown sugar, flour, pecans and butter. Sprinkle over top of casserole. Bake in preheated oven 350° for 30 to 45 minutes.

Good anytime, but everyone looks for this at Thanksgiving.

Sweet Potato Casserole

3 cups raw sweet potatoes, shredded
2 cups milk
2 eggs, beaten
¾ cup brown sugar
1 teaspoon cinnamon
1 teaspoon allspice
½ teaspoon nutmeg
⅓ teaspoon ginger
2 tablespoons butter, melted
Dash of salt

Mix all ingredients together and bake in 2-quart casserole dish at 325° for one hour. Serves 4.

Yemassee Yam and Apple Casserole

6 to 8 yams, boiled until tender-firm
5 to 6 apples, sliced thin
1 cup brown sugar
3 tablespoons butter
3 cups orange juice
4 tablespoons cornstarch
1 teaspoon salt
1 cup raisins (optional)

Cook together the brown sugar, orange juice, salt and cornstarch until thickened, then add raisins and butter to melt. Pour over yams and apples that have been peeled, sliced and layered in alternating layers in large 2-quart casserole dish. Bake at 300° for approximately 30 to 40 minutes. Serves 6 to 8.

VARIATION: May be topped with 1 small bag of miniature marshmallows.

Cajun Beans and Rice

2 (16-ounce) cans kidney beans, undrained
1 cup green onions, sliced
1 large green pepper, diced
1 teaspoon oregano
1 teaspoon thyme
1 teaspoon paprika
½ teaspoon salt
Dash of cayenne pepper
¼ cup red wine
1 cup parsley, chopped
1 teaspoon vinegar
Dash of Tabasco sauce
1 cup celery, sliced
6 cups cooked brown rice

In a large skillet, combine beans, onion, celery, pepper and seasonings. Simmer until mixture thickens (about 1 hour). Stir in red wine, parsley, vinegar and Tabasco sauce. Serve over hot rice. Serves 8 to 10.

Fried Rice

6 slices bacon, cooked and crumbled
2 cups rice, cooked and cooled
½ cup green pepper, chopped
1 cup celery, chopped
1 cup onion, chopped
2 eggs, beaten well
2 tablespoons soy sauce
1 teaspoon sugar
1 teaspoon MSG

Sauté peppers, celery, and onions in 1 tablespoon bacon grease. In a large saucepan add rice, bacon and sautéed vegetables. In a small bowl combine eggs, soy sauce, sugar and MSG. Add the liquid to the rice, bacon and vegetables. Cook on medium heat, stirring constantly, until egg pieces are cooked. If desired, add 2 cups cooked shrimp or 2 cups cubed ham. Serves 6 to 8.

Hoppin' John

1 cup small, dried beans such as cowpeas or black-eyes
5 to 6 cups water
1 dried hot pepper, if desired
1 smoked ham hock
1 medium onion, chopped
1 cup raw, long grain white rice

Wash and sort the beans, add the water, and discard any peas that float. Gently boil the peas with the pepper, ham hock, and onion until they are tender but not mushy - about 1½ hours - or until two cups of liquid remain. Add the rice to the pot, cover, and simmer over low heat for about twenty minutes, never lifting the lid. Remove from the fire and allow to steam, still covered, for another ten minutes. Remove the cover, fluff with a fork, and serve immediately.

... The classic Charleston New Year's recipe makes for a very dry version of the dish, but it is served with greens and their juices and with a side dish or more peas and pot likker.

Red Rice

- 2 cups long grain raw rice
- 1 (12-ounce) can tomato paste
- 1 small onion, chopped
- 9 slices of bacon
- 2 teaspoons sugar
- 2 teaspoons salt
- ½ teaspoon pepper

Fry bacon in frying pan, remove and drain. Save 2 tablespoons of bacon drippings. Add chopped onion to bacon grease. Fry onion until limp. Add tomato paste. Fill empty tomato paste can twice with water and add to onion and grease in frying pan. Stir carefully and add sugar, salt and pepper. Simmer 10 minutes. Add mixture in rice steamer with washed rice. Add bacon, crumbling in little pieces. Let water in bottom of steamer come to a full boil then reduce to medium heat and cook for about 45 minutes stirring rice and mixture several times. Serves 6 to 8.

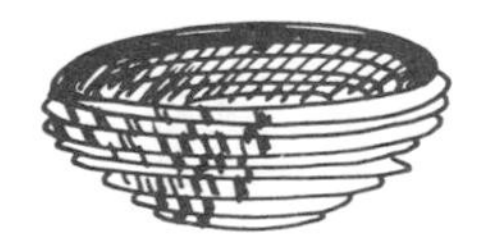

Take-Along Baked Beans

- 1 pound great Northern dry beans
- ½ pound bacon, chopped
- 1 can tomato soup
- 1 cup brown sugar
- 1 large onion, chopped

Soak beans 8 hours or overnight in water that is 3-inches above beans. Boil beans 5 minutes in same water, scooping off scum that forms. Drain and reserve liquid. Put beans in a beanpot, add all other ingredients. Add some of reserved water to cover. Bake covered at 300° 8 to 10 hours until brown and tender, adding water as needed. Serves 6.

This recipe takes some planning ahead but it's worth it.

Rice Primavera

- **1½ cups bouillon or chicken broth**
- **1 tablespoon margarine**
- **2 teaspoons basil leaves, crushed**
- **¼ cup onion, finely chopped**
- **1½ cups fresh vegetables (small broccoli florets, cubed yellow squash and grated carrots)**
- **1½ cups instant rice**
- **2 tablespoons Parmesan cheese**

Combine broth, butter, basil, onion and other vegetables in medium saucepan. Bring to a boil. Stir in the rice, cover and remove from the heat. Let stand 5 minutes, or until all liquid is absorbed. Stir in cheese before serving. Serves 4.

Wild Rice Pilaf

- **1 (6-ounce) package long grain rice**
- **1 (6-ounce) package wild rice**
- **5 cups orange juice**
- **⅔ cup onion, chopped**
- **2 tablespoons margarine**
- **⅔ cup dark raisins**
- **1 tablespoon grated orange rind**

Cook all rice together according to package directions, using orange juice in place of water. Sauté onion in butter in small skillet until tender, about 3 to 5 minutes. Stir in raisins and orange rind. Cook 1 minute. Stir onion mixture into cooked rice. Serves 8.

Corn Pie

- **1 can cream corn**
- **¼ cup butter**
- **3 eggs, beaten**
- **2 tablespoons sugar**
- **2 tablespoons flour**
- **Salt to taste**

Melt butter in 1½-quart casserole dish. Mix corn, eggs, flour and sugar together. Pour over melted butter. DO NOT STIR. Bake at 325° for 1 hour. Serves 4.

A favorite for young and old.

Eggplant Soufflé

- **1 large eggplant**
- **4 eggs**
- **½ cup half and half**
- **¼ cup butter, melted**
- **½ teaspoon salt**
- **½ teaspoon white pepper**
- **¼ cup parsley, finely chopped**
- **1 small onion, finely minced**
- **½ cup Parmesan cheese**
- **½ cup breadcrumbs**

Peel and cut eggplant into one-inch cubes. Cook in boiling salted water until tender. Drain well. (Important) Whip until smooth. Add all ingredients except cheese. Beat until fluffy. Pour into shallow baking dish. Sprinkle with cheese and bake at 325° for 35 minutes. Serves 8.

Baked Carrot and Apple Casserole

- **2 cups cooked carrots**
- **5 apples, thinly sliced**
- **6 tablespoons sugar**
- **2 tablespoons all-purpose flour**
- **Salt to taste**
- **1 tablespoon cornstarch**
- **¾ cup orange juice**
- **½ cup chopped pecans**
- **¼ cup brown sugar**

Place layer of apples in 11x7-inch baking dish, alternating with carrots until all are used. Mix sugar with salt and flour and sprinkle over vegetables. Mix cornstarch with juice and pour over dish. Crumble brown sugar and pecans over vegetables and bake at 350° for 20 to 30 minutes.

Green Bean Supreme

- 1 (4-ounce) can mushrooms
- 1 medium onion, diced
- ¼ cup margarine
- 2 (10¾-ounce) cans cream of mushroom soup
- ¾ cup sharp Cheddar cheese, shredded
- 2 teaspoons soy sauce
- ⅛ teaspoon hot pepper sauce
- ¼ teaspoon pepper
- 1 (8-ounce) can water chestnuts, sliced
- 3 packages French style frozen green beans (or 3 cans)
- ¼ cup shredded almonds
- Salt to taste

Sauté mushrooms and onions in margarine. Add soup, cheese, soy sauce, pepper sauce, salt and pepper. Cook in double boiler stirring constantly. Add beans and water chestnuts; mix thoroughly. Place in casserole dish and sprinkle with almonds. Bake 20 minutes at 325°. Serves 10.

Great for company dinners!

Sweet & Sour Green Beans

- 3 strips bacon
- 1 small onion
- 1 can water chestnuts, sliced
- 1 (16-ounce) can French style green beans
- 2 teaspoons cornstarch
- ½ teaspoon salt
- ¼ teaspoon dry mustard
- 1 tablespoon brown sugar
- 1 tablespoon vinegar
- 3 tablespoons chopped pimiento

Fry bacon until crisp; remove, drain and crumble. In bacon drippings, sauté onion and water chestnuts, stirring frequently. Drain green beans, reserving ½ cup liquid. Combine bean liquid, cornstarch, salt, mustard, brown sugar and vinegar. Add to skillet. Cook, stirring constantly, until mixture thickens. Add green beans and pimiento. Heat. Garnish with crumbled bacon. Serves 4.

Mrs. B's Green Beans

- **1 pound bulk hot sausage**
- **1 medium onion, chopped**
- **2 (17-ounce) cans cut green beans, drained**
- **1 (15-ounce) can tomato sauce**
- **½ teaspoon salt**
- **½ teaspoon sugar**
- **½ teaspoon oregano**

Lightly brown sausage, drain. Add onion and sauté until tender. Add beans, tomato sauce, salt, sugar and oregano. Bring to boil and serve. Serves 4 to 6.

A great way to dress-up canned beans. The men love it.

Italian Broccoli

- **2 (10-ounce) packages frozen cut broccoli**
- **2 eggs, beaten**
- **1 can cheese soup**
- **½ teaspoon oregano, crushed**
- **1 (8-ounce) can stewed tomatoes, cut up**
- **3 tablespoons grated Parmesan cheese**

Cook frozen broccoli for 5 to 7 minutes until just crisp. Drain. Combine eggs, cheese soup, and oregano. Stir in tomatoes and cooked broccoli. Turn into a 10x6-inch baking dish. Sprinkle with cheese. Bake uncovered at 350° for 30 minutes. Serves 4 to 6.

Broccoli Puff

- **2 packages frozen chopped broccoli**
- **1 cup buttermilk baking mix**
- **1 cup milk**
- **2 eggs**
- **½ teaspoon salt**
- **1 cup shredded Cheddar cheese**

Preheat oven to 325°. Butter 1½-inch quart casserole dish. Cook broccoli and drain. Beat buttermilk baking mix, milk, eggs and salt until smooth. Stir in broccoli and cheese. Pour in casserole. Bake until knife inserted half between center and edge comes out clean, approximately 1 hour. Serves 4 to 6.

This can be cut in half without a problem.

Pembrooke Broccoli

- **1 medium onion, chopped**
- **½ cup melted butter or margarine, divided**
- **1 can cream of mushroom soup, undiluted**
- **1 (4-ounce) can chopped mushrooms, drained**
- **8 ounces Velveeta cheese, cut in small cubes**
- **1 teaspoon parsley, chopped**
- **½ teaspoon garlic powder**
- **Salt and pepper to taste**
- **2 (10-ounce) packages of frozen chopped broccoli, partially cooked and well-drained**
- **2 cups herb-seasoned stuffing mix**

Sauté onion in ¼ cup butter until tender. Combine onion, soup, mushrooms, cheese, seasonings and broccoli. Mix well and spoon into 2-quart casserole. Combine stuffing mix and ¼ cup butter and spoon over broccoli mixture. Bake at 350° for 30 minutes. Serves 6.

This can be easily doubled for a large group.

Cabbage Soufflé

1 large head cabbage, chopped
3 slices white bread
3 teaspoons margarine
4 eggs, beaten
2 cups milk
2½ cups shredded sharp cheese
1 teaspoon salt
1 teaspoon pepper

Cook cabbage in salted water until tender and drain-set aside. Spread bread with butter and place in large mixing bowl. Combine eggs, milk and mix well. Pour over bread and allow to stand 5 minutes, add cabbage and 1½ cups of cheese. Salt and pepper and mix well. Spoon into greased 2-quart dish and bake at 250° for 1½ hours. Remove and sprinkle remaining cheese on top. Return to oven and bake until cheese melts. Serves 8.

This can be made ahead and frozen.

Spinach Cheese Pie

1 9-inch deep-dish frozen pie shell, thawed
4 eggs
1 (10-ounce) package frozen chopped spinach
1 small onion, chopped
2 tablespoons margarine
Salt and pepper to taste
¼ teaspoon parsley flakes (optional)
¼ teaspoon basil flakes (optional)
1 (8-ounce) package cream cheese, softened
½ cup feta cheese (or cottage cheese)

Pierce pie shell and bake at 450° for 5 minutes until pale golden color. Cool and set aside. Heat oven to 350°. Sauté onion in margarine. In large bowl beat eggs. Add spinach which has been thawed and excess liquid squeezed out, onion, salt, pepper, parsley and basil flakes, cream cheese (cut in small pieces) and ½ cup crumbled feta cheese or cottage cheese. Mix well and pour filling in pie crust. Bake about 50 minutes or until filling is set (when knife inserted in center comes out clean). Serves 6 to 8.

Easy to make 2 or 3 at a time; freezes well. Freeze before cooking.

Spinach Elegantè

- 2 (10-ounce) packages frozen spinach, chopped
- 3 slices bacon, cooked and crumbled
- 1 (6-ounce) can sliced mushrooms, drained
- ¼ teaspoon marjoram, crushed
- ½ cup sour cream
- ¼ cup shredded sharp cheese

Cook spinach according to package directions. Drain well. Spread in a 10x7-inch baking dish. Arrange bacon and mushrooms over spinach. Sprinkle with marjoram. Bake at 325° for 15 minutes. Cover with sour cream and sprinkle with cheese. Return to oven for five minutes until cheese melts. Serves 4 to 6.

Cauliflower Bake

- 2 heads of cauliflower
- ¼ cup margarine
- 1 can cream of shrimp soup
- 1 (8-ounce) container sour cream
- 4 to 5 packages slivered almonds

Steam cauliflower for 5 to 7 minutes. Melt margarine, soup and sour cream in microwave for 2 minutes. Arrange cauliflower in 9x13-inch baking dish. Pour mixture over cauliflower. Toast almonds for 3 to 5 minutes in 350° oven. Sprinkle on top and bake casserole for 20 minutes at 325°. Serves 6 to 8.

Cauliflower Sauté

- 2 cups cauliflower flowerets
- 2 cloves garlic, minced
- 1 small onion, sliced
- 2 tablespoons olive oil
- 1 cup snow peas
- 1 red pepper, sliced
- 1 cup sliced mushrooms
- 1 teaspoon oregano

Steam cauliflower until just tender. Set aside. In large skillet or wok, sauté garlic and onion in olive oil until soft. Add steamed cauliflower, snow peas, red pepper, mushrooms and oregano. Stir until heated through. Serves 6 to 8.

Okra Pilau

5 strips bacon
3 cups okra, chopped
1 medium onion, chopped
2 cups chicken broth
1 cup rice
Salt and pepper to taste

Fry bacon in heavy dutch oven, drain and crumble. Sauté onion in bacon drippings until tender. Add okra and bacon and toss until okra is well-coated (about 3 minutes). Add chicken broth, rice and seasonings. Bring to a boil, cover and cook for 30 minutes on low heat. Let stand 15 minutes covered. Fluff with a two-prong fork before serving. Serves 4 to 6.

Perhaps even Ashley Cooper would enjoy this??? (We said, "Perhaps")

Simple Asparagus Divine

1 large can long white asparagus spears
½ cup butter
1½ cups mayonnaise
2 tablespoons horseradish
1 teaspoon onion, minced
¼ teaspoon dry mustard
¼ teaspoon cayenne pepper
½ teaspoon salt
½ tablespoon vinegar

Heat asparagus gently until hot. Combine other ingredients in top of double boiler over hot water and stir until well blended. Pour over drained asparagus on platter. Serves 2.

Asparagus Soufflé

1 (8¼-ounce) can asparagus, cut, drained
4 eggs, slightly beaten
1 can mushroom soup
1 cup mayonnaise
1 cup sharp Cheddar cheese, grated

Mix above ingredients with fork and place in a 10-inch greased casserole dish. Bake for one hour at 350°. Can be used as a quiche also. Good with chopped ham or bacon. Serves 4 to 6.

Spaghetti Squash

- **1 spaghetti squash**
- **3 tablespoons margarine**
- **1 teaspoon salt**
- **1 cup grated Cheddar cheese**
- **1 cup spaghetti sauce**

Cut squash in half lengthwise. In a 13x9-inch pan place 2-inches water with salt. Scoop seeds from squash. Place squash upside down in pan. Bake at 350° for about 45 minutes. With a fork separate squash from shell. It will come out in little strings like angel hair spaghetti. Place squash in 1½-quart baking dish. Mix in spaghetti sauce, margarine and Cheddar cheese. Sprinkle a little more cheese on top. Return to 350° oven for 15 to 20 minutes until cheese melts. Serves 4 to 6.

A new treat.

Favorite Squash Casserole

- **2 to 3 pounds yellow squash, sliced in rounds**
- **1 medium carrot, grated**
- **1 medium onion, finely minced**
- **1 cup sour cream**
- **1 can cream of chicken soup**
- **½ cup melted margarine**
- **1 small jar chopped pimientos**
- **1 can water chestnuts, sliced (optional)**
- **1 cup seasoned bread crumbs**
- **2 cups Pepperidge Farm cornbread dressing**
- **Dash of white pepper**

Cook squash until tender, but still firm. Drain thoroughly. Mix sour cream and soup, onions, carrot, drained pimientos, water chestnuts, and pepper together. Fold in drained squash. Mix melted butter with cornbread and crumbs. Grease a glass baking dish, and put half of crumb mixture in bottom. Add squash mixture, and top with remaining crumbs. Bake uncovered at 350° for 30 to 35 minutes. Serves 8.

For color, mix yellow squash and zucchini.

Mushroom Stuffed Summer Squash

6 to 8 small summer squash
4 tablespoons butter
4 tablespoons all-purpose flour
1½ cups milk
1 teaspoon onion, grated
½ cup grated sharp cheese
1 (8-ounce) can mushroom pieces
Salt and pepper to taste

Wash the squash and boil it whole for 10 minutes. Drain. In a saucepan heat the butter until melted and blend in flour. Add the milk and stir until smooth. Add the onion, cheese and mushroom pieces. Simmer 15 minutes, stirring occasionally. Add salt and pepper to taste. Cut the squash lengthwise in halves. Scoop out seeds. Place the squash skin side down in a greased baking dish (or spray with Pam). Fill the center with the sauce. Cover and bake at 350° for 20 minutes. Uncover and bake for 10 minutes more until golden on top. Serves 3 to 6.

Ranch Squash

2 pounds yellow squash
1 medium onion, chopped
2 eggs, beaten
½ cup mayonnaise
1 small package Hidden Valley Ranch dressing, original style
1 cup grated cheese
12 saltines, crumbled
Salt and pepper to taste
½ cup Cheese Nips, crumbled for top

Cook squash and onion in water till soft. Drain well. In large shallow 10x10x2-inch casserole dish put drained squash and onion, beaten eggs, mayonnaise, dressing, cheese, saltines, salt and pepper and stir until mixed together. Put Cheese Nips on top and bake for 30 minutes at 350°. Serves 6 to 8.

This casserole is good served with a formal dinner such as Thanksgiving or Christmas or even just a special Sunday dinner. I have passed this recipe on to many friends, it is that good! Nice disguise for non-squash lovers!

Baked Vermont Acorn Squash

2 small acorn squash
2 teaspoons butter
1 cup heavy cream
1 cup maple syrup

Cut the acorn squash in half, remove the seeds and slice a sliver from the bottom of each squash so that it does not wiggle around in the pan. Lay the squash halves on a buttered tray close together. Butter the exposed flesh of the squash using ½ teaspoon butter on each squash. Into each half squash pour ¼ cup heavy cream and ¼ cup maple syrup or enough to fill the cavity almost level with the top in equal quantities. Bake in a moderate oven (350°) without stirring at least 45 minutes. Begin testing with a fork. Some squash take as much as an 1½ hours to bake and some are done in 1 hour. If the liquid cooks away, add a little more cream and maple syrup. Serves 4.

Surprising Squash

1 butternut squash, medium to large, peeled and seeded and cut into chunks
2 cups of apple juice
3 Bartlett pears, peeled, seeded and cut into chunks
2 tablespoons brown sugar
2 tablespoons butter

Put squash in large saucepan with apple juice and cook for about 15 minutes on medium heat. Add pears, butter and brown sugar. Cook until soft. Put through food processor and serve. Serves 6.

Apples may be used instead of pears.

Squash Puffs

1 cup squash, cooked, mashed, and well drained
1 egg, beaten
⅓ cup all-purpose flour
⅓ cup cornmeal
1 teaspoon baking powder
½ teaspoon salt

Combine squash and egg. Combine flour, baking powder and cornmeal. Add flour mixture to squash. Cook in wok at 375° in 1-quart oil or fry in frying pan. Drop by teaspoonfuls into hot oil. Turn over until brown. You may add onion to squash before cooking. Season squash to taste. Serves 4.

Tomatoes Florentine

- **3 (10-ounce) packages frozen chopped spinach**
- **1 cup breadcrumbs**
- **1 small onion, finely chopped**
- **3 eggs, slightly beaten**
- **½ cup sharp cheese, grated**
- **½ tablespoon garlic salt**
- **¼ teaspoon thyme**
- **⅛ teaspoon red pepper**
- **½ teaspoon black pepper**
- **½ cup Parmesan cheese**
- **8 medium tomatoes**
- **1 tablespoon oil**
- **½ cup water**

Cook spinach according to directions on package, drain thoroughly and set aside. Remove top of tomatoes, scoop out and invert to drain. Mix together all ingredients except tomatoes, spinach, Parmesan cheese, oil and water. Add drained spinach to mixture and place into tomatoes. Sprinkle Parmesan cheese on top. Put in casserole. Add water to which oil has been added. Cover casserole with foil. Bake at 325° for 20 minutes. Remove foil and place dish under broiler for one to two minutes. Remove tomatoes carefully with slotted spoon. Serves 6 to 8.

Tomato Pie

- **1 9-inch deep dish pie shell, baked**
- **2 to 3 large tomatoes thickly sliced**
- **2 to 3 green onions, chopped**
- **Salt and pepper**
- **Basil**
- **Chives**
- **1 cup mayonnaise**
- **1 cup sharp cheese, grated**
- **3 slices bacon, fried crisp**
- **Parmesan cheese**

Fill cooled pie shell with alternating layers of tomatoes and onions. Sprinkle with salt, pepper, basil and chives. Combine mayonnaise and cheese and spread over tomatoes. Sprinkle top with crushed bacon and Parmesan cheese. Bake at 350° for 30 minutes.

A wonderful way to use the over-abundance of tomatoes when they're in season.

Zucchini Creole

- 2 medium zucchini, cut into ½-inch rounds
- 3 tablespoons butter
- 3 tablespoons all-purpose flour
- 3 large tomatoes, chopped
- 1 small green pepper, seeded and chopped
- 1 small onion, chopped
- 1 teaspoon salt
- 1 tablespoon firmly packed brown sugar
- ½ bay leaf
- 2 cloves
- ½ cup breadcrumbs
- ½ cup freshly grated Parmesan cheese

Cook zucchini until tender, but firm (about 5 minutes). Drain and place in greased 2-quart casserole. Melt butter over medium heat in medium saucepan and add flour; stir until smooth and bubbly. Add tomatoes, green pepper, onion, salt, brown sugar, bay leaf and cloves. Cook for 5 or 6 minutes. Remove cloves and bay leaf and pour mixture on top of zucchini. Top with breadcrumbs and cheese mixed. Bake uncovered at 350° for 30 minutes. Serves 4 to 6.

Vegetable Medley Supreme

- 1 (11-ounce) can white shoepeg corn, drained
- 1 (16-ounce) can French cut string beans, reserve about half of liquid
- ½ cup celery, chopped
- ½ cup onion, chopped
- 1 cup grated sharp cheese
- 1 cup sour cream
- Salt and pepper

Mix together ingredients including the bean liquid and place in a large 9x13-inch casserole.

Topping:

- 1 stack Ritz crackers, crushed
- ¼ cup butter (you may use margarine, but butter is better)
- ½ cup slivered almonds

Mix the above ingredients and place on top of the vegetables. Bake for 45 minutes at 350°. Serves 4 to 6.

Versatile Vegetable Casserole

- **3 cans asparagus spears or 3 packages leaf spinach or fresh spinach**
- **3 cans artichoke hearts**
- **1 (8-ounce) can sliced water chestnuts**
- **8 ounces fresh mushrooms**
- **1 medium onion**
- **½ pound sharp New York cheese, grated**
- **1 cup sherry**
- **⅓ cup flour**
- **1 cup butter**
- **Coarse pepper**
- **Paprika**

Drain all vegetables, but save the asparagus or spinach juice. Make a sauce of ½ cup butter, ⅓ cup flour and vegetable juice. Sauté mushrooms and onion in ½ cup butter. Add to sauce and blend. Add sherry, pepper and all but ½ cup cheese. Place asparagus or spinach in a casserole. Top with artichoke hearts and chestnuts. Pour sauce over the top and sprinkle with cheese and paprika. Bake 35 to 40 minutes at 350°. Serves 6 to 8.

Very rich and needs no salt except in the cooking of the spinach.

Crowd Pleasing Vegetables

- **2 (16-ounce) cans Veg-All, drained**
- **½ cup onion, chopped**
- **1 cup celery, chopped**
- **1 can cream of chicken soup**
- **1 can water chestnuts, chopped**
- **2 cups Pepperidge Farm dressing**
- **1 cup mayonnaise**
- **½ cup margarine, melted**

Mix first five ingredients and place in 2-quart casserole dish. Mix dressing, mayonnaise and margarine. Add ¾ of dressing mixture to vegetables. Sprinkle ¼ dressing over top of casserole. Bake at 350° for 25 to 30 minutes. Serves 6 to 8.

Judy's Green Rice

3 cups cooked rice
1 chopped spinach, thawed
2 eggs, well beaten
1 cup milk
1 teaspoon Worcestershire sauce
1 teaspoon salt
2 teaspoons onion, grated
¼ cup margarine
½ cup grated sharp cheese
1 package slivered almonds

Toss rice and spinach together with fork. Add eggs, milk, Worcestershire sauce, salt and onions. Toss gently to mix, using care not to mash rice. Pour into greased 2-quart baking dish. Dot with butter and sprinkle cheese on top. Bake in slow oven, 325° for 30 to 40 minutes; sprinkle with chopped almonds. Serves 8 to 10.

Missy's Cornbread Dressing

Cornbread mix (made according to directions)
2 onions, chopped
1 green pepper, chopped
2 ribs celery, chopped
½ cup butter
½ teaspoon salt
½ teaspoon pepper
½ teaspoon poultry seasoning
2 hard boiled eggs, chopped
Neck and gizzard of turkey

Place neck and gizzard in small pan, cover with water and simmer 1 hour. Reserve this liquid to moisten dressing. Sauté onions, green pepper, and celery in ½ cup butter and seasonings. Combine cornbread and vegetables in medium bowl. Add chopped eggs and about half of turkey stock. Bake in greased 9x9-inch pan at 350° for 40 minutes or until done. Use remaining stock to moisten dressing if needed. Serves 6.

Oyster Dressing

- 1 (9-inch) round corn bread
- ¼ cup sugar
- 1 cup breadcrumbs
- 3 cups onions, chopped
- 2 cups celery, chopped
- 1 cup bell pepper, chopped
- 2 cups green onions, chopped
- ½ cup bacon drippings
- 1 pint oysters, chopped and drained
- ¼ cup dried parsley
- 1 teaspoon poultry seasoning
- ¼ teaspoon red pepper
- 1 tablespoon paprika
- 2 teaspoons onion salt
- 1 (16-ounce) can chicken broth

Add ¼ cup sugar to cornbread mixture and bake according to directions. Cool and crumble the cornbread and add breadcrumbs. Add next twelve ingredients, and add enough chicken broth to wet the mixture. Put mixture into buttered 4-quart casserole dish and top with breadcrumbs. Bake at 350° for 35 minutes or until sides of casserole are golden brown. Serves 6 to 8.

Bread Stuffing

- 3 giant loaves stale bread (2 white, 1 brown)
- 1 cup butter
- 1 egg, slightly beaten
- ½ cup boiling water
- 3 medium onions, chopped
- 6 ribs of celery, chopped
- 1 teaspoon poultry seasoning
- 1 teaspoon thyme
- 1 teaspoon salt
- ½ teaspoon pepper
- Optional ingredients: nuts, mushrooms, apples, sausage, oysters

The day before, set the bread out to dry. Cube the bread and put in a large mixing bowl. Place butter and seasonings in bowl with bread. Pour boiling water over bread - cover until bread is moistened. Add optional ingredients. Toss gently. Loosely stuff cavity and neck of turkey. Sew up with large needle and thread. Makes enough for 10 to 12-pound turkey.

Beer Batter Fry Mix

- **1½ cups unbleached all-purpose flour**
- **¾ cup plus 2 tablespoons beer**
- **2 large egg yolks (save the whites)**
- **½ tablespoon oil**
- **1 teaspoon salt**
- **Pinch of sugar**
- **2 egg whites, at room temperature**

Combine first six ingredients except the egg whites until smooth. Cover with damp cloth and refrigerate for 2 hours. Heat oil to 375°. Whip egg whites until stiff but not dry. Gently fold into beer batter. (Batter will be stiff). Dip veggies into batter and fry. Use for onion rings, mushrooms, zucchini, etc. Cook in oil until medium brown color, drain on paper towels. Serve hot.

Great for appetizer with honey-mustard dip.

Mock Hollandaise

- **2 tablespoons lemon juice**
- **2 tablespoons water**
- **4 tablespoons sour cream**
- **2 egg yolks**
- **½ teaspoon salt**
- **1 dash cayenne pepper**

Combine all ingredients and cook in top of double boiler, stirring until desired consistency. Be sure to keep water in bottom part of double boiler at a simmer. Makes 1 cup.

PASTA

Pasta

Cannelloni À La Capri

- **12 jumbo macaroni shells, cooked**
- **12 ounces mozzarella cheese, shredded**
- **1 tablespoon butter**
- **1 (6-ounce) can sliced mushrooms, drained**
- **1 (8-ounce) can tomato sauce**
- **Grated Parmesan cheese**

Cook shells as per directions in salted water. Drain and set aside. Sauté mushrooms in butter, cool. Fill pasta shells with cheese and mushrooms. Place with open side down on oven-proof dish or platter. Spoon tomato sauce, sparingly, on top of each shell. Sprinkle abundantly with Parmesan cheese. Cover with foil and heat in moderate oven 300° for about 20 to 25 minutes. Serve lukewarm to enjoy the delicate flavor of the filling.

For a complete meal on a platter, broil 4 chicken breasts and steam tops from one bunch of broccoli. Place chicken in middle of platter. Surround chicken with filled pasta. Spoon tomato sauce on pasta and chicken. Arrange broccoli around outside of pasta. Cover and heat when ready. Serves 3 to 4.

Charleston Macaroni Pie

- **4 cups water**
- **1 cup elbow macaroni**
- **1 teaspoon salt**
- **¼ cup margarine**
- **2 eggs**
- **1 teaspoon dry mustard**
- **1¼ cups milk**
- **8 ounces medium sharp Cheddar cheese, cubed**
- **½ teaspoon pepper**

Bring water and salt to boil, add macaroni and boil for 15 minutes, stirring occasionally. Drain. Add margarine to hot macaroni. In small bowl, beat eggs, dry mustard and milk with whisk and add to macaroni. Stir and add cheese which has been cut into small cubes. Pour into buttered 2-quart casserole dish. Sprinkle pepper on top. Bake uncovered at 350° for 30 to 35 minutes or until lightly browned around edges but still soft in center. Serves 6.

Everybody likes this old favorite standby.

Company Spaghetti Casserole

- 1 package Lipton dried onion soup
- 2 pounds ground beef, browned
- 3 (6-ounce) cans tomato paste
- 3 (6-ounce) cans of water
- 1 (16-ounce) can tomatoes
- 2 teaspoons garlic salt
- ¾ teaspoon sugar
- 1 teaspoon salt
- 1 teaspoon oregano
- 1 teaspoon basil
- 1 teaspoon thyme
- 1 (6-ounce) can sliced mushrooms
- ½ cup red wine
- 1 pound box vermicelli
- 1 pound Cheddar cheese, grated
- 1 small can Parmesan cheese

Mix first thirteen ingredients and simmer for 30 minutes. Cook vermicelli according to package directions. Mix sauce, vermicelli and grated Cheddar cheese. Place in a 2 to 3-quart casserole. Sprinkle with Parmesan cheese. Heat until bubbly in a 350° oven about 30 to 45 minutes. Serves 8.

NOTE: This casserole freezes well for later use.

Fix ahead and enjoy the Super Bowl!

Father Robert Kelly's Special

- 8 ounces fettuccine noodles
- ½ cup butter or margarine
- ½ cup whipping cream
- 1 cup grated Parmesan cheese
- 1 tablespoon parsley flakes
- ¼ teaspoon salt
- 1 teaspoon pepper
- 1 pound scallops
- 1 pound medium shrimp
- 2 teaspoons lemon juice

Peel shrimp, sauté in hot pan with l teaspoon lemon juice, drain and set aside. Sauté scallops in hot pan with 1 teaspoon lemon juice, drain and set aside. Cook noodles in boiling water until done, approximately 4 to 5 minutes. While noodles cook, beat butter and cream in small saucepan over low heat until butter is melted. Stir in cheese, parsley, salt and pepper. Keep warm over low heat. Return drained noodles to pan. Add shrimp and scallops. Pour sauce over stirring gently until well coated. Serve immediately. Serve with green salad and bread. Serves 6.

Grecian Shrimp Supreme

- 3 tablespoons ultra virgin olive oil
- 3 green onions, diced (also dice ½ green part for color)
- 2 cloves garlic, minced
- ½ cup fresh parsley, finely chopped (divide into ¼ cup each)
- 1 green pepper, diced
- 2 heaping tablespoons oregano
- 2 cups fresh tomatoes, chopped or 1 (16-ounce) can Italian Plum tomatoes, well drained and chopped
- ¼ cup tomato paste
- 1 pound of shrimp, peeled and deveined
- Pinch of crushed red pepper
- Butter for casserole
- 1 cup of feta cheese, crumbled
- Cooked linguine, ziti or rice

Preheat oven to 425°. In large skillet, heat olive oil and sauté onions and garlic until onion is soft. Add ¼ cup of parsley, green pepper, tomatoes, tomato paste, and oregano. Simmer covered for 20 minutes. Add shrimp and sauté for 2 minutes. Do not overcook. Stir in red pepper. Place mixture in buttered 1½-quart casserole, and sprinkle with crumbled cheese. Bake at 425° for 10 to 15 minutes, or until cheese melts and is bubbly. Remove and allow to sit for 5 to 8 minutes. Sprinkle with remaining chopped parsley. Serve over cooked linguine, ziti, or rice. (May be made in advance). Serves 4.

Colorful and flavorful!

Pesto Sauce for Pasta

- 2 cups fresh basil
- 3 tablespoons pine nuts
- 2 cloves garlic, grated
- ½ teaspoon salt
- Dash pepper
- ½ cup Parmesan cheese, cut into hunks
- ¼ cup Romano cheese, cut into hunks
- ⅔ cup olive oil
- 2 tablespoons butter

Toast pine nuts in a small skillet in a bit of butter. Wash and drain the basil, removing the stems. Put all ingredients in a food processor and blend until smooth. Refrigerate. Makes 1½ cups.

Lasagna

1 tablespoon oil or 3 tablespoons margarine
1 medium onion, chopped
2 pounds ground beef
2 (16-ounce) cans tomatoes
2 (6-ounce) cans tomato paste
Salt and pepper
2 tablespoons parsley
2 tablespoons oregano
2 bay leaves (remove after cooking)
1 pound package lasagne noodles
1 pound cottage cheese
½ pound grated sharp Cheddar cheese
1 large package grated Swiss cheese
1 large package grated mozzarella cheese
Parmesan cheese

Brown meat and onions in oil. Add tomatoes, tomato paste, salt, pepper, parsley, oregano, bay leaves. Simmer 20 minutes. Cook noodles following package directions. Drain and put in cold water. In 9x13-inch baking pan, put **small** amount of sauce. Place a layer of noodles on top. Layer sauce, then put Cheddar cheese, followed by cottage cheese. Add another layer of noodles, more sauce, then Swiss cheese, another layer of noodles, followed by more sauce and mozzarella. End with sauce. Sprinkle with Parmesan cheese. Bake at 350° for 30 minutes. Serve with tossed salad, bread sticks, and red wine. Serves 6 to 8.

Shrimp Marinara

2 pounds fresh shrimp, cleaned
1 onion, chopped
½ teaspoon garlic powder
2 tablespoons olive oil
1 teaspoon dried parsley
Salt and pepper to taste
1 (14½-ounce) can plum (wedge) tomatoes
1 (6-ounce) can tomato paste
1 (6-ounce) can water
1 tablespoon oregano
1 tablespoon sugar
½ cup sherry

Brown onion in olive oil in saucepan. Add garlic powder, tomatoes, tomato paste, water, parsley, salt and pepper, oregano and sugar. Simmer 15 minutes. Add raw deveined shrimp and cook until shrimp is pink. Add sherry 10 minutes before serving. Serve over fettuccine. Serves 4 to 6.

Mother's Best Tomato Macaroni

- 2 tablespoons margarine
- ½ cup onions, chopped
- ½ cup bell pepper, chopped
- ½ cup celery, chopped
- 1 (8-ounce) can tomato purée
- ½ cup water
- Salt and pepper to taste
- 1 (8-ounce) box elbow macaroni
- 8 to 10 ounces grated medium Cheddar cheese
- Dash of hot sauce for taste

Sauté onion, bell pepper, celery in margarine. Add tomato purée, water, salt and pepper. Cook until it bubbles. Cook noodles according to box directions, drain. Mix macaroni and vegetables and all but ¼ of cheese. Transfer to a 2-quart greased casserole dish. Top with remaining cheese and bake for 30 minutes at 350°. Serves 8.

Linguine with White Clam Sauce

- ¼ cup pure olive oil
- 2 cloves garlic
- 1¼ cups clam juice
- ¼ cup parsley, chopped
- Salt and pepper to taste
- 2 cups minced clams
- 1 dozen fresh clams
- Linguine

In large skillet, brown garlic in oil for one minute over moderate heat. Add clam juice and bring to boil. Add parsley, salt, pepper, and minced clams. Heat through. Prepare linguine and drain. Pour sauce over linguine and garnish with fresh steamed whole clams in shell. Serves 6 to 8.

A pasta delight!

Beef Neapolitan

- 3 pounds stew meat
- 1½ teaspoons salt
- ¼ teaspoon pepper
- 1 clove garlic, minced
- 1 teaspoon parsley
- ¼ teaspoon oregano
- ½ teaspoon basil
- 1 large onion, chopped
- 1 (16-ounce) can tomatoes (Progresso)

Brown meat, and add rest of ingredients. Cover and simmer 4 hours. Serve on cooked spaghetti. Serves 6 to 8.

Pasta Primavera

- 2 small zucchini, thinly sliced
- 1 bunch broccoli (1-pound) cut into florets
- 8 ounces asparagus (fresh) cut into 1-inch pieces
- 1 pound linguine
- 12 to 14 cherry tomatoes, halved
- 1 large clove garlic, peeled and minced
- ¼ cup olive oil
- ½ pound mushrooms, sliced thinly
- 1 teaspoon basil
- ½ cup frozen peas, thawed
- ¼ cup parsley, minced
- 1½ teaspoons salt
- ¼ teaspoon pepper
- ¼ teaspoon crushed red pepper
- ¼ cup butter
- ¾ cup heavy cream
- ⅔ cup freshly grated Parmesan cheese
- 1 small can pitted ripe olives
- 1 medium red onion, sliced into rings

Cook zucchini, broccoli, and asparagus in boiling salted water to cover. Cook just until tender but still crisp. (About 5 minutes.) Drain well. In large pot, cook linguine in 5-quarts boiling water until tender, but firm. Drain the cooked linguine well. In large heavy skillet sauté tomatoes and garlic in olive oil for 2 minutes. Stir in sliced onions, mushrooms, and basil and continue cooking 3 minutes. Add peas, parsley, salt and pepper, and red pepper. Mix well, and cook 1 minute. Remove from heat, drain well and combine with zucchini, broccoli, and asparagus and toss lightly. Melt butter in skillet drippings, stir in cream and ⅓ cup Parmesan cheese, cooking over moderate heat until smooth. Add linguine, tossing lightly, then add vegetables and toss again lightly. Continue heating slowly just until vegetables are warm. Serve immediately. Garnish with remaining ⅓ cup cheese and sliced olives. Makes 6 servings. (complete meal).

Simply wonderful!

Simple Linguine

- 1 (8-ounce) package linguine
- ¼ pound bacon
- 1 cup onion
- 5 slices boiled ham, cut in strips
- ½ cup frozen peas
- ⅓ cup mushrooms
- ½ cup butter, melted
- ¾ cup chicken broth
- 2 eggs, well beaten
- ½ cup Parmesan cheese
- ½ cup parsley

Cook linguine. Fry bacon and set aside. Sauté onion in a little bacon grease. Stir in ham, peas, bacon, and mushrooms. Add drained linguine to vegetable mixture. Pour in melted butter and toss gently until linguine is well mixed. Add chicken broth and heat briefly. Remove from heat and quickly add eggs and blend well. Add parsley and sprinkle with Parmesan cheese. Season with pepper and serve. Serves 6 to 8.

Spaghetti Sauce À La Revel
Father McInerny's Favorite

- 1 pound hamburger or ground round
- 1 medium onion
- 1 bell pepper
- 1 small can mushrooms (optional)
- 1 or 2 cloves garlic
- 1 (16-ounce) can tomatoes
- 1 (16-ounce) can tomato sauce
- 1 (6-ounce) can tomato paste
- Oregano or Italian seasoning

Place hamburger, onion, bell pepper and garlic in frying pan on low heat and gently brown meat; drain grease. Add all of the above to remainder of ingredients (except mushrooms and oregano) to large pot or saucepan and simmer at least two hours. If using mushrooms, add them at end and be sure to drain the fluid from the can first. Also, add salt and pepper to taste and oregano after simmering. Serve over very thin spaghetti with lots of Parmesan cheese.

COMMENTS: Sauce is best when cooked the day before and allowed to simmer for two hours, refrigerated overnight then simmered some more the next day before serving. Can be doubled or tripled easily. Serves 6 to 8.

Father says, "Make sure you have plenty of bread, so your guests can sop up all the sauce."

Truly Southern Chicken Spaghetti

2 large onions, chopped
1 large bell pepper, chopped
1 stalk of celery, chopped
1 to 2 tablespoons of oil
4 (16-ounce) cans of tomatoes
2 small cans of tomato paste
2 small paste cans water
2 tablespoons oregano
2 tablespoons basil
2 teaspoons thyme
1 tablespoon salt
1 teaspoon pepper
1 tablespoon Worcestershire (can use more for flavor)
1 tablespoon of sugar
1 to 2 bay leaves
8 chicken breasts
Spaghetti noodles

In a large pot sauté your vegetables in oil, then add your tomatoes, tomato paste and cans of water. Add spices. Bring to a boil and add chicken breasts with the skin on. (The skin helps give flavor to sauce while cooking, when you take chicken out, discard skin). Turn down to simmer and cook until chicken breasts are done, approximately 25 minutes. Take chicken out, let cool, take off skin and discard. Cut chicken off bone and cut into bite-size pieces and add back to sauce. Continue cooking for another 1 to 1½-hours and add more spices until you get the flavor you want. Serve over noodles. Serves 8.

This is best if made at least a day in advance and sits in refrigerator overnight. Also good to make and freeze. You can use your own recipe and add chicken as above.

This was my mother's recipe and a favorite of our family.

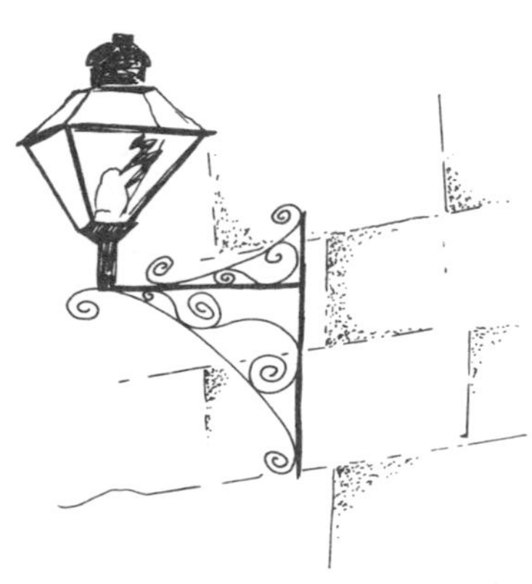

Vegetable Lasagna

- 1 cup onion, chopped
- 1 tablespoon garlic, minced
- 1 cup green pepper, chopped
- 2 teaspoons basil
- 1 teaspoon oregano
- 2 bay leaves
- 3 tablespoons olive oil
- 29 ounces tomato purée
- 1 (6-ounce) can tomato paste
- 2 tablespoons dry red wine
- 1 cup fresh tomatoes, chopped
- ½ teaspoon black pepper
- ½ cup fresh cut parsley
- 12 lasagna noodles, cooked, drained and rinsed in cold water

Filling:

- 2 cups low-fat cottage cheese
- ½ pound raw spinach, chopped
- 3 cups kidney beans, cooked
- ½ pound shredded mozzarella cheese (part skim)
- ½ cup Parmesan cheese, grated

Sauté first six ingredients in olive oil and add purée, paste, wine, tomato and peppers. Cover and simmer 45 minutes, stirring occasionally. Add parsley.

Spread sauce over bottom of 9x13-inch pan. Cover with ⅓ of noodles, ½ cup of cottage cheese, ½ of spinach, ½ of beans, ⅓ of remaining sauce and ½ of mozzarella cheese. Continue to layer as listed above. On top layer, put noodles and sauce, and top with Parmesan cheese. Bake at 350° for 35 to 45 minutes.

Station 9 Seafood Fettuccine

- **½ pound fresh mushrooms, sliced**
- **1¼ pounds zucchini, cut into julienne strips**
- **1½ sticks of real butter, divided**
- **1½ pounds uncooked shrimp, peeled and deveined and cut into bite size pieces**
- **1 pound fresh scallops, uncooked and cut into bite size pieces (if you do not want scallops, add a little more shrimp)**
- **1 cup half and half**
- **1 pound fettuccine**
- **Salt and pepper**
- **¾ cup of fresh grated Parmesan cheese**

In a large skillet sauté the mushrooms and zucchini in ½ stick of butter until soft. Remove from skillet and put in large pot. Then sauté shrimp and scallops in ½ stick of butter for a few minutes until done. Add this to large pot with sautéed vegetables, add your remaining ½ stick of butter and cup of half and half. Bring to a boil, then turn down and simmer for about five minutes. Season with salt and pepper.

In a large pot cook a pound of fettuccine according to directions on package. Have this cooked and drained and ready while your sauce is cooking. (I find that the curly noodles are better for this than the flat ones).

Take your cooked fettuccine and add to your pasta sauce. You may need to transfer all of this to a larger pot then add your Parmesan cheese, mix well and serve. Top with parsley if desired. All you need to go with this is a salad and rolls.

You will find this easier to prepare if you have your vegetables cut up and your shrimp peeled, deveined and cut up. I do all of this earlier in the day so when I go to prepare pasta most of the preparation is done and it probably takes only about 20 to 30 minutes to have ready to serve. Serves 8.

This is delicious.

Cheese, Eggs, & Grits

Cheese, Eggs & Grits

Bishop's Brunch Casserole

- 1 to 2 pounds sausage, cooked and drained
- 2 cups milk
- 4 eggs, slightly beaten (egg substitute may be used)
- 1 small can mushrooms, drained
- 3 cups Cheddar cheese, grated
- 1 teaspoon dry mustard
- 1 teaspoon onion powder
- 1 teaspoon Worcestershire sauce
- 1½ tablespoons dry onion or ⅓ cup onion, finely chopped
- 8 slices bread, cut off crust and cut in slices (give crusts to the birds)
- 1 can cream of mushroom soup
- ⅓ cup milk
- Paprika

Combine first nine ingredients and set aside. Butter a 9x13-inch glass casserole and line with bread strips. Pour mixture over bread strips. Cover and let set 6 hours or overnight in the refrigerator. May be frozen at this point. Before baking pour the mushroom soup mixed with the milk over the casserole and sprinkle with the paprika. Bake uncovered in a preheated 325° oven for 1½ hours or until firm enough to spoon easily. Enjoy!

Brunch Casserole

- 2½ cups seasoned croutons
- 1½ pounds bulk sausage
- 4 eggs, beaten
- 2¼ cups milk
- 1 (10-ounce) can cream of mushroom soup
- 1 (4-ounce) can sliced mushrooms, drained
- ¾ teaspoon dry mustard
- 2 cups Cheddar cheese, shredded
- Cherry tomatoes, halved
- Parsley sprigs

Spread croutons in lightly greased 13x9x2-inch baking dish. Brown sausage, crumble and drain. Sprinkle over croutons. Mix together eggs, milk, soup, mushrooms and mustard. Pour over sausage. Cover and refrigerate and let stand 30 minutes before baking. Bake uncovered at 325° for 50 to 55 minutes. Sprinkle cheese on top and bake for an additional 5 minutes. Cut cherry tomatoes in halves. Make a design with tomatoes and parsley to garnish. Serves 8 to 10.

Concerned about fat and cholesterol? Substitute turkey sausage, egg beaters and low-fat cheese.

Country Brunch

16 slices firm white bread
2½ cups cooked ham, cubed (about 1-pound)
16 ounces Cheddar cheese, shredded
16 ounces mozzarella cheese, shredded
6 eggs
3 cups whole milk
½ teaspoon dry mustard
⅛ to ¼ teaspoon onion powder

Trim crust from bread and cut slices in half. Grease 13x9x2-inch baking pan and layer as follows: ½ the bread, ½ the ham and ½ of each cheese. Repeat. Combine eggs, milk, mustard and onion powder and pour over layers. Refrigerate overnight. Remove 30 minutes before baking.

Topping:
2 cups corn flakes, uncrushed
½ cup butter, melted

Add topping. Bake at 375° for 45 minutes uncovered. Remove from oven. Cover loosely with foil and let stand 15 minutes. Serves 6 to 8.

Sunnyside Egg and Sausage Casserole

6 to 8 hard boiled eggs
1 pound hot sausage
1½ cups sour cream
¼ cup breadcrumbs
1½ cups Cheddar cheese

Slice eggs and place in buttered 11x7-inch casserole. Cook and drain sausage. Spread over eggs. Spread sour cream over sausage. Combine breadcrumbs and cheese and sprinkle over sour cream. Bake at 350° 20 to 30 minutes until heated through and bubbly. Serves 6.

A teachers' brunch during exams.

Brunch Party Eggs

- **3 dozen eggs**
- **2 cans cream of mushroom soup**
- **2 cups sliced mushrooms**
- **2 cups sharp cheese, grated**
- **¼ cup sherry**
- **½ cup onion, finely chopped**
- **½ cup ground pepper**

Using two large skillets, scramble eggs until just set. Place in large bowl. Mix other ingredients well. Toss gently with eggs. Bake in three 13x9-inch casseroles for 30 minutes at 350°. Bring to room temperature before baking. Serves 20.

Serve with fresh fruit bowl.

Baked Cheese Grits

- **1 cup grits (not instant)**
- **½ cup margarine or butter**
- **1 (6-ounce) package Kraft garlic cheese spread**
- **2 eggs**
- **½ cup milk (skim or regular)**
- **1 cup mild Cheddar cheese, grated**

Cook grits according to directions on box. Add margarine and garlic cheese spread. Stir until melted. Beat eggs and milk together. Add to mixture. Pour into 2-quart Pyrex baking dish. Top with grated Cheddar cheese. Bake at 350°, uncovered, until set, about 45 minutes. Serve hot. Serves 6 to 8.

Mimi's Fried Grits

- **1 cup hominy grits**
- **6 tablespoons bacon drippings or vegetable oil**
- **2 eggs, beaten**
- **1½ cups breadcrumbs**

Cook grits according to directions. Spread in loaf pan or pour into tall glasses and refrigerate until thoroughly chilled and molded. Cut into ½-inch slices. Melt the bacon drippings in skillet. Dip the slices of grits in the egg mixture and then in breadcrumbs coating both sides thoroughly. Fry in skillet 3 minutes on each side or until hot and golden brown. Serves 2 to 4.

Serve with eggs, bacon and maple syrup for breakfast, or as a side dish with a meal.

Grits 'N Shrimp

- **2 slices bacon**
- **1 medium sweet onion, sliced**
- **2 cups medium raw shrimp, peeled and deveined**
- **¼ cup lemon juice**
- **1 egg yolk**
- **Grits, cooked according to directions on package**

Fry bacon in fry pan until crisp, remove and crumble bacon. Sauté onion in bacon drippings until translucent. Add shrimp and toss until pink. Remove shrimp from pan with slotted spoon and set aside. Mix the egg yolk and lemon juice in measuring cup and add to the shrimp liquid. Stir constantly over medium heat until thickened (two or three minutes). Return shrimp and bacon to fry pan, bring to simmer (but do not cook) and serve on hot grits. Serves 4 to 6.

VARIATION: In place of lemon juice and egg yolk, mix 1 tablespoon flour and ¼ teaspoon instant coffee in ½ cup water and add to shrimp liquid. Makes brown gravy.

Quiche Olé

- **2 (9-inch) flour tortillas**
- **1½ cups Monterey Jack cheese, shredded**
- **3 eggs, slightly beaten**
- **1 cup sour cream**
- **1 (4-ounce) can green chiles, chopped**
- **¼ teaspoon salt**
- **¼ teaspoon cumin**

Line a greased 9-inch pie pan with the tortillas overlapping. Mix other ingredients and put into this shell. Bake at 350° for 45 minutes. Serve hot or cold. Travels well for tailgate or picnic. Serves 6.

NOTE: Tortillas are more flexible to work with if you warm them slightly.

Low Country Ham Quiche

- (9-inch) pastry for quiche or pie pan
- ½ cup mayonnaise
- 2 tablespoons flour
- 4 eggs, beaten
- ½ cup milk
- 1 cup cooked ham, diced
- 1 cup Cheddar cheese, shredded
- 1 cup Swiss cheese, shredded
- ⅓ cup onion, grated (optional

Line quiche or pie pan with pastry (or use frozen deep dish pie shell). Bake for 3 minutes at 400°. Remove from oven and prick with fork. Bake 5 minutes longer; let cool on a rack.

Combine mayonnaise, flour, eggs and milk. Mix thoroughly; stir in the ham and cheeses and onion. Pour into pastry shell and bake at 350° for 45 to 50 minute. Enjoy! Serves 6.

Sausage Cheddar Quiche

- Pastry for 9-inch pie pan
- 1 pound pork sausage, hot or regular
- 1 (4-ounce) can sliced mushrooms, drained
- ½ cup onion, chopped
- ¼ cup green pepper, chopped
- 1 teaspoon minced parsley
- ½ teaspoon whole basil leaves
- Dash of granulated garlic
- ⅛ teaspoon salt
- 1½ cups Cheddar cheese, shredded
- 1 cup whipping cream
- 2 eggs
- Paprika

Prick shell and bake until brown, cool. Cook sausage until browned, drain. Combine next seven ingredients in a large bowl and mix well. Spoon into shell and top with cheese. Combine cream and eggs beating until foamy. Pour over cheese and sprinkle with paprika. Bake at 325° for 50 minutes or until cheese is lightly brown and quiche is set. Serves 6.

Serve with fresh fruit, warm rolls and dessert for an easy baby shower.

Crabmeat Quiche

- **1 (8-inch) pie shell, unbaked**
- **2 eggs**
- **1 cup light cream (half and half)**
- **1 teaspoon MSG**
- **¾ teaspoon salt**
- **1 dash cayenne pepper**
- **3 ounces Swiss cheese, grated**
- **3 ounces Gruyère cheese, grated**
- **1 tablespoon flour**
- **1 (6½-ounce) can crabmeat, flaked (1 cup chopped shrimp or tuna may be substituted)**

Prick bottom and sides of pie shell with a fork. Bake at 450° for 10 minutes or until delicate brown. Combine eggs, cream, MSG, salt and cayenne pepper, beat well. Combine cheeses, flour and crabmeat, sprinkle evenly into pie shell. Pour cream mixture into pie shell. Bake at 325° for 45 minutes to 1 hour until tip of knife inserted into center comes out clean. Cut into small wedges. Serves 6 to 8.

Turkey Strata

- **1 pound fresh mushrooms, sliced (or 8-ounce can, drained)**
- **½ cup onion, finely chopped**
- **¼ cup butter**
- **10 slices white bread**
- **2 cups processed American cheese, shredded**
- **2 cups cooked turkey, diced**
- **5 eggs, slightly beaten**
- **2¾ cups milk**
- **1 teaspoon salt**
- **⅛ teaspoon pepper**

Sauté mushrooms and onions in butter until soft. Trim crust off bread, and reserve crust. With cookie cutter, cut 3-inch rounds from bread slices. Tear the bread crusts and the excess after cutting rounds, and place in bottom of greased 3-quart casserole dish. Cover the bread with mushroom-onion mix. Sprinkle a layer of cheese and layer of turkey over the mushroom-onion mix. Arrange the rounds of bread, overlapping around the outer section of casserole dish. Combine the eggs, milk, salt and pepper, and pour over the casserole, being sure to moisten the bread rounds well. Bake at 350° for 1 hour and 15 minutes until top is lightly brown and center is set. Serves 8.

Great way to use left-over turkey.

Vegetable Quiche

2 tablespoons butter or margarine
1 package frozen chopped broccoli (or spinach), thawed
½ teaspoon salt
Dash white pepper
½ teaspoon dill
½ teaspoon shallots, dried
3 eggs
1 cup heavy cream
8 ounces Swiss cheese, grated (Cheddar cheese or 4-ounces of both)
Parmesan cheese

Melt butter or margarine in skillet. Add thoroughly drained broccoli, salt, pepper, dill and shallots and cook until tender. Set aside. Whisk eggs and heavy cream together; set aside.

Prepare pastry:
1½ cups plain flour
½ teaspoon salt
½ cup butter or margarine (use cold butter sliced into 8 pieces)
4 to 5 tablespoons cold water

Combine flour, salt and butter in food processor; mix until fine crumbs. Add water 1 tablespoon at a time until pastry forms ball while mixing. Roll crust to fit quiche pan or 9-inch pie pan. Place cold mixture over crust; sprinkle grated cheese over top; pour in liquid mixture and sprinkle Parmesan cheese on top. Bake in oven at 350° for 30 to 40 minutes until golden brown and firm. Serves 8.

Plantation Grits and Sausage

½ cup uncooked grits
2 pounds mild bulk sausage
4 cups extra sharp Cheddar cheese, grated
4 eggs, beaten
1 cup milk
½ teaspoon thyme
⅛ teaspoon garlic salt

Cook and drain sausage, set aside. Cook grits as per directions on package. Mix cheese and grits in a large mixing bowl. Combine eggs, milk, thyme, and garlic salt in medium bowl. Add a small amount of hot grits and mix well, then add to grits and cheese. Mix well and pour into a 13x9-inch baking dish. Cover and refrigerate overnight. Remove from refrigerator and let stand 15 minutes before baking. Bake at 350° for about one hour. Serves 8 to 10.

Overnight Eggnog French Toast

9 eggs
3 cups half and half or milk
⅓ cup sugar
½ teaspoon nutmeg
1½ teaspoons rum extract
24 (¾-inch) slices French bread
Powdered sugar
Praline sauce

Grease two 15x10-inch baking pans (Teflon is best). In large bowl combine eggs, half and half, sugar, nutmeg, vanilla and rum extract. Beat until well blended. Arrange bread slices in greased baking pans. Pour egg mixture over bread. Lift and move bread slices until all egg mixture is absorbed. Cover with foil. Refrigerate overnight or freeze up to one week. Preheat oven to 500°. Remove foil and place in oven straight from refrigerator or freezer. Bake one pan for 15 minutes or until golden brown. Sprinkle with powdered sugar or serve with praline sauce. Repeat with second pan. Makes 24 slices.

Praline Sauce:

1½ cups brown sugar
½ cup light corn syrup
½ cup water
2 tablespoons butter
½ cup chopped pecans

Combine sugar, corn syrup and water in a small saucepan. Bring to a boil. Simmer 2 to 3 minutes stirring occasionally. Add butter and pecans and heat one minute. Serve hot.

And you thought it was impossible to serve everyone "hot" French toast at one time!

Easy Brunch

2 cups plain croutons
4 ounces Cheddar cheese
4 slices bacon, crumbled
7 eggs
½ teaspoon salt
½ teaspoon prepared mustard
⅛ teaspoon onion powder
Dash pepper

Cook 4 slices of bacon, drain and crumble. Place croutons in 10x16-inch greased casserole. Sprinkle with cheese. Beat eggs and add seasonings. Pour mixture over croutons and cheese. Sprinkle with bacon. Place in preheated 325° oven. Cook 55 to 60 minutes. Serves 6.

COOKIES & CANDY

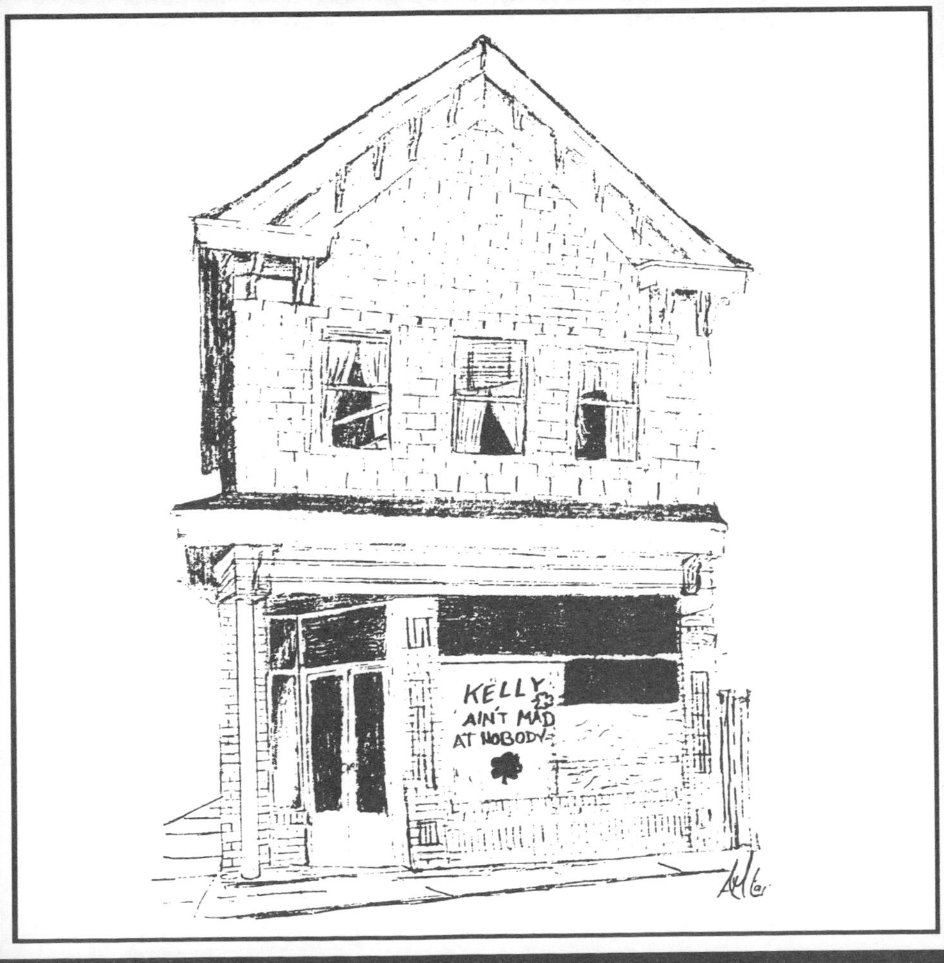

KELLY
AIN'T MAD
AT NOBODY

Cookies & Candy

Pat's Candy Supreme (Penuche)

1 box brown sugar (light or dark)
1 cup powdered sugar
1 cup less 1 tablespoon evaporated milk
3 tablespoons butter
½ teaspoon vanilla
1 cup pecans or walnuts

In heavy saucepan mix sugars and evaporated milk, bring to a boil over medium heat, stirring constantly. Add 1 tablespoon butter, boil, stirring constantly, until mixture forms soft ball when dropped in cold water. Remove from heat. Let cool down a few minutes. While still warm, add the remaining 2 tablespoons butter and vanilla. Beat vigorously until the mixture is smooth and loses its sheen. Add nuts. Pour on well-buttered pan or platter. When almost cool, cut into squares.

Mary Ann's Pralines

1 box light brown sugar
6 ounces of evaporated milk
1 tablespoon butter
1 pinch salt
1 teaspoon vanilla
1 cup nuts, chopped

Mix together sugar, milk, butter and salt and bring to a soft ball stage. Take off heat and beat until smooth (about 110 strokes). Add vanilla and nuts. Spoon out by teaspoon on wax paper. Makes 2 to 3 dozen.

Chocolate Toffee Crunch

- **1 cup walnuts, chopped**
- **¾ cup brown sugar**
- **½ cup butter**
- **1 cup semi-sweet chocolate chips**

Sprinkle walnuts on bottom of greased 9x9-inch pan. Combine sugar and butter in a saucepan. Bring to a boil and boil 7 minutes, stirring constantly. Spread over nuts. Sprinkle chips on top so that they will melt, then spread with a knife. Refrigerate to set. Cut into pieces; will crack apart. Makes 16 to 24 pieces.

Mounds

- **1 cup butter**
- **1 can Eagle Brand milk**
- **2 boxes powdered sugar**
- **2½ cups pecans, chopped**
- **1 (14-ounce) bag of coconut**
- **3 large packages of semi-sweet chocolate chips**
- **¾ stick paraffin wax**

Melt butter with the milk over low heat. Add sugar, pecans and coconut. Spread mixture into a jelly roll pan. Use waxed paper to press this mixture evenly in pan. Freeze for 45 minutes. Cut into small 1½-inch fingers. Melt the chocolate and paraffin in pot over low heat. Dip the squares into the chocolate using a toothpick. Let excess chocolate drip back into pan and then place on waxed paper.

Simply delicious!! A wonderful "gracious" gift!

Old Fashioned Chocolate Fudge

- **3 cups sugar**
- **4 heaping tablespoons cocoa**
- **1 cup evaporated milk**
- **4 tablespoons butter**
- **1 cup nuts (optional)**

Combine sugar, cocoa and milk in saucepan, place on low heat stirring occasionally. This takes awhile so do something in the kitchen while this cooks. Cook until a drop forms a soft ball in water. Remove from heat and add butter—beat by hand until thick. Pour into a greased 9x9-inch pan.

Enjoy!! It's worth the trouble!

Chocolate Fudge

- **1 large can evaporated milk**
- **4½ cups sugar**
- **3 (9-ounce) Hershey bars, broken into pieces**
- **2 (6-ounce) packages bittersweet chocolate chips**
- **1 (8-ounce) jar marshmallow creme**
- **2 teaspoons vanilla**
- **1½ cups nuts**

Mix milk and sugar. Bring to a boil, stirring constantly. Boil for 4½ minutes. Remove from heat. Pour hot mixture over other ingredients in large bowl and mix only long enough to melt chocolate. Pour in buttered 9x13-inch dish. Makes 5 pounds.

"Satisfied a houseful of chocoholics."

Turtles

- **1 package of candy caramel squares**
- **1 tablespoon of butter**
- **1 tablespoon of water**
- **1 cup pecans, chopped**
- **1 (6-ounce) package semi-sweet chocolate chips**
- **½ block paraffin**

Melt caramels with butter and water in top of double boiler. Add nuts. Drop by teaspoon onto a buttered cookie sheet to cool. Melt chocolate chips and paraffin in the top of a double boiler. When thoroughly blended dip cooled caramels into chocolate to cover completely. Place on waxed paper and cool. Store in cool place. Makes 2 to 3 dozen.

What-Cha-Ma-Call-Its (Date Nut Log)

- **½ cup margarine**
- **1 cup sugar**
- **1 cup dates, chopped**
- **1 teaspoon vanilla**
- **2 cups Rice Krispies**
- **¾ cup nuts, chopped**
- **Coconut**

Heat margarine over low heat. Stir in sugar until dissolves. Add dates and mix well. Remove from heat and add Rice Krispies, vanilla and nuts. When cool enough to handle shape into two 1½x12-inch logs. Roll in coconut pressing coconut into log while rolling. Wrap in waxed paper. Cool for 1 hour in refrigerator. Slice and keep in cool place. Makes about 36 pieces.

Peanut Butter Fudge

- **4 cups sugar**
- **1 cup butter or margarine**
- **3 tablespoons white corn syrup**
- **1 (5-ounce) can evaporated milk**
- **2 cups peanut butter**
- **1 (7-ounce) jar marshmallow creme**
- **1 teaspoon vanilla**
- **1 cup nuts, chopped (any kind)**

In saucepan, melt butter and add sugar, syrup and milk. Bring to bubbling boil; reduce heat to medium. Cook and stir constantly 5 minutes. Remove from heat; add peanut butter, marshmallow creme, nuts and vanilla. Blend until thoroughly mixed and thick enough to pour. Pour into buttered 13x9-inch pan. Makes 3 to 4 dozen pieces.

Delicious!! "I brought a plate of this to the lunchroom and it was gone in minutes."

"You Won't Believe 'Em" (Toffee)

- **1 cup butter**
- **1 cup light brown sugar**
- **1 (11-ounce) package Nestles milk chocolate chips**
- **40 saltine crackers**
- **1 cup pecans, chopped**
- **Jelly roll pan**

Line jelly roll pan with aluminum foil and spray with Pam. Lay saltines flat on foil. Melt sugar and butter together, heat until "foamy". Pour mixture over crackers evenly. Put in oven and bake 350° for 10 minutes. Take out and while still hot, pour chocolate chips over crackers. Let melt a minute or two and then spread with spoon to coat crackers. Sprinkle pecans over this. Let cool and then put in refrigerator until hard. Crack up and put in your favorite candy dish, Mason jar decorated for a special holiday or in a tin!! Store in a cool place. Makes 1 jelly roll pan.

This is a wonderful gift for Christmas. Excellent for the boss or your favorite physician. Always a big hit!!!

Almond Cookies

- **2 cups all-purpose flour**
- **1 teaspoon baking powder**
- **1 teaspoon baking soda**
- **1 cup shortening**
- **1 cup sugar**
- **1 teaspoon vanilla extract**
- **½ teaspoon almond extract**
- **1 egg**
- **1 egg yolk**
- **1 tablespoon water**
- **4 dozen whole almonds (about ½ cup)**

Combine first three ingredients. Set aside. Cream shortening, gradually add sugar, beating until light and fluffy. Stir in vanilla and almond extract. Add whole egg, beating well. Add dry ingredients and mix well. Combine egg yolk and water, mix well. Shape dough into ¾-inch balls. Press an almond into center of each cookie. Brush with egg yolk mixture. Bake on ungreased cookie sheet at 350° for 10 to 12 minutes. Cool on wire racks. Makes about 4 dozen.

Aunt Ag's Oatmeal Cookies

- **1 cup all-purpose flour, sifted**
- **1 teaspoon baking powder**
- **½ teaspoon salt**
- **1 teaspoon cinnamon**
- **1 teaspoon allspice**
- **1 teaspoon nutmeg**
- **¾ cup soft shortening or margarine**
- **1 cup brown sugar**
- **2 eggs**
- **⅓ cup milk**
- **1 cup nuts, chopped**
- **3 cups old fashioned oatmeal**
- **1 cup raisins (optional)**

Sift flour, baking powder, salt and spices, Cream shortening, sugar and eggs. Add dry ingredients in thirds, alternating with milk. Mix in oatmeal, nuts and raisins (if used). Drop by teaspoonful onto ungreased cookie sheet. Bake at 375° for 12 to 15 minutes. Makes 6 dozen.

Crescent Cookies

1 cup butter or margarine
2 cups all-purpose flour
2 cups pecans, chopped
5 tablespoons sugar
2 teaspoons vanilla
1 tablespoon water
½ teaspoon salt

Cream butter and add sugar, vanilla, and water. Sift flour and salt together and stir into mixture. Add pecans and mix thoroughly. Using portions about size of small walnut, roll into crescent shaped cookies. Bake in slow oven (325°) about 20 minutes. While warm, roll in powdered sugar. Makes 2 to 3 dozen.

Yummie! Perfect for Holiday parties!

Crisp Ginger Snaps

¾ cup butter
1 cup sugar
¼ cup light molasses
1 egg, beaten
2 cups all-purpose flour
2 teaspoons soda
¼ teaspoon salt
1 teaspoon cinnamon
1 teaspoon ground cloves (optional)
1 teaspoon ginger
Sugar for dipping

Cream together sugar and butter. Beat egg lightly. Add egg and molasses to sugar and butter mixture. Combine dry ingredients and add to above. Mix well. Chill dough. Roll into small balls. Dip in sugar. Place 2-inches apart on cookie sheet. Bake at 375° for approximately 12 minutes until done. Makes 4 dozen.

This recipe makes the old fashioned cracked on top variety. For crisp, flat ones, wet the bottom of a glass, dip in a sugar cinnamon mixture. Mash balls flat before baking.

Farmer's Daughter Chocolate Chip Cookies

1 cup white sugar
1 cup brown sugar
1 cup Crisco
2 eggs
1 teaspoon vanilla
1 tablespoon water
2 cups all-purpose flour
1 teaspoon salt
1 teaspoon baking soda
1 (12-ounce) bag of chocolate chips
1 cup nuts

Preheat oven at 300°. Do not use mixer—Must stir by hand. Cream sugars and Crisco, add eggs one at a time stirring after each egg. Add vanilla and water. Gradually add the flour, salt and soda — mixing well. Stir in chocolate chips and nuts.

Place oven rack on second shelf from top. Line the bottom rack with foil. Bake the cookies on an ungreased cookie sheet 10 to 15 minutes until light brown or golden. Makes 3 dozen.

Winnie's Peanut Butter Cookies

½ cup margarine
½ cup peanut butter (smooth or crunchy)
½ cup sugar
½ cup brown sugar
1 egg
1¼ cups sifted all-purpose flour
½ teaspoon baking powder
¾ teaspoon baking soda
¼ teaspoon salt

In large bowl of electric mixer, cream together margarine, peanut butter, sugar and brown sugar until smooth. Add egg, blend. Sift together remaining ingredients. Add in thirds to creamed mixture until smooth. Chill dough, covered, about 1 hour or longer. (Dough may be made a day or so ahead.) Roll into balls size of large walnuts. Place 3-inches apart on lightly greased baking sheet. Flatten with fork dipped in flour, crisscross. Bake in 375° oven 10 to 12 minutes, until set, but not hard. Makes 3 dozen.

VARIATION: Before baking, press ½ peanut in middle of each cookie; or, immediately after baking, press chocolate kiss in middle of each cookie.

Maureen's A #1 Cookie

2 cups all-purpose flour
1 teaspoon soda
½ teaspoon salt
1 cup margarine
½ cup sugar
¾ cup brown sugar
1 teaspoon vanilla
1 egg
½ cup nuts, chopped
½ cup raisins
½ cup oatmeal

Mix dry ingredients together and set aside. In large bowl mix butter, sugars and vanilla. Beat in the egg. Gradually add dry ingredients. Add raisins and oatmeal last. Drop by tablespoons onto ungreased baking sheets. Bake 8 to 10 minutes at 375°. Let cool slightly and remove with spatula. You can omit oatmeal and raisins and add chocolate chips. Makes about 36 large cookies.

With glass of cold milk, these are "Gone with the wind".

Monster Cookies

½ cup butter
1 cup sugar
1 cup and 2 tablespoons brown sugar
3 eggs
2 cups crunchy peanut butter
¾ tablespoon light corn syrup
¼ teaspoon vanilla
4½ cups oatmeal
2 teaspoons baking soda
¼ teaspoon salt
1 cup M & M's
1 (6-ounce) bag chocolate chips
1 cup raisins (optional)

Cream butter with sugars and eggs one at a time. Mix well and add the peanut butter, corn syrup, vanilla, oatmeal, baking soda and salt. Again mix well. Stir in M & M's, chocolate chips and raisins. Bake at 350° for 12 to 15 minutes. Makes about 6 dozen cookies.

An Irish Grandmother's Baklava

- **1 pound pecans, finely chopped (don't make a powder)**
- **½ cup sugar**
- **1 tablespoon vanilla**
- **1 tablespoon orange water**
- **1 pound unsalted butter, clarified**
- **1 package phyllo dough**
- **1 or 2 pastry brushes (depending on how many making baklava)**

Syrup:

- **1 cup water**
- **3 cups sugar**
- **2 tablespoons lemon juice**

Heat oven to 325°. Mix pecans, sugar, vanilla and orange water for filling and set aside. Clarify butter by placing over low heat until butter is clear. Make syrup by combining water, sugar and lemon juice over low heat until mixture thickens. To assemble, unfold phyllo and cut carefully in half, crosswise. Cover phyllo with damp cloth. Gently lift one piece of phyllo and place narrow side toward you. Brush with melted butter, and place 1 teaspoon of filling in center of dough closest to you. Fold long sides in ¼-inch, then fold bottom of phyllo over filling. Roll like a pencil into a cigar like cylinder. Place roll on cookie sheet. Continue until all dough is used. Bake about 25 minutes at 325° until golden. Brush each pastry with cooled syrup. Place each pastry into cupcake papers and store in tins. Can be frozen. Makes 6 dozen.

Kevin's Brownie Drop Cookies

- **4 (4-ounce) bars German chocolate**
- **2 tablespoons butter**
- **4 eggs**
- **1½ cups sugar**
- **½ cup all-purpose flour**
- **½ teaspoon baking powder**
- **½ teaspoon salt**
- **½ teaspoon cinnamon**
- **½ teaspoon vanilla**
- **1½ cups pecans, chopped**

Melt chocolate and butter over double boiler slowly or in microwave at half-power. **Cool**. Beat eggs, adding one at a time, until thick and foamy; add sugar gradually. Beat 5 minutes. Blend in **cooled** chocolate. Add flour, baking powder, salt and cinnamon. Add vanilla and nuts. Mix until well-blended. Chill at least one hour. Drop by teaspoon on a lightly greased cookie sheet. Bake at 350° until cookie looks set and shiny (8 to 10 minutes). Cool slightly before removing from pan. Makes 4 dozen.

Snickerdoodles

- 1 cup margarine
- 1½ cups sugar
- 2 eggs
- 2¾ cups all-purpose flour
- 1 teaspoon baking soda
- ¼ teaspoon salt
- 2 teaspoons cream of tartar
- 1 teaspoon vanilla

Mixture to roll dough in:

- 2 tablespoons sugar
- 2 tablespoons cinnamon

Cream margarine and sugar well. Beat in eggs thoroughly. Sift dry ingredients together. Add to creamed mixture in thirds. Add vanilla. Chill dough. Roll into walnut size balls. Roll in sugar/cinnamon mixture. Place 2-inches apart on ungreased baking sheet. Bake at 350° for 8 to 10 minutes. (Cookies puff up at first, then flatten out.) Do not overbake. Makes about 5 dozen 2-inch cookies.

Sour Cream Twists

- 3½ cups all-purpose flour
- 2 eggs
- 8 ounces sour cream
- 1 teaspoon vanilla
- 1 package yeast (dissolved in warm water)
- ½ cup butter
- ½ cup Crisco
- 1 cup sugar

Mix the above ingredients by hand until well-blended. Cover with a wet dish towel and let it rise in the refrigerator for 2 hours. Divide the dough in half. Cover unused portion and refrigerate. Sprinkle sugar on counter and roll half the dough to measure approximately 8x16-inches. Sprinkle with sugar. Fold ends to center and roll out to 8x16-inches again and sprinkle with sugar. Make both ends meet in the middle. Repeat this 3 times. Cut in the middle; then strips. This should yield 12 to 16 pieces. Twist into horseshoe shape. Bake at 375° until lightly brown.

Don't forget the second portion of dough in the refrigerator.

BEHS' Favorite Brownies

Brownies:

- **1 cup margarine**
- **1 cup water**
- **4 heaping tablespoons cocoa**
- **2 cups sifted all-purpose flour**
- **2 cups sugar**
- **½ teaspoon salt**
- **½ cup sour cream**
- **1 teaspoon baking soda**
- **2 eggs**

Combine butter, water and cocoa in saucepan. Heat to boiling stirring occasionally. Remove from heat and add to flour, sugar and salt in mixing bowl. Beat with mixer until well mixed. Add sour cream, soda and eggs. Mix until blended. Put into greased 15x11x2-inch pan. Bake in preheated oven at 375° for 22 minutes. Meanwhile prepare frosting. Remove from oven when baked. Spread frosting over cake while hot. Cool in pan or rack. Cut into squares. Store in refrigerator.

Icing:

- **½ cup margarine**
- **6 tablespoons milk**
- **4 tablespoons cocoa**
- **1 pound box powdered sugar**
- **1 teaspoon vanilla**
- **1 cup nuts, chopped**

Combine margarine, milk and cocoa in saucepan. Heat to boiling, stirring frequently until mixture bubbles, remove from heat. Beat in powdered sugar, vanilla and chopped nuts. Spread on hot cake. Makes 3 dozen squares.

NOTE: Frosting can be prepared in same saucepan as brownie mixture.

Cheesecake Squares

Crust:

- **1 cup all-purpose flour**
- **¼ cup light brown sugar, packed**
- **1 cup pecans, finely chopped**
- **½ cup butter, melted**

In a small bowl mix flour, brown sugar, pecans and butter and press into bottom of 13x9-inch glass baking dish. Bake at 325° for 10 to 15 minutes or until brown.

Filling:

- **16 ounces cream cheese**
- **1 cup sugar**
- **1 teaspoon vanilla**
- **3 eggs**

In a bowl beat cream cheese, sugar and vanilla. Add eggs and beat well. Pour over crust. Bake 20 minutes or until set.

Glaze:

- **6 tablespoons sugar**
- **1 teaspoon vanilla**
- **2 cups sour cream**

In a small bowl mix sour cream, sugar and vanilla and pour over baked filling. Bake 3 to 5 minutes. Cool and refrigerate before cutting into squares. Makes 4 dozen.

Chinese Chews

- **1⅔ cups all-purpose flour**
- **½ cup and 1 tablespoon butter or margarine**
- **3 eggs**
- **2 teaspoons baking powder**
- **1 pound light brown sugar**
- **1 teaspoon vanilla**
- **½ to 1 cup nuts, chopped**
- **Powdered sugar**

Mix first seven ingredients until well-blended. Pour into greased and floured baking pan (approximately 9x13-inch). Bake at 325° for 30 to 35 minutes or until golden brown. Sift powdered sugar on top while warm. Cut in squares when cooled. This makes about 36 squares. A larger pan may be used to get more pieces.

Chocolate Sherry Cream Bars

Bars:

- **4 ounces unsweetened baking chocolate**
- **1 cup margarine**
- **4 eggs**
- **2 cups sugar**
- **1 cup all-purpose flour**
- **½ teaspoon salt**
- **1 teaspoon vanilla**

Melt chocolate and margarine over hot water, cool slightly. Beat eggs until light. Cream in sugar. Add remaining ingredients. Beat 1 minute. Pour into greased and floured 10x14-inch pan. Bake 25 minutes in moderate oven. Cool.

Filling:

- **½ cup butter**
- **4 cups powdered sugar**
- **¼ cup half and half**
- **¼ cup sherry**
- **1 cup nuts, chopped**

Beat butter and sugar together gradually adding cream and sherry. Should be light and fluffy. Mix in nuts. Spread over bars and chill.

Topping:

- **1 (6-ounce) package semi-sweet morsels**
- **4 tablespoons water**
- **4 tablespoons butter**

Melt chocolate with butter and water over hot water. Mix well. Drizzle over filling. Chill until firm. Cut into 1-inch bars. Store in refrigerator. Makes 5 dozen.

Sure to please chocolate lovers.

Halfway Squares

- 1 cup shortening
- ½ cup brown sugar
- ½ cup granulated sugar
- 2 egg yolks, slightly beaten
- 1 tablespoon water
- 2 teaspoons vanilla
- ¼ teaspoon salt
- 1 teaspoon baking powder
- ¼ teaspoon baking soda
- 2 cups sifted all-purpose flour
- 1 (6-ounce) package butterscotch chips
- 1 cup brown sugar

Cream sugar and shortening, add egg yolks, water and vanilla. Blend well. Sift flour three times with soda, salt and baking powder. Mix with creamed mixture and blend well. Dough will be stiff. Pat it in a greased 10x14-inch baking pan. Sprinkle with butterscotch chips. Spread with topping (see below). Bake at 350° for 25 minutes. Cool. Cut into squares. Makes 4 dozen.

Topping:

- 2 egg whites
- 1 cup brown sugar

Beat egg whites stiff gradually adding brown sugar.

Judy's Lemon Squares

- 2 sticks butter
- 2 cups plain flour
- ½ cup of sugar
- 6 eggs
- 4 lemons (juice and grated rind)
- 3 cups of sugar
- 8 tablespoons self-rising flour
- Powdered sugar

Cream together first three ingredients, spread in a 10x14-inch pan and bake at 350° for 15 minutes. Next, beat the eggs, add the juice and grated lemon rind of 4 lemons. Add the 3 cups of sugar and self-rising flour. Mix and spread over pastry already prepared. Bake at 350° for 35 minutes. Cool in pan. Sprinkle with 10X powdered sugar on top. Makes 36.

SUBSTITUTION PERMITTED: You may use ½ cup of real lemon juice and 2½ teaspoons of instant lemon peel for the four lemons already mentioned.

King's Ransom Bars

½ cup brown sugar
1 cup all-purpose flour
½ cup margarine

Cream butter and sugar, blend in flour and press into 9x13-inch ungreased pan. Bake 350° for 10 minutes.

Filling:
2 eggs
2 tablespoons flour
½ teaspoon salt
1½ teaspoons vanilla
6 ounces chocolate chips
1 cup brown sugar
1 teaspoon baking powder
1 cup nuts, chopped

Beat eggs, add sugar and beat until well-blended. Add flour, baking powder, salt, vanilla and nuts. Spread evenly over bottom layer and sprinkle with chocolate chips. Bake at 350° for 25 minutes. Cut while slightly warm. Makes 12-16.

These are awesome!

Chocolate-Peanut Butter Squares

½ bar paraffin
1 cup margarine
1 cup peanut butter
1 (16-ounce) box powdered sugar
1½ cups graham cracker crumbs
1 (12-ounce) package semi-sweet chocolate chips, melted

Melt margarine and paraffin in saucepan. Remove from heat and stir in next three ingredients. Press mixture into a 13x9x2-inch baking pan and spread melted chocolate chips over top. Chill for 30 minutes, then cut into squares. Makes 24.

Mint Strips

- **1 cup butter or margarine**
- **3 squares dark unsweetened chocolate**
- **4 eggs**
- **2 cups white sugar**
- **2½ cups all-purpose flour, sifted**
- **1 teaspoon vanilla**
- **½ teaspoon salt**
- **1 package or can creamy white frosting mix**
- **Peppermint flavoring**
- **Green food coloring**
- **1 package dark chocolate frosting mix, can icing or make your own favorite chocolate frosting**
- **¼ teaspoon peppermint**

First Layer:
Melt chocolate squares and butter. Blend and set aside. Combine eggs and sugar. Beat until sugar is dissolved. Add flour, salt, vanilla and chocolate mixture to the eggs and sugar. Mix thoroughly. Spread in bottom of large greased 15x10-inch jelly roll pan with 1-inch sides. Bake at 350° for 12 minutes and cool.

Second Layer:
Prepare white frosting by directions. Add peppermint flavoring to taste and green food coloring for a medium color. Spread on cooled first layer and chill.

Third Layer:
1 package of dark chocolate frosting mix or can or your own frosting should be spread over the second layer. Chill and cut into strips. Makes 6 dozen.

This may be frozen.

Congo Squares

- **1 box light brown sugar**
- **2½ cups all-purpose flour**
- **1 cup oil**
- **3 eggs**
- **1 teaspoon baking powder**
- **1 teaspoon salt**
- **1 teaspoon vanilla**
- **1 (6-ounce) package chocolate chips**
- **1 cup nuts, chopped**

Mix all together with wooden spoon. Bake at 350° in greased 16x11-inch pan for 25-30 minutes. Makes 36.

Easy - great for teenagers.

Pasta Flora Squares

- 1 cup shortening
- 3 cups plain flour
- 3 teaspoons baking powder
- 2 tablespoons sugar
- 1 teaspoon salt
- 2 jiggers brandy or whiskey
- 2 eggs, slightly beaten
- 1 (1-pound) jar apricot preserves (or peach, pineapple or strawberry)

Cut shortening into dry ingredients until evenly mixed. With fork, stir in brandy and beaten eggs. Knead slightly. Chill. Roll our ⅔ of the dough to fit bottom of 9x12-inch baking dish. Spread with fruit preserves or marmalade. Cut remainder of dough into strips and put on top of fruit, lattice fashion. Brush top with milk. Bake at 375° about 20 minutes. Cut in squares. Makes 3 dozen.

Pecan Pie Squares

Crust:

- 3 cups flour
- ¼ cup plus 2 tablespoons sugar
- ¾ cup butter, softened
- ¾ teaspoon salt

Grease 15½x10½x1-inch jelly roll pan. Beat on medium speed until crumbly. Press firmly in pan. Bake 20 minutes at 350°.

Filling:

- 4 eggs, slightly beaten
- 1½ cups sugar
- 1½ cups Karo light or dark syrup
- 1½ teaspoons vanilla
- 2½ cups pecans, chopped
- 3 tablespoons butter, melted

Mix until well blended. Add nuts. Pour over baked layer. Bake until set, 25 to 30 minutes. Cool and cut into 1½-inch squares. Makes 70 squares.

Plantation Brownies

Cream Cheese Mixture:

- **¾ pound cream cheese**
- **¼ cup butter**
- **1 cup sugar**
- **4 large eggs**
- **2 teaspoons vanilla extract**
- **¼ cup flour**

Beat cream cheese and butter together until soft. Add sugar, beat well. Add eggs one at a time, beating well. Add vanilla. Fold in flour. Set aside.

Chocolate Mixture:

- **1 (16-ounce) package semi-sweet chocolate**
- **1½ sticks margarine**
- **8 large eggs**
- **3 cups sugar**
- **1 tablespoon plus 1 teaspoon vanilla extract**
- **½ teaspoon almond extract**
- **2 cups all-purpose flour**
- **2 teaspoons baking powder**
- **2 teaspoons salt**
- **2 cups pecans, chopped**

Melt chocolate and margarine in a double boiler. Beat eggs, gradually adding sugar, until thick and light in color. Blend in chocolate/margarine mixture. Add vanilla and almond extracts. Combine flour, baking powder and salt. Fold into above mixture. Stir in nuts. Pam or grease two 13x9½-inch baking pans. Reserve 4 cups of chocolate mixture. Divide the rest between the 2 pans. Divide the cream cheese mixture between the 2 pans, spreading it on top of the chocolate mixture. Spoon reserved chocolate mixture on top of the cream cheese layers. To achieve a marble effect and the binding of the two layers, swirl them with a knife or icing spatula. Bake at 325° for 30 to 35 minutes or until a cake tester comes out clean. Makes 5 to 6 dozen.

These are very rich and very wonderful.

Rocky Road Squares

- ½ cup butter
- ½ cup brown sugar
- 1 cup all-purpose flour
- ½ cup graham cracker crumbs
- 2 cups miniature marshmallows
- 1 (6-ounce) package semi-sweet chocolate chips
- ½ cup nuts, chopped

Combine butter and sugar and beat until light and fluffy. Mix flour and graham crumbs together and add to creamed mixture. Pat into greased 9x9-inch cake pan. Sprinkle marshmallows, chocolate chips, and nuts on top of crust. Bake at 375° for 15 to 20 minutes. Cool and cut into squares. Makes 16.

Yummies

- 1 yellow cake mix
- 1 stick butter, melted
- 1 egg
- 1 (8-ounce) package cream cheese
- 2 eggs
- 1 pound powdered sugar
- 1 teaspoon vanilla

Mix first three ingredients together and put in bottom of a 9x13-inch pan. Next, beat together cream cheese, eggs, sugar and vanilla. Pour over above mixture. Bake at 350° for 35 to 40 minutes. Cool, cut into squares and refrigerate. Makes 36.

Cake Cones

- 1 box cake mix
- ½ cup cold water
- 2 eggs
- 3 tablespoons water
- 1 teaspoon vanilla
- 1 tablespoon cooking oil
- 24 flat bottomed ice cream cones

Combine cake mix and ½ cup cold water. Beat 1 minute. Beat in eggs, water, vanilla and oil. Mix well. Place ice cream cones in muffin tins or on cookie sheet and fill each half full of batter. Bake 15 minutes at 350° or until cake springs back when lightly touched. Frost when cool. Makes 24.

Perfect for children to decorate for any occasion. (Valentine, Birthday, Halloween, Christmas, etc.)

California Tarts

Tart Shells:

1 small cream cheese
½ cup butter
1 cup all-purpose flour

Cream together cream cheese, butter, flour. Roll crust thin and line small muffin tins.

Filling:

1 cup raisins
1 cup pecans
1 cup sugar
½ cup butter
2 egg yolks, beaten
1 teaspoon vanilla extract

Mix ingredients all together, then fill each tart shell ¾ full. Bake at 350° until brown (approximately 20 minutes). Dust with powdered sugar while warm. Makes 3 dozen.

Traveling Cupcakes

4 squares semi-sweet chocolate
1 cup butter or margarine
1¾ cups nuts, broken
1¾ cups sugar
1 cup unsifted plain flour
4 large eggs, beaten slightly
1 teaspoon vanilla

Melt chocolate and butter in heavy pan over low heat. Add nuts and stir until well coated. Combine sugar, flour, eggs, vanilla in separate bowl, but DO NOT BEAT. Add chocolate mixture to flour mixture. Fold in but do not beat. Line muffin pans with paper liners and fill to ⅔ full. Bake at 325° for 25 minutes. Makes 2 dozen.

VARIATION: Press miniature peanut butter cups into batter until candy is even with batter.

These are called traveling cupcakes because they do not have any frosting and they travel well.

Cherry Cheese Tarts

- **2 eggs**
- **2 (8-ounce) packages cream cheese**
- **Dash of vanilla**
- **¾ cup sugar**
- **1 (2-inch) package foil muffin cups**
- **1 box vanilla wafers**
- **1 (21-ounce) can cherry pie filling**

Place muffin cups on cookie sheet and place one vanilla wafer in each cup. Combine eggs, cream cheese, vanilla and sugar in mixing bowl. Beat until smooth. Pour mixture into cups, ¾ full. Bake at 350° for 12 minutes. When cool, top each tart with 1 to 2 cherries. Refrigerate until serving. Makes 4 dozen.

You can't eat just one!

Teacher Proof Peanut Butter Cupcakes

- **1 box Jiffy golden cake mix**
- **1 egg**
- **¼ cup water**
- **½ cup peanut butter**

Follow directions on back of box for mixing. After blending add peanut butter. If mixture is too thick add a bit more water. Pour into muffin/cupcake pan with paper liners. Bake according to directions. When cool, frost with chocolate or fudge frosting. Makes 12.

NOTE: Crunchy peanut butter may be used instead of smooth.

Chinese Candy

2 (6-ounce) packages butterscotch chips
1 can Chinese noodles
1 cup cashew nuts
1 cup raisins (if desired)

Melt butterscotch chips in top of double boiler. Add other ingredients. Remove from heat. Mix well. Drop by teaspoon on waxed paper. Cool, place in covered tins. Makes 4 dozen.

NOTE: Chocolate chips may be used instead of butterscotch chips.

Simply delicious! This is a candy that needs to resurface again. Children love them.

Fancy Cheez-Its

Cheez-Its crackers
Peanut butter
White chocolate

Put dab of peanut butter between two crackers. Melt white chocolate in double boiler. Dip crackers in chocolate and let cool on waxed paper. Will freeze.

Sugared Pecans

⅓ cup margarine
¼ cup sugar
½ teaspoon cinnamon
¼ teaspoon ginger
¼ teaspoon nutmeg
1 pound pecan halves

Place nuts in large flat pan. Melt margarine, stir in sugar and spices. Mix well. Pour over nuts and mix to coat well. Bake at 275° for 30 minutes stirring every 10 minutes. Store in tight tins. Makes 1 pound.

VARIATION: Add 2 teaspoons vanilla, 1 teaspoon rum flavoring, and 2 tablespoons honey in place of cinnamon, ginger and nutmeg.

GRACIOUS ENDINGS

Gracious Endings

Dr. Bird Cake

Cake:

- **3 cups all-purpose flour**
- **1 teaspoon baking soda**
- **1 teaspoon salt**
- **1 teaspoon baking powder**
- **1 teaspoon cinnamon**
- **2 cups sugar**
- **1½ cups cooking oil**
- **1 (8-ounce) can crushed pineapple and juice**
- **1½ teaspoons vanilla**
- **3 eggs, beaten**
- **2 cups ripe bananas, diced**

Measure and sift dry ingredients. Add all other ingredients to dry mixture. Stir to blend, but DO NOT beat. Spoon into 3 greased and floured 9-inch pans. Bake at 350° for 25 to 30 minutes or until wooden pick inserted in center comes out clean. Cool in pans 10 minutes. Remove from pans and COOL COMPLETELY before frosting. Spread frosting on tops and sides. Sprinkle with nuts, if desired.

Cream Cheese Frosting:

- **1 (8-ounce) package cream cheese, softened**
- **½ cup butter**
- **1 (16-ounce) box powdered sugar**
- **1 teaspoon vanilla**
- **Chopped nuts (optional)**

Cream butter and cream cheese until fluffy. Then add sugar and vanilla. Top with the nuts if desired. Serves 12.

Fresh Apple Cake

- **3 cups apples, cut in small pieces**
- **2 cups sugar**
- **2 eggs, slightly beaten**
- **1 tablespoon vanilla**
- **1½ cups Crisco oil**
- **3 cups self-rising flour, sifted**
- **2 tablespoons cinnamon**
- **1 cup pecans or walnuts**

Mix apples, 1 cup sugar and eggs in bowl and set aside. In a separate bowl combine 1 cup sugar, vanilla and oil. To this add the flour and cinnamon combination. Add the apple mixture to the sugar mixture and mix well. Pour into a **greased** tube pan and bake at 350° for 1 hour and 15 minutes. Serves 12 to 16.

It is so easy, but it looks like you worked hard all day. So enjoy!

Gingerbread with Lemon Sauce

- **1 package Betty Crocker Super Moist carrot cake mix**
- **⅔ cup water**
- **⅓ cup molasses**
- **⅓ cup margarine or butter, softened**
- **3 eggs**
- **1 teaspoon ground ginger**
- **½ teaspoon ground allspice**
- **¼ teaspoon ground cloves**
- **Lemon Sauce**

Heat oven to 350°. Grease and sugar (about 1 tablespoon granulated sugar) 12-cup bundt cake pan. Blend cake mix, water, molasses, margarine, eggs, ginger, allspice and cloves in large bowl on low speed, scraping bowl constantly, until moistened. Beat on medium speed, scraping bowl frequently, 2 minutes. Pour into pan. Bake as directed on package. Cool 10 minutes. Invert on wire rack. Remove pan and cool cake completely. Dust with powdered sugar if desired; serve with Lemon Sauce.

Lemon Sauce:

- **½ cup sugar**
- **1 tablespoon plus 2 teaspoons cornstarch**
- **1 cup water**
- **1 tablespoon margarine or butter**
- **1 tablespoon lemon peel, grated**
- **1 tablespoon lemon juice**

Mix sugar and cornstarch in saucepan. Gradually stir in water. Cook over medium heat, stirring constantly until mixture thickens and boils. Boil and stir 1 minute, remove from heat. Stir in margarine or butter, grated lemon peel and lemon juice. Serve warm or cool. About 1¼ cups sauce.

Hootenholler Whiskey Cake

- 3 eggs
- ½ cup butter, softened
- 1 cup sugar
- 1 cup all-purpose flour
- ½ teaspoon baking powder
- ¼ teaspoon salt
- ½ teaspoon ground nutmeg
- ¼ cup milk
- ¼ cup pancake syrup
- ¼ teaspoon baking soda
- ¼ cup bourbon
- 2 cups raisins
- 2 cups pecans or walnuts, chopped

Cream butter. Gradually add sugar, beating until light and fluffy. Add eggs one at a time, beating well after each addition. Combine next four ingredients. Add to creamed mixture, alternately with milk beginning and ending with dry ingredients. Combine pancake syrup and baking soda and add to creamed mixture. Stir in remaining ingredients. Pour into 13x9x2-inch greased and floured sheet pan. Bake in a 300° oven for one hour. Check after 45 minutes. Baking time may vary according to your oven. Done when wooden pick inserted in center comes out clean. Serves 12 to 16.

Out of This World Cake

Cake:

- 1 box graham crackers, crushed
- 1 cup butter, melted
- 2 cups sugar
- 1 cup milk
- 1 teaspoon baking powder
- 5 eggs, well beaten
- 1 cup coconut
- 1 cup nuts, chopped
- 2 teaspoons vanilla

Mix all ingredients well by hand. Bake in a greased and floured tube pan at 350° for 1½ hours. **Do not preheat oven!**

Icing:

- 1 box powdered sugar
- 1 small can crushed pineapple with juice
- 1 stick of butter, melted and cooled

Mix and pour half over cake while hot and still in pan. Let stand for 10 minutes. Turn cake on plate and pour remaining icing over cake. Serves 12.

Italian Cream Cake

Cake:

- **½ cup margarine**
- **½ cup Crisco**
- **2 cups sugar**
- **5 eggs, separated**
- **2 cups sifted all-purpose flour**
- **1 teaspoon soda**
- **1 cup buttermilk**
- **1 tablespoon vanilla**
- **1 (3½-ounce) can coconut**
- **1 cup pecans, chopped**

Cream margarine, Crisco and sugar. Add egg yolks, one at a time, beating well after each addition. Add flour, soda, buttermilk and vanilla and mix well. Add nuts and coconut and mix well. Beat egg whites until stiff and **gently fold** into batter. Bake in 3 round 9-inch greased and floured pans at 350° for 30 minutes.

Frosting:

- **1 (8-ounce) package cream cheese**
- **¼ cup margarine**
- **1 box powdered sugar**
- **1 teaspoon vanilla**

Cream margarine and cream cheese. Add sugar and vanilla. Mix well. If too stiff, add a touch of milk using 1 teaspoon at a time until right consistency. Serves 12 to 16.

Pistachio Marble Cake

- **1 package yellow cake mix**
- **⅔ cup oil**
- **4 eggs**
- **1 package pistachio instant pudding mix**
- **½ pint sour cream**
- **5½ ounces chocolate syrup**
- **¼ cup nuts, chopped**
- **½ cup semi-sweet chocolate chips**

Beat cake mix, eggs and oil together. Add pudding and sour cream to batter and beat for 10 minutes. Grease bundt pan and sprinkle with nuts and chips. Pour ¾ batter into pan. Add syrup to remaining batter and drop by tablespoon on top of original batter. Using a knife, marble the chocolate. Bake at 325° 50 to 60 minutes testing with toothpick. **Cool in pan** at least one hour. Serves 12.

Rose Marie's Carrot Cake

Cake:

2½ cups all-purpose sifted flour
2 cups sugar
2 teaspoons baking powder
1½ teaspoons baking soda
2 teaspoons cinnamon
1 teaspoon salt
4 eggs
1½ cups cooking oil
2 cups carrots, grated coarsely
1 cup crushed pineapple, with syrup
1 teaspoon vanilla
1 package frozen coconut, thawed

In large bowl, stir together dry ingredients. Add oil, eggs, carrots, pineapple with syrup, vanilla and coconut. Mix until all ingredients are moistened. Beat with electric beater 2 minutes at medium speed. Pour batter into greased (I use Pam) and floured 9x13-inch pan or bundt pan. Bake at 350° for 60 minutes. Cool and frost with Cream Cheese Frosting. Serves 12 to 16.

Cream Cheese Frosting:

1 (8-ounce) package cream cheese, at room temperature
4 tablespoons butter or margarine, softened
1 tablespoon vanilla
Dash of salt
1 box powdered sugar, sifted
1 cup walnuts, coarsely chopped

Cream together cream cheese and butter. Beat in vanilla and salt. Gradually add powdered sugar and blend well. Stir in chopped nuts.

George Bullwinkel's Nut Cake

1 pound butter
1 pound sugar
10 eggs
1 tablespoon vanilla
4 cups walnuts, chopped
1 pound self-rising flour

Cream together butter and sugar. Add eggs one at a time, beating well after each egg. Add vanilla. Sift part of the flour over chopped nuts, mixing well. Add remaining flour to the cake batter. Mix well. Add floured nuts a few at a time mixing well. Bake at 325° for about 45 minutes in 8½x4½-inch loaf pans. Will make 3 or 4 loaves.

Another Christmas tradition in many Charleston homes.

The Charleston Cake Lady

Pumpkin Cake

Cake:

- **2 cups sugar**
- **2 cups self-rising flour**
- **3 teaspoons cinnamon**
- **4 eggs**
- **1 can pumpkin**
- **1 cup oil**

Mix sugar and oil. Add eggs and pumpkin. Mix flour and cinnamon then add to mixture. Bake at 350° for 1 hour in a greased and floured tube pan. Serves 12 to 16.

Icing:

- **2 (3-ounce) packages cream cheese**
- **1 cup margarine**
- **1 box powdered sugar**
- **2 teaspoons vanilla**

Cream margarine and cream cheese. Add powdered sugar and vanilla. Spread on top and sides of cake.

Strawberries in the Mist

- **1 quart firm medium sized strawberries, washed and hulled**
- **1 cup fresh pineapple chunks, cut small**
- **½ cup sugar**
- **½ cup Cointreau**
- **1 cup heavy cream, whipped**
- **2 tablespoons fresh orange zest and juice**
- **Fresh mint leaves**

Chill whole strawberries and pineapple tossed in mixture of sugar, juice, zest and Cointreau for at least 3 hours. Spoon into champagne glasses and top with whipped cream. Garnish with mint leaves. Serves 4.

Light and easy.

Sister Mary's Dark Rum Cake

Cake:

- **1 cup nuts, chopped**
- **1 (3-ounce) package instant vanilla pudding**
- **½ cup cold water**
- **½ cup dark rum**
- **1 package yellow cake mix**
- **4 eggs**
- **½ cup Crisco oil**

Preheat oven to 325°. Grease and flour a 10-inch tube pan. Sprinkle nuts over the bottom of pan. Mix all other ingredients. Pour batter over nuts. Bake for 1 hour or until done. Set on a rack to cool. Invert on a serving plate. Prick top and drizzle or brush glaze evenly over the top.

Glaze:

- **¼ pound butter or margarine**
- **1 cup granulated sugar**
- **½ cup water**
- **½ cup dark rum**

Melt butter in pan. Stir in water and sugar. Boil 5 minutes, stirring constantly. Stir in rum.

You could ring the pan with cherries around the edge before you put in the nuts. Serves 12.

This is great for Christmas!

Winnie's Macaroon Cake

- **1 cup Crisco shortening**
- **2 cups sugar**
- **2 cups all-purpose flour**
- **6 eggs**
- **2 tablespoons almond extract**
- **1 cup pecans, chopped**

Cream shortening and sugar. Add eggs one at a time alternating with flour. Beat well after each addition. Add almond extract and pecans. Bake in greased tube pan at 250° for 1 hour and 35 to 40 minutes or until golden—**not brown**. Test cake for doneness with toothpick. Serves 12.

Old family favorite.

Summer Fruit Cake

Cake:

- **2 cups sugar**
- **3 eggs**
- **1¼ cups Mazola oil**
- **¼ cup concentrated orange juice**
- **3 cups plain flour**
- **¼ teaspoon salt**
- **1 teaspoon baking soda**
- **1 teaspoon cinnamon**
- **1 teaspoon vanilla**
- **1 cup fresh apples, finely chopped**
- **1 (8-ounce) can coconut**
- **1 cup nuts, chopped**

Mix first twelve ingredients in order named. Bake in a greased tube pan at 325° for 1½ hours.

Sauce:

- **½ cup margarine**
- **1 cup sugar**
- **½ teaspoon soda**
- **½ cup buttermilk**

Melt margarine, combine other ingredients. Bring to a boil and pour over cake in pan. Let cool. Makes 1 tube pan.

Very good at Christmas for the non-fruit cake lovers!!!! This is a favorite. Make a few days ahead. It tastes better with age.

Zwieback Cake

- **1 (6-ounce) package Zwieback, crushed**
- **6 eggs, separated**
- **1 cup nuts, chopped**
- **2 teaspoons baking powder**
- **1 cup sugar**
- **1 teaspoon vanilla**
- **1 pint heavy cream, whipped and sweetened**

Separate eggs. Cream, sugar and egg yolks together. Crush Zwieback finely between 2 sheets wax paper. Add crushed Zwieback to egg and sugar. Mix baking powder and chopped nuts; add to Zwieback mixture. Gently fold in stiffly beaten egg whites and vanilla. Divide evenly into 2 8x8-inch square Pam sprayed pans. Bake at 400° 10 to 12 minutes. Layer and top with whipped cream. Top with cherry if desired. Store in refrigerator. Serves 10 to 12.

Banana Split Cake

- ½ cup butter
- 2 cups graham craker crumbs
- 2½ cups powdered sugar
- 8 ounces cream cheese
- 2 tablespoons hot water
- 1 teaspoon vanilla
- 3 to 5 bananas
- 1 (20-ounce) can crushed pineapple, drained
- 12 ounces Cool Whip
- 1 small package pecan pieces
- 1 small bottle maraschino cherries

Melt butter in a 13x9-inch pan. Add graham cracker crumbs. Mix well. Press into pan to form crust.

Beat together until creamy the cream cheese, hot water, vanilla and powdered sugar. Spread mixture on crumb crust. Slice bananas on top of mixture. Spoon drained pineapple over bananas. Spread Cool Whip on pineapple. Top with chopped pecans and maraschino cherries. Cover and refrigerate two hours or overnight. Serves 12 to 16.

Serve and enjoy.

Legare Street Lemon Delight

- 30 ladyfingers, separated
- 1 pint whipping cream
- 1 each (8-ounce and 3-ounce) packages cream cheese, softened
- ¾ cup sugar
- 1 (20-ounce) can lemon pie filling

Chill bowl and beaters, whip cream and set aside. Cream sugar and cream cheese. Fold whipped cream into cream cheese mixture. Stand ladyfingers around sides of trifle bowl or 10-inch spring form pan. Put layer of ladyfingers on bottom of pan, add ⅓ cream mixture, add ½ pie filling. Repeat layers ending with cream mixture. Chill several hours before serving. (Recipe was originally submitted with pineapple pie filling which was unavailable in this area.) Serves 10 to 12.

Can be made the day before for easy, elegant entertaining.

Bullwinkel's Whipped Cream Cake

- 1 pound, 1 ounce granulated sugar
- 4 ounces whole eggs
- 4 ounces egg yolks
- 4½ ounces skim milk
- Dash vanilla
- ⅛ ounce baking powder
- 12 ounces cake flour
- ⅛ ounce salt
- 1½ quarts whipping cream
- 6 ounces powdered sugar, sifted
- Raspberry jelly

(For your information, 1 cup equals 8 ounces and 2 tablespoons equal one ounce.) Mix granulated sugar, eggs, yolks, milk and dash of vanilla in mixing bowl. Beat at second speed for 45 minutes. (Yes! 45 minutes). Sift together flour, baking powder and salt. Add flour mixture to sugar mixture by hand and mix well. Spread in three 12-inch cake pans. Bake at 390° for about 12 minutes. Cool.

Whip cream by mixer until prints form on the beater. Add powdered sugar and dash of vanilla. Spread raspberry jelly on the bottom and middle layer. Then spread the whipped topping on the top of the three layers. Stack layers and garnish with a few cherries on top. Serves 12 to 16.

Mr. Bullwinkel's Whipped Cream Cake has been a Christmas family tradition for many, many years around Charleston. At the printing of this book, he is 77 years of age and still works full-time during the holidays to keep this tradition alive.

Coconut Cake

- 1 package butter cake mix
- 1 cup sour cream
- 2 cups sugar
- 3 packages frozen coconut

Bake cake according to package directions using three round 8-inch pans. Mix sour cream and sugar together and refrigerate for 2 hours. Add 2½ packages frozen coconut to mixture. Spread between layers and on top. Sprinkle ½ package frozen coconut on top. Refrigerate for three days. Serves 12.

Should be called "Excellence in Coconut." Always a big hit with the coconut lover. Will melt in your mouth and you'll be ready for another.

Chocolate Eclair Delight

- **1 pound box of graham crackers**
- **2 (3-ounce) packages vanilla instant pudding mix**
- **3 cups milk**
- **1 (8-ounce) container Cool Whip**

Lay crackers flat in 9x13-inch pan. Add 3 cups milk to instant pudding and beat until thick, fold in 8-ounces Cool Whip. Layer pudding on top of graham crackers, cover pudding with another layer of graham crackers.

Icing:

- **1 cup sugar**
- **⅓ cup cocoa**
- **½ cup evaporated milk**
- **½ cup margarine**
- **1 teaspoon vanilla**

Boil together for 1 minute: sugar, cocoa and evaporated milk. Add margarine and vanilla and beat until thick. Pour over top layer of graham crackers—refrigerate for several hours. Cut in squares and serve. Serves 12 to 16.

Delicious and light!!

Kahlúa Angel Food Cake

- **1 angel food cake**
- **¼ cup plus 2 tablespoons Kahlúa**
- **½ cup Nestles Quick**
- **¼ cup half and half**
- **¼ cup dinner mints, crushed**
- **1 (16-ounce) container Cool Whip**

Poke holes in top of cake with a thin knife. Combine two tablespoons Kahlúa and half and half and slowly pour half of this mixture into cake holes. Refrigerate two hours. Remove cake from refrigerator and pour remainder of cream mixture into the holes of the cake. Refrigerate for two more hours.

Combine Cool Whip, Nestles Quick and ¼ cup Kahlúa in a small bowl. Spread over top and sides of cake. Sprinkle crushed mints on top of cake, then refrigerate until serving time.

Chocolate Mint - Whipped Cream Cake

Cake:

1½ cups all-purpose flour, sifted
1 teaspoon baking soda
½ teaspoon salt
¼ teaspoon baking powder
½ cup butter, softened
1¼ cups sugar
2 eggs
½ cup unsweetened cocoa, sifted
1 cup hot water

Sift flour, soda, salt and baking powder together and set aside. In a large bowl, beat butter, sugar and eggs at high speed for 3 minutes or until light and fluffy. Combine cocoa and water. Add flour mixture and cocoa alternately to butter mixture. Beat just until smooth. Pour into 3 greased and floured 8-inch pans. Bake at 350° for 25 minutes or until cake springs back when lightly pressed with fingertips. Cool in pans 10 minutes. Remove from pans and cool on wire racks.

Filling:

1 pint whipping cream
3 to 4 tablespoons powdered sugar
⅛ teaspoon peppermint extract
Green food coloring

In a medium size bowl, combine cream, sugar, peppermint extract and enough food coloring to tint to a pale green. Whip just until soft peaks form. Spread between layers.

Frosting:

2 squares unsweetened chocolate, melted
2 cups powdered sugar
3½ tablespoons hot water
¼ cup butter, softened
½ teaspoon vanilla

In a small bowl, combine melted chocolate , sugar, and hot water. Beat until smooth and well-blended. Add butter and vanilla. Continue to beat until frosting is thick. Set bowl of frosting in ice water and beat with a wooden spoon until frosting is of spreading consistency. Frost sides and top of cake. Refrigerate until ready to serve. Serves 12 to 16.

Worth the time for a special occasion.

Fresh Strawberry Bavarian

- **2 cups fresh strawberries, sliced**
- **1 tablespoon unflavored gelatin**
- **⅔ cup granulated sugar**
- **¼ cup cold water**
- **½ cup boiling water**
- **1 tablespoon lemon juice**
- **2 egg whites**
- **2 tablespoons granulated sugar**
- **Dash of salt**
- **¾ cup heavy cream**
- **Sweetened whipped cream and strawberries for garnish**

Combine strawberries and ⅔ cup sugar, blend well and let stand for 30 minutes. Soften gelatin in cold water for 5 minutes, then pour boiling water over softened gelatin and stir until gelatin is dissolved. Add gelatin mixture and lemon juice to strawberry mixture and chill until slightly thickened. Meanwhile beat 2 egg whites until frothy; gradually add 2 tablespoons of sugar and salt. Continue beating until egg whites form soft peaks. Fold egg whites into berry mixture and chill again, stirring occasionally so berries do not sink to bottom. Whip cream until stiff and fold in berry mixture. Pour into lightly oiled 1½-quart mold and chill overnight. Unmold onto serving dish and garnish with strawberries and whipped cream. Serves 6 to 8.

Lemon Lush

- **½ cup margarine or butter**
- **1 cup all-purpose flour**
- **1 cup nuts, chopped and divided**
- **1 cup powdered sugar**
- **1 (8-ounce) package cream cheese, softened**
- **1 large container Cool Whip, divided**
- **2 (3¼-ounce) packages instant lemon pudding mix**
- **3 cups milk**
- **1 small can coconut**

Mix margarine, flour and ¾ cup nuts. Spread in a 13x9-inch pan, patting it down until flattened to a thin layer. Bake at 300° for 25 minutes and cool. Mix sugar and cream cheese until thoroughly blended. Fold in ½ of the Cool Whip and spread over crust. Mix lemon pudding with milk. Beat until thick. Spread over Cool Whip layer. Spread remainder of Cool Whip on pudding and sprinkle with ¼ cup nuts and coconut. Serves 8 to 10.

Substitute chocolate or butterscotch for the lemon pudding, it's hard to decide which is the best!

Mint Cake

- **25 Oreo cookies (large pack)**
- **½ cup butter**
- **3 squares unsweetened chocolate**
- **3 eggs, beaten**
- **½ gallon vanilla ice cream**
- **½ cup green crème de menthe**
- **2 cups powdered sugar**

Crush cookies in blender 3 or 4 at a time. Spread crumbs in 9x13-inch pan. In a double boiler over low heat, stir butter, chocolate, eggs and sugar until mixture looks like fudge. Spread mixture over cookie crumbs, put in freezer for 20 minutes. Soften ½ gallon vanilla ice cream and mix with ½ cup crème de menthe. Spread over top of fudge mixture. Put 5 or 6 more cookies in blender and crush. Sprinkle over top of ice cream. Freeze for 3 hours. Serves 12 to 16.

Refreshing dessert!

Pistachio Delight

- **1 cup all-purpose flour**
- **½ cup margarine, softened**
- **2 tablespoons sugar**
- **½ cup nuts, chopped**
- **1 (8-ounce) package cream cheese**
- **⅔ cup powdered sugar**
- **1 large container Cool Whip**
- **2 small packages instant pistachio pudding mix**
- **2½ cups milk**

Mix flour, margarine, sugar and nuts. Press in 13x9-inch ungreased pan. Bake at 350° until brown, (about 9 to 10 minutes). Cool. Mix softened cream cheese, sugar and 1 cup Cool Whip and spread on crust. Beat pudding and milk until thickened, pour on cream cheese mixture. Cover with remainder of Cool Whip. Refrigerate and cut into squares. Make this into a chocolate delight by substituting chocolate pudding for the pistachio and topping with toasted pecans. Serves 12.

Great for a luncheon dessert or bridge party.

Lorna Doone Dessert

- **1 package Lorna Doone cookies, crushed**
- **¼ cup butter**
- **2 (3½-ounce) boxes instant vanilla pudding**
- **1¼ cups milk**
- **1 quart butter pecan ice cream**
- **1 medium carton Cool Whip**
- **3 Heath bars, crushed**

Crush cookies in plastic bag. Combine with butter and press into 13x9-inch pan. Set aside. Combine pudding, milk, and ice cream. Mix well by hand. Spoon onto crust mixture. Freeze about 4 hours. Before serving, spoon on Cool Whip and crushed Heath bars. Store in refrigerator until ready to serve. Serves 12 to 16.

Rave Reviews Coconut Cake

Cake:

- **1 package yellow cake mix**
- **1⅓ cups water**
- **¼ cup oil**
- **1 cup walnuts or pecans, chopped**
- **1 small package vanilla instant pudding mix**
- **4 eggs**
- **2 cups angel flake coconut**

Blend cake mix, pudding mix, water, eggs and oil in large mixing bowl. Beat at medium speed for 4 minutes. Stir in coconut and walnuts. Pour into 3 greased and floured 9-inch layer pans. Bake at 350° for 35 minutes. Cool in pans 15 minutes; remove and cool on rack. Fill and frost with Coconut-Cream Cheese Frosting.

Coconut-Cream Cheese Frosting:

- **4 tablespoons butter or margarine**
- **2 cups angel flake coconut**
- **1 (8-ounce) package cream cheese**
- **2 teaspoons milk**
- **3½ cups powdered sugar, sifted**
- **½ teaspoon vanilla**

Melt 2 tablespoons butter in skillet. Add coconut; stir constantly over low heat until golden brown. Spread coconut on absorbent paper to cool. Cream 2 tablespoons butter with cream cheese. Add milk and sugar alternately, beating well. Add vanilla. Stir in 1¾ cups coconut and spread on tops and sides of cake layers. Sprinkle with remaining coconut. Serves 10 to 12.

Mrs. Swain's Ice Box Fruitcake

- **1 quart nuts, chopped**
- **½ pound glazed cherries**
- **½ pound raisins**
- **1 (8-ounce) package dates, chopped**
- **1 box vanilla wafers**
- **1 can condensed cream**

Mix together the first four ingredients, then add the cream. Crush the entire box of vanilla wafers and add to the creamed mixture. Pack firmly into a loaf pan that has been buttered or foil lined. Place in the refrigerator for at least 48 hours. Slice when needed, but remember to return the fruitcake to the refrigerator. Serves 10 to 12.

Too Good To Be Yogurt Cake

Cake:

- **½ cup butter**
- **1 cup sugar**
- **2 eggs**
- **2 cups all-purpose flour, sifted**
- **1 teaspoon baking powder**
- **1 teaspoon soda**
- **½ teaspoon cinnamon**
- **1 cup thick plain yogurt**
- **1 cup nuts, chopped**
- **1 teaspoon vanilla**

Cream softened butter and sugar until fluffy. Add eggs and blend thoroughly. Sift dry ingredients and add alternately with yogurt to creamed mixture. Add nuts and flavoring. Mix well. Pour into greased 9x13-inch pan. Bake in oven at 350° for 40 to 45 minutes or until done.

Syrup:

- **1½ cups sugar**
- **¾ cup water**
- **1 tablespoon lemon or orange juice**
- **3 tablespoons brandy or rum (optional)**

Mix all ingredients in saucepan. Boil for 15 minutes. Cool and pour over warm cake.

This cake is better after it sits a few hours or when served the next day.

Chocolate Pound Cake

- **1 cup margarine**
- **½ cup Crisco shortening**
- **3 cups sugar**
- **5 eggs**
- **3 cups cake flour**
- **4 tablespoons cocoa**
- **½ teaspoon baking powder**
- **½ teaspoon salt**
- **1 cup milk**
- **1 tablespoon vanilla**

Cream margarine and Crisco. Add sugar and blend. Add eggs, one at a time, beating after each addition. Sift together flour, cocoa, baking powder and salt. Add flour mixture, alternating with milk and vanilla. Bake at 350° for 1½ hours or longer in a greased and floured tube pan.

A friendly tip: May use a can of chocolate icing. Try melting it a little in microwave and drizzle over cake. Works very well.

Katherine's Pound Cake

- **2 sticks butter**
- **½ cup Crisco**
- **3 cups sugar**
- **5 eggs**
- **1 teaspoon vanilla flavoring**
- **1 teaspoon butter flavoring**
- **1 teaspoon rum flavoring**
- **½ teaspoon baking powder**
- **½ teaspoon salt**
- **3 cups plain flour, sifted**
- **1 cup milk**

Combine butter and Crisco and beat. Add sugar and beat until fluffy. Add eggs, one at a time, and beat until well mixed. Add flavorings and beat. Sift flour with baking powder and salt and add alternately with milk to mixture. Start with flour and end with flour. Line tube pan with wax paper and grease and flour. Bake at 325° for 1 hour and 15 minutes or until golden brown. Serves 12 to 16.

NOTE: 2 loaf pans can be used instead of tube pan, or for birthday cake, use 10x14-inch sheet cake.

Three Flavor Pound Cake

3 cups sugar
1 cup butter or margarine
6 eggs
3 cups all-purpose flour
½ teaspoon salt
¼ teaspoon baking soda
1 cup whipping cream
½ teaspoon lemon extract
½ teaspoon orange extract
1 teaspoon vanilla

Cream together sugar and butter until light and fluffy. Add eggs one at a time, beating well after each addition. Sift together flour, salt and baking soda. Add to creamed mixture alternately with whipping cream, beating after each addition. Add extracts and vanilla. Beat well. Pour batter into a well greased and floured bundt or tube pan. Bake at 350° for 1½ hours or until cake tests done. Cool 15 minutes before removing from pan. When cool, sprinkle with powdered sugar if desired. Serves 12 to 16.

Amaretto Chocolate Cheesecake

Cheesecake:

1 9-inch chocolate wafer crust
Amaretto
2 (8-ounce) packages cream cheese, at room temperature
1½ cups sugar
⅓ cup cocoa
2 *large* eggs, room temperature
1 teaspoon vanilla
Fresh strawberries
Whipped cream

Prepare chocolate wafer crust in springform pan as per directions on package. Sprinkle with amaretto. Set aside. Whip cream cheese. Add sugar, cocoa, eggs and vanilla. Whip until blended. Pour into crust and bake 45 minutes at 350°. (It may puff and appear to crack.)

Topping:

½ cup sour cream
2 tablespoons amaretto
½ cup brown sugar

Combine the sour cream, amaretto and brown sugar. Mix well. Pour on top of cheesecake and spread from center out to sides. Bake for 10 minutes at 350°. Refrigerate overnight. Remove from 9" springform pan. Decorate with real whipped cream and fresh strawberries. Serves 10.

Sour Cream Pound Cake

- **1 cup butter or margarine**
- **3 cups sugar**
- **6 eggs**
- **3 cups all-purpose flour**
- **1 cup sour cream**
- **¼ teaspoon soda**
- **1 teaspoon vanilla**
- **½ teaspoon lemon extract**

Preheat oven to 300°. Cream butter and sugar. (Creaming of butter and sugar and beating very well after addition of each egg is very important.) Add eggs one at a time beating after each addition. Add soda to sour cream. Add flour one cup at a time alternately with sour cream mixture. Add vanilla and lemon extract. Bake in bundt or tube pan for 1½ hours or until done. When cooled, sprinkle powdered sugar over top and sides of cake. (1 teaspoon almond extract can be substituted for lemon extract.) Serves 12 to 16.

This freezes very well so it can be made anytime and is just as moist as when first made.

Fabulous Cheese Cake

Crust:

- **1¼ cups graham cracker crumbs**
- **¼ cup margarine**
- **2 tablespoons sugar**

Combine graham cracker crumbs, margarine and sugar, press into bottom of 10-inch pie pan.

Filling:

- **3 eggs**
- **½ cup sugar**
- **2 (8-ounce) packages cream cheese, softened**
- **2 teaspoons vanilla, divided**
- **4 tablespoons sugar**
- **1 pint sour cream**

Beat eggs well at high speed and then add ½ cup sugar, cream cheese (a little at a time) and 1 teaspoon vanilla. Pour filling into crust. Bake at 350° for 25 minutes. Cool for 10 minutes (leave the oven on). Mix 4 tablespoons sugar with sour cream and add 1 teaspoon vanilla. Pour this on top of cheese cake when cool. Bake 10 more minutes. Delicious topped with cherries, pineapple or blueberries. Serves 10 to 12.

My family loves this more than any other dessert.

No Fault New York Cheesecake

- **⅓ cup margarine, melted**
- **1¼ cups graham cracker crumbs**
- **¼ cup sugar**
- **4 (8-ounce) packages cream cheese**
- **2 tablespoons flour**
- **1 (14-ounce) can sweetened condensed milk (Eagle Brand)**
- **4 eggs**
- **¼ cup lemon juice concentrate**

Preheat oven to 350°. Combine butter, crumbs and sugar; pat firmly onto bottom of 9-inch springform pan. Beat cream cheese until fluffy. Beat in 2 tablespoons flour, then 4 eggs. Gradually add sweetened milk; beat until smooth. Add the lemon juice and mix well. Pour into prepared pan and bake 1 hour or until golden brown. Cool to room temperature and/or refrigerate. Serves 12.

Wonderful cheesecake - perfect everytime!

Praline Cheese Cake

Crust:

- **1½ cups cinnamon graham cracker crumbs**
- **3 tablespoons butter or margarine, melted**
- **3 tablespoons sugar**

Combine above ingredients mixing well. Press into a 9-inch springform pan. Bake at 350° for 10 minutes.

Filling:

- **3 (8-ounce) packages cream cheese**
- **¾ cup brown sugar, firmly packed**
- **2 tablespoons all-purpose flour**
- **3 eggs**
- **2 teaspoons vanilla extract**
- **½ cup pecans, finely chopped**
- **Whipped cream (optional)**
- **Pecan halves (optional)**

Beat cream cheese until smooth; gradually add brown sugar and flour, mixing well. Add eggs, one at a time. Stir in vanilla and pecans. Pour into cracker crust. Bake at 350° for 40 to 45 minutes. Let cool on wire rack. Refrigerate overnight. Remove from pan and top with whipped cream and pecan halves, if desired. Serves 10 to 12.

Pumpkin Cheesecake

- **¾ cup graham cracker crumbs**
- **½ cup ground pecans**
- **2 tablespoons sugar**
- **2 tablespoons brown sugar**
- **¼ cup butter or margarine, melted**
- **¾ cup sugar**
- **¾ cup canned pumpkin**
- **3 egg yolks**
- **1½ teaspoons ground cinnamon**
- **½ teaspoon ground mace**
- **½ teaspoon ground ginger**
- **¼ teaspoon salt**
- **3 (8-ounce) packages cream cheese, softened**
- **¼ cup plus 2 tablespoons sugar**
- **1 egg**
- **1 egg yolk**
- **2 tablespoons cornstarch**
- **½ teaspoon vanilla extract**
- **½ teaspoon lemon extract**
- **Whipping cream (optional)**
- **Pecan halves (optional)**

Combine first five ingredients. Mix well. Firmly press mixture into 9-inch springform pan. Combine ¾ cup sugar, pumpkin, egg yolks, spices and salt in medium bowl, mix well and set aside. Beat cream cheese with electric mixer until light and fluffy. Gradually add ¼ cup plus 2 tablespoons sugar, mixing well. Add egg and egg yolk. Add cornstarch and extracts. Beat until smooth. Add pumpkin mixture and mix well. Pour into prepared pan. Bake at 350° for 50 to 55 minutes. Center may be soft but will firm when chilled. Let cool on a wire rack. Chill thoroughly. Garnish with whipping cream and pecans, if desired. Makes 9-inch cheesecake.

Delicious and a wonderful idea for Thanksgiving dinner dessert.

Ashley Bakery Chocolate Pecan Pie

- **1 cup pecans**
- **½ cup margarine**
- **1 cup sugar**
- **¾ cup light corn syrup**
- **3 eggs, slightly beaten**
- **1 teaspoon vanilla**
- **2 tablespoons chocolate syrup**
- **Pinch of salt**
- **1 9-inch pie crust**

Sprinkle nuts into pie shell. Cream sugar, butter and salt. Add corn syrup, eggs and vanilla. Stir in chocolate syrup. Pour over nuts. Bake at 375° for 40 to 45 minutes. Serves 8 to 10.

A favorite in BE Lunchroom.

Brenda's Fresh Peach Pie

- 4 cups fresh peaches, sliced
- 2 9-inch baked pie shells, sprinkled with powdered sugar
- 1 cup sugar
- 1 cup boiling water
- 3 tablespoons cornstarch
- ½ teaspoon almond flavoring
- 3 tablespoons Jello (use any flavor as long as it is red) mixed with 2 teaspoons of the boiling water

Cook sugar, water, and cornstarch until thickened. Mix in Jello. Add peaches and flavoring. Put in baked pie crusts. Chill for several hours. Top with whipped cream. Makes 2 pies.

Chocolate Fudge Pie

- 2 squares unsweetened Bakers' chocolate
- ½ cup evaporated milk
- ½ stick butter
- 1½ cups sugar
- 2 teaspoons vanilla
- 2 eggs
- Dash of salt
- Unbaked pie shell
- ½ pint whipped cream

Preheat oven to 325°. Melt the chocolate and butter together. Mix all other ingredients and add the chocolate mixture. Beat until blended. Pour into unbaked pie shell. Bake at 325° for 45 minutes on bottom oven rack. Serve each slice with a scoop of whipped cream. Serves 8.

Crunchy Apple Pie

- 1 cup graham cracker crumbs
- 1 cup sugar
- ½ cup all-purpose flour
- ½ cup pecans
- ¼ teaspoon salt
- ½ teaspoon cinnamon
- 6 apples, peeled, cored and sliced
- 1 (10-inch) unbaked pie shell
- ½ cup butter

Combine crumbs, sugar, flour, pecans, salt and cinnamon. Arrange apples in pie shell and sprinkle with this mixture. Pour melted butter evenly over the top. Bake at 350° for 1 hour. Top with whipped cream or ice cream. Serves 8 to 10.

Candy Bar Pie

1⅓ cups coconut, grated
2 tablespoons margarine, melted
1 teaspoon instant coffee powder (optional)
2 tablespoons water
1 (7½-ounce) milk chocolate candy bar with almonds, broken (or 2 (4-ounce) bars)
4 cups (12-ounce) container frozen whipped dessert topping, thawed

Combine coconut and margarine; press into 8-inch pie plate. Bake in 325° oven for 10 minutes or until coconut is golden. Cool thoroughly.

Dissolve coffee powder in water; add chocolate bar. Stir chocolate mixture over low heat until melted. Cool. Fold in whipped topping; pile into coconut crust. Chill in freezer several hours or overnight (will not freeze solid). May be eaten frozen. Serves 6 to 8.

To make this easy dessert elegant, top with curled chocolate.

Edith's Grasshopper Pie

1 package Famous Chocolate Wafers
½ cup butter
¾ of ½ gallon vanilla ice milk
3 tablespoons crème de menthe
1 pint whipping cream
1 (4-ounce) Elmers New Orleans Old Birch Crunchy Chocolate Pecan Topping or Smucker's Chocolate Magic Shell

Melt butter, mix with crushed Famous Chocolate Wafers. Press mixture into a 9-inch pie plate and freeze. Soften ¾ of ½ gallon vanilla ice milk. Mix crème de menthe into softened ice milk. Put into frozen pie shell and return to freezer. When ready to serve, whip the cream. Heat the sauce according to directions on package. Spread the whipped cream over the ice cream and drizzle the chocolate over the top of cream. Enjoy! Serves 6 to 8.

Cloud Nine Chocolate Pie

Pie Shell:

- **2 egg whites**
- **⅛ teaspoon salt**
- **⅛ teaspoon cream of tartar**
- **½ cup sugar**
- **⅛ teaspoon vanilla**
- **½ cup nuts, finely chopped**

Beat egg whites with salt and cream of tartar until foamy. Add sugar, 2 tablespoons at a time, beating well after each addition. Continue beating until stiff peaks form. Fold in vanilla and nuts. Spoon into lightly greased 8-inch pie pan to form nest-like shell. Build sides up ½ inch above edge of pan. Bake approximately 50 minutes at 300°. Cool completely.

Chocolate Cream Filling:

- **1 (4-ounce) bar German sweet chocolate**
- **3 tablespoons water**
- **1 teaspoon vanilla**
- **1½ cups heavy cream, whipped**

Stir chocolate in water over low heat until melted. Cool until thick, and add vanilla. Fold in 1 cup whipped cream. Pile into cooled pie shell and cover with remaining whipped cream. Garnish with chocolate curls. To make chocolate curls, use vegetable peeler and chilled chocolate bar, such as Bakers' chocolate. Serves 6 to 8.

Father Charles Kelley's Favorite

Deep Dish Apple Crumb Pie:

- **1 can sliced apples (not apple pie filling)**
- **¼ cup brown sugar**
- **½ cup granulated sugar**
- **1 teaspoon cinnamon**
- **Pinch of salt**

Butter a 9x9-inch deep square dish. Empty apples into dish. Mix brown sugar, granulated sugar, cinnamon, salt and spread over the apples.

Topping:

- **1 cup self-rising flour**
- **¾ cup granulated sugar**
- **1 teaspoon baking powder**
- **1 egg**
- **½ cup butter**

Mix first four ingredients until mixture is crumbly then spread over the top. Melt butter and pour over the mixture. Bake in 350° oven until brown, about 25 minutes. Serves 6.

Lord Calvert Mudd Pie

- 18 Oreo cookies
- 1 quart coffee ice cream, softened
- 5 tablespoons butter, melted
- ⅓ cup evaporated milk
- 1 cup whipping cream
- 6 ounces chocolate morsels
- 4 tablespoons Kahlúa
- 1 tablespoon sugar
- 1 cup pecans, chopped

Crush Oreos in blender and mix with melted butter. Press in a springform pan or 9-inch pie pan and freeze. Spread softened ice cream in pie crust and freeze. Melt milk and morsels over low heat and pour over pie. Freeze. Whip cream and put on pie. Mix Kahlúa and sugar and drip over whipped cream. Garnish with pecans. Keep frozen until ready to serve. Serves 8.

Heavenly Strawberry Pie

- 1 tablespoon margarine
- 1 cup sugar
- 4 tablespoons cornstarch
- Red food coloring
- 1½ cups 7-Up
- 2 cups fresh strawberries, sliced
- 1 (9-inch) baked pie shell or graham crust
- Whipped cream

Combine margarine, sugar, cornstarch, red food coloring, and 7-Up in saucepan. Stir over medium heat until very thick. Cool. Fold in strawberries and pour into pie shell. Chill and serve with whipped cream. Serves 8 to 10.

Macaroon Pie

- 12 saltines, rolled into crumbs
- 12 dates, chopped
- ½ cup pecans, cut into small pieces
- ¼ teaspoon baking powder
- 1 teaspoon almond extract
- 1 cup sugar
- 3 egg whites, beaten until stiff
- ½ pint whipping cream

Mix first six ingredients together. Fold into stiff egg whites. Bake in a greased 8-inch pie tin at 350° for 30 minutes. Top with whipped UNSWEETENED cream. Serves 6 to 8.

Joey's Lemon Meringue Pie

Pie:

- **1¼ cups sugar**
- **⅓ cup cornstarch**
- **3 egg yolks**
- **1½ cups water**
- **½ cup lemon juice**
- **3 tablespoons butter or margarine**
- **2 teaspoons vinegar**
- **1½ teaspoons lemon extract**
- **1 (9-inch) baked pastry shell**
- **Cooked meringue**

In top of double boiler, mix sugar and cornstarch. Add egg yolks, lemon juice and water. Mix well. Put water in bottom of double boiler and bring to a boil, reduce heat and cook lemon mixture over hot water, stirring constantly until thickened. Remove from heat, stir in butter, vinegar and lemon extract. Pour immediately into pastry shell. Spread meringue over warm filling sealing to edge of pastry. Bake at 425° for 5 to 8 minutes or until lightly browned. Cool before serving. Serves 8.

Meringue:

- **¼ cup plus 2 tablespoons sugar**
- **1 tablespoon cornstarch**
- **¾ cup water**
- **3 egg whites at room temperature**
- **Pinch of salt**
- **1 teaspoon vanilla extract**

Combine sugar and cornstarch in a small bowl, add water and mix well. Heat in microwave, stirring occasionally until clear and thickened. In a separate bowl, combine egg whites and salt; beat until foamy. Add vanilla, and continue beating while gradually pouring cooked mixture into egg whites. Beat 3 minutes or until stiff but not dry. Do not overbeat.

Tart and wonderful - just like a homemade lemon pie should be!

Nana's Apple Pie

1 package Pillsbury ready to use pie crust
3 pounds McIntosh or Granny Smith apples, peeled, cored and sliced
1 tablespoon lemon juice
1 teaspoon lemon peel, grated
¾ cup sugar
⅓ cup all-purpose flour
1 teaspoon cinnamon
⅛ teaspoon salt
½ teaspoon nutmeg
2 tablespoons butter, cut into small pieces
½ cup raisins (optional)

Preheat oven to 425°. Remove pastry from box and place one layer in 9-inch pie plate - allow sides to over hang. In a large bowl toss apples with lemon juice and peel. Combine dry ingredients in small bowl. Add to apple mixture and toss to completely coat apples. Place apple slices in pie crust laying slices first along the outside and work towards inside until entire pastry is covered. Continue adding layers of apples until all are used. Pour any juices over filling. Dot with butter. Take remaining crust and gently place over filling. Press the top crust to the lower crust. You may press firmly with a fork or flute the crust as desired all the way around to seal. Slash vents in the center of crust. (My mother always etched my dad's name Jim.) Place pie on shelf of oven, lower ⅓. Put foil on oven floor to catch drips. Bake 40 to 50 minutes or until golden.

Glaze:
1 cup powdered sugar
2 tablespoons milk

Combine to make thin paste. Pour over hot pie. Serves 8 to 10.

Peanutty Pie

- **1 cup peanut butter**
- **1 (3-ounce) package cream cheese**
- **1 cup powdered sugar**
- **1 (8-ounce) tub frozen whipped topping**
- **1 graham cracker pie shell**

Cream together peanut butter, cream cheese, and sugar. Fold in whipped topping and spoon into shell.

Topping:

- **⅓ cup peanut butter**
- **⅔ cup powdered sugar**

Mix together and spoon over the top of pie. Refrigerate. You may drizzle caramel or hot fudge sauce to garnish pie. Serves 6 to 8.

You've never had peanut butter so good!

Snickers Pie With Mocha Fudge Sauce

- **3 (9-inch) graham cracker pie shells**
- **1 gallon natural vanilla ice cream, slightly softened**
- **2 to 4 Snickers bars**
- **Any good quality hot fudge sauce**
- **2 ounces coffee**

Chop Snickers into about 8 pieces per bar. In a large mixing bowl, "smoosh" Snickers into ice cream until until evenly incorporated. Spoon ice cream mix into pie shells and freeze 4 hours or overnight. Heat hot fudge as per directions, add coffee to fudge. Cut pie into six slices and top each with a generous ladle of mocha fudge sauce. Can be frozen for that surprise occasion when you need something special. Serves 6 to 8.

The best selling dessert at Tommy Condon's Irish Pub and Restaurant is this famous Snickers Pie. They make batches that will feed multitudes of hungry Irishmen, women and of course wee little ones.

Elegantè Almond Torte

- **4 eggs, separated**
- **½ cup powdered sugar**
- **½ cup granulated sugar**
- **½ cup shortening**
- **¾ cup powdered sugar**
- **3 tablespoons milk**
- **1 cup all-purpose flour**
- **1 teaspoon baking powder**
- **¼ teaspoon salt**
- **½ cup unblanched almonds, sliced**
- **2 tablespoons granulated sugar**
- **1 teaspoon cornstarch**

Heat oven to 325°. Grease and flour two 8x1½-inch round layer pans. Beat egg whites until foamy. Beat in ½ cup each granulated sugar and powdered sugar, (I like to add 1 teaspoon of cornstarch to prevent "weeping"), continue beating until stiff and glossy. Set meringue aside.

Measure shortening, ¾ cup powdered sugar, the egg yolks and milk into large mixer bowl. Blend ½ minute on low speed, scraping bowl constantly. Add flour, baking powder, and salt. Blend and spread in pans. (will be thick) Spread half the meringue on batter in each pan. Sprinkle each with half the almonds, then with 1 tablespoon sugar. Bake 35 to 40 minutes or until meringue is set. Cool away from draft.

Prepare Almond Cream Filling. Let cool completely. with spatulas, carefully remove layers from pans. Place 1 layer meringue side up on serving plate. Spread with filling. Top with other layer, meringue side up. Chill at least 1 hour.

Serves 12.

Almond Cream Filling:

- **½ teaspoon salt**
- **½ cup sugar**
- **3 tablespoons flour**
- **1¼ cups milk**
- **2 egg yolks, slightly beaten**
- **1 tablespoon butter**
- **½ teaspoon vanilla**
- **1 teaspoon almond flavoring**

In small saucepan, combine sugar, flour and salt. Gradually add milk; mix well. Cook over medium heat until mixture boils, stirring constantly; boil 1 minute. Blend small amount (about ¼ cup) hot mixture into egg. Return egg mixture to saucepan; mix well. Cook until mixture starts to bubble, stirring constantly. Stir in margarine and vanilla and almond extract. Cover and cool. Fills a 2-layer cake.

Stono Cup Pie

- ½ teaspoon instant coffee crystals
- 2 tablespoons bourbon
- 1 to 1½ cups pecans, chopped
- 1 cup sugar
- 3 eggs
- 1 cup white corn syrup
- 4 tablespoons butter, melted
- ½ cup semi-sweet chocolate chips
- Whipped cream

Preheat oven to 425°. Prick bottom of pie crust and place in oven 4 or 5 minutes until dry. Remove from oven and cool. Reduce oven heat to 350°. Dissolve coffee crystals in bourbon and pour over the pecans. Set aside. Beat eggs until frothy, and add sugar and continue to beat. Add corn syrup, melted butter, chocolate chips and pecan mixture. Pour into semi-cooked pie crust. Bake at 350° for 40 to 45 minutes until golden. Serves 8.

Serve with whipped cream if you dare!!

Mandarin Orange-Pineapple Torte

- 1 box Duncan Hines Butter Recipe Golden Cake mix
- 4 eggs
- ¾ cup Crisco oil
- 1 (11-ounce) can mandarin oranges and its juice

Mix all ingredients and beat at medium speed 3 to 4 minutes. Bake in four 9-inch pans at 350° for 20 to 30 minutes or until brown.

Filling - Frosting:

- 1 (20-ounce) can crushed pineapple and juice
- 1 (4-ounce) box instant vanilla Jello pudding
- 1 (8-ounce) container Cool Whip

Mix pudding and let stand a few minutes in the refrigerator. When the pudding has set a little, add the pineapple and juice. Fold in the Cool Whip. Fill between layers very generously and frost the cake with the remainder. This torte should stand in refrigerator at least 48 hours before cutting. Serves 12 to 16.

After cutting the first piece, this will not last long.

Loretta Croghan's Lemon Torte

Meringue Layers:

4 eggs, separated
1 cup flour
1 pinch salt
1 teaspoon vanilla
¾ cup powdered sugar
1 teaspoon baking powder
3 tablespoons milk
1 cup pecans, thinly sliced

Beat the egg yolks with powdered sugar, add all dry ingredients, and then vanilla and milk. Pour the batter into 2 lightly greased round layer pans and set aside while making the meringue. Whip the 4 egg whites with 1 cup of sugar until stiff. Spread this meringue over each unbaked layer and top with sliced pecans. Bake at 325° for 35 to 40 minutes or until set.

Lemon Filling:

4 eggs
1 cup sugar
Juice of 2 lemons
Rind of 1 lemon

Beat the eggs, sugar, lemon juice and rind until combined. Pour into a double boiler and cook until thick. Completely cool the filling before using.

To Combine:

Put first layer on cake plate and spread ½ filling on top. Gently place second layer on top of first and spread remaining filling on top. Serve with freshly whipped cream.

This was Monsignor William Croghan's favorite.

Chocolate-Chocolate Truffle Torte

8 eggs, separated
¾ cup sugar
¼ cup pecans, ground
½ tablespoon vanilla
2½ squares unsweetened chocolate
6 tablespoons unsalted, unsweetened butter, melted
1 cup fine breadcrumbs
⅓ cup cake flour

Place egg yolks, ½ of the sugar and vanilla in a large bowl. Beat until triple in volume - fold in nuts.

In a double boiler, melt chocolate. When cool, add to yolk mixture. Stir until chocolate in color. Slowly add cooled butter to mixture.

Beat egg whites until soft peaks - add sugar. (Do not beat until stiff, just soft peaks.) Fold egg whites into chocolate batter. Sprinkle with flour and breadcrumbs. Gently fold until mixed.

Pour into a greased and lined 9" springform pan. Bake at 350° for 35 to 40 minutes. When cooled, remove from pan and slice into three layers.

Genaise Cream:

1 cup heavy cream
1 (4-ounce) white chocolate, chopped
6 tablespoons butter, melted
5 tablespoons light rum

Place heavy cream in heavy bowl in top of double boiler. (Metal will do). Heat until the cream barely boils, whisk in chocolate until melted. Stir in butter and rum. Cool in refrigerator about one hour. When cool whip light and fluffy. Spread Genaise between layers and frost tops and sides of cake. Decorate with shaved chocolate and crushed pecans. Refrigerate cake.

Sour Cream Fudge Torte

1 package devils food cake mix
3 eggs
1 cup water
⅓ cup oil

Combine ingredients in large bowl. Bake cake according to directions on package. Pour into two 8-inch round greased and floured cake pans. Cool completely and split each layer in half. Fill and frost each layer with Sour Cream Coconut Filling.

Filling:
2 cups sour cream
1 cup sugar
3 cups coconut, flaked
3 cups non-dairy whipped topping

Combine all above ingredients. Frost all layers and top of cake. Serves 12.

A feast for chocolate lovers!

Market Place Pecan Torte

1 cup shortening
2 cups dark-brown sugar
4 eggs, separated
3 cups self-rising flour
1 cup milk
1 teaspoon vanilla
1 cup pecans, chopped
4 tablespoons sugar
½ pint of whipping cream, whipped

Cream shortening and brown sugar. Add egg yolks, then flour and milk, alternately. Add vanilla and nuts. Spread in two 9-inch layer pans. Beat egg whites, adding 4 tablespoons sugar slowly, and spread on top of cake. Bake at 325° for 50 minutes. Cool. Spread first layer with half of whipped cream and place second layer on top. Cover it with remainder of whipped cream and decorate with nuts and cherries if desired. Serves 6 to 8.

Ambrosia Crumble

- **1½ cups shredded coconut**
- **1 cup all-purpose flour**
- **1 cup granulated sugar**
- **½ cup brown sugar, packed firmly**
- **½ cup unsalted butter, softened**
- **½ large ripe pineapple, cut into 1-inch cubes**
- **3 large navel oranges, peeled and sectioned**
- **3 ripe bananas, cut into ½-inch slices**
- **2 tablespoons fresh lemon juice**
- **1 pint vanilla ice cream**

Preheat oven to 350°. Generously butter a shallow 3-quart baking dish. In a medium bowl, combine 1 cup of coconut, the flour, ¾ cup granulated sugar and all the brown sugar. Using your hands, pinch the butter into the flour mixture to form coarse crumbs. In another bowl, toss together the pineapple, oranges and bananas with the remaining coconut, ¼ cup sugar and lemon juice. Place the fruit in the baking dish and sprinkle the crumb topping evenly over the fruit. Bake for 45 minutes or until the top is golden. Serve with a scoop of vanilla ice cream. Serves 12.

A good dessert for brunch.

Blueberry Crisp

- **2 cans blueberry pie filling**
- **1½ teaspoons lemon juice**
- **½ cup margarine, melted**
- **1 package yellow cake mix**
- **¾ cup nuts, chopped**

Spread pie filling in the bottom of 9x13-inch baking dish. Sprinkle with lemon juice. Combine dry cake mix, nuts and melted margarine. Sprinkle over pie filling. Bake at 350° for about 45 minutes until golden brown. Serve warm with ice cream or whipped cream. Serves 12.

A favorite with the little children ...(and big kids, too).

Cranberry Apple Crisp

1 can whole cranberry sauce
1 cup light brown sugar
1 tablespoon cornstarch
3 cups Winesap or Granny Smith apples

Mix sugar and cornstarch together and add apples. Pour cranberry sauce over this mixture. Put into 1½-quart baking dish and set aside.

Topping:
1 stick margarine
½ cup light brown sugar
1 package instant regular oatmeal
½ cup pecans, chopped

Melt margarine and add other ingredients. Pour over apple mixture. Bake at 350° for 30 minutes. Serves 4.

A true comfort food - makes the whole house smell good!

Fruit Cobbler

⅔ to 1 cup sugar
1 tablespoon cornstarch
¼ cup water or fruit juice
3 cups fresh fruit or 1 quart
Butter
Cinnamon

Mix sugar and cornstarch. Gradually add water or juice. Bring to a boil. Boil 1 minute stirring constantly. Add fruit and remaining juice. Pour into 1½-quart baking dish. Dot with butter and sprinkle with cinnamon.

Topping:
1½ cups all-purpose flour
1 tablespoon sugar
1½ teaspoons baking powder
½ teaspoon salt
3 tablespoons shortening
½ cup milk

Measure flour and stir in sugar, baking powder and salt. Cut in shortening until mixture looks like meal. Stir in milk and drop by spoonful onto hot mixture. Bake 25 to 30 minutes at 400°. Serves 6 to 8.

This is a family original and favorite. Delicious with peaches or blackberries.

Trifle

- 1 pound cake
- 1 cup raspberry jam
- 1 cup sliced almonds, toasted
- ¾ cup Harvey's Bristol Cream
- ¼ cup cognac
- 2 (12-ounce) packages frozen raspberries (or fresh if available)
- Vanilla custard (recipe below)
- 2 cups heavy cream, whipped and sweetened
- Fresh strawberries, raspberries and almonds for top of Trifle

Slice cake into 1½-inch slices. Spread jam between 2 slices and put them together to make "sandwich". Continue with rest of cake and jam, and layer the "sandwiches" on sides and bottom of large footed glass bowl. Sprinkle with almond slices, and pour over the Harvey's Bristol Cream and the cognac. Wash and drain the raspberries.

Custard Sauce:

- 1½ tablespoons cornstarch
- 2 cups whole milk
- 4 egg yolks
- ½ cup sugar
- 1½ teaspoons vanilla

In a small bowl, mix together cornstarch and ¼ cup milk. Beat egg yolks until light and combine with cornstarch mixture. Heat remaining milk in a saucepan. DO NOT BOIL. Stir in sugar until dissolved. Very slowly, stir in about 1 cup of hot milk into egg yolks. Return all to saucepan and continue to stir constantly over low heat for 10 minutes until slightly thickened. Remove from heat, stir in vanilla and cool to room temperature.

Put the raspberries over the cake, pour on the cooled custard, and chill thoroughly 4 to 5 hours. When ready to serve, top with whipped cream and decorate with almonds and fruit. Serves 12 to 16.

A Christmas Tradition!

Mocha Coeur À La Crème

- **1 cup whipping cream**
- **1 (8-ounce) package cream cheese, softened**
- **⅓ cup sugar**
- **Dash of salt**
- **½ teaspoon instant espresso coffee**
- **1 tablespoon water**
- **1 teaspoon vanilla extract**
- **1 (6-ounce) package semi-sweet chocolate chips, melted and cooled**
- **Chocolate curls, for garnish**
- **Powdered sugar**

Line a 7-inch coeur à la crème mold or heart-shaped basket with a single layer of damp cheesecloth, allow a 4-inch overhang all around the pan. In a large mixing bowl, whip cream until soft peaks form; set aside. In another large mixing bowl, combine cream cheese, sugar and salt. Beat until light and fluffy. Dissolve coffee in water and add to the cream cheese with the vanilla. Beat until well blended. Add chocolate. Beat just until thoroughly blended; scraping the sides of bowl with rubber spatula. Fold in whipped cream. Spoon into mold, spreading evenly to edges. Fold cheesecloth over the top. Set mold in shallow pan and refrigerate overnight.

When ready to serve, fold back cheesecloth from the top of mold. Invert mold onto serving plate; remove mold and cheesecloth. Garnish with chocolate curls and sprinkle with powdered sugar, if desired. Makes 10 to 12 servings, and contains 285 calories.

This is easier to make than the name sounds!

Orange Sherbet

- **2½ cups sugar**
- **3 cups fresh orange juice (8 oranges)**
- **4 cups milk**
- **1 pint evaporated milk**
- **Pinch of salt**

Combine sugar and orange juice. Gradually add milk, cream and a pinch of salt. Freeze. Serves 10 to 12.

Very easy and very delicious!

Peach Crumble Parfait

- 1 cup sugar
- 1 egg, beaten
- 1 cup pecans, chopped
- 1 cup sour cream
- 1 cup milk
- 1 cup peaches, peeled and diced
- 1 (3⅝-ounce) package instant vanilla pudding mix

Thoroughly combine sugar, egg, pecans, and spread mixture in a foil-lined 15x10x1½-inch baking pan. Bake at 350° for 18 to 20 minutes, or until golden brown. Cool to room temperature. Coarsely crumble baked nut mixture and divide ½ the crumb mix among 6 sherbet glasses. Combine pudding mix, sour cream, and milk. Beat on low speed for 1 to 2 minutes or until well blended. Fold in peaches and spoon the mixture over the crumbs in glasses. Top with remaining crumbs. Chill several hours before serving. Serves 6.

Brownie Chocolate Pudding

- 1 cup all-purpose flour
- ¾ cup sugar
- 2 tablespoons unsweetened cocoa
- 2 teaspoons baking powder
- ⅛ teaspoon salt
- ½ cup milk
- 2 tablespoons butter
- 1 teaspoon vanilla
- 1 cup brown sugar
- ¼ cup cocoa
- 1¾ cups hot water
- ½ cup nuts
- ½ cup semi-sweet chocolate pieces

Mix flour, sugar, unsweetened cocoa, baking powder and salt together. Add milk, butter, and vanilla. Then add nuts and semi-sweet chocolate pieces. Pour batter in ungreased 9x9-inch pan, and sprinkle with brown sugar and cocoa which have been mixed together. Pour hot water over batter. **Don't stir.** Bake at 350° for 40 minutes. Serve in dessert dish. Serves 4 to 6.

Great when warm with a scoop of ice cream on top!

Top Gun Banana Pudding

- **1 large package vanilla instant pudding**
- **3 cups milk**
- **1 large tub Cool Whip**
- **1 can condensed milk**
- **10 ripe bananas**
- **1½ to 2 boxes vanilla wafers**
- **1 small tub Cool Whip (optional)**

Make instant pudding according to package directions, add condensed milk, stir, and add large tub of whipped topping. Stir again and set aside. Cut bananas in rounds about ¼- to ½-inch thick in separate bowl. In large bowl layer vanilla wafers, bananas and pudding mixture as many times as necessary ending with the pudding mixture on top. If desired you can spread small container of whipped topping on top for added decoration. Refrigerate 1 hour before serving. Serves 6 to 8.

Everyone will want this recipe!

Sullivan's Island Bread Pudding

Pudding:

- **2 cups bread, broken in small pieces**
- **4 cups milk**
- **½ cup sugar**
- **4 large eggs**
- **¼ cup butter**
- **½ teaspoon salt**
- **1 teaspoon vanilla**

Soak bread in milk for 4 minutes. Add sugar, eggs, butter, salt and vanilla. Mix well. Pour into a 10x10-inch buttered pan and place in a pan of warm water. Bake at 350° for 1 hour.

Hard Sauce:

- **2 cups powdered sugar**
- **¼ cup butter**
- **2 teaspoons vanilla**

Beat hard sauce ingredients for 3 minutes. Serve pudding topped with sauce. Serves 8.

Schill's Sweet Surprise

- **1 (20-ounce) can crushed pineapple, drained**
- **1 can any flavor pie filling**
- **1 yellow box cake mix, use dry**
- **2 sticks butter, chopped**
- **1 cup pecans, chopped**
- **9x13 or 10x10-inch baking dish**

Place ingredients in order given in baking dish. **Do not mix,** just layer. Bake at 350° for 55 minutes. Let cool and serve in same dish it was baked in. Great to serve warm, in winter, topped with vanilla ice cream. Serves 12 to 16.

Make sure you try this with blueberry pie filling.

Macaroon Mousse

- **2 dozen plain macaroons (from bakery)**
- **1 pint whipping cream**
- **Sherry wine**
- **2 tablespoons sugar (optional)**

Break up macaroons and put in small bowl. Cover with sherry - about 1½-ounces. Stir with fork to break up. Let stand in refrigerator overnight (cover with plastic wrap). Should be mushy by A.M.

Whip cream until stiff, adding sugar gradually. Omit sugar or use sparingly. Mash and stir macaroons - fold into whipped cream. Put mixture into a loaf pan or other suitable container and return to freezer to freeze. Remove from freezer about 1 hour before serving. Stir before serving. Should be completely thawed. Serve in champagne glasses and garnish with cherries and strawberries. Serves 6 to 8.

Delicious but rich.

Southern Fudge Cake

Cake:

2 cups sugar
2 cups all-purpose flour
1 teaspoon soda
1 cup margarine or butter
1 cup water
4 tablespoons cocoa
½ cup buttermilk
1 teaspoon vanilla
2 eggs, beaten

Mix sugar, flour, and soda in large bowl. Set aside. Combine butter, cocoa and water in saucepan, bring to a boil, but do not boil. Pour over sugar mixture and mix well. Add buttermilk, vanilla and eggs and mix well. Pour into greased 9x13-inch pan. Bake at 400° for 20 to 25 minutes.

Icing:

½ cup margarine or butter
4 tablespoons cocoa
⅓ cup milk
1 (16-ounce) box powdered sugar
1 teaspoon vanilla
1 cup nuts, chopped

Combine butter, cocoa and milk in saucepan. Bring to a boil, but do not boil. Add sugar, vanilla and nuts and spread on cake while hot.

Tom's Marvelous Mousse

6 ounces semi-sweet chocolate
¼ teaspoon salt
2. tablespoons water
4 large eggs, separated
2 teaspoons vanilla
½ pint heavy cream
Optional garnish: candied violets, fresh mint leaves or chocolate curls

Combine first three ingredients in top of double boiler over hot water (medium heat). Stir until chocolate is completely melted. Remove from heat. Beat egg yolks until light and lemon colored, gradually beat in melted chocolate. Stir in vanilla. Beat egg whites until they stand in stiff peaks. Using a spatula very gently fold into chocolate mixture until all traces of egg whites disappear. Whip cream reserving ¼ cup and fold gently into chocolate mixture. Spoon into crystal bowls. Chill covered until ready to serve. Garnish with dollops of reserved whipped cream, using violets, mint leaves or chocolate curls. Serves 6 to 8.

"Death by chocolate."

Brownie Pie

- **3 egg whites**
- **Dash salt**
- **¾ cup sugar**
- **½ pint whipped cream (may substitute Cool Whip)**
- **¾ cup fine chocolate snap crumbs, rolled**
- **½ cup nuts, chopped**
- **½ teaspoon vanilla**

Beat egg whites and salt until it forms soft peaks. Add sugar, beat until stiff. Fold in chocolate crumbs, nuts and vanilla. Spread evenly in lightly buttered 9-inch pie plate. Bake at 325° for 35 minutes. Cool. Spread whipped cream on top and cool in refrigerator for about 4 hours. Serves 6 to 8.

Delicious - and easy to make. Great dessert for those who like chocolate.

Easy Brownie Pizza

- **¾ cup light corn syrup**
- **⅓ cup whipping cream**
- **1 (8-ounce) package semi-sweet chocolate**
- **½ cup butter or margarine**
- **½ cup sugar**
- **2 eggs**
- **½ teaspoon vanilla**
- **¾ cup unsifted flour**
- **½ teaspoon salt**
- **½ cup walnuts, chopped**

Grease and flour 12-inch pizza pan. In 3-quart saucepan bring corn syrup and whipping cream to boil over medium heat, stirring occasionally. Add chocolate, stir until melted. Set aside ⅔ cup of the chocolate sauce for topping. Add butter and sugar to remaining sauce; stir until butter melts.Remove from heat. Stir in eggs and vanilla. Gradually stir in flour, salt and nuts. Pour into pan. Bake at 350° for 20 minutes or until firm. Cool in pan on rack for 10 minutes. Remove from pan and place on rack until cool. Top with ice cream, fruit, nuts and chocolate sauce. Serves 12.

GRACIOUSLY LIGHT

Graciously Light

Almost Piña Coladas

- 1 (8-ounce) can unsweetened crushed pineapple
- 1 large banana, sliced
- 15 ice cubes
- 1 (12-ounce) can evaporated skimmed milk
- ½ cup pineapple-orange banana juice
- ½ teaspoon rum extract
- ½ teaspoon coconut extract

Combine all ingredients and process in blender until smooth. Serves 6.

Calories	99	Protein	5	Fat	0.3
Carbohydrate	20	Cholesterol	2	Sodium	66

Hot Spinach Dip Loaf

- 1 (1-pound) round loaf sourdough bread
- 1 (10-ounce) package frozen chopped spinach, thawed
- 1 (8-ounce) package Neufchâtel cheese, softened
- 1 (8-ounce) carton plain nonfat yogurt
- 5 ounces 40% less-fat Cheddar cheese, shredded
- ½ cup low-fat sour cream
- 1 (1-ounce) package no-oil Italian dressing mix
- 1 (2-ounce) jar sliced pimiento, drained

Cut off top ¼ of loaf. Set aside. Hollow out center of loaf and cut bread into 1-inch cubes. Place bread cubes on ungreased baking sheet. Bake at 350° for 15 minutes until golden brown. Set aside.

Drain spinach; press between paper towels to remove excess moisture. Combine spinach and remaining ingredients in bowl and stir well. Spoon mixture into bread cavity. Cover with top of loaf. Wrap in heavy aluminum foil, place on ungreased baking sheet and bake at 325° for 1½ hours or until thoroughly heated. Unwrap and serve with bread cubes. (One tablespoon dip and one bread cube per serving). Makes 3 cups dip and 48 bread cubes.

Calories	36	Protein	2	Fat	2
Carbohydrate	4	Cholesterol	5	Sodium	38

Crab-Stuffed Mushrooms

- 1 pound raw mushroom caps
- ½ cup low-cal Italian dressing
- 1 teaspoon margarine
- ½ teaspoon salt
- 7½ ounces cooked crab
- ½ cup dry breadcrumbs, divided
- 1 large raw egg
- ¼ cup chopped onions
- ¼ cup low-cal mayonnaise (dressing type)
- 1 teaspoon lemon juice

Marinate mushroom caps in Italian dressing for one hour. Mince stems, sauté in margarine. Drain mushroom caps. Mix crabmeat, ½ of the breadcrumbs, egg, onion, mayonnaise, lemon juice, salt, and mushroom stems. Place mushroom caps in shallow baking dish, fill caps with crab mixture. Top with remaining breadcrumbs. Bake at 350° for 15 minutes. Serves 35.

Calories	48	Protein	4	Fat	2
Carbohydrate	4	Cholesterol	26	Sodium	188

Creamy Orange Dip

- 1 (8-ounce) package Neufchâtel cheese, softened
- 2 tablespoons powdered sugar
- 2 tablespoons plain nonfat yogurt
- 2 tablespoons unsweetened orange juice
- 2 tablespoons orange rind, grated

Combine all ingredients. Stir until smooth. Cover and chill thoroughly. Makes 1⅓ cups. (1 tablespoon per serving).

Calories	28	Protein	1	Fat	2
Carbohydrate	1	Cholesterol	7	Sodium	39

Serve with fresh fruit or unsalted crackers.

Zucchini Pizzas

- ¾ cup commercial spaghetti sauce
- 2 ounces part-skim mozzarella cheese, shredded
- 2 tablespoons Parmesan cheese, grated
- 2 tablespoons green onions, minced
- ¼ teaspoon pepper, freshly ground
- ¼ teaspoon dried whole oregano
- 24 slices fresh zucchini, ½-inch thick
- 24 slices fresh mushrooms
- 24 slices ripe olives

Combine spaghetti sauce, cheeses, onions, pepper and oregano. Stir well. Spoon rounded teaspoons of cheese mixture on each zucchini slice. Top each with a slice of mushroom and slice of olive. Broil 6 inches from heat 3 to 5 minutes or until thoroughly heated. Serve immediately. Makes 24.

Calories	19	Protein	1	Fat	1
Carbohydrate	2	Cholesterol	1	Sodium	62

Entertain with this tasty, yet healthy, appetizer.

Delightful Crab Soup

- ½ pound fresh crabmeat
- ¼ cup onion, diced
- 2 tablespoons reduced-calorie margarine, melted
- ½ teaspoon Beau Monde seasoning
- ⅛ teaspoon white pepper
- Dash of mace
- ½ teaspoon hot sauce
- 1 (12-ounce) can evaporated skimmed milk
- 2 tablespoons cornstarch
- 2 cups skim milk
- ¼ cup dry sherry
- 2 teaspoons fresh chives, minced

Remove and discard cartilage from crabmeat; set aside. Sauté onion in margarine in a large saucepan until tender. Stir in Beau Monde seasoning and next four ingredients; cook, stirring constantly; cook 1 minute. Reduce heat, and stir in crabmeat and sherry. Garnish with chives. Makes 5 cups.

Calories	97	Protein	9	Fat	2
Carbohydrate	8	Cholesterol	25	Sodium	160

Garden Vegetable Soup

- 1 beef bouillon cube
- 2 cups tomato juice
- 3 cups water
- 2 medium potatoes, diced
- 2 medium carrots, diced
- 1 cup green beans, diced
- 1 medium onion, diced
- 1 medium zucchini, diced
- 2 celery stalks, diced
- 3 medium tomatoes, diced
- ½ green bell pepper, diced
- ¼ teaspoon dried leaf basil
- ¼ teaspoon dried leaf marjoram

In a large pot over medium heat, dissolve bouillon cube in tomato juice and water. Add the vegetables and herbs. Bring to a boil. Reduce heat. Simmer until the vegetables are tender, about 20 minutes. Serves 6.

Calories	97	Protein	4	Fat	1
Carbohydrate	19	Cholesterol	0	Sodium	463

Fruit Temptation Salad

- ½ cup apple, unpeeled and cubed
- ½ cup fresh pineapple chunks
- ½ cup strawberries, sliced
- ½ cup green grapes
- ¼ cup celery, chopped
- 1 tablespoon pecans, chopped
- 1 tablespoon unsweetened apple juice
- 1 tablespoon plain nonfat yogurt
- 1 tablespoon reduced-calorie mayonnaise
- 4 lettuce leaves

Combine first six ingredients in a bowl. Toss gently. Combine apple juice, yogurt and mayonnaise stirring with a whisk until smooth. Pour over fruit mixture. Toss well. Serve on lettuce-lined salad plates. Serves 4.

Calories	60	Protein	1	Fat	3
Carbohydrate	10	Cholesterol	1	Sodium	39

Speedy Caesar Salad

- 6 cups loosely packed torn romaine lettuce
- 2 tablespoons grated Parmesan cheese
- 2 tablespoons water
- 2 tablespoons red wine vinegar
- 2 teaspoons olive oil
- 2 teaspoons anchovy paste
- 1 clove garlic
- ⅓ cup seasoned croutons

Place torn romaine lettuce in a large bowl; set aside. Combine Parmesan cheese and next five ingredients in container of an electric blender; cover and process until smooth. Pour over lettuce; toss well. Top with croutons. Serves 5.

Calories	57	Protein	3	Fat	3
Carbohydrate	4	Cholesterol	2	Sodium	318

Asparagus-Spinach Salad

- 1 pound asparagus spears
- ½ cup bottled poppy seed dressing or Italian dressing
- 1 teaspoon grated orange peel
- 1 tablespoon orange juice
- 8 cups torn fresh spinach
- 2 cups sliced fresh strawberries
- ¾ to 1 pound cooked turkey, cubed
- ¼ cup pecan halves

Snap off and discard woody bases from asparagus. Cut into 1-inch pieces. Place in 1-quart microwave baking dish with 2 tablespoons water. Cover and microwave on high for 5 to 7 minutes or until tender but still crisp, stirring once. Drain and rinse with cold water. Let stand in cold water until cool. Drain. In a medium mixing bowl stir together dressing, orange peel and orange juice. Set aside. In a salad bowl, combine asparagus, spinach, berries and turkey. Add dressing mixture, toss. Sprinkle pecans on top. Serve with your favorite crackers for a light summer supper. Serves 4.

Calories	390	Protein	33	Fat	26
Carbohydrate	18	Cholesterol	59	Sodium	289

Aloha Pineapple Salad

Curly leaf lettuce leaves
1 medium-size fresh pineapple
2 medium kiwi fruits, peeled
2 tablespoons grated coconut

Place lettuce leaves on a serving platter. Set aside. Prepare pineapple and slice into 6 slices. Arrange on lettuce leaves. Cut kiwi into 6 slices and arrange on pineapple. Pour 2 tablespoons Poppy Seed Dressing over each and sprinkle with coconut. Serves 6.

Poppy Seed Dressing:
¾ cup unsweetened orange juice
2 teaspoons cornstarch
1 tablespoon honey
1 tablespoon corn oil
1½ teaspoons poppy seeds
¼ teaspoon grated orange rind

Combine orange juice and cornstarch in a 2 cup glass measuring cup. Stir well. Microwave at high for 2½ minutes or until thickened, stirring once. Add honey, oil, poppy seeds, and orange rind. Stir well. Cover and chill. Makes ¾ cup.

Calories	95	Protein	1	Fat	1
Carbohydrate	26	Cholesterol	0	Sodium	4

Blue Cheese Dressing

½ cup plain low-fat yogurt
½ cup low-fat sour cream
2 tablespoons blue cheese, crumbled
1 teaspoon lime rind, grated
2 tablespoons lime juice
¼ teaspoon garlic powder
⅛ teaspoon ground white pepper
2 drops of hot sauce

Combine all ingredients in a small bowl, stirring well. Cover and chill thoroughly. Serve with salad greens. Makes 1¼ cups.

Calories	17	Protein	1	Fat	1
Carbohydrate	1	Cholesterol	4	Sodium	26

Honey Mustard Dressing

- 1 tablespoon white wine vinegar
- 1 teaspoon water
- 1 teaspoon olive oil
- 1 teaspoon Dijon mustard
- 1 teaspoon honey

Mix all ingredients in jar, shake well. Serve on fresh spinach leaves or your favorite salad fixings.

Calories	**33**	**Protein**	**.13**	**Fat**	**2.4**
Carbohydrate	**3.5**	**Cholesterol**	**0**	**Sodium**	**33**

Chicken Mandarin

- 1 (9-ounce) package frozen broccoli spears
- 2 whole chicken breasts, boned, halved, and skinned
- ¼ cup flour
- ½ teaspoon garlic powder
- ¼ teaspoon paprika
- 3 tablespoons margarine
- ¾ cup orange juice
- 2 tablespoons white wine
- 1 teaspoon dried tarragon
- 1 teaspoon cornstarch
- ¼ teaspoon grated orange peel
- 1 (11-ounce) can mandarin orange segments, drained
- 2 tablespoons toasted almonds, sliced

Thaw broccoli and drain. Flatten chicken breasts by pounding lightly between sheets of waxed paper. In small bowl, combine flour, garlic powder and paprika. Coat chicken with flour mixture. In medium skillet, brown chicken in margarine. Place in 8-inch square baking dish. In same skillet, combine orange juice, wine, tarragon, cornstarch and orange peel. Cook until mixture boils and thickens, stirring constantly. Pour sauce over chicken. Bake at 350° for 15 minutes. Divide broccoli in four equal portions and arrange on top of chicken breasts. Top each serving with ¼ of the mandarin oranges and almonds. Cover and bake an additional 15 minutes. Serves 4.

Calories	**330**	**Protein**	**29**	**Fat**	**13**
Carbohydrate	**21**	**Cholesterol**	**72**	**Sodium**	**280**

The mandarin orange gives a different and delightful flavor to the chicken and the broccoli.

Whole Wheat Pasta Primavera

- 3 tablespoons olive oil
- 3 ounces pea pods
- 2½ ounces broccoli, chopped
- 4 ounces zucchini, sliced and quartered
- 3½ ounces caulifloweretes
- ¼ cup onion, chopped
- 2½ ounces sweet red pepper, sliced
- 2 cloves garlic, minced
- ¼ pound cherry tomatoes, cut in half
- Pinch basil
- Sea salt (optional)
- Pepper to taste
- 1 pound whole wheat spaghetti
- ½ cup low-fat milk
- ½ cup low-sodium chicken consommé (prepared)
- ⅓ cup Parmesan cheese

In medium pan, heat oil. Add all vegetables except garlic and cherry tomatoes. Stir over high heat until vegetables are tender, about 4 minutes. Add garlic, tomatoes and seasonings. Stir for 1 minute; remove from heat.

Cook spaghetti according to package. Drain.

In another pan, heat milk and consommé. Add spaghetti and cheese, toss gently. Reheat vegetables. Serve vegetables over spaghetti. Garnish with parsley. Serves 8.

Calories	235	Protein	10	Fat	7
Carbohydrate	37	Cholesterol	4	Sodium	92

Sweet Potato Circle

- **1½ tablespoons margarine**
- **1 tablespoon olive oil**
- **3 medium sweet potatoes**
- **1 teaspoon ginger**
- **2 tablespoons brown sugar**
- **¾ teaspoon salt**

Melt margarine and oil together. Line a 9-inch glass pie plate with aluminum foil and lightly brush with margarine mixture. Set balance of oil mixture aside. In small cup, mix ginger, sugar and salt. Peel potatoes and slice very thin, preferably with food processor. Place a layer of potatoes in a decorative circular design in pie plate. Sprinkle with sugar mixture, then margarine mixture. Make second layer of potatoes, sprinkle with balance of sugar mixture, then margarine mixture. Spray a sheet of aluminum foil with non-stick spray and cover potatoes. Place a heavy pie pan on top of aluminum foil and cook at 400° for 30 minutes. Uncover and bake for an additional 30 minutes or until brown and crisp on top. Invert onto serving platter. Serves 6.

Calories	**143**	**Protein**	**1**	**Fat**	**5**
Carbohydrate	**23**	**Cholesterol**	**0**	**Sodium**	**312**

Savory Rice Casserole

- **2 cups cooked brown rice**
- **¼ cup shredded Cheddar cheese (1-ounce)**
- **¼ cup shredded part-skim mozzarella (1-ounce)**
- **⅓ cup green onions including tops, sliced**
- **2 egg whites, beaten slightly**
- **½ teaspoon Italian seasoning**
- **½ teaspoon salt or to taste**
- **1 teaspoon lemon juice**
- **¼ teaspoon hot pepper sauce**
- **¼ cup cooked shrimp, chopped (1 ounce, optional)**

Preheat oven to 375°. Combine all ingredients in large mixing bowl and stir until well mixed. Coat a 1-quart baking dish with nonstick cooking spray and press mixture in evenly. Bake for 15 minutes. Serves 4.

This tasty casserole makes a satisfying lunch with sliced tomatoes or a good accompaniment to a light dinner of cold turkey and a salad.

Calories	**164**	**Protein**	**7**	**Fat**	**3**
Carbohydrate	**26**	**Cholesterol**	**21**	**Sodium**	**352**

Spinach Soufflé

- 3 tablespoons low-fat margarine
- 3 tablespoons all-purpose flour
- 1 cup skim milk
- 2 egg yolks, beaten
- ½ cup chopped spinach, drained
- 1 cup part-skim ricotta cheese
- 1 teaspoon onion, chopped
- ¼ teaspoon salt
- ⅛ teaspoon pepper

Make aluminum foil collar for 2-quart soufflé dish extending about 3 inches above rim of dish. Spray dish and foil with non-stick spray. Lightly flour dish. In small saucepan, melt margarine, add flour and stir until blended. Gradually add milk and cook over low heat until thickened. Stir 3 tablespoons of milk mixture into egg yolks. Return yolk mixture to milk mixture and set aside. In food processor, mix spinach (thoroughly squeezed and drained) cheese, onion, salt and pepper. Blend until smooth. Add milk mixture. Process just until well mixed. Beat egg whites until stiff, gently fold in spinach mixture. Pour into soufflé dish. Bake at 400° 45 to 50 minutes or until golden color. Serves 5.

This soufflé, served with a broiled chicken breast and fresh fruit makes a wonderful brunch.

Calories	**158**	**Protein**	**9**	**Fat**	**9**
Carbohydrate	**9**	**Cholesterol**	**99**	**Sodium**	**283**

Apple Butter

- 1 cup stewed chopped apples
- ⅛ teaspoon cloves
- ¼ teaspoon ginger
- ½ teaspoon cinnamon
- 12 packages artificial sweetener

While apples are still hot, mix all ingredients together until well blended. Spoon into 8 ounce container. Store in refrigerator. Serves 24. (2 teaspoons per serving).

Calories	**8**	**Protein**	**.027**	**Fat**	**.012**
Carbohydrate	**2**	**Cholesterol**	**0**	**Sodium**	**2**

Dina's Stuffed Potatoes

- 3 medium baking potatoes
- ¾ cup plain lowfat yogurt
- ⅛ teaspoon salt
- ¼ teaspoon black pepper
- Vegetable cooking spray
- ¼ cup green onions, thinly sliced
- ¼ cup Swiss cheese, shredded
- 1 tablespoon chopped chives
- Paprika

Wash potatoes; prick with fork. Bake at 400° for 1 hour or until done. Let cool slightly. Cut in half lengthwise. Scoop out pulp, leaving a ¼-inch shell. Set shells aside. Combine potato pulp, yogurt, salt and pepper in medium bowl. Mash until light and fluffy. Set aside. Coat a small skillet with cooking spray; place over medium heat until hot. Add green onions, sauté until tender. Remove from heat. Add onions, cheese and chives to potato mixture. Stir well. Spoon potato mixture into shells. Place on ungreased baking sheet. Bake at 350° uncovered for 10 minutes or until thoroughly heated. Sprinkle with paprika before serving. Serves 6.

VARIATION: Use sliced mushrooms and yellow onions.

Calories	**148**	**Protein**	**5**	**Fat**	**2**
Carbohydrate	**28**	**Cholesterol**	**6**	**Sodium**	**94**

Lightly-Scalloped Potatoes

- Vegetable cooking spray
- 2 cloves garlic, minced
- ⅓ cup onion, diced
- 1½ tablespoons flour
- 1 (12-ounce) can evaporated skimmed milk
- 1½ cups skim milk
- 1 teaspoon salt
- ½ teaspoon crushed red pepper
- 9 cups red potatoes, thinly sliced and unpeeled (about 4 pounds)
- ¾ cup (3-ounces) Gruyère cheese
- ⅓ cup Parmesan cheese, freshly grated

Coat a dutch oven with cooking spray; place over medium-high heat until hot. Add garlic and onion, sauté until tender. Add flour, milk, salt and pepper, cook 1 minute, stirring constantly, until mixture boils. Add potatoes, and return to boil, stirring occasionally. Layer half each of potatoes, Gruyère cheese and Parmesan cheese in a 13x9x2-inch baking dish coated with cooking spray. Repeat layers. Bake at 350° for 45 minutes or until bubbly and golden brown. Let stand 30 minutes before serving. Serves 16. (½ cup per serving).

Calories	**138**	**Protein**	**7**	**Fat**	**3**
Carbohydrate	**22**	**Cholesterol**	**8**	**Sodium**	**240**

Baked Vegetables with Tofu Marinara

- 2 carrots, sliced
- 1 medium zucchini, cut into slices
- 1½ cups broccoli, chopped
- 2 tablespoons olive oil
- 2 fresh garlic cloves, pressed
- ½ teaspoon oregano
- ½ teaspoon basil
- 1 tablespoon parsley, chopped
- 2 scallions, chopped
- ½ pound firm tofu cut into ½-inch cubes
- 2 cups tomato sauce
- 4 large mushrooms, quartered
- 3 tablespoons Parmesan cheese

Preheat oven to 375°. In small pan steam carrots, zucchini and broccoli until tender, set aside. In pan, heat olive oil and sauté the garlic, oregano, basil, parsley, and scallions for 1 minute and then add tofu. Carefully sauté an additional 3 to 4 minutes turning occasionally. Remove from heat and transfer to medium bowl. Add vegetables, tomato sauce, and mushrooms to bowl and toss. Transfer to four small baking dishes or crocks. Sprinkle with cheese. Bake 20 to 25 minutes on top rack of oven until cheese has browned and mixture is bubbly. Serves 4.

Calories	**196**	**Protein**	**10**	**Fat**	**11**
Carbohydrate	**18**	**Cholesterol**	**3**	**Sodium**	**839**

Chicken 'N Lemon

- ¾ cup chicken broth
- ¼ cup lemon juice
- 2 chicken breasts, skinned
- 2 teaspoons olive oil
- ½ teaspoon salt
- ½ teaspoon oregano leaves
- White pepper to taste
- Dash garlic powder

Pour broth and lemon juice into small baking pan. Rub each chicken breast with oil and place in pan. Sprinkle with seasonings and bake 20 to 25 minutes. Baste with drippings. Serves 2.

Calories	**238**	**Protein**	**35**	**Fat**	**9**
Carbohydrate	**2**	**Cholesterol**	**96**	**Sodium**	**640**

Quick and easy and very filling.

Cheesy Broccoli Casserole

- 1½ pounds fresh broccoli
- 2 eggs, slightly beaten
- ¾ cup cottage cheese
- ½ cup Cheddar cheese, shredded (2-ounces)
- 2 tablespoons onion, finely chopped
- 1 teaspoon Worcestershire sauce
- ¼ teaspoon salt
- ⅛ teaspoon pepper
- ¼ cup fine dry breadcrumbs
- 1 tablespoon margarine or butter, melted

Wash and trim broccoli; cut into spears. Cook broccoli, covered, in a small amount of unsalted boiling water about 10 minutes or until crisp-tender; drain.

Meanwhile, in bowl combine beaten eggs, cottage cheese, Cheddar cheese, onion, Worcestershire sauce, salt and pepper. Arrange broccoli in shallow 1½-quart baking dish; spoon cheese mixture on top. Stir together breadcrumbs and margarine; sprinkle over cheese mixture. Bake, uncovered, in a 350° oven 15 to 20 minutes or until heated through and egg mixture is set. Serves 6.

This mild and flavorful cheese sauce proves broccoli and cheese are a perfect match. Serve with eggs for a brunch menu or just add a baked potato for a nice, light lunch or dinner.

Calories	**154**	**Protein**	**11**	**Fat**	**9**
Carbohydrate	**9**	**Cholesterol**	**106**	**Sodium**	**372**

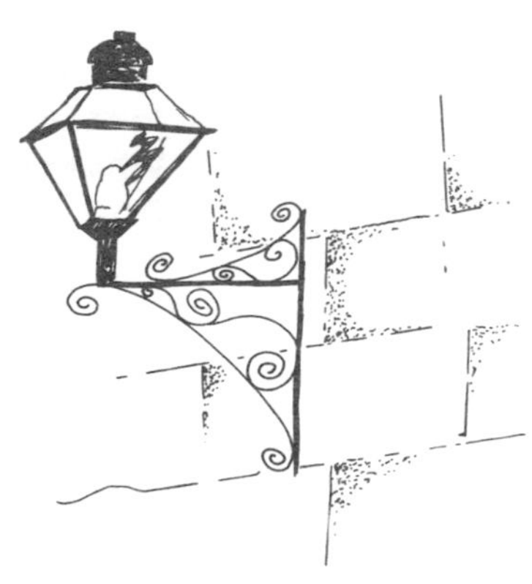

Curried Turkey

- ¼ cup oil
- 1 bunch green onions
- 1 small stalk celery
- 1 green pepper, sliced
- 2 tablespoons slivered almonds
- 2 cups water chestnuts, thinly sliced
- 2 cups diced, cooked turkey
- 2 tablespoons flour
- 1 teaspoon curry powder
- 1 teaspoon paprika
- ½ teaspoon sweet basil
- 1½ cups chicken broth
- ¼ cup pimento, chopped
- 1 cup drained pineapple tidbits (juice pack)

Slice green onions and celery diagonally, about ½-inch thick. Heat oil in a skillet and sauté onions, celery, and peppers until slightly browned. Add almonds, water chestnuts, and cooked turkey. Mix well with flour, paprika, curry powder, and basil. Sauté slightly, stirring constantly, until well blended. Mix in broth, pimento, and pineapple. Cover and let steam briefly. Season with pepper. Delicious served on rice. Serves 6.

Calories	230	Protein	16	Fat	13
Carbohydrate	11	Cholesterol	36	Sodium	239

Peanut Butter Cookies

- ¼ cup plus 2 tablespoons margarine, softened
- ¼ cup plus 2 tablespoons creamy peanut butter
- ½ cup firmly packed brown sugar
- 2 cups all-purpose flour
- ½ teaspoon ground cinnamon
- 1 egg
- 2 tablespoons skim milk
- ½ teaspoon vanilla extract

Cream margarine and peanut butter in a medium bowl. Add sugar, beating well.

Combine flour and cinnamon; add to creamed mixture, mixing until well blended. Add remaining ingredients, and beat well.

Press dough from a cookie press into 2-inch strips onto ungreased cookie sheets, following manufacturer's instructions. Bake at 400° for 6 minutes or until edges are lightly browned. Remove from cookie sheets, and cool completely on wire racks. Makes 9 dozen.

Calories	24	Protein	1	Fat	1
Carbohydrate	3	Cholesterol	2	Sodium	13

Breast of Chicken À La Raspberry

- 4 (5-ounce) boneless chicken breasts, skin removed
- 1 cup white raspberry flavored vinegar
- ½ teaspoon sea salt (optional)
- Pepper to taste
- ½ cup half and half
- ½ cup low-sodium chicken stock
- 2 teaspoons cornstarch
- 2 tablespoons margarine
- 1 tablespoon corn oil
- 12 fresh red raspberries
- 4 sprigs watercress

Combine vinegar, salt, and pepper. Marinate chicken in mixture for 3 hours. Drain and discard vinegar. In a double boiler, combine ¼ cup half and half and chicken stock. In a small bowl, mix cornstarch with ¼ cup half and half. Add to above mixture. Simmer until sauce is creamy. Set aside. Melt margarine in skillet with oil. Sauté chicken breasts until fully cooked. Drain fat. Pour sauce over chicken. Cook until hot and bubbly. When serving, garnish with raspberries and watercress or use lemon twist and watercress. Serves 4.

Calories	**277**	**Protein**	**34**	**Fat**	**12**
Carbohydrate	**8**	**Cholesterol**	**10**	**Sodium**	**364**

Creole Snapper

- ⅓ cup low-fat mayonnaise
- ½ teaspoon cumin
- ½ teaspoon onion powder
- ¼ teaspoon red pepper
- ¼ teaspoon garlic powder
- 1 pound snapper fillets
- 8 sesame crackers, crushed
- Non-stick spray

Mix mayonnaise and seasonings in bowl. Brush snapper with mayonnaise mixture, coat with cracker crumbs. Place in baking dish that has been coated with non-stick spray. Bake at 400° for 15 to 20 minutes or until done. Serves 4.

Calories	**192**	**Protein**	**24**	**Fat**	**7**
Carbohydrate	**7**	**Cholesterol**	**47**	**Sodium**	**226**

So quick and easy, yet very tasty. Serve with boiled new potatoes and steamed vegetables.

Chicken Kabobs

- 1 (8-ounce) can pineapple chunks in their own juice
- 1 tablespoon low-sodium soy sauce
- 2 tablespoons unsweetened apple juice concentrate, thawed
- 2 garlic cloves, minced
- ½ teaspoon ground ginger
- ½ cup dry sherry or white wine
- 1 medium onion, cut into 16 chunks
- 1 green pepper, cut into 16 chunks
- 16 mushrooms, stems removed
- 4 skinned, boneless chicken breast halves, cut into 32 pieces
- 8 kabob skewers

Drain pineapple and set juice aside. Combine pineapple juice with soy sauce, apple juice, garlic, ginger and wine. Marinate chicken in this mixture for 30 minutes. On each skewer, thread and alternate 2 onion pieces, 2 green pepper pieces, a few pineapple pieces and 4 chicken pieces. Cook on grill 3 to 5 minutes per side, basting with marinade, until chicken is done. Serves 8.

Calories	164	Protein	21	Fat	3
Carbohydrate	8	Cholesterol	54	Sodium	114

Baked Potato Topper

- 2 ounces farmer's cheese
- ¼ cup skim milk
- 2 tablespoons green onion, finely chopped
- ⅛ teaspoon salt
- ⅛ teaspoon pepper
- 1 tablespoon chives, finely chopped

In food processor, mix cheese, milk, onion, salt and pepper until well blended. Spoon sauce on baked potato and garnish with chives. Serves 4.

Calories	40	Protein	3.5	Fat	2
Carbohydrate	1	Cholesterol	13	Sodium	274

For something different, try this on steamed cauliflower or broiled chicken breasts.

Potato Skin Tuna Melt

- 2 baking potatoes
- 1 tablespoon butter, melted
- 1 egg, beaten
- 7 ounces white, water-packed tuna, flaked
- 2 tablespoons diet mayonnaise
- ¼ cup celery hearts, finely diced
- 2 tablespoons onion, diced
- 2 tablespoons lemon juice
- ½ teaspoon veg-it seasoning
- 2 ounces Lorraine cheese, cut in thin strips
- 1 teaspoon parsley, chopped
- Ground pepper to taste

Bake potatoes at 375° for about 45 minutes. Cool. Halve potatoes lengthwise and scoop out. Save inside for another favorite dish. Brush inside of potato skins liberally with butter and bake additional 10 minutes. Mix tuna, mayonnaise, celery, onion and lemon juice. Fill each about half full with tuna mixture. Crisscross cheese strips over tuna. Sprinkle with parsley and paprika. Place in non-stick shallow pan. Bake uncovered 15 to 20 minutes until hot and bubbly. Serves 4.

Calories	**282**	**Protein**	**19**	**Fat**	**10**
Carbohydrate	**28**	**Cholesterol**	**100**	**Sodium**	**329**

Berry Cream Pie

- 6 phyllo-pastry leaves
- Nonstick cooking spray
- 2 cups strawberries, sliced
- 1 cup blueberries
- 1 cup raspberries
- 1 tablespoon lemon juice
- 2 large egg whites
- 3 tablespoons sugar
- 2 cups nondairy whipped topping

Preheat oven to 350°. With cooking spray, grease 9-inch pie plate; lay one phyllo leaf in pie plate, allowing edges to hang over outside of plate. Lightly spray phyllo inside plate only. Repeat with remaining phyllo to line plate. Bake 15 minutes or until golden; cool.

In bowl, mix berries with lemon juice; refrigerate 30 minutes. In bowl, with electric mixer at high speed, beat egg whites until soft peaks form when beaters are raised. Beat in sugar, 1 tablespoon at a time; beat until stiff. Fold in nondairy topping; gently fold in berries. Place in phyllo shell. Serves 8.

Calories	**161**	**Protein**	**3**	**Fat**	**5**
Carbohydrate	**27**	**Cholesterol**	**0**	**Sodium**	**82**

Veal Scallopini

- 2 tablespoons olive oil
- 4 (3½-ounce) scallopini of veal
- 1 egg, well beaten
- 2 ounces low-fat milk
- ½ cup breadcrumbs
- ½ teaspoon dried basil
- ¼ teaspoon oregano
- ½ teaspoon garlic powder
- ½ cup Chablis
- 1 large onion, chopped
- 1 cup beef stock
- 1 tablespoon lemon juice
- 1 teaspoon Worcestershire sauce

Heat oil in medium non-stick skillet. Flatten veal to ¼-inch thickness. In small bowl, mix together egg and milk. Mix breadcrumbs on a piece of waxed paper with basil, oregano, and garlic powder. Dip veal into egg mixture then in breadcrumb mixture. Sauté in oil for 2 minutes on each side over medium-high heat. Add wine and cook additional 2 minutes, turning once. Remove veal to warm plate. Add onion, beef stock, lemon juice and Worcestershire sauce to pan drippings. Bring to a boil over high heat and cook uncovered 3 to 4 minutes until onions are soft. Serve veal with warm onion sauce. Serves 4.

Calories	291	Protein	30	Fat	11
Carbohydrate	12	Cholesterol	162	Sodium	379

Amaretto Chocolate Mousse

- **1 envelope unflavored gelatin**
- **2 egg yolks**
- **¼ cup sugar**
- **2 tablespoons amaretto or other almond-flavored liqueur**
- **4 egg whites**
- **1½ cups skim milk, divided**
- **⅓ cup sugar**
- **⅓ cup cocoa**
- **Strawberry halves**

Combine gelatin and ½ cup milk in a medium saucepan, stirring well; let stand 1 minute. Cook over medium heat, stirring constantly, 1 minute or until gelatin dissolves. Combine remaining 1 cup milk and egg yolks, beating well. Add yolk mixture, ¼ cup sugar, and cocoa to saucepan; stir well. Cook over medium heat, stirring constantly, 8 minutes or until smooth and thickened. Remove from heat; stir in amaretto, and chill 20 minutes.

Beat egg whites (at room temperature) in a medium bowl until foamy. Gradually add ⅓ cup sugar, 1 tablespoon at a time, beating until stiff peaks form. Gradually add chilled chocolate mixture to beaten egg whites, folding gently. Spoon mixture into 1½-inch quart serving dish. Chill at least 2 hours. Garnish with strawberry halves, if desired. Serves 10.

Calories	**87**	**Protein**	**4**	**Fat**	**2**
Carbohydrate	**13**	**Cholesterol**	**68**	**Sodium**	**101**

Chocoholics Chocolate Fluff

- ¾ cup water
- ⅔ cup nonfat dry milk
- 1 tablespoon plus 1 teaspoon cocoa, unsweetened
- ½ teaspoon vanilla butternut flavor
- 1 envelope unflavored gelatin
- Sweetener equivalent to 8 teaspoons sugar
- 1½ teaspoons vanilla extract
- 7 ice cubes

Place water in a small saucepan. Sprinkle gelatin over water and let soften a few minutes. Heat, stirring frequently, over low heat, until gelatin is completely dissolved. Remove from heat. In a blender container, combine dry milk, sweetener, cocoa, and extracts. Add gelatin mixture. Turn on blender. Add ice cubes, 1 at a time, while blending. Blend one minute, or until ice is gone. Divide into 4 servings. This may be eaten right away or, if a firmer texture is desired, chilled for at least 15 minutes.

VARIATION: For Mocha Fluff, add 1½ teaspoons instant coffee granules with the cocoa. Serves 4.

Calories	66	Protein	7	Fat	0
Carbohydrate	7	Cholesterol	2	Sodium	68

Better Than Chocolate Chip Cookies

- 2¼ cups whole wheat flour
- ⅓ cup butter or margarine
- ¼ cup sugar
- 2 eggs
- ½ cup chopped nuts
- 1 teaspoon baking soda
- ¼ cup brown sugar, firmly packed
- 10 packages Sweet One™ sweetener
- 1 cup semisweet chocolate morsels
- ¾ cup wheat bran

In a small bowl, combine flour and baking soda; set aside. In large bowl, cream butter, sugars, and sweetener. Beat in eggs. Gradually add flour mixture and wheat bran, mixing well. Stir in morsels and nuts. Drop by rounded teaspoons onto ungreased cookie sheets. Bake at 375° for 8 to 10 minutes. Makes 4 dozen.

Calories	68	Protein	1	Fat	4
Carbohydrate	9	Cholesterol	12	Sodium	32

Chocolate-Mint Torte

- ¼ cup margarine, softened
- 2 egg whites
- 1¼ cups cake flour, sifted
- ¼ teaspoon baking soda
- 1 (8-ounce) carton plain nonfat yogurt
- ¾ cup sugar
- ½ teaspoon vanilla extract
- ¼ cup unsweetened cocoa
- ¼ teaspoon baking powder
- Vegetable cooking spray
- 1 teaspoon crème de menthe
- 1 cup vanilla ice milk, softened
- 1 tablespoon powdered sugar

Cream margarine; gradually add sugar, beating well at medium speed of an electric mixer. Add egg whites (at room temperature) and vanilla; beat well. Combing flour, cocoa, soda, and baking powder; add to sugar mixture alternately with yogurt, beating well after each addition. Pour batter into an 8-inch round cake pan that has been coated with cooking spray. Bake at 350° for 30 minutes, or until a wooden pick inserted in center comes out clean. Cool in pan 10 minutes; remove from pan, and let cool completely on a wire rack.

Combine ice milk and crème de menthe, stirring well. Line one 8-inch round cake pan with wax paper, leaving an overhang around edges, Spread ice milk mixture evenly into pan. Freeze 2 hours or until firm. Carefully cut cake horizontally into two layers. Place bottom layer of cake on a serving plate. Invert frozen ice milk layer onto cake; remove wax paper. Top with remaining cake layer. Cover and freeze several hours or until firm. Let stand 5 minutes. Dust with powdered sugar before serving. Serves 10.

Calories	**192**	**Protein**	**4**	**Fat**	**6**
Carbohydrate	**31**	**Cholesterol**	**2**	**Sodium**	**120**

Cinnamon Raisin Pretzels

- 1 package hot roll mix
- ½ cup raisins
- 1 tablespoon brown sugar
- 1 teaspoon cinnamon
- 1 cup hot water
- 2 tablespoons oil
- 1 egg

In food processor, mix yeast, flour mixture, sugar and cinnamon. Blend well. Add water, oil, egg and raisins. Process until dough forms ball and sides of bowl are clean. On floured surface, knead dough until smooth, about 3 minutes. Cover dough and let rest 5 minutes. Flatten dough and divide into 10 pieces. Roll each piece into one 18-inch rope. (Keep remaining pieces covered). Tie each piece into pretzel shape. Moisten and press ends to secure. Place on ungreased cookie sheet, cover with towel and let rise 5 minutes in warm place. Uncover dough and bake at 400° for 15 to 20 minutes or until golden brown. Remove from cookie sheet immediately. Makes 10 pretzels.

A wonderful snack, and try it toasted for a quick breakfast.

Calories	**220**	**Protein**	**6**	**Fat**	**4**
Carbohydrate	**41**	**Cholesterol**	**21**	**Sodium**	**320**

Pumpkin-Scream Muffins

- 1 cup whole wheat flour
- ½ cup unprocessed wheat bran flakes
- 1 tablespoon sugar
- 2 teaspoons baking powder
- ½ teaspoon baking soda
- ½ teaspoon ground cinnamon
- 2 tablespoons vegetable oil
- ½ cup cooked or canned pumpkin
- 1 egg or 2 egg whites
- ¾ cup orange juice
- ⅓ cup dark or golden raisins
- 1 tablespoon wheat germ or bran flakes

Combine all ingredients, except the wheat germ, in a mixing bowl. Stir to blend. Spoon into lightly oiled muffin tins. Sprinkle on the wheat germ. Bake at 400° for 10 to 15 minutes. Makes 8 muffins.

Calories	**148**	**Protein**	**3**	**Fat**	**4**
Carbohydrate	**25**	**Cholesterol**	**34**	**Sodium**	**123**

Pineapple Upside-down Cake

- 1 (8-ounce) can sliced pineapple in juice
- 3½ tablespoons margarine, melted, divided
- 1½ tablespoons brown sugar, packed to measure
- 6 packets Sweet One™, granulated sugar substitute, divided
- ¼ cup pecan halves
- 2 large eggs, separated, at room temperature
- 1 teaspoon vanilla extract
- ¾ cup cake flour
- ¾ teaspoon baking powder
- ¼ teaspoon salt
- 3 tablespoons granulated sugar

Preheat oven to 325°. Drain pineapple, reserving ⅓ cup juice. Set aside. Pat pineapple slices dry with paper towel. In 8-inch cake pan, combine 1½ tablespoons melted margarine, brown sugar and 2 packets Sweet One™. Spread evenly in bottom of pan. Place pineapple slices on top of sugar mixture. Arrange pecan halves decoratively in center of each pineapple ring and around edges. Set aside. Sift together flour, baking powder and salt. Set aside. Combine reserved pineapple juice, 2 tablespoons melted margarine, 4 packets Sweet One™, egg yolks and vanilla in mixing bowl and mix until just blended. Add flour mixture and mix until smooth.

Beat egg whites and sugar until stiff peaks form. Gently fold into batter. Spoon batter over pineapple and pecans. Bake 18 to 20 minutes. Test for doneness with wooden pick. Place wire rack over cake pan; invert and cool in pan 2 to 3 minutes. Remove pan and cool completely. With spatulas, gently lift onto serving platter. Serves 8.

Calories	**168**	**Protein**	**3**	**Fat**	**9**
Carbohydrate	**21**	**Cholesterol**	**53**	**Sodium**	**144**

Celebration Blueberry Ring

- 1 cup oat bran
- ¾ cup all-purpose flour
- ¾ cup sugar
- ½ cup whole wheat flour
- 1 teaspoon baking soda
- 1¼ cups plain low-fat yogurt
- 1 teaspoon vanilla
- ½ teaspoon grated lemon rind
- 1 egg, lightly beaten
- 1 egg white, stiffly beaten
- 1 cup fresh blueberries
- Non-stick spray
- ½ cup powdered sugar
- 2 teaspoons skim milk

Mix oat bran, flour, sugar, wheat flour, and soda. Make a well in center, set aside. Mix yogurt, vanilla, lemon rind and whole egg and add all at once to dry mixture. Mix just until dry ingredients are moistened. Gently fold in beaten egg white and blueberries. Spoon batter into bundt pan which has been coated with non-stick spray. Bake at 350° for about 45 minutes. Let sit in pan for 10 minutes. Mix powdered sugar and milk until well blended. Remove cake from pan and drizzle sugar mixture over cake.

Calories	143	Protein	4	Fat	1.3
Carbohydrate	29	Cholesterol	15	Sodium	83

Chocolate Almond Crisps

- 2 egg whites
- 3 tablespoons plus 1½ teaspoons unsweetened cocoa
- ¼ cup finely chopped blanched almonds
- ¼ cup semisweet chocolate mini-morsels
- ¾ cup plus 2 tablespoons sifted powdered sugar
- ½ teaspoon almond extract
- Vegetable cooking spray

Beat egg whites (at room temperature) at high speed of an electric mixer 1 minute. Combine sugar and cocoa; gradually add sugar mixture to egg whites, 1 tablespoon at a time, beating until stiff peaks form and sugar dissolves (2 to 4 minutes). Fold in mini-morsels, almonds, and almond extract. Drop by teaspoonfuls, 1-inch apart, onto cookie sheets that have been coated with cooking spray. Bake at 300° for 40 minutes or until set. Cool slightly on cookie sheets; gently remove to wire racks, and cool completely. Makes 3 dozen.

Calories	32	Protein	1	Fat	1
Carbohydrate	6	Cholesterol	0	Sodium	3

Carrot Cake

- 1¾ cups all-purpose flour
- ⅔ cup whole wheat flour
- 2 teaspoons baking soda
- 1 teaspoon ground cinnamon
- ¾ teaspoon ground allspice
- ¼ teaspoon ground nutmeg
- ⅛ teaspoon salt
- ¾ cup firmly packed brown sugar
- 3 tablespoons vegetable oil
- 2 eggs
- 3 cups carrots, coarsely shredded
- ½ cup raisins
- ⅔ cup nonfat buttermilk
- 1 (8-ounce) can crushed pineapple in juice, drained
- 2 teaspoons vanilla
- Vegetable non-stick spray

Combine first seven ingredients in bowl, mix well. Set aside. Combine sugar and oil, stir well. Add eggs, one at a time, beating well after each addition. Stir in carrots and next four ingredients. Add flour mixture, stir well. Spoon batter into 13x9x2-inch baking pan coated with non-stick spray. Bake at 350° for 35 minutes or until done. Cool completely in pan on rack. Spread Cream Cheese Frosting over top of cake. Serves 18. (3x2-inch piece per serving).

Cream Cheese Frosting:

- 8 ounces Neufchâtel cheese, softened
- 3 tablespoons powdered sugar
- 2 tablespoons skim milk
- ½ teaspoon grated orange peel
- 1 teaspoon vanilla

Cream cheese, sugar and milk. Add orange peel and vanilla, stir until well blended. Spread on cooled cake.

Calories	208	Protein	5	Fat	6
Carbohydrate	35	Cholesterol	32	Sodium	183

Traditional carrot cake has 511 calories in one slice. This wonderful light recipe has only 208 calories.

Apple Crisp

Fruit Layer:

- **4 cups peeled apple slices**
- **¼ cup water**
- **Artificial brown sugar equivalent to 4 teaspoons sugar**
- **2 teaspoons lemon juice**
- **¾ teaspoon ground cinnamon**

For fruit layer, combine all ingredients in a medium bowl. Toss lightly to coat apples. Spread in an ungreased 8-inch square baking dish.

Topping:

- **½ cup oat bran cereal or quick cooking oats or old fashioned rolled oats**
- **2 tablespoons chopped walnuts**
- **Artificial brown sugar equivalent to 1 tablespoon sugar**
- **1 tablespoon margarine, melted**

For topping, preheat oven to 375°. In a small bowl, combine the oat bran cereal or rolled oats, nuts and brown sugar substitute. Add margarine and mix well.

To complete, sprinkle topping over the apples. Bake for about 30 minutes or until the apples are tender and the topping is lightly browned. Serve warm or chilled. Serves 4.

Calories	**144**	**Protein**	**3**	**Fat**	**6**
Carbohydrate	**19**	**Cholesterol**	**0**	**Sodium**	**40**

Try this for breakfast. What a wonderful way to start the day! Fresh peaches, blueberries, etc., are a good substitute for the apples.

Granny's Peach Bread

- 1½ cups all-purpose flour
- ½ cup whole wheat flour
- ½ cup wheat germ
- ¼ cup firmly packed brown sugar
- 2 teaspoons baking powder
- ½ teaspoon baking soda
- ½ teaspoon ground cinnamon
- ¼ teaspoon salt
- ¼ teaspoon ground cloves
- ¼ teaspoon ground allspice
- 1 egg, beaten
- 1 (8-ounce) carton lemon low-fat yogurt
- ⅓ cup skim milk
- ¼ cup vegetable oil
- 1 teaspoon vanilla extract
- 2 cups fresh peaches, peeled and sliced
- Vegetable cooking spray

Combine first ten ingredients in a large bowl; stir well. Make a well in center of mixture. Combine egg, yogurt, milk, oil, and vanilla in a small bowl; stir well. Add liquid ingredients to dry ingredients, stirring just until moistened.

Position knife blade in food processor bowl. Add peaches; top with cover, and process until smooth. Fold peaches into flour mixture. Spoon into an 8½x4½x3-inch loaf pan that has been coated with cooking spray. Bake at 350° for 1 hour or until a wooden pick inserted in center comes out clean. Cool in pan 10 minutes; remove from pan and cool on a wire rack. Serves 16. (½-inch slices = 1 serving).

Calories	143	Protein	4	Fat	5
Carbohydrate	22	Cholesterol	18	Sodium	124

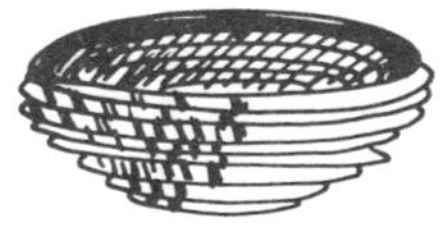

Lemon Tea Loaf

- **1¼ cups cake flour**
- **1 teaspoon baking powder**
- **1 teaspoon baking soda**
- **½ cup margarine, softened**
- **¼ cup granulated sugar**
- **6 packets Sweet One™ granulated sugar substitute**
- **1 large egg**
- **2 tablespoons lemon juice**
- **1 tablespoon grated lemon peel**
- **⅓ cup buttermilk**
- **2 large egg whites, at room temperature**
- **¼ teaspoon cream of tartar**

Preheat oven to 350°. Sift together cake flour, baking powder and soda, set aside. In large bowl beat margarine, sugar, Sweet One™, egg, lemon juice and lemon peel until well blended. Add flour mixture alternately with buttermilk, beginning and ending with flour and beating until smooth. Set aside. Beat egg whites and cream of tartar until stiff peaks form. Fold into batter. Pour batter into 8x5-inch loaf pan sprayed with non-stick cooking spray. Bake 35 to 40 minutes until done. Cool on wire rack 10 minutes before removing from pan. Cool completely on wire rack.

Glaze:

- **1 tablespoon granulated sugar**
- **2 packets Sweet One™**
- **1 tablespoon water**
- **2 teaspoons lemon juice**

In small saucepan over medium heat, combine sugar, Sweet One™, water and lemon juice. Bring to a boil. Cook 2 to 3 minutes or until mixture is thick and syrupy. Brush on top of tea loaf. For a garnish, use sliced strawberries, blueberries, and other fruit in season. Serves 12.

Calories	**126**	**Protein**	**2**	**Fat**	**8**
Carbohydrate	**11**	**Cholesterol**	**18**	**Sodium**	**206**

043

Raspberry Fudge Brownies

- 1 (10-ounce) package frozen raspberries in light syrup, thawed and not drained
- ¼ cup plus 2 tablespoons unsalted margarine
- ¼ cup plus 2 tablespoons unsweetened cocoa
- ⅔ cup sugar
- 2 eggs, beaten
- ½ teaspoon vanilla extract
- ½ cup all-purpose flour
- ⅛ teaspoon salt
- Vegetable cooking spray

Drain raspberries, reserving 3 tablespoons juice. Set raspberries and juice aside. Combine margarine and cocoa in a large saucepan. Cook over low heat, stirring constantly, until margarine melts and mixture becomes smooth. Remove from heat, let cool slightly.

Add sugar, eggs, and vanilla to cocoa mixture, stirring well to combine. Stir in 3 tablespoons reserved raspberry juice. Combine flour and salt; add flour mixture to cocoa mixture, stirring well to combine. Gently fold raspberries into cocoa mixture.

Spoon batter into an 8-inch square baking pan that has been coated with cooking spray. Bake at 350° for 20 minutes or until a wooden pick inserted in center comes out clean. Let brownies cool completely; cut into 2-inch squares. Cut squares in half to form triangles. Makes 32 brownies.

Calories	**61**	**Protein**	**1**	**Fat**	**3**
Carbohydrate	**8**	**Cholesterol**	**13**	**Sodium**	**14**

Since there are many concerns over nutrition in today's world and consumers are interested in preparing healthier meals, Mrs. Marti Chitwood has graciously assisted us with this section in giving special nutrient information following each recipe. Additionally, she has supplied us with the following chart. Mrs. Chitwood is a registered dietitian, with more than 15 years experience in the fields of nutrition and diabetes counseling. She currently has a private practice in Charleston, South Carolina.

A general note about adjusting a recipe:

To improve the nutritional quality of a recipe, study the ingredients. Do you see excessive amount of rich ingredients such as cream cheese, sugar, salt, etc.? Is the recipe visibly lacking in color and texture? If so, try adding nutrient-dense foods and try reducing (or replacing) empty calorie ingredients.

Hints to Improve the Nutritional Quality of Your Favorite Recipes

Dietary Goal	If Recipe Calls For	Try This
	shortening or butter	**-reduce amount or eliminate** -oil or margarine -calorie-reduced margarine
	-use no more than 1 to 2 tablespoons of added oil or fat per cup of flour, and compensate by increasing or adding a low-fat moist ingredient such as buttermilk or yogurt, to add moisture.	
	milk	-skim milk
	cream	-undiluted evaporated skim milk -"double milk" (1 dry skim milk w/ 1 cup fluid skim milk)
	sour cream	-low-fat or non-fat yogurt -lite sour cream -whipped low-fat cottage cheese
Reduce fat, saturated fat, cholesterol	**cream cheese**	-yogurt cheese -lite cream cheese or Neufchâtel -whipped low-fat cottage cheese -whipped tofu

Dietary Goal	If Recipe Calls For	Try This
Reduce fat, saturated fat, cholesterol	**whole milk cheese (such as Cheddar)**	-reduce amount or substitute -low fat cheese
	cottage cheese	-low-fat cottage cheese
	ricotta cheese	-part skim ricotta -low-fat cottage cheese
	whipped cream	-yogurt cheese whipped, sweetened w/Equal and vanilla -whipped evaporated milk -lite dairy topping
	mayonnaise	-calorie-reduced mayonnaise -substitute ½ low-fat yogurt, whipped tofu or low-fat cottage cheese
	red meat	-reduce amount, trim visible fat -choose leanest cuts
Avoid too much sodium	**salt**	-reduce amount -"lite" salt in reduced amounts -herbs, spices, flavorings
	canned creamed soups	-make your own cream sauce base adding appropriate seasonings
	soups	-use reduced sodium broths, -use reduced sodium soups
Avoid too much sugar	**sugar, brown sugar honey, molasses**	-reduce amount or eliminate -concentrated frozen apple, orange, pineapple juice - adjusting liquid in recipe appropriately
Eat foods with adequate starch and fiber	**flour**	-substitute at least ½ with whole grain flour -replace ¼ flour w/unprocessed miller's bran flakes
	white rice	-brown rice or part wild rice
	-add mildly flavored vegetables or fruits to casseroles, breads, muffins, stuffings, etc. to increase fiber and nutrient content, and to make portions more generous. **Examples:** shredded zucchini or yellow squash in cookies, breads or casseroles; add extra celery, green pepper, onions to stuffings, rice dishes, pasta dishes.	

GRACIOUS GIFTS

Gracious Gifts

*All of our gift recipes are not confined to this section. They are scattered throughout the book and designated by our ***Charleston Gift Basket.***

Aunt Sarah's Squash Pickles

8 cups small squash, thinly sliced (packed tight in measuring cup)
2 cups onions, sliced
4 medium green peppers, sliced
2 teaspoons mustard seed
2 teaspoons celery seed

Mix the above ingredients and sprinkle lightly with salt. Set aside for 1 hour covered.

3 cups sugar
2 cups white vinegar
1 teaspoon pickling spice

Put pickling spices in a cheese cloth bag. Drop into mixture of sugar and vinegar. Bring to full boil. Add squash mixture and bring to full boil again until onions are clear and the peppers turn color. Spoon into sterile jars and seal in the usual manner. Makes 4 pints.

Hot Pepper Jelly

6 green peppers
20 hot peppers
5 pounds sugar
3 cups white vinegar
2½ (6-ounce) bottles liquid pectin
10 drops green food coloring
30 drops red food coloring

Remove seeds from green peppers. Trim stems from hot peppers. Place peppers in blender and process until smooth. Combine sugar and vinegar in large pot, stirring to mix well. Add peppers. Boil 8 to 10 minutes stirring as needed. Remove from heat and strain into another large pot. Discard pepper residue. Put large pot of strained pepper liquid over heat and add liquid pectin and food coloring, stir—do not mix. Bring to a boil. Ladle into half-pint jars and seal. Makes 12 to 14 half-pints.

Make sure to wear gloves when handling peppers or be prepared to itch! Also, keep hands away from eyes while preparing this jelly!

Dad's Mustard Sauce

1 cup dry mustard (Coleman's preferred)
1 cup white vinegar
2 eggs
1 cup sugar
Pinch salt

The night before: Mix dry mustard with vinegar. (Hint: Make a smooth paste with small amount of vinegar to dry mustard. Then gradually add rest of vinegar to avoid lumps.) Let this mixture stand overnight, covered loosely. Next day stir in well-beaten eggs, sugar and salt. Bring this to a slow boil and cook till thickened and coats spoon, stirring constantly (about 15 minutes). Cool, place in jars and refrigerate. Makes about 1 pint.

Hot Tomato Pickles

Fresh green tomatoes, sliced
1 teaspoon whole dill seed per jar
1 jalapeño pepper per jar
1 clove of garlic per jar
2 quarts hot water
1 quart white vinegar
¾ cup non-iodized salt

Pack prepared jars with seed, pepper, and garlic. Add sliced green tomatoes. Add vinegar and salt to hot water, pour over tomatoes in quart jars, leaving ½-inch headspace in each jar. Cap jars and boil in water bath canner for about 5 minutes. Remove from canner and allow pickles to season for one week before eating. Store in dark place to prevent color change.

Kahlúa

2 cups water
3½ cups sugar
6 tablespoons instant coffee
1 vanilla bean, crushed
1 pint inexpensive brandy

Mix sugar, water and coffee in a saucepan. Heat to boiling point, however, **DO NOT BOIL**. Remove from heat and add vanilla bean. Cool completely. Add 1 pint brandy and let stand 30 days in liightly capped bottles. Makes 2 to 3 pints.

A great Christmas gift for friends and neighbors.

Pickled Okra

- **2 pounds tender fresh okra**
- **5 pods hot red or green peppers**
- **5 hot red chiles (or 1 teaspoon cayenne pepper)**
- **5 cloves garlic, peeled**
- **1½ quarts white vinegar**
- **1 cup water**
- **9 tablespoons salt**
- **2 tablespoons celery seed**

Sterilize 5 pint jars and lids. Into each jar place 1 pepper pod, 1 hot chili (or 1 teaspoon cayenne pepper, if chili not available) and 1 clove of garlic, peeled. Pack the whole, small fresh okra into each jar (standing up).

In a pan, combine the vinegar, water, salt and celery seed. Bring to a boil. Pour over each jar of okra. Seal the jars. Makes 5 pints.

Do not open the jars for 8 weeks.

The Best Cheese Log

- **1 (8-ounce) package cream cheese**
- **1 (10-ounce) package mild Cheddar cheese**
- **1 (5-ounce) jar Kraft Old London cheese**
- **4 ounces blue cheese**
- **½ to 1 teaspoon garlic salt**
- **¼ teaspoon pepper**
- **2 cups pecans, chopped**

Soften all cheese at room temperature. Blend with mixer, add seasonings and mix well. Shape into ball or log and roll in pecans. Chill. Serve with crackers.

The perfect gift when wrapped in plastic wrap, tied with a pretty ribbon and placed in a basket with a box of gourmet crackers.

Sliced Cucumber Pickles

4 quarts unpeeled medium cucumber slices, ⅛-inch thick
7 tablespoons salt
1½ quarts of vinegar
1 tablespoon celery seed
2 tablespoons mustard seed
1½ teaspoons curry powder
4 cups granulated sugar

Sprinkle cucumber slices with salt, cover with cold water, and let stand overnight. Drain off brine and wash cucumber slices in several waters. Bring vinegar and remaining ingredients to a boil and add cucumber slices. Heat 4 minutes, stirring constantly, being careful not to let mixture boil. Pour at once into hot sterilized preserve jars and seal at once as jar manufacturer directs. Makes 5 pints.

Spiced Apple Jelly

1 quart good bottled apple juice
6 cups sugar
2 sticks cinnamon (optional)
2 to 3 cloves
1 package powdered pectin

Mix apple juice, pectin and spices in large kettle. Heat until it comes to a rolling boil. Add sugar all at once. Continue heating until mixture comes to a rolling boil. (Cannot be stirred down.) Boil 1 to 1½ minutes. Remove from heat. Skim spices and foam from jelly. Put into sterilized jars and seal.

Basically this is following directions on pectin box. The taste of the juice is the taste of the jelly so choose well. The bottled natural unstrained juice works well also.

Strawberry & Fig Jam

3 cups figs, mashed
3 cups sugar
2 (3-ounce) packages strawberry Jello

Mix and let stand 30 minutes to blend flavor. Bring to slow boil. Cook and stir for 5 minutes or until jam consistency. Pour into hot jars and seal.

VARIATION: Try orange Jello with peaches for a change.

Russian Tea

- **2½ cups orange flavored instant breakfast drink**
- **1 cup instant tea**
- **1 teaspoon cloves**
- **1 teaspoon cinnamon**

Combine all ingredients, mix well. Store in an airtight jar. Place 2 teaspoons of tea mixture in cup, fill with boiling water. Stir until tea mixture is dissolved. Pour in best china and enjoy with a friend.

Makes a nice little thank-you gift when put in a fancy jar.

Pear Relish

- **18 to 22 pears cored but not peeled**
- **8 large green and red bell peppers**
- **1 pound onions**
- **5 hot peppers**
- **1 quart cider vinegar**
- **4 cups sugar**
- **2 tablespoons salt**
- **3 tablespoons dry mustard**
- **3 tablespoons celery seed**
- **3 tablespoons turmeric**

Grind together pears, onion, peppers and hot pepper. In large saucepan, combine vinegar, sugar, salt, mustard, celery seed and turmeric. Add ground pear mixture.

Cook 30 minutes on low boil stirring constantly. Pour into warm sterile jars. Seal—Do Not Disturb for 6 weeks. Makes 10 pints.

The ***Gracious Goodness, Charleston*** committee wishes to express their deep appreciation to the hundreds of alumni, faculty and friends who generously contributed over 1200 of their best kept secret recipes.

Unfortunately, due to our cost limitations and similarity of recipes, we were unable to publish all recipes received. We do hope our friends will understand this compromise and share in our enthusiasm for the finished product of ***Gracious Goodness, Charleston.***

The Typing Committee

Helen Maginn Allen
Dee Dee Maginn Cooper
Alice Danehey Gatch
Dossie Molony Ostapeck
Dotty Mixson Maginn
Ann Montgomery Stafford
Pat Jaskiewicz Swain
Rosie White Ryan
Virginia Jones Wolfe

Contributors

Cissy Mallard Alexander
Helen Maginn Allen
Carol Ann Bunch Allison
Abbey Anger
Joy Blanchard Ardrey
A. W. Shucks
Joyce Garrett Bailey
Coleen Baker
Sara McKerley Barrett
Angela Rowland Basha
Joey Basha
Helena Griffith Bastain
Ellen C. Beckman
Angel Urban Beers
Jean Graf Bello
Kathy Garner Bendt
Rene Moluf Betros
Barbara Walsh Bianchi
Bette Farmer Blanchard
Kathy O'Hagan Blanchard
Mary Santos Blanchard
Rae Ann Grubman Blyth
Mrs. Thomas Blyth, Jr.
Alice Bockhold
Maureen Calder Bolchoz
Chumpsie Simons Bonnoitt
Mary Brooks
Kay Pace Broome
Kit Brownell
Claudia Bissey Budds
George Bullwinkel
Cornelia Townsend Burn
Madeline Leinbach Burns
Sheila Johnson Burris
Jeannette Campomenosi
Rosemary Melfi Cantey
Sherry Capitan
Peggy Conroy Carey
Patricia M. Carter, MD
Marti McGowan Chitwood
Cheryl Pitts Clair
Dena Glenn Clair
Brenda Bolchoz Clarey
Helen Ehrhardt Clawson
Elsie Wolfrum Clees
Robert Closson
Anne Frizelle Coleman
Patsy Colligan
Tommy Condon's
Gladys Garrard Condon
Ingrid Blum Condon
Sandra M. Condon
Danny & Ryan Cooper
Dee Dee Maginn Cooper
Ryan Cooper
Vera Barnett Couturier
Roseann Cramer
Andrea Riols Crites
Jan Crites
Pati Crosby Croffead
Joan Runey Croghan
James Dangerfield
Cindy Wilson Daniel
Mrs. Robert F. DeAntonio
Liz Deloach
Patty Maginn Dhooge
Alma Runey Donato
Mary Donnelly
Jessie Doran
Kathy Keenan Dornetto
Jackqulin Cardwell Doscher
Fred Downs
Edith Wheeler Doyle
Corrie Harper Duffy
Kathy Hostetter Duffy
Mary Ellen Duffy
Carolyn Schill Eiserhardt
Dooley Bell Fava
Eileen Calder Ferri
Margaret Maginn Ferri
Rose Marie Conroy Finnegan
Ann Driver Fitts
Claire Fredericks Fray
Mrs. Kathleen Fredericks
Berta Way Freeman
Frances Maginn Frizelle
Suzanne Snyder Frizelle
Joan Webber Frye
Jenny Linville Fulwiler
Donna Joseph Furlong
Alice Danehey Gatch
Carlton Gay
Karen Joseph Geckle
Millie Moore Geilfuss
Ann Leitgob Gerken
Beth Carter Gibson
Linda Moluf Gilfillan
Bette Smith Griffith
Patricia Sullivan Gustafson
Jean Ricketts Hairfield
Sissy Magee Hall
Charlotte Irwin Hanna
Coach Ron Hanna
Mrs. Henry Hay
Mariana Ramsay Hay
Nancy McNurlin Heath
Donna Donnelly Heissenbuttle
Patricia Puckhaber Henrikson
Henry's Restaurant

Pat Holper
William B. Hooffstetter
Hoppin' John's
Sally Way Howle
Sarah Johnston Hudson
Steve Hudson
Margaret Clarke Hutchinson
James Igoe
Judy Brown Jameson
Margaret Johnson
Carol Jones
Jenny Joseph
Molly Joseph
Peggy Conroy Joseph
Becky Kassis
Joann Jones Kassis
Nouha Saikaly Kassis
Carolyn H. Keenan
Bunny Kerr
Evangeline Bouvette Kerr
Mary Kennerty King
Natalie Johnson Knisley
Dianne Wasko Kochamba
Mary Michel Kuhn
LaBrasca's
Linda Crawford Lambert
Joan Roth Lannan
Joan Holling LaTorre
Mary Verble Lavelle
Mary Lee Demetre Lavelle
Mary Ellen Eiserhardt Lenhardt
Camille Lewis
Alberta Sottile Long
Betty Long
T. Love
Dorothy Lewis Maastricht
Mary Cisa Magee
Helen (Buddy) Maginn
Dotty Mixson Maginn
Laura Sevearingen Maginn
Ruth Hills Mallard
Cindy Molony Masters
Ann Lauro Mayhall
Pat Holstein McAlister
Pat Trudell McDougald
Father Lawrence McInerny
Helena Blanchard McKay
Carole Shahid McMahon
Lorice Adry McMahon
Marla McMahon
Janet Messina
St. Clair Shahid Michel
Corinne Gayard Mills
Catharine Cranford Mintzer
Ann Boniface Molony
Kathy Gibson Molony
Sadie Brown Molony
Olga Shahid Moluf
Kathleen Condon Montgomery
Miffy Montano Moore
Kathleen Dixon Murphy
Deborah Robinson Nelson
Suzanne Mims Newkirk
Emaline Nimmer
Helen O'Hagan
Kitty O'Neill
Mary E. O'Neill
Muriel Gaffney O'Neill
Dossie Molony Ostapeck
Darlene Ring Ostrander
Bette Thomas Owens
Betty Montgomery Palmer
Judy Papadimitriou
Deborah Pawley
Joe Pomer
Sarah Pomer
Florence Pommering
Teresa Whetsell Pregnall
Sandra V. Pye
Kathy Kennerty Rackley
Mary Loretta Croghan Ramsay
Ginny Condon Ravenel
Maureen Holseberg Ray
Patti Bailey Regan
Robert Register
Mary Condon Register
Peter Rix
Robert's of Charleston
Roitzsch Family
Carol Seignious Roper
Rosemary Conway Rowland
Frances M. Rumpf
Aubyn Chance Runey
Audrey Meyer Runey
Desiree Hall Runey
Elsie Condon Runey
Dr. Michael Runey
Patty Davis Runey
Mrs. Reba Runey
Renee Couturier Runey
Rosie White Ryan
Sally Mullen Sakre
Peggy Salvo
Judy Fredricks Santos
Yvonne Keating Santos
Jean Schultze
Judy Hagstrom Schwerin
Ellen Armstrong Scoggin
Priscilla Robertson Scoggin
Kim Reese Seabrook
Jane Seymour
Janie Joseph Shahid
Julia Khoury Shahid
Marcia Bernstein Shealey
B. J. Kirkland Shoe
Gloria Seithel Silcox
Catherine Maginn Simmons
Frances Bowick Simmons
Buddy Sirisky
Sister Alice Joseph Brady
Sister Bridget Sullivan
Sister Enrica Federal
Sister M. Margaretta Molony
Sister Mary Pavonarius
Ann Smith
Barbara Smith
Kathleen Blanchard Smith
Susan Smith
Judy Frizelle Snyder
Mary Maginn Soffera
Eleanor Sottile
Rosena Termini Spollane
Ann Montgomery Stafford
Ashley Ann Stafford
Station 9 Restaurant
Marshall Stith
Louise Storen
Mary Storen
Charlotte Brainard Straney
Mary Ann Sullivan
Pat Jaskiewicz Swain
Jean Shahid Taylor
John M. Taylor
Julia Terry Templeton
Marilyn Buero Tezza
Helen Malis Theos
Katherine Gigis Theos
Paul A. Theos
Neyle Scoggin Thompson
Thelma Laurey Thompson
Town & Country Inn
Charles Pete Trapalis
Sylvia Trapalis
Peggy Velissarios
Anne Bellinger Villeponteaux
Mary Villeponteaux
Mary Laurey Villeponteaux
Ruth Laurey Villeponteaux
Ted Villeponteaux
Barbara Campbell Wade
Noreen Walker
Lynn Ward
Mary Ellen Long Way
Mary Ellen Way
Barbara & Harold Weaver
Harriet & David Weaver
Charlotte Rexroad Werkmeister
Winnie Budds White
Anita Williams
Martha Taylor Williams
Pat Willis
Lisa Johnston Wilson
Trevor Wilson
Kay Brandenburg Wolfe
Robbie Wolfe
Marie Doscher Woodard
Kathy Konrad Yonce

Testing Committee

Helen Maginn Allen
Joyce Garrett Bailey
Ruth Scarborough Baker
Allene Phillips Barans
Angela Rowland Basha
Helena Griffith Bastian
Leigh Young Bastian
Lynn Smith Beltz
Kathy Garner Bendt
Fran Seabrook Bennett
Renee Moluf Betros
Barbara Walsh Bianchi
Bette Farmer Blanchard
Kathy O'Hagan Blanchard
Mary Santos Blanchard
Cheryl Basha Bolchoz
Mary Anne Bolchoz
Maureen Calder Bolchoz
Theresa Forsberg Bolchoz
Celsus Bergin Bollinger
Chumpsie Simons Bonnoitt
Mary Beth Molony Bunch
Madeline Leinbach Burns
Angel Frizelle Butler
Dolly Santos Calvert
Erin Harrell Carter
Cheryl Pitts Clair
Dena Glenn Clair
Brenda Bolchoz Clarey
Caroline Ehrhardt Condon
Ingrid Condon
Kathy Cope Condon
Mindy Cope Condon
Sandra M. Condon
Dee Dee Maginn Cooper
Amy Sullivan Copeland
Beth Bolchoz Corbett
Kathleen Cantwell Couturier
Vera Barnett Couturier
Joan Runey Croghan
Peggy Frizelle Curry
Kathryn Harrell Dabney
Tammy Basha Daniels
Maryann Yarborough Dieter
Alma Runey Donato
Corrie Harper Duffy
Mary Stall Ferrara
Eileen Calder Ferri
Rose Marie Conroy Finnegan
Mary Cuomo Fisher
Ann Driver Fitts
Lisa Mikell Fosberry
Frannie Maginn Frizelle
Jenny Linville Fulwiler
Karen Joseph Geckle
Stacy Tollison Griffith
Patricia Sullivan Gustafson
Jean Ricketts Hairfield
Cissy Magee Hall
Mary Bolchoz Harrell
Bonnie Kennerly Hartnett
Barbara Evans Hayes
Nancy McNurlin Heath
Christine Yarborough Hill
Mamie Frizelle Stoughton
Sally Way Howle
Sarah Johnston Hudson
Judi Brown Jameson
Amy Joseph
Kathy Joseph
Kevin Joseph
Molly Joseph
Peggy Conroy Joseph
Joann Jones Kassis
Nouha Saikaly Kassis
Julianne Harrell Khoury
Kelly Yarborough Knobbs
Susan Wulbern Koval
Peggy Leinbach LaBoone
Joan Roth Lannan
Joan Holling LaTorre
Mary Verble Lavelle
Mary Lee Lavelle
Elizabeth Griffith Loy
Dorothy Lewis Maastricht
Helen (Buddy) Maginn
Dotty Mixson Maginn
Ruth Hills Mallard
Cindy Molony Masters
Ann Gould McCrary
Lorrice Adry McMahon
Gail Bolchoz McQueeney
Carol Ring Meyer
St. Clair Shahid Michel
Patty Duc Mikell
Peggy Armstrong Miller
Corrine Gayard Mills
Kathy Gibson Molony
Sadie Brown Molony
Sister Margaretta Molony
Sandra Martin Moore
Allyson Harrell Moring
Christine Ostapeck Mullinax
Chrissie Michel Murphy
Deborah Robinson Nelson
Susan Mims Newkirk
Mary Ellen Kehoe Ondo
Bette Thomas Owens
Kathy Kennerty Rackley
Ginny Condon Ravenel
Maureen Holseberg Ray
Patty Bailey Regan
Carol Seignious Roper
Lori Mikell Rowland
Rosemary Conway Rowland
Aubyn Chance Runey
Audrey Meyer Runey
Donna Hutchinson Runey
Patty Davis Runey
Rene Couturier Runey
Rosie White Ryan
Jackie Hancock Salmonsen
Judy Fredricks Santos
Julie Smith Santos
Eileen Schleelein
Judy Hagstrom Schwerin
Sib Robertson Scoggin
Carolyn Brearey Shahid
Janie Joseph Shahid
Mary Raynes Shahid
Marcia Bernstein Shealey
Patsy Ankersen Sheppard
B. J. Kirkland Shoe
Gloria Seithel Silcox
Beth Zwingmann Sloan
Ann Molony Smith
Barbara Smith
Janice Michel Smith
Kathleen Blanchard Smith
Judy Frizelle Snyder
Marie Joseph Snyder
Delores Sander Soffera
Mary Maginn Soffera
Charlotte Brainard Straney
Pam Ott Straughn
Sandra Riols Tawes
Eileen McCrary Thames
Helen Malis Theos
Sylvia Trapalis
Barbara Campbell Wade
Daisy Prince Walsh
Martha Taylor Williams
Rosie Cahill Windham
Kathy Konrad Yonce

INDEX

Index

C

D

T

Bishop England Endowment Fund
363 Seven Farms Drive
Charleston, SC 29492-7534
(843) 849-9599, Ext. 21
Fax (843) 849-9221 • E-Mail: abasha@behs.com

Please send _____ copy(ies) @ $17.95 each _________
Postage and handling @ $4.00 each _________
South Carolina residents add sales tax @ $1.08 each _________
Total _________

Name ____

Address ____

City ______________________________ State _______ Zip __________

Make checks payable to ***Gracious Goodness Charleston.***

Bishop England Endowment Fund
363 Seven Farms Drive
Charleston, SC 29492-7534
(843) 849-9599, Ext. 21
Fax (843) 849-9221 • E-Mail: abasha@behs.com

Please send _____ copy(ies) @ $17.95 each _________
Postage and handling @ $4.00 each _________
South Carolina residents add sales tax @ $1.08 each _________
Total _________

Name ____

Address ____

City ______________________________ State _______ Zip __________

Make checks payable to ***Gracious Goodness Charleston.***

Bishop England Endowment Fund
363 Seven Farms Drive
Charleston, SC 29492-7534
(843) 849-9599, Ext. 21
Fax (843) 849-9221 • E-Mail: abasha@behs.com

Please send _____ copy(ies) @ $17.95 each _________
Postage and handling @ $4.00 each _________
South Carolina residents add sales tax @ $1.08 each _________
Total _________

Name ____

Address ____

City ______________________________ State _______ Zip __________

Make checks payable to ***Gracious Goodness Charleston.***

Please take a minute and send us names and addresses of bookstores or gift shops in your area. Thank you.

Name of Store ____

Buyer's Name ____

Address ______________________ City ___________ State _____ Zip ______

Name of Store ____

Buyer's Name ____

Address ______________________ City ___________ State _____ Zip ______

- -

Please take a minute and send us names and addresses of bookstores or gift shops in your area. Thank you.

Name of Store ____

Buyer's Name ____

Address ______________________ City ___________ State _____ Zip ______

Name of Store ____

Buyer's Name ____

Address ______________________ City ___________ State _____ Zip ______

- -

Please take a minute and send us names and addresses of bookstores or gift shops in your area. Thank you.

Name of Store ____

Buyer's Name ____

Address ______________________ City ___________ State _____ Zip ______

Name of Store ____

Buyer's Name ____

Address ______________________ City ___________ State _____ Zip ______